THE TRAVELS OF MARK TWAIN

THE TRAVELS OF

MARK TWAIN

Edited by

CHARLES NEIDER

Cooper Square Press

First Cooper Square Press edition 2000

This Cooper Square Press paperback edition of *The Travels of Mark Twain* is an unabridged republication of the edition first published in New York in 1961, with the addition of one textual emendation. It is reprinted by arrangement with the editor.

Published by Cooper Square Press,
An Imprint of Rowman & Littlefield Publishers, Inc.
150 Fifth Avenue, Suite 911
New York, New York 10011

Distributed by National Book Network

Library of Congress Cataloging-in-Publication Data

Twain, Mark, 1835–1910
The travels of Mark Twain / edited by Charles Neider.
p. cm.
ISBN 0-8154-1039-5 (pbk. : alk. paper)
1. Twain, Mark, 1835–1910—Journeys. 2. Authors, Amercan—19th century—Biography. 3. Voyages and travels. I. Neider, Charles, 1915– II. Title.

PS1303 .N37 2000
818'.409—dc21

The paper used in this publication meets the minimum requirements of American National Standard for Information Sciences—Permanence of Paper for Printed Library Materials, ANSI/NISO Z39.48–1992.
Manufactured in the United States of America.

To Penny and Peter Kenez

Editor's Note

Mark Twain wrote five books of travel—three of foreign travel (*The Innocents Abroad, A Tramp Abroad* and *Following the Equator*) and two of domestic (*Roughing It* and *Life on the Mississippi*). I have included ample selections from all of these works. Under each heading the material is presented in the chronological and sequential order in which it was first published in book form.

C. N.

The Itinerary of The Travels of Mark Twain

INTRODUCTION

by Charles Neider

1

For a man who claimed to "loathe all travel, except on foot," Samuel Clemens had a strong digestion for it. His travels began early, in his eighteenth year, when, telling his mother he was going up to St. Louis to earn a little money, he went *through* St. Louis to New York, where the Crystal Palace Fair was in progress in the hot months of 1853. It must have been quite an experience for the Missouri boy, who had been working for his brother Orion on the Hannibal *Journal,* to make his way from his lodgings on Duane Street up to Sixth Avenue and 42nd Street, to where Bryant Park now stands, and to stare at the progress of nations as displayed there, at an admission price of fifty cents.

"The visitors to the Palace average 6,000 daily—double the population of Hannibal," he wrote to his sister Pamela Moffett at two o'clock one morning. He would get up at six and be at work at seven. Where did he spend his evenings? "Where do you suppose, with a free printers' library containing more than 4,000 volumes within a quarter of a mile of me, and nobody at home to talk to?" There was not only the future, as represented by the Palace, in that metropolis of a century ago, but also the vivid national past. "I saw a large company of soldiers of 1812 the other day, with a '76 veteran scattered here and there in the ranks." In an October 1853 letter to Pamela he called the city an "abominable place" but it intrigued him. "It is as hard on my conscience to leave New York, as it was easy to leave Hannibal." Later, in 1867, he would write to the *Alta California* of San Francisco what a hard place New York was to live in, how it caught and tore and ripped and spewed out one's time, how noisy and distracting and death to peace of mind it was. Which did not prevent him, in his later years, from cheerfully taking up residence in it.

One gathers from his early letters that he was alert, industrious and curious. His letters are informative but without the vein of humor which was later to characterize him. One imagines, however, that his conversation must have contained it amply, flavored by his southwestern drawl and country manners.

He worked in New York at the printing trade, then in Philadelphia, made a brief trip to Washington and returned to Missouri after an absence of almost fifteen months. He was a fellow who slept and ate well almost anywhere and who did not easily succumb to depression. He took up his trade in St. Louis awhile, then joined Orion in Keokuk, Iowa, for a two-year printing stint on another of Orion's ill-fated ventures. When he tired of life in Keokuk under the melancholy and restrictive influence of Orion, ten years his senior, he was at no loss to decide how to make his fortune. He would go to the headwaters of the Amazon, collect coca and return home rich. The inspiration had come from reading about Lt. Herndon's experiences on that mighty river.

It pained him to tell Orion of his plans, for he knew he would receive only arguments, sincerely offered—for Orion was not easily capable of insincerity—yet difficult to deflect without hurting Orion's feelings. In a letter to his brother Henry he wrote: "But you know what Orion is. When he gets a notion into his head, and more especially if it is an erroneous one, the Devil can't get it out again." He was always an outspoken critic of Orion, at times to Orion himself. He had confided his Amazon plans to his mother. She advised him to handle the matter as he had handled an earlier one, the trip to New York. She reminded him of how diplomatic he had been with *her*. Why not tell Orion that he was going as far as New York —or whatever the port was going to be?

He went to Cincinnati and worked at his trade until April 1857 (he was not yet twenty-two), then took a boat down the Mississippi to New Orleans, ready to sail for South America and the Amazon. The only trouble was, as he explained much later in his *Autobiography,* "When I got to New Orleans I inquired about ships leaving for Pará and discovered that there weren't any and learned that there probably wouldn't be any during that century." There was only one thing to do: to make his fortune by piloting; and so he persuaded a relucant Horace Bixby to take him on as a cub and to teach him the sinuous, treacherous, shifting day life and night life of that other great river, the Mississippi.

He was taught the river, and in the process he learned a cross section of American life he could hardly have studied elsewhere. He got to know shoals, bars and towheads; towns and hamlets by the score; men by the hundred who would teem in his memory, types found on the river and in the river's basin; and he got to know the cosmopolis of New Orleans, with its foreign flavor. The river commingled American types as California does today. He learned the taste of independence and high pay, both of which were the rewards of Mississippi piloting. But the real fortune he made was not yet evident. It consisted of the optimism of his best years and of a keen sense of the American condition, qualities of mind and character which were to determine the output of his genius.

When the Civil War put a period to piloting on the river, Clemens, after a two-week stint in the Confederate Army in Missouri (during which he was exhausted by continual retreating, as he claimed later), decided to sit out the war. Orion had recently been appointed Secretary of Nevada Territory, and so Clemens accompanied him on a stagecoach journey to Nevada. The brothers took the stage at St. Joseph on July 26, 1861, and it was five and one-half years of roaming in Nevada, California, and the Hawaiian Islands, with a trip across the Isthmus to New York, before Clemens saw St. Louis and Hannibal again.

These were the years later to be recorded in *Roughing It,* the determining years of literary apprenticeship, of gathering materials, of learning the trades of newspaper correspondence and lecturing. No longer a printer and a pilot, Clemens became an amateur miner and scribbler, meanwhile observing and memorizing the life of the silver-mining frontier as he had observed and memorized the life of the river and its basin. Prospecting and mining became a passion which died, but the writing, beginning with letters to the Virginia City *Territorial Enterprise* signed "Josh," grew to the proportions of regular correspondence under the name of "Mark Twain." Clemens was a reporter in San Francisco, a correspondent in Hawaii for the Sacramento *Union,* a successful Pacific Coast lecturer and the author of the Jumping Frog story. In those years he was steadily approaching the threshold of fame.

By 1867 he had almost gained the fortune which he had lost by not collecting coca along the Amazon. He had made it by giving up printing as a trade in favor of journalism, and dialect humor in favor of the plain, deeper humor which had already established his fame as "the wild humorist of the Pacific slope." He was now ready to blow upon the embers of his destiny and to light a great conflagration in the literary skies of his native land.

2

Shortly before sailing from San Francisco for New York on December 15, 1866, the thirty-one-year-old Clemens had got the notion to go around the world and to write a series of newspaper letters as he went, letters which would pay his way, act as raw material for possible lectures, and perhaps even serve as the basis of a book. By the time he sailed his idea was more than a notion: a prominent San Francisco paper, the *Alta California,* had agreed to print his letters at $20 each. It was no great risk for the *Alta* to take, for Clemens was by now known to be one of the best correspondents available, with a brilliant and idiomatic descriptive gift in addition to what was even rarer, an apparently inexhaustible store of humor, a usually kind humor which when the need was felt could transform itself into an awesome invective—all with a flavor uniquely American.

Clemens's letters began at once, at sea, and continued from New York. In New York, having learned of the Quaker City excursion to the Holy Land, he abruptly changed his plans and prepared to join it. The excursion was well suited to his genius and became the basis of his extraordinary first book of travel, *The Innocents Abroad.* The excursion lasted from June 8 to November 19, 1867, and the immediate result for Clemens was some fifty letters to the *Alta,* half a dozen to the New York *Tribune* and one to the New York *Herald.*

As a majestic, revered old man, living on comfortable terms with his fictitious name, Clemens let his memory wander over the important events of his life. When it came to the *Alta* letters and the writing of *The Innocents Abroad,* it curiously betrayed him. It seemed to him, as he wrote in his *Autobiography,* that he had used only "several" of the letters, "ten or twelve, perhaps." He said he had found "they were newspaper matter, not book matter." And he imagined himself in San Francisco, a bright, healthy young man, writing *The Innocents Abroad* in sixty days, largely at night. "I could have added a fortnight's labor with the pen and gotten along without the letters altogether."

A comparison of the letters with the book shows how misled he was. Without them he would have had no book at all, for his notebooks were mere jottings and could not have supported the weight of fact and description of the book. They were excellent letters and he used them wholesale, improving diction and grammar, occasionally toning down slang, eliminating references which were too locally Californian, and in general giving the material a more polished look, yet without trying to "write up" to eastern readers. Sometimes he merely rearranged the order of the letters. For example, in the letters he presented Pompeii before Naples; in the book he reversed the order. In many cases he stepped away from the foreground by changing "I" to "we," adding to the effect of modesty as well as of breadth of experience. With his basic materials secure, he could relax, expand and invent. His chief additions were comic sequences, dialogue, and such American color as his vituperation on the subject of the name Tahoe.

He was angry when he recalled the *Alta* letters as an old man. While writing the first ten chapters of the volume in Washington he learned from a western friend that the *Alta* proprietors had copyrighted the letters and were planning to issue them in book form. This news sent him to San Francisco to persuade the proprietors to relinquish book rights in the letters. He never forgave them for the fright they had caused him. Recollecting his youth, it seemed to him that he was boundlessly strong in those halcyon days and could accomplish anything, even the writing of *The Innocents Abroad* in sixty nights with only the smallest help from the letters.

The truth was that much of his work in San Francisco was of an editorial nature and that the true brilliance of his achievement was the writing of the letters under the difficulties of travel. The *Alta* letters are important in Clemens's literary career as none of his other newspaper letters are. The *Enterprise* letters, the *Union* letters, the *Tribune* letters and the *Sun* letters all figure in his biography, but nowhere near as prominently as the *Alta* ones.

The Innocents Abroad was composed in the first half of 1868 and was issued by the American Publishing Company of Hartford in July 1869. Clemens was now in his thirty-fourth year. Between the completion of the manuscript and its publication Clemens traveled extensively on a lecture tour and also successfully courted his future wife, Olivia Langdon, becoming engaged to her February 4, 1869. *The Innocents Abroad* was a great success. America had been on the receiving end of a procession of sour-eyed visitors from Europe and had got the wincing habit as a result. Now it was time to return the compliment with a flourish. Clemens had the apprenticeship and the background for the task. Above all, he had the appetite and the skill.

What is perhaps most surprising to the modern reader is the fresh, tireless language energy of the book: the broad and sophisticated vocabulary and the easy ability to achieve many kinds of effect. Nor can one overlook the book's technical skill—for example, the subtle shifts of tense from past to present to give sudden vividness to scene and description, or the wise, sly avoidance of much use of the first-person pronoun, suggesting that the author's opinions and reactions are typical.

Clemens's fellow excursionists had much to do with the creation of the book. They constituted a microcosm of American humanity on European and Asiatic and African soil and gave the author a chance to satirize traveling Americans while he was satirizing such time-encrusted cultures as those of Italy and Egypt. His association with that assemblage of some sixty persons no doubt was partly responsible for the sudden flowering of his literary ideas—through the ferment of study, of language, character and manners which he could intimately share and observe.

The journalistic atmosphere of San Francisco influenced the tone and content of the book as it did those of the letters. It helped give the book its fresh view of older cultures. The mood of the country at large also profoundly affected the book, which refreshed readers saddened by war and eager to escape into the apparently ludicrous world abroad.

The Innocents Abroad is a charming title but its accuracy is open to some inspection. How innocent could a group of Americans be a scant two years after a fratricidal war? Perhaps it is more likely that many members of the group were going to seek innocence, not in Europe but in the Holy Land. Some were traveling as pilgrims. Wasn't the voyage touted as the Holy Land excursion, and wasn't the steam-propelled sidewheeler named the *Quaker City?* In not mentioning the Civil War in his book Clemens was being faithful to his slim relations with it; but he was also noting and adhering to the mood of the nation as he knew it. Of course, he was not obliged to mention it in a book about a Holy Land excursion; but then he was not obliged to expatiate on Lake Tahoe, on the advantages of life in the United States, and on a quaint stay in the Benton House back home.

The five years from 1865 to Clemens's marriage in February 1870 were the miraculous years of Mark Twain's life. They set the tone and structure of it. In them he found his mature style, left journalism for literature, embraced fame and affluence, transferred the scene of his actual activity from the West to the East, and married the woman who was to have so great an influence upon his life and work.

3

After his marriage in 1870 Clemens settled in Buffalo and wrote humorous sketches for the Buffalo *Express* (of which he had become part owner) and for a New York monthly magazine, *The Galaxy*. But before long his publisher, Bliss, urged him to follow up the phenomenal success of *The Innocents Abroad* with a book about his western experiences, to be called *Roughing It*. Clemens was willing; the book, however, was not. He seemed to have forgotten the details of the overland stage trip and feared he had lost touch with the slang and idiom of its time and place. In a letter to Orion he said he could remember nothing at all; could Orion recollect the route and any of the incidents? Orion sent a memorandum book but the notes were on the meager side and the frontier book clearly showed it had no intention of easily relenting.

There were other matters pressing Clemens—deaths in the family, the uncongeniality of Buffalo to a man of his interests and temperament, and the considerable outgo of money for domestic expenses. He did not remain in Buffalo long, deciding in favor of Hartford, then a literary center. In the meantime he spent the summer of 1871 at Quarry Farm outside Elmira, struggling to give life to Bliss's notion. He had no newspaper letters to lean on now—at any rate for the early chapters—and the events were now a decade old. He did have his writings for the Virginia City *Territorial Enterprise* and the Sacramento *Union* but they were of no direct help in starting the book. He made progress, however, while enduring a kind of stage fright.

And then one day he received a visit from Joe Goodman, editor of the *Enterprise,* who had given Clemens the job of city editor in the absence on leave of Dan de Quille. Goodman read the early chapters at the author's request and said, why they were excellent. It was all the mercurial Clemens needed, and soon he was crying that *The Innocents Abroad* would have to get up early in the morning to beat *Roughing It,* and that the latter would straightway sell 100,000 copies—no, a million. He persuaded Goodman to stay a month and they talked and talked of those colorful times which to Clemens had seemed so faded but which now took on great vividness.

He completed the volume in the autumn of 1871 and it was issued the following February, not as a trade but as a subscription book. *The Innocents Abroad* had also been sold on the subscription plan. *Roughing It* was the first book written after his marriage and settling in the East. (One discounts "Mark Twain's Burlesque Autobiography," published in 1871, on the grounds that it was too slim to be truly called a book.) Like *The Innocents Abroad, Roughing It* was greeted with friendly and favorable reviews. He was becoming a national figure. The literary elect, however, was largely myopic regarding his true, great qualities.

Roughing It is of course an invaluable social history of the silver mining days; for even if its facts are sometimes open to question, the essential truth of its portrait is not. Its language is looser, thinner, freer and more idiomatic than that of *The Innocents Abroad.* If the greater variety of scenes of *The Innocents Abroad* is part of the latter's charm, the more poetic vein, and the tone of a great fable, are to the advantage of *Roughing It.* The sales of the western book were considerable—40,000 copies in the first three months—but they fell far behind those of *The Innocents Abroad.* The latter sold 100,000 copies in its first three years; it took *Roughing It* a decade to reach that figure. (When the first royalty check arrived Clemens did not forget Orion's memorandum book. For its use he sent his brother $1,000.)

4

In the winter of 1871-72 Mark Twain went on another domestic lecture tour. The following August he sailed alone for England with the intention of collecting material for a book on that country. But the warm welcome he received and the extensive socializing he enjoyed put an end to note-taking for the project, which he abandoned. In the middle of November he left for home.

In April of 1873 he brought his family to England. In November he escorted them home, returning alone almost immediately for a lecture tour, and remaining until the middle of January. For the next three years he did not travel much.

In May 1877 he went to Bermuda with his friend Reverend Joseph Twichell, jotting in a notebook that it was "the first actual pleasure trip" he had ever taken. Meanwhile the complexity and expense of his Hartford way of life were beginning to tax his strength and his optimism. In a letter to his mother written in February of 1878 he said: "Life has come to be a very serious matter with me. I have a badgered, harassed feeling a good part of my time. It comes mainly of business responsibilities and annoyances, and the persecution of kindly letters from well meaning strangers—to whom I must be rudely silent or else put in the biggest half of my time bothering over answers. There are other things also that help to consume my time and defeat my projects. Well, the consequence is, I cannot write a book at home. This cuts my income down. Therefore, I have about made up my mind to take my tribe and fly to some little corner of Europe and budge no more until I shall have completed one of the half dozen books that lie begun, up stairs."

And in one of the notebooks of that time we find this jotting: "To go abroad has something of the same sense that death brings—'I am no longer of ye; what ye say of me is now of no consequence—but of how much consequence when I am with ye and of ye.' I know you will refrain from saying harsh things *because* they cannot hurt me, since I am out of reach and cannot hear them. This is why we say no harsh things of the dead."

Clemens and his family sailed for Germany April 11, 1878. Clemens went to Europe with the plan of taking a walking tour with Twichell which would be the basis of a new book of travels. While waiting for Twichell, Clemens and his family settled down in Germany, where they continued their assiduous study of the language, begun in the Hartford house. Twichell arrived early in August and he and Clemens set out for the Black Forest. Twichell remained in Europe, as Mark Twain's guest, for about six weeks, after which the Clemens family went down to Italy, staying three weeks in Venice, a week in Florence and a fortnight in Rome. Then they went to Munich, where Clemens began working on *A Tramp Abroad,* writing and destroying much in the winter of 1878-79. He could not seem to work up enthusiasm for the book as a whole, although he wrote many sections which pleased him.

The Clemenses tried Paris at the end of February 1879. They encountered a cold wet winter, and Clemens's work on *A Tramp Abroad* continued heavy and plaguing. As usual, he found himself indulging in much social life. The summer arrived; it was cold too. The Clemenses made their way to London via the Low Countries but London was no respite; it was as cold and wet as Paris had been. They sailed for America August 23, 1879.

Work on *A Tramp Abroad,* continued at home, seemed at times like a nightmare and Clemens was infinitely relieved when the job was done. The book was published the middle of March 1880. It was fairly well received. William Dean Howells, his friend and editor of the *Atlantic Monthly,* praised it, which was music to Clemens. In later years Brander Matthews pronounced it superior to *The Innocents Abroad,* a judgment with which few readers would agree today.

The Innocents Abroad reflected the author's joy in writing it. *A Tramp Abroad* reflected his labors and uncertainty. The latter lacks the tension, the fire, the brilliant detail, the vocabulary, the energy and the invective of the earlier book. But *A Tramp Abroad* has stretches of sustained humor and heights of humor the earlier book lacks. In *The Innocents Abroad* the text is serious; the embroidery is enlivened by jokes. In *A Tramp Abroad* the text itself is often a series of jokes.

5

The January 1875 issue of the *Atlantic* was no ordinary issue, for in addition to containing two poems by Longfellow, an essay on Weimar by Bayard Taylor, and an essay on "The Americanized European" by Oliver Wendell Holmes, it contained the opening of *Roderick Hudson,* by Henry James, and the first installment of "Old Times on the Mississippi," by Mark Twain. Howells many years later recalled that the *Atlantic* had hoped to increase its sales due to the Mississippi sketches (which appeared in seven issues of the magazine) but that the lax observance of copyright in those days had frustrated its hopes. According to his testimony, *The New York Times* and the St. Louis *Democrat* benefited from the advance copies of the magazine which they regularly received by reprinting the Mississippi sketches and placing them on the market before the magazine was on the stands. These two papers pretty well covered the nation, Howells said, and they, if anybody, benefited from the sketches for which the *Atlantic* had paid $20 a page, high rates for the magazine at that time.

However, perhaps Howells's memory betrayed him, for it seems reasonable to assume that if the magazine had looked forward to a substantial increase in sales it would have displayed the Mississippi sketches prominently. The first page of the January issue opened with the *Roderick Hudson* installment, and almost all of the other contributions began with a full page. There was a full page for Taylor; for "Wilhelmina," by Constance Fenimore Woolson; and even one for the anonymous "Touching Visitants from a Higher Life." When it came to the Mark Twain contribution a middle or half-page beginning (on page 69) sufficed—a precedent that was followed in the subsequent issues—which recalls the fact that at those subdued Boston dinners where Twain was so sought after as a speaker, for some time he was not thought worthy enough to sit on the dais with the other literary giants: Whittier, Bryant, Longfellow and the others.

The seven installments of "Old Times on the Mississippi" were each the equivalent of two chapters of the book which appeared several years later, and specifically were Chapters 4 to 17 of the book. They did not entirely comprise the "first half" of the book (the recollected half); for Chapters 1 to 3 were written later, as well as 18 and 19 (Clemens's relations with the pilot Brown), 20 (the explosion of the *Pennsylvania* and the death of his younger brother Henry), and a short chapter, 21, headed "A Section of My Biography." The text of the installments was almost identical with that of the book.

The appearance of the installments renewed in Mark Twain an early desire to go down the river to collect material for a book. As usual he disliked traveling alone. Because neither Howells, nor Osgood (now Clemens's publisher), nor John Hay was free to accompany him, he postponed revisiting the Mississippi. It was not until April 17, 1882, that he finally set out for a journey of six weeks. He went to St. Louis, down the river to New Orleans and up the river to St. Paul. He was accompanied by Osgood and a male stenographer. Many details of the trip are given in *Life on the Mississippi,* which he completed that summer and autumn at Quarry Farm and in Hartford.

The book was published in May 1883. "Upon the whole," wrote

Howells after his friend's death in 1910, "I have the notion that Clemens thought this his greatest book. . . ." In it Mark Twain for the first and only time in his travel books struck and sustained the autobiographical note. A long, sustained calm and a profound reservoir of power supplanted the ebullience of *The Innocents Abroad.* In the river book humor for the most part was subdued. This period piece of an aspect of the nation's youth could not have been done better by another hand. Clemens owed the river years much. They had given him two great disciplines from which he had benefited as a writer: close observation and memory practice. He repaid the debt by creating a masterpiece. *Life on the Mississippi* enlarged his reputation, especially in Europe, as an author who was a good deal more than just an inspired wit or buffoon. Thomas Hardy remarked to Howells at a dinner in England, "Why don't people understand that Mark Twain is not merely a great humorist? He's a very remarkable fellow in a very different way." And he went on to praise the Mississippi book.

6

The winter of 1884-85 Clemens spent platforming with George Washington Cable. In August 1890 he went to Keokuk, Iowa, to see his dying mother. The following spring he closed the manorial Hartford house and took his family to Europe in order to live a quieter and a less expensive life. He and his wife were suffering from rheumatism; the Paige typesetter bubble was threatening to burst; and his publishing house was in serious financial trouble. The Clemenses sailed on June 6, 1891, for France. Not long afterward Clemens wrote to his business manager that he intended to write another travel book and would take a year or two to collect the materials for it. Then followed a long and hectic period of hopes, despairs and troubles, punctuated by frequent transatlantic crossings by Clemens for business, not professional, reasons. He accomplished little sustained work during this time.

The winter of 1891-92 was spent in Berlin. The following spring was spent in the south of France. Then the Clemenses tried Venice, Berlin again, and finally a villa on a hill near Florence. In the summer of 1892 Clemens visited the United States for less than two weeks. On March 22, 1893, he returned to his homeland for two months; on August 29 he returned for seven. He went to Europe again in March 1894, spent about three weeks with his family, and was back in New York by the middle of April.

On April 18 his publishing house, Charles L. Webster & Co., failed. In May he returned to Europe for a summer in southern France. By the end of the year the Paige typesetter affair, in which he had invested heavily, ended in a fiasco. On February 23, 1895, he sailed for New York, returning to Europe the end of March. It was then he decided to make his lecture tour around the world. He was now sixty and very tired. He still, as always, loathed lecturing.

On May 11 the Clemenses embarked for the United States, Mrs. Clemens and her children having been abroad continuously for four years. In July Clemens, his wife, and his daughter Clara left Elmira for the trip around the world, arriving in Vancouver August 16, sailing for Australia August 23, and arriving in England the middle of the following July. Clemens was alone in London when he was handed a cable informing him of the unexpected death of his favorite daughter, Susy. (His wife and Clara were on the seas, hurrying to Susy's bedside; Susy died of spinal meningitis on August 18.) His cup was running over.

A little later the Clemenses settled down in a house in Tedworth Square in London, and there he wrote his last book of travels, *Following the Equator*. On October 26, 1896, he remarked in his notebook, "Wrote the first chapter of the book today." On April 13, 1897, he jotted, "I finished my book today," and on May 18 wrote: "Finished the book *again*. Addition of 30,000 words." In January he had written to Twichell, "I am working, but it is for the sake of the work—the 'surcease of sorrow' that is found there. I work all the days, and trouble vanishes away when I use that magic. This book will not long stand between it and me, now; but that is no matter, I have many unwritten books to fly to for my preservation; the interval between the finishing of this one and the beginning of the next will not be more than one hour, at most."

Following the Equator was published in September 1897. Together with the lecture tour, it enabled Clemens to pay his debts to the last cent. The miracle is that it got done at all, considering the circumstances of its composition. A book to be good must have an inspiration of its own. In this case the lecture tour was the chief spirit and the book merely a poor, tight-lipped, disjointed, wandering, aching record of it. It is strange how the feeling of weariness and age can make its way into prose—by a grayness, by a loss of lilt in phrasing and of daring in invention, by a sputtering in choice of words, a falling off of metaphor, a tendency to meander, a turning of energy inward. It is kinder to say no more, except that there were fine things in it, more than enough to witness that a giant had breathed upon it.

7

Because we think of Mark Twain as *the* American author above all others we do not readily imagine him spending years away from his country. We easily recall Herman Melville's voyages, or images of Henry James in London, Paris, Venice. When Mark Twain comes to mind it is usually the Mississippi that we think of or the Far West; at least it is Hartford, Elmira, Buffalo, New York. Yet on reflection it turns out that he crossed the Atlantic a fair number of times (twenty-seven) and spent more than a decade away from his homeland.

He was on the whole a conventional traveler who treasured his comforts and was content to go where others had gone before. One suspects that he went to California mainly because of its proximity to Nevada and that he liked San Francisco largely because he could pursue his trade there while enjoying a society which by the standards of his childhood and youth was extremely cosmopolitan. As far as I know he did not visit Monterey (the old Pacific capital), the missions, Sutter's fort, or the village of Los Angeles. It is a pity; his impressions would be worth having. He made no effort to penetrate into Africa. He did not bother to record his week in Spain near the end of the Holy Land excursion. In later years, despite many visits to Europe, he did not go to Spain, Greece, Russia or any of the other places where travel was likely to be uncomfortable. He liked the well-padded trails: England, Germany, Switzerland, Austria, Italy.

His views on travel were set down forcefully in an interview which he granted to a reporter for the New York *World* in London on October 6, 1900. The interview appeared in the *World* on October 14. It has never before been reprinted. I quote the relevant passages.

"Is it true that you have resolved never to leave the United States again?"

"Not a word of truth in it. Perhaps we may spend the rest of our days at home. I don't know and no consideration on earth could induce me to give a pledge about that or anything else. That is another of my rules of life. I never give pledges or promises about things of that sort. If I felt myself under the constraint of a pledge the situation would become so irksome to me that only on that account alone I would be irresistibly compelled to come away again. No—as far as I am able to speak about a subject on which other people have the controlling voice more or less—I propose to stay the winter in New York, and then go back to Hartford in the spring."

"But do you really think that such an indefatigable traveller as you have been can settle down at home? Won't you feel restless?"

"An indefatigable traveller! That's where I am misunderstood. Now I have made thirty-four long journeys in my life, and thirty-two of them were made under the spur of absolute compulsion. I mean it—under nothing but sheer compulsion. There always was an imperative reason. I had to gather material for books or sketches, I had to stump around lecturing to make money, or I had to go abroad for the health or the education of my family. For love of travel—never any of these thirty-two journeys. There is no man living who cares less about seeing new places and peoples than I. You are surprised—but it's the gospel truth. I had a surfeit of it.

"When I started out, in 1867, for a six months' tour in the Quaker City I was a voracious sightseer. With nearly all the rest of that gang I said to myself: 'This is the opportunity of my life—never again shall I have the chance, the time or the money to see the Old World.' We lived up to that idea. We went in for seeing everything that was to be seen. In a city of inexhaustible treasures like Rome we got up at six in the morning and throughout the whole day, in rain or shine, we made a perpetual procession through picture galleries, churches, museums, palaces—looking at things which for the most part did not interest us one cent but which we thought we had to see. And we saw them. If our meals interfered with our seeing any old thing our meals were put aside. At nine or ten at night we returned to our hotel, our brains and our bodies reeling with fatigue and utter exhaustion. My head used to ache, my eyes to swim, but I would not succumb to the terrible temptation to throw myself on the bed, as if I did so I could not rise from it again before morning. I had to resist because we had to see something else by moonlight or because there was no moon or some other foolish reason. The only rest we had was when we went a short voyage from one port to another in the Mediterranean, and then I slept all the time. What was the result of this insensate sightseeing? Why, that I was so fagged that I lost the capacity to appreciate most of what I saw or to carry away any coherent idea of it. Since then only hard necessity has ever driven me to travelling. When I went around the world, five years ago, it was because I wanted money to pay off debts that were a nuisance to me—they burdened my conscience. People say that it was to relieve my creditors. Not at all. It was far more to relieve Clemens than creditors. I could not be happy until I got rid of that debt. I have never recovered from the Quaker City surfeit of sightseeing, and don't think there is any reasonable prospect of my doing so now."

8

Mark Twain's journey around the world was not the last of his travels. There was the summer of 1897 in Switzerland; a long stretch in Vienna; the summer of 1899 in Sweden; then London. On January 8, 1900, Clemens wrote to his financier friend, H. H. Rogers, "I am tired to death of this everlasting exile." The summer of that year was spent outside London. In the first week of October the Clemens family finally left for their homeland. Mark Twain said to a reporter: "If I ever get ashore I am going to break both of my legs so I can't get away again."

In 1902 he went to Missouri to accept an honorary doctorate. In October 1903 he took his family to Italy for his wife Livy's health (she died there), returning July 1904. Early in 1907 he went to Bermuda. In June of the same year he went to Oxford to accept a coveted doctorate. In 1908 he went to Bermuda again; also in 1909; again in 1910. On April 12, 1910, he left Bermuda for the last time. He died on April 21 of that year.

1 / *At Home*

1 : *Stage-coaching on the Overland**

As THE SUN WENT DOWN and the evening chill came on, we made preparation for bed. We stirred up the hard leather letter-sacks, and the knotty canvas bags of printed matter (knotty and uneven because of projecting ends and corners of magazines, boxes and books). We stirred them up and redisposed them in such a way as to make our bed as level as possible. And we *did* improve it, too, though after all our work it had an upheaved and billowy look about it, like a little piece of a stormy sea. Next we hunted up our boots from odd nooks among the mail-bags where they had settled, and put them on. Then we got down our coats, vests, pantaloons and heavy woolen shirts, from the armloops where they had been swinging all day, and clothed ourselves in them—for, there being no ladies either at the stations or in the coach, and the weather being hot, we had looked to our comfort by stripping to our underclothing, at nine o'clock in the morning. All things being now ready, we stowed the uneasy Dictionary where it would lie as quiet as possible, and placed the water-canteen and pistols where we could find them in the dark. Then we smoked a final pipe, and swapped a final yarn; after which, we put the pipes, tobacco, and bag of coin in snug holes and caves among the mail-bags, and then fastened down the coach curtains all around and made the place as "dark as the inside of a cow," as the conductor phrased it in his picturesque way. It was certainly as dark as any place could be—nothing was even dimly visible in it. And finally, we rolled

* In July 1861 Sam Clemens headed for Nevada on what he thought was going to be a trip of three months. He did not return home until some five and a half years later. On this journey he was an unknown former printer and former river pilot, with his future decidedly uncertain. When he returned home he was widely known as the "wild humorist of the Pacific slope"—at any rate he was widely known in the West—and was on the threshold of a great career.—C. N.

ourselves up like silkworms, each person in his own blanket, and sank peacefully to sleep.

Whenever the stage stopped to change horses, we would wake up, and try to recollect where we were—and succeed—and in a minute or two the stage would be off again, and we likewise. We began to get into country, now, threaded here and there with little streams. These had high, steep banks on each side, and every time we flew down one bank and scrambled up the other, our party inside got mixed somewhat. First we would all be down in a pile at the forward end of the stage, nearly in a sitting posture, and in a second we would shoot to the other end, and stand on our heads. And we would sprawl and kick, too, and ward off ends and corners of mail-bags that came lumbering over us and about us; and as the dust rose from the tumult, we would all sneeze in chorus, and the majority of us would grumble, and probably say some hasty thing, like: "Take your elbow out of my ribs!—can't you quit crowding?"

Every time we avalanched from one end of the stage to the other, the Unabridged Dictionary would come too; and every time it came it damaged somebody. One trip it "barked" the Secretary's [1] elbow; the next it hurt me in the stomach, and the third it tilted Bemis's nose up till he could look down his nostrils—he said. The pistols and coin soon settled to the bottom, but the pipes, pipe-stems, tobacco, and canteens clattered and floundered after the Dictionary every time it made an assault on us, and aided and abetted the book by spilling tobacco in our eyes, and water down our backs.

Still, all things considered, it was a very comfortable night. It wore gradually away, and when at last a cold gray light was visible through the puckers and chinks in the curtains, we yawned and stretched with satisfaction, shed our cocoons, and felt that we had slept as much as was necessary. By and by, as the sun rose up and warmed the world, we pulled off our clothes and got ready for breakfast. We were just pleasantly in time, for five minutes afterward the driver sent the weird music of his bugle winding over the grassy solitudes, and presently we detected a low hut or two in the distance. Then the rattling of the coach, the clatter of our six horses' hoofs, and the driver's crisp commands, awoke to a

[1] The Secretary was Mark Twain's older brother, Orion, a man whose luck and destiny would be as bleak as Mark Twain's were bright.—C. N.

louder and stronger emphasis, and we went sweeping down on the station at our smartest speed. It was fascinating—that old Overland stage-coaching.

We jumped out in undress uniform. The driver tossed his gathered reins out on the ground, gaped and stretched complacently, drew off his heavy buckskin gloves with great deliberation and insufferable dignity—taking not the slightest notice of a dozen solicitous inquiries after his health, and humbly facetious and flattering accostings, and obsequious tenders of service, from five or six hairy and half-civilized station-keepers and hostlers who were nimbly unhitching our steeds and bringing the fresh team out of the stables—for, in the eyes of the stage-driver of that day, station-keepers and hostlers were a sort of good enough low creatures, useful in their place, and helping to make up a world, but not the kind of beings which a person of distinction could afford to concern himself with; while, on the contrary, in the eyes of the station-keeper and the hostler, the stage-driver was a hero—a great and shining dignitary, the world's favorite son, the envy of the people, the observed of the nations. When they spoke to him they received his insolent silence meekly, and as being the natural and proper conduct of so great a man; when he opened his lips they all hung on his words with admiration (he never honored a particular individual with a remark, but addressed it with a broad generality to the horses, the stables, the surrounding country *and* the human underlings); when he discharged a facetious insulting personality at a hostler, that hostler was happy for the day; when he uttered his one jest—old as the hills, coarse, profane, witless, and inflicted on the same audience, in the same language, every time his coach drove up there—the varlets roared, and slapped their thighs, and swore it was the best thing they'd ever heard in all their lives. And how they would fly around when he wanted a basin of water, a gourd of the same, or a light for his pipe!—but they would instantly insult a passenger if he so far forgot himself as to crave a favor at their hands. They could do that sort of insolence as well as the driver they copied it from—for, let it be borne in mind, the Overland driver had but little less contempt for his passengers than he had for his hostlers.

The hostlers and station-keepers treated the really powerful *conductor* of the coach merely with the best of what was their idea of civility, but the *driver* was the only being they bowed down to and worshiped. How admiringly they would gaze up at him in his high seat as he gloved himself with lingering deliberation, while some happy hostler held the bunch of reins aloft, and waited patiently for him to take it! And how they would bombard him with glorifying ejaculations as he cracked his long whip and went careering away.

The station buildings were long, low huts, made of sun-dried, mud-colored bricks, laid up without mortar (*adobes,* the Spaniards call these bricks, and Americans shorten it to *'dobies*). The roofs, which had no slant to them worth speaking of, were thatched and then sodded or covered with a thick layer of earth, and from this sprung a pretty rank growth of weeds and grass. It was the first time we had ever seen a man's front yard on top of his house. The buildings consisted of barns, stable-room for twelve or fifteen horses, and a hut for an eating-room for passengers. This latter had bunks in it for the station-keeper and a hostler or two. You could rest your elbow on its eaves, and you had to bend in order to get in at the door. In place of a window there was a square hole about large enough for a man to crawl through, but this had no glass in it. There was no flooring, but the ground was packed hard. There was no stove, but the fireplace served all needful purposes. There were no shelves, no cupboards, no closets. In a corner stood an open sack of flour, and nestling against its base were a couple of black and venerable tin coffee-pots, a tin teapot, a little bag of salt, and a side of bacon.

By the door of the station-keeper's den, outside, was a tin washbasin, on the ground. Near it was a pail of water and a piece of yellow bar-soap, and from the eaves hung a hoary blue woolen shirt, significantly—but this latter was the station-keeper's private towel, and only two persons in all the party might venture to use it—the stage-driver and the conductor. The latter would not, from a sense of decency; the former would not, because he did not choose to encourage the advances of a station-keeper. We had towels—in the valise; they might as well have been in Sodom and Gomorrah. We (and the conductor) used our handkerchiefs, and the driver his pantaloons and sleeves. By the door, inside, was fastened a small old-fashioned looking-glass frame, with two little fragments of the original mirror lodged down in one corner of it. This arrangement afforded a pleasant double-barreled portrait of you when you looked into it, with one half of your head set up a couple of inches above the other half. From the glass frame hung the half of a comb by a string—but if I had to describe that patriarch or die, I believe I would order some sample coffins. It had come down from Esau and Samson, and had been accumulating hair ever since—along with certain impurities. In one corner of the room stood three or four rifles and muskets, together with horns and pouches of ammunition. The station-men wore pantaloons of coarse, country-woven stuff, and into the seat and the inside of the legs were sewed ample additions of buckskin, to do duty in place of leggings, when the man rode horseback—so the pants were half dull blue and half yellow, and unspeakably picturesque. The pants were stuffed into the tops of high boots, the heels whereof were armed with great Spanish spurs, whose little iron clogs and chains jingled with every step. The man wore a huge beard and mustachios, an old slouch hat, a blue woolen shirt, no suspenders, no vest, no coat—in a leathern sheath in his belt, a great long "navy" revolver (slung on right side, hammer to the front), and projecting from his boot a horn-handled bowie-knife. The furniture of the hut was neither gorgeous nor much in the way. The rocking-chair and sofas were not present, and never had been, but they were represented by two three-legged stools, a pine-board bench four feet long, and two empty candle-boxes. The table was a greasy board on stilts, and the table-cloth and napkins had not come—and they were not looking for them, either. A battered tin platter, a knife and fork, and a tin pint cup, were at each man's place, and the driver had a queens-ware saucer that had seen better days. Of course, this duke sat at the head of the table. There was one isolated piece of table furniture that bore about it a touching air of grandeur in misfortune. This was the caster. It was German silver, and crippled and rusty, but it was so preposterously out of place there that it was suggestive of a tattered exiled king among barbarians, and the majesty of its native position compelled respect even in its degradation. There was only one cruet left, and that was a stopperless, fly-specked, broken-necked thing, with two inches of vinegar in it, and a dozen preserved flies with their heels up and looking sorry they had invested there.

The station-keeper up-ended a disk of last week's bread, of the shape and size of an old-time cheese, and carved some slabs from it which were as good as Nicholson pavement, and tenderer.

He sliced off a piece of bacon for each man, but only the experienced old hands made out to eat it, for it was condemned army bacon which the United States would not feed to its soldiers in the forts, and the stage company had bought it cheap for the sustenance of their passengers and employees. We may have found this condemned army bacon further out on the Plains than the section I am locating it in, but we *found* it—there is no gainsaying that.

Then he poured for us a beverage which he called *"Slumgullion,"* and it is hard to think he was not inspired when he named it. It really pretended to be tea, but there was too much dish-rag, and sand, and old bacon-rind in it to deceive the intelligent traveler. He had no sugar and no milk—not even a spoon to stir the ingredients with.

We could not eat the bread or the meat, nor drink the "Slumgullion." And when I looked at that melancholy vinegar-cruet, I thought of the anecdote (a very, very old one, even at that day) of the traveler who sat down to a table which had nothing on it but a mackerel and a pot of mustard. He asked the landlord if this was all. The landlord said:

"All! Why, thunder and lightning, I should think there was mackerel enough there for six."

"But I don't like mackerel."

"Oh—then help yourself to the mustard."

In other days I had considered it a good, a very good, anecdote, but there was a dismal plausibility about it, here, that took all the humor out of it.

Our breakfast was before us, but our teeth were idle.

I tasted and smelt, and said I would take coffee, I believed. The station-boss stopped dead still, and glared at me speechless. At last, when he came to, he turned away and said, as one who communes with himself upon a matter too vast to grasp:

"Coffee! Well, if that don't go clean ahead of me, I'm d—d!"

We could not eat, and there was no conversation among the hostlers and herdsmen—we all sat at the same board. At least there was no conversation further than a single hurried request, now and then, from one employee to another. It was always in the same form, and always gruffly friendly. Its Western freshness and novelty startled me, at first, and interested me; but it presently grew monotonous, and lost its charm. It was:

"Pass the bread, you son of a skunk!" No, I forget—skunk was not the word; it seems to me it was still stronger than that; I know it was, in fact, but it is gone from my memory, apparently. However, it is no matter—probably it was too strong for print, anyway. It is the landmark in my memory which tells me where I first encountered the vigorous new vernacular of the occidental plains and mountains.

We gave up the breakfast, and paid our dollar apiece and went back to our mail-bag bed in the coach, and found comfort in our pipes. Right here we suffered the first diminution of our princely state. We left our six fine horses and took six mules in their place. But they were wild Mexican fellows, and a man had to stand at the head of each of them and hold him fast while the driver gloved and got himself ready. And when at last he grasped the reins and gave the word, the men sprung suddenly away from the mules' heads and the coach shot from the station as if it had issued from a cannon. How the frantic animals did scamper! It was a fierce and furious gallop—and the gait never altered for a moment till we reeled off ten or twelve miles and swept up to the next collection of little station huts and stables.

So we flew along all day. At 2 P.M. the belt of timber that fringes the North Platte and marks its windings through the vast level floor of the Plains came in sight. At 4 P.M. we crossed a branch of the river, and at 5 P.M. we crossed the Platte itself, and landed at Fort Kearney, *fifty-six hours out from St. Joe*—THREE HUNDRED MILES!

Now that was stage-coaching on the great Overland, ten or twelve years ago, when perhaps not more than ten men in America, all told, expected to live to see a railroad follow that route to the Pacific.

From *Roughing It,* 1872.

2 : *Salt Lake City*

WE HAD A FINE SUPPER, of the freshest meats and fowls and vegetables—a great variety, and as great abundance. We walked about the streets some, afterward, and glanced in at shops and stores; and there was fascination in surreptitiously staring at every creature we took to be a Mormon. This was fairyland to us, to all intents and purposes—a land of enchantment, and goblins, and awful mystery. We felt a curiosity to ask every child how many mothers it had, and if it could tell them apart; and we experienced a thrill every time a dwelling-house door opened and shut as we passed, disclosing a glimpse of human heads and backs and shoulders —for we so longed to have a good satisfying look at a Mormon family in all its comprehensive ampleness, disposed in the customary concentric rings of its home circle.

By and by the Acting Governor of the territory introduced us to other "Gentiles," and we spent a sociable hour with them. "Gentiles" are people who are not Mormons. Our fellow-passenger, Bemis, took care of himself, during this part of the evening, and did not make an overpowering success of it, either, for he came into our room in the hotel about eleven o'clock, full of cheerfulness, and talking loosely, disjointedly, and indiscriminately, and every now and then tugging out a ragged word by the roots that had more hiccups than syllables in it. This, together with his hanging his coat on the floor on one side of a chair, and his vest on the floor on the other side, and piling his pants on the floor just in front of the same chair, and then contemplating the general result with superstitious awe, and finally pronouncing it "too many for *him*" and going to bed with his boots on, led us to fear that something he had eaten had not agreed with him.

But we knew afterward that it was something he had been drinking. It was the exclusively Mormon refresher, "valley tan." Valley tan (or, at least, one form of valley tan) is a kind of whisky, or first cousin to it; is of Mormon invention and manufactured only in Utah. Tradition says it is made of (imported) fire and brimstone. If I remember rightly, no public drinking-saloons were allowed in the kingdom by Brigham Young, and no private drinking permitted among the faithful, except they confined themselves to "valley tan."

Next day we strolled about everywhere through the broad, straight, level streets, and enjoyed the pleasant strangeness of a city of fifteen thousand inhabitants with no loafers perceptible in it; and no visible drunkards or noisy people; a limpid stream rippling and dancing through every street in place of a filthy gutter; block after block of trim dwellings, built of "frame" and sunburned brick —a great thriving orchard and garden behind every one of them, apparently—branches from the street stream winding and sparkling among the garden-beds and fruit trees—and a grand general air of neatness, repair, thrift, and comfort, around and about and over the whole. And everywhere were workshops, factories, and all manner of industries; and intent faces and busy hands were to be seen wherever one looked; and in one's ears was the ceaseless clink of hammers, the buzz of trade and the contented hum of drums and fly-wheels.

The armorial crest of my own state consisted of two dissolute bears holding up the head of a dead and gone cask between them and making the pertinent remark, "UNITED, WE STAND—(hic!)—DIVIDED WE FALL." It was always too figurative for the author of this book. But the Mormon crest was easy. And it was simple, unostentatious, and fitted like a glove. It was a representation of a GOLDEN BEEHIVE, with the bees all at work!

The city lies in the edge of a level plain as broad as the state of Connecticut, and crouches close down to the ground under a curving wall of mighty mountains whose heads are hidden in the clouds, and whose shoulders bear relics of the snows of winter all the summer long. Seen from one of these dizzy heights, twelve or fifteen miles off, Great Salt Lake City is toned down and diminished till it is suggestive of a child's toy village reposing under the majestic protection of the Chinese wall.

On some of these mountains, to the southwest, it had been raining every day for two weeks, but not a drop had fallen in the city. And on hot days in late spring and early autumn the citizens could quit fanning and growling and go out and cool off by looking at the luxury of a glorious snow-storm going on in the mountains. They could enjoy it at a distance, at those seasons, every day, though no snow would fall in their streets, or anywhere near them.

Salt Lake City was healthy—an extremely healthy city. They declared that there was only one physician in the place and he was arrested every week regularly and held to answer under the vagrant act for having "no visible means of support." They always give you a good substantial article of truth in Salt Lake, and good measure and good weight, too. Very often, if you wished to weigh one of their airiest little commonplace statements you would want the hay-scales.

We desired to visit the famous inland sea, the American "Dead Sea," the great Salt Lake—seventeen miles, horseback, from the city—for we had dreamed about it, and thought about it, and talked about it, and yearned to see it, all the first part of our trip; but now when it was only arm's-length away it had suddenly lost nearly every bit of its interest. And so we put it off, in a sort of general way, till next day—and that was the last we ever thought of it. We dined with some hospitable Gentiles; and visited the foundation of the prodigious temple; and talked long with that shrewd Connecticut Yankee, Heber C. Kimball (since deceased), a saint of high degree and a mighty man of commerce. We saw the "Tithing-House," and the "Lion House," and I do not know or remember how many more church and government buildings of various kinds and curious names. We flitted hither and thither and enjoyed every hour, and picked up a great deal of useful information and entertaining nonsense, and went to bed at night satisfied.

The second day, we made the acquaintance of Mr. Street (since deceased) and put on white shirts and went and paid a state visit to the king. He seemed a quiet, kindly, easy-mannered, dignified, self-possessed old gentleman of fifty-five or sixty, and had a gentle craft in his eye that probably belonged there. He was very simply dressed and was just taking off a straw hat as we entered. He talked about Utah, and the Indians, and Nevada, and general American matters and questions, with our secretary and certain government officials who came with us. But he never paid any attention to me, notwithstanding I made several attempts to "draw him out" on federal politics and his high-handed attitude toward Congress. I thought some of the things I said were rather fine. But he merely looked around at me, at distant intervals, something as I have seen a benignant old cat look around to see which kitten was meddling with her tail. By and by I subsided into an indignant silence, and so sat until the end, hot and flushed, and execrating him in my heart for an ignorant savage. But he was calm. His conversation with those gentlemen flowed on as sweetly and peacefully and musically as any summer brook. When the audience was ended and we were retiring from the presence, he put his hand on my head, beamed down on me in an admiring way and said to my brother:

"Ah—your child, I presume? Boy or girl?"

Mr. Street was very busy with his telegraphic matters—and considering that he had eight or nine hundred miles of rugged, snowy, uninhabited mountains, and waterless, treeless, melancholy deserts to traverse with his wire, it was natural and needful that he should be as busy as possible. He could not go comfortably along and cut his poles by the roadside, either, but they had to be hauled by ox-teams across those exhausting deserts—and it was two days' journey from water to water, in one or two of them. Mr. Street's contract was a vast work, every way one looked at it; and yet to comprehend what the vague words "eight hundred miles of rugged mountains and dismal deserts" mean, one must go over the ground in person—pen-and-ink descriptions cannot convey the dreary reality to the reader. And after all, Mr. S.'s mightiest difficulty turned out to be one which he had never taken into the account at all. Unto Mormons he had sublet the hardest and heaviest half of his great undertaking, and all of a sudden they concluded that they were going to make little or nothing, and so they tranquilly threw their poles overboard in mountain or desert, just as it happened when they took the notion, and drove home and went about their customary business! They were under written contract to Mr. Street, but they did not care anything for that. They said they would "admire" to see a "Gentile" force a Mormon to fulfil a losing contract in Utah! And they made themselves very merry over the matter. Street said—for it was he that told us these things:

"I was in dismay. I was under heavy bonds to complete my contract in a given time, and this disaster looked very much like ruin. It was an astounding thing; it was such a wholly unlooked-for difficulty, that I was entirely nonplussed. I am a business man—have always been a business man—do not know anything *but* business—and so you can imagine how like being struck by lightning it was to find myself in a country where *written contracts were worthless!*—that main security, that sheet-anchor, that absolute necessity, of business. My confidence left me. There was no use in making new contracts—that was plain. I talked with first one prominent citizen and then another. They all sympathized with me, first rate, but they did not know how to help me. But at last a Gentile said, 'Go to Brigham Young!—these small fry cannot do you any good.' I did not think much of the idea, for if the *law* could not help me, what could an individual do who had not even anything to do with either making the laws or executing them? He might be a very good patriarch of a church and preacher in its tabernacle, but something sterner than religion and moral suasion was needed to handle a hundred refractory, half-civilized subcontractors. But what was a man to do? I thought if Mr. Young could not do anything else, he might probably be able to give me some advice and a valuable hint or two, and so I went straight to him and laid the whole case before him. He said very little, but he showed strong interest all the way through. He examined all the papers in detail, and whenever there seemed anything like a hitch, either in the papers or in my statement, he would go back and take up the thread and follow it patiently out to an intelligent and satisfactory result. Then he made a list of the contractors' names. Finally he said:

" 'Mr. Street, this is all perfectly plain. These contracts are strictly and legally drawn, and are duly signed and certified. These men manifestly entered into them with their eyes open. I see no fault or flaw anywhere.'

"Then Mr. Young turned to a man waiting at the other end of the room and said: 'Take this list of names to So-and-so, and tell him to have these men here at such-and-such an hour.'

"They were there, to the minute. So was I. Mr. Young asked them a number of questions, and their answers made my statement good. Then he said to them:

" 'You signed these contracts and assumed these obligations of your own free will and accord?'

" 'Yes.'

" 'Then carry them out to the letter, if it makes paupers of you! Go!'

"And they *did* go, too! They are strung across the deserts now, working like bees. And I never hear a word out of them. There is a batch of governors, and judges, and other officials here, shipped from Washington, and they maintain the semblance of a republican form of government—but the petrified truth is that Utah is an absolute monarchy and Brigham Young is king!"

Mr. Street was a fine man, and I believe his story. I knew him well during several years afterward in San Francisco.

Our stay in Salt Lake City amounted to only two days, and therefore we had no time to make the customary inquisition into the workings of polygamy and get up the usual statistics and deductions preparatory to calling the attention of the nation at large once more to the matter. I had the will to do it. With the gushing self-sufficiency of youth I was feverish to plunge in headlong and achieve a great reform here—until I saw the Mormon women. Then I was touched. My heart was wiser than my head. It warmed toward these poor, ungainly, and pathetically "homely" creatures, and as I turned to hide the generous moisture in my eyes, I said, "No—the man that marries one of them has done an act of Christian charity which entitles him to the kindly applause of mankind, not their harsh censure—and the man that marries sixty of them has done a deed of open-handed generosity so sublime that the nations should stand uncovered in his presence and worship in silence."

It is a luscious country for thrilling evening stories about assassinations of intractable Gentiles. I cannot easily conceive of anything more cozy than the night in Salt Lake which we spent in a Gentile den, smoking pipes and listening to tales of how Burton galloped in among the pleading and defenseless "Morisites" and shot them down, men and women, like so many dogs. And how Bill Hickman, a Destroying Angel, shot Drown and Arnold dead for bringing suit against him for a debt. And how Porter Rockwell did this and that dreadful thing. And how heedless people often come to Utah and make remarks about Brigham, or polygamy, or some other sacred matter, and the very next morning at daylight such parties are sure to be found lying up some back alley, contentedly waiting for the hearse. And the next most interesting thing is to sit and listen to these Gentiles talk about polygamy; and how some portly old frog of an elder, or a bishop, marries a girl—likes her, marries her sister—likes her, marries another sister—likes her, takes another—likes her, marries her mother—likes her, marries her father, grandfather, great grandfather, and then comes back hungry and asks for more. And how the pert young thing of eleven will chance to be the favorite wife, and her own venerable grandmother have to rank away down toward D 4 in their mutual husband's esteem, and have to sleep in the kitchen, as like as not. And how this dreadful sort of thing, this hiving together in one foul nest of mother and daughters, and the making a young daughter superior to her own mother in rank and authority, are things which Mormon women submit to because their religion teaches them that the more wives a man has on earth, and the more children he rears, the higher the place they will all have in the world to come—and the warmer, maybe, though they do not seem to say anything about that.

According to these Gentile friends of ours, Brigham Young's harem contains twenty or thirty wives. They said that some of them had grown old and gone out of active service, but were comfortably housed and cared for in the hennery—or the Lion House, as it is strangely named. Along with each wife were her children—fifty altogether. The house was perfectly quiet and orderly, when the children were still. They all took their meals in one room, and a happy and homelike sight it was pronounced to be. None of our party got an opportunity to take dinner with Mr. Young, but a Gentile by the name of Johnson professed to have enjoyed a sociable breakfast in the Lion House. He gave a preposterous account of the "calling of the roll," and other preliminaries, and the carnage that ensued when the buckwheat-cakes came in. But he embellished rather too much. He said that Mr. Young told him several smart sayings of certain of his "two-year-olds," observing with some pride that for many years he had been the heaviest contributor in that line to one of the Eastern magazines; and then he wanted to show Mr. Johnson one of the pets that had said the last good thing, but he could not find the child. He searched the faces of the children in detail, but he could not decide which one it was. Finally, he gave it up with a sigh and said: "I thought I would know the little cub again, but I don't." Mr. Johnson said further, that Mr. Young observed that life was a sad, sad thing—"because the joy of every new marriage a man contracted was so apt to be blighted by the inopportune funeral of a less recent bride." And Mr. Johnson said that while he and Mr. Young were pleasantly conversing in private, one of the Mrs. Youngs came in and demanded a breastpin, remarking that she had found out that he had been giving a breastpin to No. 6, and *she,* for one, did not propose to let this partiality go on without making a satisfactory amount of trouble about it. Mr. Young reminded her that there was a stranger present. Mrs. Young said that if the state of things inside the house was not agreeable to the stranger, he could find room outside. Mr. Young promised the breastpin, and she went away. But in a minute or two another Mrs. Young came in and demanded a breastpin. Mr. Young began a remonstrance, but Mrs. Young cut him short. She said No. 6 had got one, and No. 11 was promised one, and it was "no use for him to try to impose on her—she hoped she knew her rights." He gave his promise, and she went. And presently three Mrs. Youngs entered in a body and opened on their husband a tempest of tears, abuse, and entreaty. They had heard all about No. 6, No. 11, and No. 14. Three more breastpins were promised. They were hardly gone when nine more Mrs. Youngs filed into the presence, and a new tempest burst forth and raged round about the prophet and his guest. Nine breastpins were promised, and the weird sisters filed out again. And in came eleven more, weeping and wailing and gnashing their teeth. Eleven promised breastpins purchased peace once more.

"That is a specimen," said Mr. Young. "You see how it is. You see what a life I lead. A man *can't* be wise all the time. In a heedless moment I gave my darling No. 6—excuse my calling her thus, as her other name has escaped me for the moment—a breastpin. It was only worth twenty-five dollars—that is, *apparently* that was its whole cost—but its ultimate cost was inevitably bound to be a good deal more. You yourself have seen it climb up to six hundred and fifty dollars—and alas, even that is not the end! For I have wives all over this territory of Utah. I have dozens of wives whose *numbers,* even, I do not know without looking in the family Bible. They are scattered far and wide among the mountains and valleys of my realm. And, mark you, every solitary one of them will hear of this wretched breastpin, and every last one of them will have one or die. No. 6's breastpin will cost me twenty-five hundred dollars before I see the end of it. And these creatures will compare these pins together, and if one is a shade finer than the rest, they will all be thrown on my hands, and I will have to order a new lot to keep peace in the family. Sir, you probably did not know it, but all the time you were present with my children your every movement was watched by vigilant servitors of mine. If you had offered to give a child a dime, or a stick of candy, or any trifle of the kind, you would have been snatched out of the house instantly, provided it could be done before your gift left your hand. Otherwise it would be absolutely necessary for you to make an exactly similar gift to all my children—and knowing by experience the importance of the thing, I would have stood by and seen to it myself that you did it, and did it thoroughly. Once a gentleman gave one of my children a tin whistle—a veritable invention of Satan, sir, and one which I have an unspeakable horror of, and so would you if you had eighty or ninety children in your house. But the deed was done—the man escaped. I knew what the result was going to be, and I thirsted for vengeance. I ordered out a flock of Destroying Angels, and they hunted the man far into the fastnesses of the Nevada mountains. But they never caught him. I am not cruel, sir—I am not vindictive except when sorely outraged—but if I had caught him, sir, so help me Joseph Smith, I would have locked him into the nursery till the brats whistled him to death. By the slaughtered body of St. Parley Pratt (whom God assoil!) there was never anything on this earth like it! *I* knew who gave the whistle to the child, but I could not make those jealous mothers believe me. They believed *I* did it, and the result was just what any man of reflection could have foreseen: I had to order a hundred and ten whistles—I think we had a hundred and ten children in the house then, but some of them are off at college now—I had to order a hundred and ten of those shrieking things, and I wish I may never speak another word if we didn't have to talk on our fingers entirely, from that time forth until the children got tired of the whistles. And if ever another man gives a whistle to a child of mine and I get my hands on him, I will hang him higher than Haman! That is the word with the bark on it! Shade of Nephi! *You* don't know anything about married life. I am rich, and everybody knows it. I am benevolent, and everybody takes advantage of it. I have a strong fatherly instinct, and all the foundlings are foisted on me. Every time a woman wants to do well by her darling, she puzzles her brain to cipher out some scheme for getting it into my hands. Why, sir, a woman came here once with a child of a curious lifeless sort of complexion (and so had the woman), and swore that the child was mine and she my wife—that I had married her at such-and-such a time in such-and-such a place, but she had forgotten her number, and of course I could not remember her name. Well, sir, she called my attention to the fact that the child looked like me, and really it did seem to resemble me—a common thing in the territory—and, to cut the story short, I put it in my nursery, and she left. And, by the ghost of Orson Hyde, when they came to wash the paint off that child it was an Injun! Bless my soul, you don't know anything about married life. It is a perfect dog's life, sir—a perfect dog's life. You can't economize. It isn't possible. I have tried keeping one set of bridal attire for all occasions. But it is of no use. First you'll marry a combination of calico and consumption that's as thin as a rail, and next you'll get a creature that's nothing more than the dropsy in disguise, and then you've got to eke out that bridal dress with an old balloon. That is the way it goes. And think of the wash-bill— (excuse these tears)—nine hundred and eighty-four pieces a week! No, sir, there is no such a thing as economy in a family like mine. Why, just the one item of cradles—think of it! And vermifuge! Soothing-syrup! Teething-rings! And 'papa's watches' for the babies to play with! And things to scratch the furniture with! And lucifer matches for them to eat, and pieces of glass to cut themselves with! The item of glass alone would support *your* family, I venture to say, sir. Let me scrimp and squeeze all I can, I still can't get ahead as fast as I feel I ought to, with my opportunities. Bless you, sir, at a time when I had seventy-two wives in this house, I groaned under the pressure of keeping thousands of dollars tied up in seventy-two bedsteads when the money ought to have been out at interest; and I just sold out the whole stock, sir, at a sacrifice, and built a bedstead seven feet long and ninety-six feet wide. But it was a failure, sir. I could *not* sleep. It appeared to me that the whole seventy-two women snored at once. The roar was deafening. And then the danger of it! That was what I was looking at. They would all draw in their breath at once, and you could actually see the walls of the house suck in—and then they would all exhale their breath at once, and you could see the walls swell out, and strain, and hear the rafters crack, and the shingles grind together. My friend, take an old man's advice and *don't* encumber yourself with a large family—mind, I tell you, don't do it. In a small family, and in a small family only, you will find that comfort and that peace of mind which are the best at last of the blessings this world is able to afford us, and for the lack of which no accumulation of wealth, and no acquisition of fame, power, and greatness can ever compensate us. Take my word for it, ten or eleven wives is all you need—never go over it."

Some instinct or other made me set this Johnson down as being unreliable. And yet he was a very entertaining person, and I doubt if some of the information he gave us could have been acquired from any other source. He was a pleasant contrast to those reticent Mormons.

From *Roughing It,* 1872.

3 : Carson City

WE WERE APPROACHING THE END of our long journey. It was the morning of the twentieth day. At noon we would reach Carson City, the capital of Nevada Territory. We were not glad, but sorry. It had been a fine pleasure trip; we had fed fat on wonders every day; we were now well accustomed to stage life, and very fond of it; so the idea of coming to a standstill and settling down to a humdrum existence in a village was not agreeable, but on the contrary depressing.

Visibly our new home was a desert, walled in by barren, snow-clad mountains. There was not a tree in sight. There was no vegetation but the endless sage-brush and greasewood. All nature was gray with it. We were plowing through great deeps of powdery alkali dust that rose in thick clouds and floated across the plain like smoke from a burning house. We were coated with it like millers; so were the coach, the mules, the mail-bags, the driver—we and the sage-brush and the other scenery were all one monotonous color. Long trains of freight-wagons in the distance enveloped in ascending masses of dust suggested pictures of prairies on fire. These teams and their masters were the only life we saw. Otherwise we moved in the midst of solitude, silence, and desolation. Every twenty steps we passed the skeleton of some dead beast of burthen, with its dust-coated skin stretched tightly over its empty ribs. Frequently a solemn raven sat upon the skull or the hips and contemplated the passing coach with meditative serenity.

By and by Carson City was pointed out to us. It nestled in the edge of a great plain and was a sufficient number of miles away to look like an assemblage of mere white spots in the shadow of a grim range of mountains overlooking it, whose summits seemed lifted clear out of companionship and consciousness of earthly things.

We arrived, disembarked, and the stage went on. It was a "wooden" town; its population two thousand souls. The main street consisted of four or five blocks of little white frame stores which were too high to sit down on, but not too high for various other purposes; in fact, hardly high enough. They were packed close together, side by side, as if room were scarce in that mighty plain. The sidewalk was of boards that were more or less loose and inclined to rattle when walked upon. In the middle of the town, opposite the stores, was the "plaza," which is native to all towns beyond the Rocky Mountains—a large, unfenced, level vacancy, with a liberty pole in it, and very useful as a place for public auctions, horse trades, and mass-meetings, and likewise for teamsters to camp in. Two other sides of the plaza were faced by stores, offices, and stables. The rest of Carson City was pretty scattering.

We were introduced to several citizens, at the stage-office and on the way up to the Governor's from the hotel—among others, to a Mr. Harris, who was on horseback; he began to say something, but interrupted himself with the remark:

"I'll have to get you to excuse me a minute; yonder is the witness that swore I helped to rob the California coach—a piece of impertinent intermeddling, sir, for I am not even acquainted with the man."

Then he rode over and began to rebuke the stranger with a six-shooter, and the stranger began to explain with another. When the pistols were emptied, the stranger resumed his work (mending a whip-lash), and Mr. Harris rode by with a polite nod, homeward bound, with a bullet through one of his lungs, and several through his hips; and from them issued little rivulets of blood that coursed down the horse's sides and made the animal look quite picturesque. I never saw Harris shoot a man after that but it recalled to mind that first day in Carson.

This was all we saw that day, for it was two o'clock, now, and according to custom the daily "Washoe Zephyr" set in; a soaring dust-drift about the size of the United States set up edgewise came with it, and the capital of Nevada Territory disappeared from view. Still, there were sights to be seen which were not wholly uninteresting to newcomers; for the vast dust-cloud was thickly freckled with things strange to the upper air—things living and dead, that flitted hither and thither, going and coming, appearing and disappearing among the rolling billows of dust—hats, chickens, and parasols sailing in the remote heavens; blankets, tin signs, sage-brush, and shingles a shade lower; door-mats and buffalo-robes lower still; shovels and coal-scuttles on the next grade; glass doors, cats, and little children on the next; disrupted lumber yards, light buggies, and wheelbarrows on the next; and down only thirty or forty feet above ground was a scurrying storm of emigrating roofs and vacant lots.

It was something to see that much. I could have seen more, if I could have kept the dust out of my eyes.

But, seriously, a Washoe wind is by no means a trifling matter. It blows flimsy houses down, lifts shingle roofs occasionally, rolls up tin ones like sheet music, now and then blows a stage-coach over and spills the passengers; and tradition says the reason there are so many bald people there is, that the wind blows the hair off their heads while they are looking skyward after their hats. Carson streets seldom look inactive on summer afternoons, because there are so many citizens skipping around their escaping hats, like chamber-maids trying to head off a spider.

The "Washoe Zephyr" (Washoe is a pet nickname for Nevada) is a peculiarly Scriptural wind, in that no man knoweth "whence it cometh." That is to say, where it *originates*. It comes right over the mountains from the West, but when one crosses the ridge he does not find any of it on the other side! It probably is manufactured on the mountain-top for the occasion, and starts from there. It is a pretty regular wind, in the summer-time. Its office-hours are from two in the afternoon till two the next morning; and anybody venturing abroad during those twelve hours needs to allow for the wind or he will bring up a mile or two to leeward of the point he is aiming at. And yet the first complaint a Washoe visitor to San Francisco makes, is that the sea-winds blow so, there! There is a good deal of human nature in that.

We found the state palace of the Governor of Nevada Territory to consist of a white frame one-story house with two small rooms in it and a stanchion-supported shed in front—for grandeur—it compelled the respect of the citizen and inspired the Indians with awe. The newly arrived Chief and Associate Justices of the territory, and other machinery of the government, were domiciled with less splendor. They were boarding around privately, and had their offices in their bedrooms.

The Secretary and I took quarters in the "ranch" of a worthy French lady by the name of Bridget O'Flannigan, a camp-follower of his Excellency the Governor. She had known him in his prosperity as commander-in-chief of the Metropolitan Police of New York, and she would not desert him in his adversity as Governor of Nevada. Our room was on the lower floor, facing the plaza; and when we had got our bed, a small table, two chairs, the government fire-proof safe, and the Unabridged Dictionary into it, there was still room enough left for a visitor—maybe two, but not without straining the walls. But the walls could stand it—at least the partitions could, for they consisted simply of one thickness of white "cotton domestic" stretched from corner to corner of the room. This was the rule in Carson—any other kind of partition was the rare exception. And if you stood in a dark room and your neighbors in the next had lights, the shadows on your canvas told queer secrets sometimes! Very often these partitions were made of old flour-sacks basted together; and then the difference between the common herd and the aristocracy was, that the common herd had unornamented sacks, while the walls of the aristocrat were overpowering with rudimental fresco—*i. e.*, red and blue mill brands on the flour-sacks. Occasionally, also, the better classes embellished their canvas by pasting pictures from *Harper's Weekly* on them. In many cases, too, the wealthy and the cultured rose to spittoons and other evidences of a sumptuous and luxurious taste.[1] We had a carpet and a genuine queen's-ware washbowl. Consequently we were hated without reserve by the other tenants of the O'Flannigan "ranch." When we added a painted oilcloth window-curtain, we simply took our lives into our own hands. To prevent bloodshed I removed up-stairs and took up quarters with the untitled plebeians in one of the fourteen white-pine cot-bedsteads that stood in two long ranks in the one sole room of which the second story consisted.

It was a jolly company, the fourteen. They were principally voluntary camp-followers of the Governor, who had joined his retinue by their own election at New York and San Francisco, and came along, feeling that in the scuffle for little territorial crumbs and offices they could not make their condition more precarious than it was, and might reasonably expect to make it better. They were popularly known as the "Irish Brigade," though there were only four or five Irishmen among all the Governor's retainers. His good-natured Excellency was much annoyed at the gossip his henchmen created—especially when there arose a rumor that they were paid assassins of his, brought along to quietly reduce the Democratic vote when desirable!

Mrs. O'Flannigan was boarding and lodging them at ten dollars a week apiece, and they were cheerfully giving their notes for it. They were perfectly satisfied, but Bridget presently found that notes that could not be discounted were but a feeble constitution for a Carson boarding-house. So she began to harry the Governor to find employment for the "Brigade." Her importunities and theirs together drove him to a gentle desperation at last, and he finally summoned the Brigade to the presence. Then, said he:

"Gentlemen, I have planned a lucrative and useful service for you—a service which will provide you with recreation amid noble landscapes, and afford you never-ceasing opportunities for enriching your minds by observation and study. I want you to survey a railroad from Carson City westward to a certain point! When the legislature meets I will have the necessary bill passed and the remuneration arranged."

[1] Washoe people take a joke so hard that I must explain that the above description was only the rule; there were many honorable exceptions in Carson—plastered ceilings and houses that had considerable furniture in them.—M. T.

"What, a railroad over the Sierra Nevada Mountains?"

"Well, then, survey it eastward to a certain point!"

He converted them into surveyors, chain-bearers, and so on, and turned them loose in the desert. It was "recreation" with a vengeance! Recreation on foot, lugging chains through sand and sagebrush, under a sultry sun and among cattle bones, coyotes, and tarantulas. "Romantic adventure!" could go no further. They surveyed very slowly, very deliberately, very carefully. They returned every night during the first week, dusty, footsore, tired, and hungry, but very jolly. They brought in great stores of prodigious hairy spiders—tarantulas—and imprisoned them in covered tumblers upstairs in the "ranch." After the first week, they had to camp on the field, for they were getting well eastward. They made a good many inquiries as to the location of that indefinite "certain point," but got no information. At last, to a peculiarly urgent inquiry of "How far eastward?" Governor Nye telegraphed back:

"To the Atlantic Ocean, blast you!—and then bridge it and go on!"

This brought back the dusty toilers, who sent in a report and ceased from their labors. The Governor was always comfortable about it; he said Mrs. O'Flannigan would hold him for the Brigade's board anyhow, and he intended to get what entertainment he could out of the boys; he said, with his old-time pleasant twinkle, that he meant to survey them into Utah and then telegraph Brigham to hang them for trespass!

The surveyors brought back more tarantulas with them, and so we had quite a menagerie arranged along the shelves of the room. Some of these spiders could straddle over a common saucer with their hairy, muscular legs, and when their feelings were hurt, or their dignity offended, they were the wickedest-looking desperadoes the animal world can furnish. If their glass prison-houses were touched ever so lightly they were up and spoiling for a fight in a minute. Starchy?—proud? Indeed, they would take up a straw and pick their teeth like a member of Congress. There was as usual a furious "zephyr" blowing the first night of the Brigade's return, and about midnight the roof of an adjoining stable blew off, and a corner of it came crashing through the side of our ranch. There was a simultaneous awakening, and a tumultuous muster of the Brigade in the dark, and a general tumbling and sprawling over each other in the narrow aisle between the bed-rows. In the midst of the turmoil, Bob H—— sprung up out of a sound sleep, and knocked down a shelf with his head. Instantly he shouted:

"Turn out, boys—the tarantulas is loose!"

No warning ever sounded so dreadful. Nobody tried, any longer, to leave the room, lest he might step on a tarantula. Every man groped for a trunk or a bed, and jumped on it. Then followed the strangest silence—a silence of grisly suspense it was, too—waiting, expectancy, fear. It was as dark as pitch, and one had to imagine the spectacle of those fourteen scant-clad men roosting gingerly on trunks and beds, for not a thing could be seen. Then came occasional little interruptions of the silence, and one could recognize a man and tell his locality by his voice, or locate any other sound a sufferer made by his gropings or changes of position. The occasional voices were not given to much speaking—you simply heard a gentle ejaculation of "Ow!" followed by a solid thump, and you knew the gentleman had felt a hairy blanket or something touch his bare skin and had skipped from a bed to the floor. Another silence. Presently you would hear a gasping voice say:

"Su-su-something's crawling up the back of my neck!"

Every now and then you could hear a little subdued scramble and a sorrowful "O Lord!" and then you knew that somebody was getting away from something he took for a tarantula, and not losing any time about it, either. Directly a voice in the corner rang out wild and clear:

"I've got him! I've got him!" [Pause, and probable change of circumstances.] "No, he's got me! Oh, ain't they *never* going to fetch a lantern!"

The lantern came at that moment, in the hands of Mrs. O'Flannigan, whose anxiety to know the amount of damage done by the assaulting roof had not prevented her waiting a judicious interval, after getting out of bed and lighting up, to see if the wind was done, now, up-stairs, or had a larger contract.

The landscape presented when the lantern flashed into the room was picturesque, and might have been funny to some people, but was not to us. Although we were perched so strangely upon boxes, trunks and beds, and so strangely attired, too, we were too earnestly distressed and too genuinely miserable to see any fun about it, and there was not the semblance of a smile anywhere visible.

I know I am not capable of suffering more than I did during those few minutes of suspense in the dark, surrounded by those creeping, bloody-minded tarantulas. I had skipped from bed to bed and from box to box in a cold agony, and every time I touched anything that was fuzzy I fancied I felt the fangs. I had rather go to war than live that episode over again. Nobody was hurt. The man who thought a tarantula had "got him" was mistaken—only a crack in a box had caught his finger. Not one of those escaped tarantulas was ever seen again. There were ten or twelve of them. We took candles and hunted the place high and low for them, but with no success. Did we go back to bed then? We did nothing of the kind. Money could not have persuaded us to do it. We sat up the rest of the night playing cribbage and keeping a sharp lookout for the enemy.

From *Roughing It,* 1872.

4 : Lake Tahoe

IT WAS THE END OF AUGUST, and the skies were cloudless and the weather superb. In two or three weeks I had grown wonderfully fascinated with the curious new country, and concluded to put off my return to "the States" awhile. I had grown well accustomed to wearing a damaged slouch hat, blue woolen shirt, and pants crammed into boot-tops, and gloried in the absence of coat, vest, and braces. I felt rowdyish and "bully" (as the historian Josephus phrases it, in his fine chapter upon the destruction of the Temple). It seemed to me that nothing could be so fine and so romantic. I had become an officer of the government, but that was for mere sublimity. The office was an unique sinecure. I had nothing to do and no salary. I was private secretary to his majesty the Secretary, and there was not yet writing enough for two of us. So Johnny K—— and I devoted our time to amusement. He was the young son of an Ohio nabob and was out there for recreation.

He got it. We had heard a world of talk about the marvelous beauty of Lake Tahoe, and finally curiosity drove us thither to see it. Three or four members of the Brigade had been there and located some timber-lands on its shores and stored up a quantity of provisions in their camp. We strapped a couple of blankets on our shoulders and took an ax apiece and started—for we intended to take up a wood ranch or so ourselves and become wealthy. We were on foot. The reader will find it advantageous to go horseback. We were told that the distance was eleven miles. We tramped a long time on level ground, and then toiled laboriously up a mountain about a thousand miles high and looked over. No lake there. We descended on the other side, crossed the valley and toiled up another mountain three or four thousand miles high, apparently, and looked over again. No lake yet. We sat down tired and perspiring, and hired a couple of Chinamen to curse those people who had beguiled us. Thus refreshed, we presently resumed the march with renewed vigor and determination. We plodded on, two or three hours longer, and at last the lake burst upon us—a noble sheet of blue water lifted six thousand three hundred feet above the level of the sea, and walled in by a rim of snow-clad mountain peaks that towered aloft full three thousand feet higher still! It was a vast oval, and one would have to use up eighty or a hundred good miles in traveling around it. As it lay there with the shadows of the mountains brilliantly photographed upon its still surface I thought it must surely be the fairest picture the whole earth affords.

We found the small skiff belonging to the Brigade boys, and without loss of time set out across a deep bend of the lake toward the landmarks that signified the locality of the camp. I got Johnny to row—not because I mind exertion myself, but because it makes me sick to ride backward when I am at work. But I steered. A three-mile pull brought us to the camp just as the night fell, and we stepped ashore very tired and wolfishly hungry. In a "cache" among the rocks we found the provisions and the cooking-utensils, and then, all fatigued as I was, I sat down on a boulder and superintended while Johnny gathered wood and cooked supper. Many a man who had gone through what I had, would have wanted to rest.

It was a delicious supper—hot bread, fried bacon, and black coffee. It was a delicious solitude we were in, too. Three miles away was a sawmill and some workmen, but there were not fifteen other human beings throughout the wide circumference of the lake. As the darkness closed down and the stars came out and spangled the great mirror with jewels, we smoked meditatively in the solemn hush and forgot our troubles and our pains. In due time we spread our blankets in the warm sand between two large boulders and soon fell asleep, careless of the procession of ants that passed in through rents in our clothing and explored our persons. Nothing could disturb the sleep that fettered us, for it had been fairly earned, and if our consciences had any sins on them they had to adjourn court for that night, anyway. The wind rose just as we were losing consciousness, and we were lulled to sleep by the beating of the surf upon the shore.

It is always very cold on that lake-shore in the night, but we had plenty of blankets and were warm enough. We never moved a muscle all night, but waked at early dawn in the original positions, and got up at once, thoroughly refreshed, free from soreness, and brim full of friskiness. There is no end of wholesome medicine in such an experience. That morning we could have whipped ten such people as we were the day before—sick ones at any rate. But the world is slow, and people will go to "water cures" and "movement cures" and to foreign lands for health. Three months of camp life on Lake Tahoe would restore an Egyptian mummy to his pristine vigor, and give him an appetite like an alligator. I do not mean the oldest and driest mummies, of course, but the fresher ones. The air up there in the clouds is very pure and fine, bracing and delicious. And why shouldn't it be?—it is the same the angels breathe. I think that hardly any amount of fatigue can be gathered together that a man cannot sleep off in one night on the sand by its side. Not under a roof, but under the sky; it seldom or never rains there in the summer-time. I know a man who went there to die. But he made a failure of it. He was a skeleton when he came, and could barely stand. He had no appetite, and did nothing but read tracts and reflect on the future. Three months later he was sleeping out-of-doors regularly, eating all he could hold, three times a day, and chasing game over mountains three thousand feet high for recreation. And he was a skeleton no longer, but weighed part of a ton. This is no fancy sketch, but the truth. His disease was consumption. I confidently commend his experience to other skeletons.

I superintended again, and as soon as we had eaten breakfast we got in the boat and skirted along the lake-shore about three miles and disembarked. We liked the appearance of the place, and so we claimed some three hundred acres of it and stuck our "notices" on a tree. It was yellow-pine timber-land—a dense forest of trees a hundred feet high and from one to five feet through at the butt. It was necessary to fence our property or we could not hold it. That is to say, it was necessary to cut down trees here and there and make them fall in such a way as to form a sort of inclosure (with pretty wide gaps in it). We cut down three trees apiece, and found it such heartbreaking work that we decided to "rest our case" on those; if they held the property, well and good; if they didn't, let the property spill out through the gaps and go; it was no use to work ourselves to death merely to save a few acres of land. Next day we came back to build a house—for a house was also necessary, in order to hold the property. We decided to build a substantial log house and excite the envy of the Brigade boys; but by the time we had cut and trimmed the first log it seemed unnecessary to be so elaborate, and so we concluded to build it of saplings. However, two saplings, duly cut and trimmed, compelled recognition of the fact that a still modester architecture would satisfy the law, and so we concluded to build a "brush" house. We devoted the next day to this work, but we did so much "sitting around" and discussing, that by the middle of the afternoon we had achieved only a half-way sort of affair which one of us had to watch while the other cut brush, lest if both turned our backs we might not be able to find it again, it had such a strong family resemblance to the surrounding vegetation. But we were satisfied with it.

We were landowners now, duly seized and possessed, and within the protection of the law. Therefore we decided to take up our residence on our own domain and enjoy that large sense of independence which only such an experience can bring. Late the next afternoon, after a good long rest, we sailed away from the Brigade camp with all the provisions and cooking-utensils we could carry off—borrow is the more accurate word—and just as the night was falling we beached the boat at our own landing.

If there is any life that is happier than the life we led on our timber ranch for the next two or three weeks, it must be a sort of life which I have not read of in books or experienced in person. We did not see a human being but ourselves during the time, or hear any sounds but those that were made by the wind and the waves, the sighing of the pines, and now and then the far-off thunder of an avalanche. The forest about us was dense and cool, the sky above us was cloudless and brilliant with sunshine, the broad lake before us was glassy and clear, or rippled and breezy, or black and storm-tossed, according to Nature's mood; and its circling border of mountain domes, clothed with forests, scarred with landslides, cloven by cañons and valleys, and helmeted with glittering snow, fitly framed and finished the noble picture. The view was always fascinating, bewitching, entrancing. The eye was never tired of gazing, night or day, in calm or storm; it suffered but one grief, and that was that it could not look always, but must close sometimes in sleep.

We slept in the sand close to the water's edge, between two protecting boulders, which took care of the stormy night winds for us. We never took any paregoric to make us sleep. At the first break of dawn we were always up and running foot-races to tone down excess of physical vigor and exuberance of spirits. That is, Johnny was—but I held his hat. While smoking the pipe of peace after breakfast we watched the sentinel peaks put on the glory of the sun, and followed the conquering light as it swept down among the shadows, and set the captive crags and forests free. We watched the tinted pictures grow and brighten upon the water till every little detail of forest, precipice, and pinnacle was wrought in and finished, and the miracle of the enchanter complete. Then to "business."

That is, drifting around in the boat. We were on the north shore. There, the rocks on the bottom are sometimes gray, sometimes white. This gives the marvelous transparency of the water a fuller advantage than it has elsewhere on the lake. We usually pushed out a hundred yards or so from the shore, and then lay down on the thwarts in the sun, and let the boat drift by the hour whither it would. We seldom talked. It interrupted the Sabbath stillness, and marred the dreams the luxurious rest and indolence brought. The shore all along was indented with deep, curved bays and coves, bordered by narrow sand-beaches; and where the sand ended, the steep mountainsides rose right up aloft into space—rose up like a vast wall a little out of the perpendicular, and thickly wooded with tall pines.

So singularly clear was the water, that where it was only twenty or thirty feet deep the bottom was so perfectly distinct that the boat seemed floating in the air! Yes, where it was even *eighty* feet deep. Every little pebble was distinct, every speckled trout, every hand's-breadth of sand. Often, as we lay on our faces, a granite boulder, as large as a village church, would start out of the bottom apparently, and seem climbing up rapidly to the surface, till presently it threatened to touch our faces, and we could not resist the impulse to seize an oar and avert the danger. But the boat would float on, and the boulder descend again, and then we could see that when we had been exactly above it, it must still have been twenty or thirty feet below the surface. Down through the transparency of these great depths, the water was not *merely* transparent, but dazzlingly, brilliantly so. All objects seen through it had a bright, strong vividness, not only of outline, but of every minute detail, which they would not have had when seen simply through the same depth of atmosphere. So empty and airy did all spaces seem below us, and so strong was the sense of floating high aloft in mid-nothingness, that we called these boat excursions "balloon voyages."

We fished a good deal, but we did not average one fish a week. We could see trout by the thousand winging about in the emptiness under us, or sleeping in shoals on the bottom, but they would not bite—they could see the line too plainly, perhaps. We frequently selected the trout we wanted, and rested the bait patiently and persistently on the end of his nose at a depth of eighty feet, but he would only shake it off with an annoyed manner, and shift his position.

We bathed occasionally, but the water was rather chilly, for all it looked so sunny. Sometimes we rowed out to the "blue water," a mile or two from shore. It was as dead blue as indigo there, because of the immense depth. By official measurement, the lake in its center is one thousand five hundred and twenty-five feet deep!

Sometimes, on lazy afternoons, we lolled on the sand in camp, and smoked pipes and read some old well-worn novels. At night, by the camp-fire, we played euchre and seven-up to strengthen the mind —and played them with cards so greasy and defaced that only a whole summer's acquaintance with them could enable the student to tell the ace of clubs from the jack of diamonds.

We never slept in our "house." It never occurred to us, for one thing; and besides, it was built to hold ground, and that was enough. We did not wish to strain it.

By and by our provisions began to run short, and we went back to the old camp and laid in a new supply. We were gone all day, and reached home again about nightfall, pretty tired and hungry. While Johnny was carrying the main bulk of the provisions up to our "house" for future use, I took the loaf of bread, some slices of bacon, and the coffee-pot, ashore, set them down by a tree, lit a fire, and went back to the boat to get the frying-pan. While I was at this, I heard a shout from Johnny, and looking up I saw that my fire was galloping all over the premises!

Johnny was on the other side of it. He had to run through the flames to get to the lake-shore, and then we stood helpless and watched the devastation.

The ground was deeply carpeted with dry pine-needles, and the fire touched them off as if they were gunpowder. It was wonderful to see with what fierce speed the tall sheet of flame traveled! My coffee-pot was gone, and everything with it. In a minute and a half the fire seized upon a dense growth of dry manzanita chapparal six or eight feet high, and then the roaring and popping and crackling was something terrific. We were driven to the boat by the intense heat, and there we remained, spell-bound.

Within half an hour all before us was a tossing, blinding tempest of flame! It went surging up adjacent ridges—surmounted them and disappeared in the cañons beyond—burst into view upon higher and farther ridges, presently—shed a grander illumination abroad, and dove again—flamed out again, directly, higher and still higher up the mountainside—threw out skirmishing parties of fire here and there, and sent them trailing their crimson spirals away among remote ramparts and ribs and gorges, till as far as the eye could reach the lofty mountain-fronts were webbed as it were with a tangled network of red lava streams. Away across the water the crags and domes were lit with a ruddy glare, and the firmament above was a reflected hell!

Every feature of the spectacle was repeated in the glowing mirror of the lake! Both pictures were sublime, both were beautiful; but that in the lake had a bewildering richness about it that enchanted the eye and held it with the stronger fascination.

We sat absorbed and motionless through four long hours. We

never thought of supper, and never felt fatigue. But at eleven o'clock the conflagration had traveled beyond our range of vision, and then darkness stole down upon the landscape again.

Hunger asserted itself now, but there was nothing to eat. The provisions were all cooked, no doubt, but we did not go to see. We were homeless wanderers again, without any property. Our fence was gone, our house burned down; no insurance. Our pine forest was well scorched, the dead trees all burned up, and our broad acres of manzanita swept away. Our blankets were on our usual sand-bed, however, and so we lay down and went to sleep. The next morning we started back to the old camp, but while out a long way from shore, so great a storm came up that we dared not try to land. So I bailed out the seas we shipped, and Johnny pulled heavily through the billows till we had reached a point three or four miles beyond the camp. The storm was increasing, and it became evident that it was better to take the hazard of beaching the boat than go down in a hundred fathoms of water; so we ran in, with tall white-caps following, and I sat down in the stern-sheets and pointed her head-on to the shore. The instant the bow struck, a wave came over the stern that washed crew and cargo ashore, and saved a deal of trouble. We shivered in the lee of a boulder all the rest of the day, and froze all the night through. In the morning the tempest had gone down, and we paddled down to the camp without any unnecessary delay. We were so starved that we ate up the rest of the Brigade's provisions, and then set out to Carson to tell them about it and ask their forgiveness. It was accorded, upon payment of damages.

We made many trips to the lake after that, and had many a hair-breadth escape and blood-curdling adventure which will never be recorded of any history.

From *Roughing It,* 1872.

5 : *Silver Mining in Nevada*

After leaving the Sink, we traveled along the Humboldt River a little way. People accustomed to the monster mile-wide Mississippi, grow accustomed to associating the term "river" with a high degree of watery grandeur. Consequently, such people feel rather disappointed when they stand on the shores of the Humboldt or the Carson and find that a "river" in Nevada is a sickly rivulet which is just the counterpart of the Erie canal in all respects save that the canal is twice as long and four times as deep. One of the pleasantest and most invigorating exercises one can contrive is to run and jump across the Humboldt River till he is overheated, and then drink it dry.

On the fifteenth day we completed our march of two hundred miles and entered Unionville, Humboldt County, in the midst of a driving snow-storm. Unionville consisted of eleven cabins and a liberty pole. Six of the cabins were strung along one side of a deep cañon, and the other five faced them. The rest of the landscape was made up of bleak mountain walls that rose so high into the sky from both sides of the cañon that the village was left, as it were, far down in the bottom of a crevice. It was always daylight on the mountain-tops a long time before the darkness lifted and revealed Unionville.

We built a small, rude cabin in the side of the crevice and roofed it with canvas, leaving a corner open to serve as a chimney, through which the cattle used to tumble occasionally, at night, and mash our furniture and interrupt our sleep. It was very cold weather and fuel was scarce. Indians brought brush and bushes several miles on their backs; and when we could catch a laden Indian it was well—and when we could not (which was the rule, not the exception), we shivered and bore it.

I confess, without shame, that I expected to find masses of silver lying all about the ground. I expected to see it glittering in the sun on the mountain summits. I said nothing about this, for some instinct told me that I might possibly have an exaggerated idea about it, and so if I betrayed my thought I might bring derision upon myself. Yet I was as perfectly satisfied in my own mind as I could be of anything, that I was going to gather up, in a day or two, or at furthest a week or two, silver enough to make me satisfactorily wealthy—and so my fancy was already busy with plans for spending this money. The first opportunity that offered, I sauntered carelessly away from the cabin, keeping an eye on the other boys, and stopping and contemplating the sky when they seemed to be observing me; but as soon as the coast was manifestly clear, I fled away as guiltily as a thief might have done and never halted till I was far beyond sight and call. Then I began my search with a feverish excitement that was brimful of expectation—almost of certainty. I crawled about the ground, seizing and examining bits of stone, blowing the dust from them or rubbing them on my clothes, and then peering at them with anxious hope. Presently I found a bright fragment and my heart bounded! I hid behind a boulder and polished it and scrutinized it with a nervous eagerness and a delight that was more pronounced than absolute certainty itself could have afforded. The more I examined the fragment the more I was convinced that I had found the door to fortune. I marked the spot and carried away my specimen. Up and down the rugged mountainside I searched, with always increasing interest and always augmenting gratitude that I had come to Humboldt and come in time. Of all the experiences of my life, this secret search among the hidden treasures of silver-land was the nearest to unmarred ecstasy. It was a delirious revel. By and by, in the bed of a shallow rivulet, I found a deposit of shining yellow scales, and my breath almost forsook me! A gold-mine, and in my simplicity I had been content with vulgar silver! I was so excited that I half believed my overwrought imagination was deceiving me. Then a fear came upon me that people might be observing me and would guess my secret. Moved by this thought, I made a circuit of the place, and ascended a knoll to reconnoiter. Solitude. No creature was near. Then I returned to my mine, fortifying myself against possible disappointment, but my fears were groundless—the shining scales were still there. I set about scooping them out, and for an hour I toiled down the windings of the stream and robbed its bed. But at last the descending sun warned me to give up the quest, and I turned homeward laden with wealth. As

I walked along I could not help smiling at the thought of my being so excited over my fragment of silver when a nobler metal was almost under my nose. In this little time the former had so fallen in my estimation that once or twice I was on the point of throwing it away.

The boys were as hungry as usual, but I could eat nothing. Neither could I talk. I was full of dreams and far away. Their conversation interrupted the flow of my fancy somewhat, and annoyed me a little, too. I despised the sordid and commonplace things they talked about. But as they proceeded, it began to amuse me. It grew to be rare fun to hear them planning their poor little economies and sighing over possible privations and distresses when a gold-mine, all our own, lay within sight of the cabin, and I could point it out at any moment. Smothered hilarity began to oppress me, presently. It was hard to resist the impulse to burst out with exultation and reveal everything; but I did resist. I said within myself that I would filter the great news through my lips calmly and be serene as a summer morning while I watched its effect in their faces. I said:

"Where have you all been?"

"Prospecting."

"What did you find?"

"Nothing."

"Nothing? What do you think of the country?"

"Can't tell, yet," said Mr. Ballou, who was an old gold-miner, and had likewise had considerable experience among the silver-mines.

"Well, haven't you formed any sort of opinion?"

"Yes, a sort of a one. It's fair enough here, maybe, but overrated. Seven-thousand-dollar ledges are scarce, though. That Sheba may be rich enough, but we don't own it; and, besides, the rock is so full of base metals that all the science in the world can't work it. We'll not starve, here, but we'll not get rich, I'm afraid."

"So you think the prospect is pretty poor?"

"No name for it!"

"Well, we'd better go back, hadn't we?"

"Oh, not yet—of course not. We'll try it a riffle, first."

"Suppose, now—this is merely a supposition, you know—suppose you could find a ledge that would yield, say, a hundred and fifty dollars a ton—would that satisfy you?"

"Try us once!" from the whole party.

"Or suppose—merely a supposition, of course—suppose you were to find a ledge that would yield two thousand dollars a ton—would *that* satisfy you?"

"Here—what do you mean? What are you coming at? Is there some mystery behind all this?"

"Never mind. I am not saying anything. You know perfectly well there are no rich mines here— of course you do. Because you have been around and examined for yourselves. Anybody would know that, that had been around. But just for the sake of argument, suppose—in a kind of general way—suppose some person were to tell you that two-thousand-dollar ledges were simply contemptible—contemptible, understand—and that right yonder in sight of this very cabin there were piles of pure gold and pure silver—oceans of it—enough to make you all rich in twenty-four hours! Come!"

"I should say he was as crazy as a loon!" said old Ballou, but wild with excitement, nevertheless.

"Gentlemen," said I, "I don't say anything—*I* haven't been around, you know, and of course don't know anything—but all I ask of you is to cast your eye on *that,* for instance, and tell me what you think of it!" and I tossed my treasure before them.

There was an eager scrabble for it, and a closing of heads together over it under the candle-light. Then old Ballou said:

"Think of it? I think it is nothing but a lot of granite rubbish and nasty glittering mica that isn't worth ten cents an acre!"

So vanished my dream. So melted my wealth away. So toppled my airy castle to the earth and left me stricken and forlorn.

Moralizing, I observed, then, that "all that glitters is not gold."

Mr. Ballou said I could go further than that, and lay it up among my treasures of knowledge, that *nothing* that glitters is gold. So I learned then, once for all, that gold in its native state is but dull, unornamental stuff, and that only low-born metals excite the admiration of the ignorant with an ostentatious glitter. However, like the rest of the world, I still go on underrating men of gold and glorifying men of mica. Commonplace human nature cannot rise above that. . . .

From *Roughing It,* 1872.

6 : *Striking It Rich*

I NOW COME TO A CURIOUS EPISODE—the most curious, I think, that had yet accented my slothful, valueless, heedless career. Out of a hillside toward the upper end of the town, projected a wall of reddish-looking quartz croppings, the exposed comb of a silver-bearing ledge that extended deep down into the earth, of course. It was owned by a company entitled the "Wide West." There was a shaft sixty or seventy feet deep on the under side of the croppings, and everybody was acquainted with the rock that came from it—and tolerably rich rock it was, too, but nothing extraordinary. I will remark here, that although to the inexperienced stranger all the quartz of a particular "district" looks about alike, an old resident of the camp can take a glance at a mixed pile of rock, separate the fragments and tell you which mine each came from, as easily as a confectioner can separate and classify the various kinds and qualities of candy in a mixed heap of the article.

All at once the town was thrown into a state of extraordinary excitement. In mining parlance the Wide West had "struck it rich!" Everybody went to see the new developments, and for some days there was such a crowd of people about the Wide West shaft that a stranger would have supposed there was a mass-meeting in session there. No other topic was discussed but the rich strike, and nobody thought or dreamed about anything else. Every man brought away a specimen, ground it up in a hand-mortar, washed it out in his horn spoon, and glared speechless upon the marvelous result. It was not hard rock, but black, decomposed stuff which could be crumbled in the hand like a baked potato, and when spread out on paper exhibited a thick sprinkling of gold and particles of "native" silver. Higbie [1] brought a handful to the cabin, and when he had washed it out his amazement was beyond description. Wide

[1] Calvin Higbie of California, to whom *Roughing It* was dedicated: "an honest man, a genial comrade and a steadfast friend."—C. N.

West stock soared skyward. It was said that repeated offers had been made for it at a thousand dollars a foot, and promptly refused. We have all had the "blues"—the mere skyblues—but mine were indigo, now—because I did not own in the Wide West. The world seemed hollow to me, and existence a grief. I lost my appetite, and ceased to take an interest in anything. Still I had to stay, and listen to other people's rejoicings, because I had no money to get out of the camp with.

The Wide West company put a stop to the carrying away of "specimens," and well they might, for every handful of the ore was worth a sum of some consequence. To show the exceeding value of the ore, I will remark that a sixteen-hundred-pounds parcel of it was sold, just as it lay, at the mouth of the shaft, at *one dollar a pound;* and the man who bought it "packed" it on mules a hundred and fifty or two hundred miles, over the mountains, to San Francisco, satisfied that it would yield at a rate that would richly compensate him for his trouble. The Wide West people also commanded their foreman to refuse any but their own operatives permission to enter the mine at any time or for any purpose. I kept up my "blue" meditations and Higbie kept up a deal of thinking, too, but of a different sort. He puzzled over the "rock," examined it with a glass, inspected it in different lights and from different points of view, and after each experiment delivered himself, in soliloquy, of one and the same unvarying opinion in the same unvarying formula:

"It is *not* Wide West rock!"

He said once or twice that he meant to have a look into the Wide West shaft if he got shot for it. I was wretched, and did not care whether he got a look into it or not. He failed that day, and tried again at night; failed again; got up at dawn and tried, and failed again. Then he lay in ambush in the sage-brush hour after hour, waiting for the two or three hands to adjourn to the shade of a boulder for dinner; made a start once, but was premature—one of the men came back for something; tried it again, but when almost at the mouth of the shaft, another of the men rose up from behind the boulder as if to reconnoitre, and he dropped on the ground and lay quiet; presently he crawled on his hands and knees to the mouth of the shaft, gave a quick glance around, then seized the rope and slid down the shaft. He disappeared in the gloom of a "side drift" just as a head appeared in the mouth of the shaft and somebody shouted "Hello!"—which he did not answer. He was not disturbed any more. An hour later he entered the cabin, hot, red, and ready to burst with smothered excitement, and exclaimed in a stage whisper:

"I knew it! We are rich! IT'S A BLIND LEAD!"

I thought the very earth reeled under me. Doubt—conviction—doubt again—exultation—hope, amazement, belief, unbelief—every emotion imaginable swept in wild procession through my heart and brain, and I could not speak a word. After a moment or two of this mental fury, I shook myself to rights, and said:

"Say it again!"

"It's a blind lead!"

"Cal, let's—let's burn the house—or kill somebody! Let's get out where there's room to hurrah! But what is the use? It is a hundred times too good to be true."

"It's a blind lead for a million!—hanging wall—foot wall—clay casings—everything complete!" He swung his hat and gave three cheers, and I cast doubt to the winds and chimed in with a will. For I was worth a million dollars, and did not care "whether school kept or not!"

But perhaps I ought to explain. A "blind lead" is a lead or ledge that does not "crop out" above the surface. A miner does not know where to look for such leads, but they are often stumbled upon by accident in the course of driving a tunnel or sinking a shaft. Higbie knew the Wide West rock perfectly well, and the more he had examined the new developments the more he was satisfied that the ore could not have come from the Wide West vein. And so had it occurred to him alone, of all the camp, that there was a blind lead down in the shaft, and that even the Wide West people themselves did not suspect it. He was right. When he went down the shaft, he found that the blind lead held its independent way through the Wide West vein, cutting it diagonally, and that it was inclosed in its own well-defined casing-rocks and clay. Hence it was public property. Both leads being perfectly well defined, it was easy for any miner to see which one belonged to the Wide West and which did not.

We thought it well to have a strong friend, and therefore we brought the foreman of the Wide West to our cabin that night and revealed the great surprise to him. Higbie said:

"We are going to take possession of this blind lead, record it and establish ownership, and then forbid the Wide West company to take out any more of the rock. You cannot help your company in this matter—nobody can help them. I will go into the shaft with you and prove to your entire satisfaction that it *is* a blind lead. Now we propose to take you in with us, and claim the blind lead in our three names. What do you say?"

What could a man say who had an opportunity to simply stretch forth his hand and take possession of a fortune without risk of any kind and without wronging any one or attaching the least taint of dishonor to his name? He could only say, "Agreed."

The notice was put up that night, and duly spread upon the recorder's books before ten o'clock. We claimed two hundred feet each—six hundred feet in all—the smallest and compactest organization in the district, and the easiest to manage.

No one can be so thoughtless as to suppose that we slept that night. Higbie and I went to bed at midnight, but it was only to lie broad awake and think, dream, scheme. The floorless, tumble-down cabin was a palace, the ragged gray blankets silk, the furniture rosewood and mahogany. Each new splendor that burst out of my visions of the future whirled me bodily over in bed or jerked me to a sitting posture just as if an electric battery had been applied to me. We shot fragments of conversation back and forth at each other. Once Higbie said:

"When are you going home—to the States?"

"To-morrow!"—with an evolution or two, ending with a sitting position. "Well—no—but next month, at furthest."

"We'll go in the same steamer."

"Agreed."

A pause.

"Steamer of the 10th?"

"Yes. No, the 1st."

"All right."

Another pause.

"Where are you going to live?" said Higbie.

"San Francisco."

"That's me!"

Pause.

"Too high—too much climbing"—from Higbie.

"What is?"

"I was thinking of Russian Hill—building a house up there."

"Too much climbing? Sha'n't you keep a carriage?"

"Of course. I forgot that."

Pause.

"Cal, what kind of a house are you going to build?"

"I was thinking about that. Three-story and an attic."

"But what *kind?*"

"Well, I don't hardly know. Brick, I suppose."

"Brick—bosh."

"Why? What is your idea?"

"Brown-stone front—French plate-glass—billiard-room off the dining-room—statuary and paintings—shrubbery and two-acre grass-plat—greenhouse—iron dog on the front stoop—gray horses—landau, and a coachman with a bug on his hat!"

"By George!"

A long pause.

"Cal, when are you going to Europe?"

"Well—I hadn't thought of that. When are you?"

"In the spring."

"Going to be gone all summer?"

"All summer! I shall remain there three years."

"No—but are you in earnest?"

"Indeed I am."

"I will go along too."

"Why, of course you will."

"What part of Europe shall you go to?"

"All parts. France, England, Germany—Spain, Italy, Switzerland, Syria, Greece, Palestine, Arabia, Persia, Egypt—all over—everywhere."

"I'm agreed."

"All right."

"Won't it be a swell trip!"

"We'll spend forty or fifty thousand dollars trying to make it one, anyway."

Another long pause.

"Higbie, we owe the butcher six dollars, and he has been threatening to stop our—"

"Hang the butcher!"

"Amen."

And so it went. By three o'clock we found it was no use, and so we got up and played cribbage and smoked pipes till sunrise. It was my week to cook. I always hated cooking—now, I abhorred it.

The news was all over town. The former excitement was great—this one was greater still. I walked the streets serene and happy. Higbie said the foreman had been offered two hundred thousand dollars for his third of the mine. I said I would like to see myself selling for any such price. My ideas were lofty. My figure was a million. Still, I honestly believe that if I had been offered it, it would have had no other effect than to make me hold off for more.

I found abundant enjoyment in being rich. A man offered me a three-hundred-dollar horse, and wanted to take my simple, unindorsed note for it. That brought the most realizing sense I had yet had that I was actually rich, beyond shadow of doubt. It was followed by numerous other evidences of a similar nature—among which I may mention the fact of the butcher leaving us a double supply of meat and saying nothing about money.

By the laws of the district, the "locators" or claimants of a ledge were obliged to do a fair and reasonable amount of work on their new property within ten days after the date of the location, or the property was forfeited, and anybody could go and seize it that chose. So we determined to go to work the next day. About the middle of the afternoon, as I was coming out of the post-office, I met a Mr. Gardiner, who told me that Capt. John Nye was lying dangerously ill at his place (the "Nine-Mile Ranch"), and that he and his wife were not able to give him nearly as much care and attention as his case demanded. I said if he would wait for me a moment, I would go down and help in the sickroom. I ran to the cabin to tell Higbie. He was not there, but I left a note on the table for him, and a few minutes later I left town in Gardiner's wagon.

Captain Nye was very ill indeed, with spasmodic rheumatism. But the old gentleman was himself—which is to say, he was kind-hearted and agreeable when comfortable, but a singularly violent wildcat when things did not go well. He would be smiling along pleasantly enough, when a sudden spasm of his disease would take him and he would go out of his smile into a perfect fury. He would groan and wail and howl with the anguish, and fill up the odd chinks with the most elaborate profanity that strong convictions and a fine fancy could contrive. With fair opportunity he could swear very well and handle his adjectives with considerable judgment; but when the spasm was on him it was painful to listen to him, he was so awkward. However, I had seen him nurse a sick man himself and put up patiently with the inconveniences of the situation, and consequently I was willing that he should have full license now that his own turn had come. He could not disturb me, with all his raving and ranting, for my mind had work on hand, and it labored on diligently, night and day, whether my hands were idle or employed. I was altering and amending the plans for my house, and thinking over the propriety of having the billiard-room in the attic, instead of on the same floor with the dining-room; also, I was trying to decide between green and blue for the upholstery of the drawing-room, for, although my preference was blue, I feared it was a color that would be too easily damaged by dust and sunlight; likewise while I was content to put the coachman in a modest livery, I was uncertain about a footman—I needed one, and was even resolved to have one, but wished he could properly appear and perform his functions out of livery, for I somewhat dreaded so much show; and yet, inasmuch as my late grandfather had had a coachman and such things, but no liveries, I felt rather drawn to beat him;—or beat his ghost, at any rate; I was also systematizing the European trip, and managed to get it all laid out, as to route and length of time to be devoted to it—everything, with one exception—namely, whether to cross the desert from Cairo to Jerusalem per camel, or go by sea to Beirut, and thence down through the country per caravan. Meantime I was writing to the friends at home every day, instructing them concerning all my plans and intentions, and directing them to look up a handsome homestead for my mother and agree upon a price for it against my coming, and also directing them to sell my share of the Tennessee land and tender the proceeds to the widows' and orphans' fund of the typographical union of which I had long been a member in good standing. [This Tennessee land had been in the possession of the family many years, and promised to confer high fortune upon us some day; it still promises it, but in a less violent way.]

When I had been nursing the captain nine days he was somewhat better, but very feeble. During the afternoon we lifted him into a chair and gave him an alcoholic vapor bath, and then set about putting him on the bed again. We had to be exceedingly careful, for the least jar produced pain. Gardiner had his shoulders and I his legs; in an unfortunate moment I stumbled and the patient fell heavily on the bed in an agony of torture. I never heard a man swear so in my life. He raved like a maniac, and tried to snatch a revolver from the table—but I got it. He ordered me out of the house, and swore a world of oaths that he would kill me wherever he caught me when he got on his feet again. It was simply a passing fury, and meant nothing. I knew he would forget it in an hour, and maybe be sorry for it, too; but it angered me a little, at the moment. So much so, indeed, that I determined to go back to Esmeralda. I thought he was able to get along alone, now, since he was on the war-path. I took supper, and as soon as the moon rose, began my nine-mile journey, on foot. Even millionaires needed no horses, in those days, for a mere nine-mile jaunt without baggage.

As I "raised the hill" overlooking the town, it lacked fifteen minutes of twelve. I glanced at the hill over beyond the cañon, and in the bright moonlight saw what appeared to be about half the population of the village massed on and around the Wide West croppings. My heart gave an exulting bound, and I said to myself, "They have made a new strike to-night—and struck it richer than ever, no doubt." I started over there, but gave it up. I said the "strike" would keep, and I had climbed hills enough for one night. I went on down through the town, and as I was passing a little German bakery, a woman ran out and begged me to come in and help her. She said her husband had a fit. I went in, and judged she was right—he appeared to have a hundred of them, compressed into one. Two Germans were there, trying to hold him, and not making much of a success of it. I ran up the street half a block or so and routed out a sleeping doctor, brought him down half dressed, and we four wrestled with the maniac, and doctored, drenched and bled him, for more than an hour, and the poor German woman did the crying. He grew quiet, now, and the doctor and I withdrew and left him to his friends.

It was a little after one o'clock. As I entered the cabin door, tired but jolly, the dingy light of a tallow candle revealed Higbie, sitting by the pine table gazing stupidly at my note, which he held in his fingers, and looking pale, old, and haggard. I halted, and looked at him. He looked at me, stolidly. I said:

"Higbie, what—what is it?"

"We're ruined—we didn't do the work—THE BLIND LEAD'S RELOCATED!"

It was enough. I sat down sick, grieved—broken-hearted, indeed. A minute before, I was rich and brimful of vanity; I was a pauper now, and very meek. We sat still an hour, busy with thought, busy with vain and useless self-upbraidings, busy with "Why *didn't* I do this, and why *didn't* I do that," but neither spoke a word. Then we dropped into mutual explanations, and the mystery was cleared away. It came out that Higbie had depended on me, as I had on him, and as both of us had on the foreman. The folly of it! It was the first time that ever staid and steadfast Higbie had left an important matter to chance or failed to be true to his full share of a responsibility.

But he had never seen my note till this moment, and this moment was the first time he had been in the cabin since the day he had seen me last. He, also, had left a note for me, on that same fatal afternoon—had ridden up on horseback, and looked through the window, and being in a hurry and not seeing me, had tossed the note into the cabin through a broken pane. Here it was, on the floor, where it had remained undisturbed for nine days:

> Don't fail to do the work before the ten days expire. W. has passed through and given me notice. I am to join him at Mono Lake, and we shall go on from there to-night. He says he will find it this time, sure. CAL.

"W." meant Whiteman, of course. That thrice accursed "cement"!

That was the way of it. An old miner, like Higbie, could no more withstand the fascination of a mysterious mining excitement like this "cement" foolishness, than he could refrain from eating when he was famishing. Higbie had been dreaming about the marvelous cement for months; and now, against his better judgment, he had gone off and "taken the chances" on my keeping secure a mine worth a million undiscovered cement veins. They had not been followed this time. His riding out of town in broad daylight was such a commonplace thing to do that it had not attracted any attention. He said they prosecuted their search in the fastnesses of the mountains during nine days, without success; they could not find the cement. Then a ghastly fear came over him that something might have happened to prevent the doing of the necessary work to hold the blind lead (though indeed he thought such a thing hardly possible) and forthwith he started home with all speed. He would have reached Esmeralda in time, but his horse broke down and he had to walk a great part of the distance. And so it happened that as he came into Esmeralda by one road, I entered it by another. His was the superior energy, however, for he went straight to the Wide West, instead of turning aside as I had done—and he arrived there about five or ten minutes too late! The "notice" was already up, the "relocation" of our mine completed beyond recall, and the crowd rapidly dispersing. He learned some facts before he left the ground. The foreman had not been seen about the streets since the night we had located the mine—a telegram had called him to California on a matter of life and death, it was said. At any rate he had done no work and the watchful eyes of the community were taking note of the fact. At midnight of this woeful tenth day, the ledge would be "relocatable," and by eleven o'clock the hill was black with men prepared to do the relocating. That was the crowd I had seen when I fancied a new "strike" had been made—idiot that I was. [We three had the same right to relocate the lead that other people had, provided we were quick enough.] As midnight was announced, fourteen men, duly armed and ready to back their proceedings, put up their "notice" and proclaimed their ownership of the blind lead, under the new name of the "Johnson." But A. D. Allen, our partner (the foreman), put in a sudden appearance about that time, with a cocked revolver in his hand, and said his name must be added to the list, or he would "thin out the Johnson company some." He was a manly, splendid, determined fellow, and known to be as good as his word, and therefore a compromise was effected. They put in his name for a hundred feet, reserving to themselves the customary two hundred feet each. Such was the history of the night's events, as Higbie gathered from a friend on the way home.

Higbie and I cleared out on a new mining excitement the next morning, glad to get away from the scene of our sufferings, and after a month or two of hardships and disappointment, returned to Esmeralda once more. Then we learned that the Wide West and the Johnson companies had consolidated; that the stock, thus united, comprised five thousand feet, or shares; that the foreman, apprehending tiresome litigation, and considering such a huge concern unwieldy, had sold his hundred feet for ninety thousand dollars in gold and gone home to the States to enjoy it. If the stock was worth such a gallant figure, with five thousand shares in the corporation, it makes me dizzy to think what it would have been worth with only our original six hundred in it. It was the difference between six hundred men owning a house and five thousand owning it. We would have been millionaires if we had only worked with pick and spade one little day on our property and so secured our ownership!

It reads like a wild fancy sketch, but the evidence of many witnesses, and likewise that of the official records of Esmeralda District, is easily obtainable in proof that it is a true history. I can always have it to say that I was absolutely and unquestionably worth a million dollars, once, for ten days.

A year ago my esteemed and in every way estimable old millionaire partner, Higbie, wrote me from an obscure little mining-camp in California that after nine or ten years of buffetings and hard striving, he was at last in a position where he could command twenty-five hundred dollars, and said he meant to go into the fruit business in a modest way. How such a thought would have insulted him the night we lay in our cabin planning European trips and brown-stone houses on Russian Hill!

From *Roughing It,* 1872.

7 : *Virginia City*

SIX MONTHS AFTER MY ENTRY into journalism[1] the grand "flush times" of Silverland began, and they continued with unabated splendor for three years. All difficulty about filling up the "local department" ceased, and the only trouble now was how to make the lengthened columns hold the world of incidents and happenings that came to our literary net every day. Virginia had grown to be the "livest" town, for its age and population, that America had ever produced. The sidewalks swarmed with people—to such an extent, indeed, that it was generally no easy matter to stem the human tide. The streets themselves were just as crowded with quartz-wagons, freight-teams, and other vehicles. The procession was endless. So great was the pack, that buggies frequently had to wait half an hour for an opportunity to cross the principal street. Joy sat on every countenance, and there was a glad, almost fierce, intensity in every eye, that told of the money-getting schemes that were seething in every brain and the high hope that held sway in every heart. Money was as plenty as dust; every individual considered himself wealthy, and a melancholy countenance was nowhere to be seen. There were military companies, fire companies, brass-bands, banks, hotels, theaters, "hurdy-gurdy houses," wide-open gambling-palaces, political pow-wows, civic processions, street-fights, murders, inquests, riots, a whisky-mill every fifteen steps, a Board of Aldermen, a Mayor, a City Surveyor, a City Engineer, a Chief of the Fire Department, with First, Second, and Third Assistants, a Chief of Police, City Marshal, and a large police force, two Boards of Mining Brokers, a dozen breweries, and half a dozen jails and station-houses in full operation, and some talk of building a church. The "flush times" were in magnificent flower! Large fire-proof brick buildings were going up in the principal streets, and the wooden

[1] In July 1862 Clemens was offered the job of city editor of the Virginia City *Territorial Enterprise*.—C. N.

suburbs were spreading out in all directions. Town lots soared up to prices that were amazing.

The great "Comstock lode" stretched its opulent length straight through the town from north to south, and every mine on it was in diligent process of development. One of these mines alone employed six hundred and seventy-five men, and in the matter of elections the adage was, "as the 'Gould & Curry' goes, so goes the city." Laboring-men's wages were four and six dollars a day, and they worked in three "shifts" or gangs, and the blasting and picking and shoveling went on without ceasing, night and day.

The "city" of Virginia roosted royally midway up the steep side of Mount Davidson, seven thousand two hundred feet above the level of the sea, and in the clear Nevada atmosphere was visible from a distance of fifty miles! It claimed a population of fifteen thousand to eighteen thousand, and all day long half of this little army swarmed the streets like bees and the other half swarmed among the drifts and tunnels of the "Comstock," hundreds of feet down in the earth directly under those same streets. Often we felt our chairs jar, and heard the faint boom of a blast down in the bowels of the earth under the office.

The mountainside was so steep that the entire town had a slant to it like a roof. Each street was a terrace, and from each to the next street below the descent was forty or fifty feet. The fronts of the houses were level with the street they faced, but their rear first floors were propped on lofty stilts; a man could stand at a rear first-floor window of a C Street house and look down the chimneys of the row of houses below him facing D Street. It was a laborious climb, in that thin atmosphere, to ascend from D to A Street, and you were panting and out of breath when you got there; but you could turn around and go down again like a house afire—so to speak. The atmosphere was so rarefied, on account of the great altitude, that one's blood lay near the surface always, and the scratch of a pin was a disaster worth worrying about, for the chances were that a grievous erysipelas would ensue. But to offset this, the thin atmosphere seemed to carry healing to gunshot wounds, and, therefore, to simply shoot your adversary through both lungs was a thing not likely to afford you any permanent satisfaction, for he would be nearly certain to be around looking for you within the month, and not with an opera-glass, either.

From Virginia's airy situation one could look over a vast, far-reaching panorama of mountain ranges and deserts; and whether the day was bright or overcast, whether the sun was rising or setting, or flaming in the zenith, or whether night and the moon held sway, the spectacle was always impressive and beautiful. Over your head Mount Davidson lifted its gray dome, and before and below you a rugged cañon clove the battlemented hills, making a somber gateway through which a soft-tinted desert was glimpsed, with the silver thread of a river winding through it, bordered with trees which many miles of distance diminished to a delicate fringe; and still further away the snowy mountains rose up and stretched their long barrier to the filmy horizon—far enough beyond a lake that burned in the desert like a fallen sun, though that, itself, lay fifty miles removed. Look from your window where you would, there was fascination in the picture. At rare intervals—but very rare—there were clouds in our skies, and then the setting sun would gild and flush and glorify this mighty expanse of scenery with a bewildering pomp of color that held the eye like a spell and moved the spirit like music.

The first twenty-six graves in the Virginia cemetery were occupied by *murdered* men. So everybody said, so everybody believed, and so they will always say and believe. The reason why there was so much slaughtering done, was, that in a new mining district the rough element predominates, and a person is not respected until he has "killed his man." That was the very expression used.

If an unknown individual arrived, they did not inquire if he was capable, honest, industrious, but—had he killed his man? If he had not, he gravitated to his natural and proper position, that of a man of small consequence; if he had, the cordiality of his reception was graduated according to the number of his dead. It was tedious work struggling up to a position of influence with bloodless hands; but when a man came with the blood of half a dozen men on his soul, his worth was recognized at once and his acquaintance sought.

In Nevada, for a time, the lawyer, the editor, the banker, the chief desperado, the chief gambler, and the saloon-keeper, occupied the same level in society, and it was the highest. The cheapest and easiest way to become an influential man and be looked up to by the community at large, was to stand behind a bar, wear a cluster-diamond pin, and sell whisky. I am not sure but that the saloon-keeper held a shade higher rank than any other member of society. His opinion had weight. It was his privilege to say how the elections should go. No great movement could succeed without the countenance and direction of the saloon-keepers. It was a high favor when the chief saloon-keeper consented to serve in the legislature or the board of aldermen. Youthful ambition hardly aspired so much to the honors of the law, or the army and navy as to the dignity of proprietorship in a saloon. To be a saloon-keeper and kill a man was to be illustrious. Hence the reader will not be surprised to learn that more than one man was killed in Nevada under hardly the pretext of provocation, so impatient was the slayer to achieve reputation and throw off the galling sense of being held in indifferent repute by his associates. I knew two youths who tried to "kill their men" for no other reason—and got killed themselves for their pains. "There goes the man that killed Bill Adams" was higher praise and a sweeter sound in the ears of this sort of people than any other speech that admiring lips could utter.

The men who murdered Virginia's original twenty-six cemetery occupants were never punished. Why? Because Alfred the Great, when he invented trial by jury, and knew that he had admirably framed it to secure justice in his age of the world, was not aware that in the nineteenth century the condition of things would be so entirely changed that unless he rose from the grave and altered the jury plan to meet the emergency, it would prove the most ingenious and infallible agency for *defeating* justice that human wisdom could contrive. For how could he imagine that we simpletons would go on using his jury plan after circumstances had stripped it of its usefulness, any more than he could imagine that we would go on using his candle-clock after we had invented chronometers? In his day news could not travel fast, and hence he could easily find a jury of honest, intelligent men who had not heard of the case they were called to try—but in our day of telegraphs and newspapers his plan compels us to swear in juries composed of fools and rascals, because the system rigidly excludes honest men and men of brains.

I remember one of those sorrowful farces, in Virginia, which we call a jury trial. A noted desperado killed Mr. B., a good citizen, in the most wanton and cold-blooded way. Of course the papers were full of it, and all men capable of reading read about it. And of course all men not deaf and dumb and idiotic talked about it. A jury list was made out, and Mr. B. L., a prominent banker and a valued citizen, was questioned precisely as he would have been questioned in any court in America:

"Have you heard of this homicide?"

"Yes."

"Have you held conversations upon the subject?"

"Yes."

"Have you formed or expressed opinions about it?"

"Yes."

"Have you read the newspaper accounts of it?"

"Yes."

"We do not want you."

A minister, intelligent, esteemed, and greatly respected; a merchant of high character and known probity; a mining superintendent of intelligence and unblemished reputation; a quartz-mill owner of excellent standing, were all questioned in the same way, and all set aside. Each said the public talk and the newspaper reports had not so biased his mind but that sworn testimony would overthow his previously formed opinions and enable him to render a verdict without prejudice and in accordance with the facts. But of course such men could not be trusted with the case. Ignoramuses alone could mete out unsullied justice.

When the peremptory challenges were all exhausted, a jury of twelve men was impaneled—a jury who swore they had neither heard, read, talked about, nor expressed an opinion concerning a murder which the very cattle in the corrals, the Indians in the sagebrush, and the stones in the streets were cognizant of! It was a jury composed of two desperadoes, two low beer-house politicians, three barkeepers, two ranchmen who could not read, and three dull, stupid, human donkeys! It actually came out afterward, that one of these latter thought that incest and arson were the same thing.

The verdict rendered by this jury was, Not Guilty. What else could one expect?

The jury system puts a ban upon intelligence and honesty, and a premium upon ignorance, stupidity, and perjury. It is a shame that we must continue to use a worthless system because it *was* good a thousand years ago. In this age, when a gentleman of high social standing, intelligence, and probity, swears that testimony given under solemn oath will outweigh, with him, street talk and newspaper reports based upon mere hearsay, he is worth a hundred jurymen who will swear to their own ignorance and stupidity, and justice would be far safer in his hands than in theirs. Why could not the jury law be so altered as to give men of brains and honesty an *equal chance* with fools and miscreants? Is it right to show the present favoritism to one class of men and inflict a disability on another, in a land whose boast is that all its citizens are free and equal? I am a candidate for the legislature. I desire to tamper with the jury law. I wish to so alter it as to put a premium on intelligence and character, and close the jury-box against idiots, blacklegs, and people who do not read newspapers. But no doubt I shall be defeated—every effort I make to save the country "misses fire."

My idea, when I began this chapter, was to say something about desperadoism in the "flush times" of Nevada. To attempt a portrayal of that era and that land, and leave out the blood and carnage, would be like portraying Mormondom and leaving out polygamy. The desperado stalked the streets with a swagger graded according to the number of his homicides, and a nod of recognition from him was sufficient to make a humble admirer happy for the rest of the day. The deference that was paid to a desperado of wide reputation, and who "kept his private graveyard," as the phrase went, was marked, and cheerfully accorded. When he moved along the sidewalk in his excessively long-tailed frock-coat, shiny stump-toed boots, and with dainty little slouch hat tipped over left eye, the small-fry roughs made room for his majesty; when he entered the restaurant, the waiters deserted bankers and merchants to overwhelm him with obsequious service; when he shouldered his way to a bar, the shouldered parties wheeled indignantly, recognized him, and—apologized. They got a look in return that froze their marrow, and by that time a curled and breast-pinned barkeeper was beaming over the counter, proud of the established acquaintanceship that permitted such a familiar form of speech as:

"How 're ye, Billy, old fel? Glad to see you. What 'll you take—the old thing?"

The "old thing" meant his customary drink, of course.

The best-known names in the territory of Nevada were those belonging to these long-tailed heroes of the revolver. Orators, governors, capitalists, and leaders of the legislature enjoyed a degree of fame, but it seemed local and meager when contrasted with the fame of such men as Sam Brown, Jack Williams, Billy Mulligan, Farmer Pease, Sugarfoot Mike, Pock-Marked Jake, El Dorado Johnny, Jack McNabb, Joe McGee, Jack Harris, Six-fingered Pete, etc., etc. There was a long list of them. They were brave, reckless men, and traveled with their lives in their hands. To give them their due, they did their killing principally among themselves, and seldom molested peaceable citizens, for they considered it small credit to add to their trophies so cheap a bauble as the death of a man who was "not on the shoot," as they phrased it. They killed each other on slight provocation, and hoped and expected to be killed themselves—for they held it almost shame to die otherwise than "with their boots on," as they expressed it.

I remember an instance of a desperado's contempt for such small game as a private citizen's life. I was taking a late supper in a restaurant one night, with two reporters and a little printer named—Brown, for instance—any name will do. Presently a stranger with a long-tailed coat on came in, and not noticing Brown's hat, which was lying in a chair, sat down on it. Little Brown sprang up and became abusive in a moment. The stranger smiled, smoothed out the hat, and offered it to Brown with profuse apologies couched in caustic sarcasm, and begged Brown not to destroy him. Brown threw off his coat and challenged the man to fight—abused him, threatened him, impeached his courage, and urged and even implored him to fight; and in the meantime the smiling stranger placed himself under our protection in mock distress. But presently he assumed a serious tone, and said:

"Very well, gentlemen, if we must fight, we must, I suppose. But don't rush into danger and then say I gave you no warning. I am more than a match for all of you when I get started. I will give you proofs, and then if my friend here still insists, I will try to accommodate him."

The table we were sitting at was about five feet long, and unusually cumbersome and heavy. He asked us to put our hands on the dishes and hold them in their places a moment—one of them was a large oval dish with a portly roast on it. Then he sat down, tilted up one end of the table, set two of the legs on his knees, took the end of the table between his teeth, took his hands away, and pulled down with his teeth till the table came up to a level position, dishes and all! He said he could lift a keg of nails with his teeth. He picked up a common glass tumbler and bit a semicircle out of it. Then he opened his bosom and showed us a network of knife and bullet scars; showed us more on his arms and face, and said he believed he had bullets enough in his body to make a pig of lead. He was armed to the teeth. He closed with the remark that he was Mr. ——– of Cariboo—a celebrated name whereat we shook in our shoes. I would publish the name, but for the suspicion that he might come and carve me. He finally inquired if Brown still thirsted for blood. Brown turned the thing over in his mind a moment, and then—asked him to supper. . . .

Of course there was a large Chinese population in Virginia—it is the case with every town and city on the Pacific coast. They are a harmless race when white men either let them alone or treat them no worse than dogs; in fact, they are almost entirely harmless anyhow, for they seldom think of resenting the vilest insults or the cruelest injuries. They are quiet, peaceable, tractable, free from drunkenness, and they are as industrious as the day is long. A disorderly Chinaman is rare, and a lazy one does not exist. So long as a Chinaman has strength to use his hands he needs no support from anybody; white men often complain of want of work, but a Chinaman offers no such complaint; he always manages to find something to do. He is a great convenience to everybody—even to the worst class of white men, for he bears the most of their sins, suffering fines for their petty thefts, imprisonment for their robberies, and death for their murders. Any white man can swear a Chinaman's life away in the courts, but no Chinaman can testify against a white man. Ours is the "land of the free"—nobody denies that—nobody challenges it. [Maybe it is because we won't let other people testify.] As I write, news comes that in broad daylight in San Francisco, some boys have stoned an inoffensive Chinaman to death, and that although a large crowd witnessed the shameful deed, no one interfered.

There are seventy thousand (and possibly one hundred thousand) Chinamen on the Pacific coast. There were about a thousand in Virginia. They were penned into a "Chinese quarter"—a thing which they do not particularly object to, as they are fond of herding together. Their buildings were of wood; usually only one story high, and set thickly together along streets scarcely wide enough for a wagon to pass through. Their quarter was a little removed from the rest of the town. The chief employment of Chinamen in towns is to wash clothing. They always send a bill pinned to the clothes. It is mere ceremony, for it does not enlighten the customer much. Their price for washing was $2.50 per dozen—rather cheaper than white people could afford to wash for at that time. A very common sign on the Chinese houses was: "See Yup, Washer and Ironer"; "Hong Wo, Washer"; "Sam Sing & Ah Hop, Washing." The house-servants, cooks, etc., in California and Nevada, were chiefly Chinamen. There were few white servants and no Chinawomen so employed. Chinamen make good house-servants, being quick, obedient, patient, quick to learn, and tirelessly industrious. They do not need to be taught a thing twice, as a general thing. They are imitative. If a Chinaman were to see his master break up a center-table, in a passion, and kindle a fire with it, that Chinaman would be likely to resort to the furniture for fuel forever afterward.

All Chinamen can read, write, and cipher with easy facility—pity but all our petted *voters* could. In California they rent little patches of ground and do a deal of gardening. They will raise surprising crops of vegetables on a sand-pile. They waste nothing. What is rubbish to a Christian, a Chinaman carefully preserves and makes useful in one way or another. He gathers up all the old oyster and sardine cans that white people throw away, and procures marketable tin and solder from them by melting. He gathers up old bones and turns them into manure. In California he gets a living out of old mining claims that white men have abandoned as exhausted and worthless—and then the officers come down on him once a month with an exorbitant swindle to which the legislature has given the broad, general name of "foreign" mining tax, but it is usually inflicted on no foreigners but Chinamen. This swindle has in some cases been repeated once or twice on the same victim in the course of the same month—but the public treasury was not additionally enriched by it, probably.

Chinamen hold their dead in great reverence—they worship their departed ancestors, in fact. Hence, in China, a man's front yard, back yard, or any other part of his premises, is made his family burying-ground, in order that he may visit the graves at any and all times. Therefore that huge empire is one mighty cemetery; it is ridged and wrinkled from its center to its circumference with graves —and inasmuch as every foot of ground must be made to do its utmost, in China, lest the swarming population suffer for food, the very graves are cultivated and yield a harvest, custom holding this to be no dishonor to the dead. Since the departed are held in such worshipful reverence, a Chinaman cannot bear that any indignity be offered the places where they sleep. Mr. Burlingame said that herein lay China's bitter opposition to railroads; a road could not be built anywhere in the empire without disturbing the graves of their ancestors or friends.

A Chinaman hardly believes he could enjoy the hereafter except his body lay in his beloved China; also, he desires to receive, himself, after death, that worship with which he has honored his dead that preceded him. Therefore, if he visits a foreign country, he makes arrangements to have his bones returned to China in case he dies; if he hires to go to a foreign country on a labor contract, there is always a stipulation that his body shall be taken back to China if he dies; if the government sells a gang of coolies to a foreigner for the usual five-year term, it is specified in the contract that their bodies shall be restored to China in case of death. On the Pacific coast the Chinamen all belong to one or another of several great companies or organizations, and these companies keep track of their members, register their names, and ship their bodies home when they die. The See Yup Company is held to be the largest of these. The Ning Yeong Company is next, and numbers eighteen thousand members on the coast. Its headquarters are at San Francisco, where it has a costly temple, several great officers (one of whom keeps regal state in seclusion and cannot be approached by common humanity), and a numerous priesthood. In it I was shown a register of its members, with the dead and the date of their shipment to China duly marked. Every ship that sails from San Francisco carries away a heavy freight of Chinese corpses—or did, at least, until the legislature, with an ingenious refinement of Christian cruelty, forbade the shipments, as a neat underhanded way of deterring Chinese immigration. The bill was offered, whether it passed or not. It is my impression that it passed. There was another bill—it became a law—compelling every incoming Chinaman to be vaccinated on the wharf and pay a duly-appointed quack (no decent doctor would defile himself with such legalized robbery) ten dollars for it. As few importers of Chinese would want to go to an expense like that, the lawmakers thought this would be another heavy blow to Chinese immigration.

What the Chinese quarter of Virginia was like—or, indeed, what the Chinese quarter of any Pacific coast town was and is like—may be gathered from this item which I printed in the *Enterprise* while reporting for that paper:

CHINATOWN.—Accompanied by a fellow-reporter, we made a trip through our Chinese quarter the other night. The Chinese have built their portion of the city to suit themselves; and as they keep neither carriages nor wagons, their streets are not wide enough, as a general thing, to admit of the passage of vehicles. At ten o'clock at night the Chinaman may be seen in all his glory. In every little cooped-up, dingy cavern of a hut, faint with the odor of burning Josh-lights and with nothing to see the gloom by save the sickly, guttering tallow candle, were two or three yellow, long-tailed vagabonds, coiled up on a sort of short truckle-bed, smoking opium, motionless and with their lusterless eyes turned inward from excess of satisfaction—or rather the recent smoker looks thus, immediately after having passed the pipe to his neighbor—for opium-smoking is a comfortless operation, and requires constant attention. A lamp sits on the bed, the length of the long pipe-stem from the smoker's mouth; he puts a pellet of opium on the end of a wire, sets it on fire, and plasters it into the pipe much as a Christian would fill a hole with putty; then he applies the bowl to the lamp and proceeds to smoke—and the stewing and frying of the drug and the gurgling of the juices in the stem would well-nigh turn the stomach of a statue. John likes it, though; it soothes him; he takes about two dozen whiffs, and then rolls over to dream, Heaven only knows what, for we could not imagine by looking at the soggy creature. Possibly in his visions he travels far away from the gross world and his regular washing, and feasts on succulent rats and birds'-nests in Paradise.

Mr. Ah Sing keeps a general grocery and provision store at No. 13 Wang Street. He lavished his hospitality upon our party in the friendliest way. He had various kinds of colored and colorless wines and brandies, with unpronounceable names, imported from China in little crockery jugs, and which he offered to us in dainty little miniature wash-basins of porcelain. He offered us a mess of birds'-nests; also, small, neat sausages, of which we could have swallowed several yards if we had chosen to try, but we suspected that each link contained the corpse of a mouse, and therefore refrained. Mr. Sing had in his store a thousand articles of merchandise, curious to behold, impossible to imagine the uses of, and beyond our ability to describe.

His ducks, however, and his eggs, we could understand; the former were split open and flattened out like codfish, and came from China in that shape, and the latter were plastered over with some kind of paste which kept them fresh and palatable through the long voyage.

We found Mr. Hong Wo, No. 37 Chow-chow Street, making up a lottery scheme—in fact, we found a dozen others occupied in the same way in various parts of the quarter, for about every third Chinaman runs a lottery, and the balance of the tribe "buck" at it. "Tom," who speaks faultless English, and used to be chief and only cook to the *Territorial Enterprise,* when the establishment kept bachelor's hall two years ago, said that "Sometime Chinaman buy ticket one dollar hap, ketch um two tree hundred, sometime no ketch um anyting; lottery like one man fight um seventy—maybe he whip, maybe he get whip heself, welly good." However, the percentage being sixty-nine against him, the chances are, as a general thing, that "he get whip heself." We could not see that these lotteries differed in any respect from our own, save that the figures being Chinese, no ignorant white man might ever hope to succeed in telling "t'other from which"; the manner of drawing is similar to ours.

Mr. See Yup keeps a fancy store on Live Fox Street. He sold us fans of white feathers, gorgeously ornamented; perfumery that smelled like Limburger cheese, Chinese pens, and watch-charms made of a stone unscratchable with steel instruments, yet polished and tinted like the inner coat of a sea-shell.[1] As tokens of his esteem, See Yup presented the party with gaudy plumes made of gold tinsel and trimmed with peacocks' feathers.

We ate chow-chow with chop-sticks in the celestial restaurants; our comrade chided the moon-eyed damsels in front of the houses for their want of feminine reserve; we received protecting Josh-lights from our hosts and "dickered" for a pagan god or two. Finally, we were impressed with the genius of a Chinese book-

[1] A peculiar species of the "jade-stone"—to a Chinaman peculiarly precious.—M. T.

keeper; he figured up his accounts on a machine like a gridiron with buttons strung on its bars; the different rows represented units, tens, hundreds, and thousands. He fingered them with incredible rapidity—in fact, he pushed them from place to place as fast as a musical professor's fingers travel over the keys of a piano.

They are a kindly-disposed, well-meaning race, and are respected and well treated by the upper classes, all over the Pacific coast. No Californian *gentleman or lady* ever abuses or oppresses a Chinaman, under any circumstances, an explanation that seems to be much needed in the East. Only the scum of the population do it—they and their children; they, and, naturally and consistently, the policemen and politicians, likewise, for these are the dust-licking pimps and slaves of the scum, there as well as elsewhere in America.

From *Roughing It,* 1872.

8 : San Francisco

SAN FRANCISCO, a truly fascinating city to live in, is stately and handsome at a fair distance, but close at hand one notes that the architecture is mostly old-fashioned, many streets are made up of decaying, smoke-grimed, wooden houses, and the barren sand-hills toward the outskirts obtrude themselves too prominently. Even the kindly climate is sometimes pleasanter when read about than personally experienced, for a lovely, cloudless sky wears out its welcome by and by, and then when the longed-for rain does come it *stays.* Even the playful earthquake is better contemplated at a dis—

However, there are varying opinions about that.

The climate of San Francisco is mild and singularly equable. The thermometer stands at about seventy degrees the year round. It hardly changes at all. You sleep under one or two light blankets summer and winter, and never use a mosquito-bar. Nobody ever wears summer clothing. You wear black broadcloth—if you have it—

in August and January, just the same. It is no colder, and no warmer, in the one month than the other. You do not use overcoats and you do not use fans. It is as pleasant a climate as could well be contrived, take it all around, and is doubtless the most unvarying in the whole world. The wind blows there a good deal in the summer months, but then you can go over to Oakland, if you choose—three or four miles away—it does not blow there. It has only snowed twice in San Francisco in nineteen years, and then it only remained on the ground long enough to astonish the children, and set them to wondering what the feathery stuff was.

During eight months of the year, straight along, the skies are bright and cloudless, and never a drop of rain falls. But when the other four months come along, you will need to go and steal an umbrella. Because you will require it. Not just one day, but one hundred and twenty days in hardly varying succession. When you want to go visiting, or attend church, or the theater, you never look up at the clouds to see whether it is likely to rain or not—you look at the almanac. If it is winter, it will *rain*—and if it is summer, it *won't* rain, and you cannot help it. You never need a lightning-rod, because it never thunders and it never lightnings. And after you have listened for six or eight weeks, every night, to the dismal monotony of those quiet rains, you will wish in your heart the thunder *would* leap and crash and roar along those drowsy skies once, and make everything alive—you will wish the prisoned lightnings *would* cleave the dull firmament asunder and light it with a blinding glare for *one* little instant. You would give *anything* to hear the old familiar thunder again and see the lightning strike somebody. And along in the summer, when you have suffered about four months of lustrous, pitiless sunshine, you are ready to go down on your knees and plead for rain—hail—snow—thunder and lightning—anything to break the monotony—you will take an earthquake, if you cannot do any better. And the chances are that you'll get it, too.

San Francisco is built on sand-hills, but they are prolific sand-hills. They yield a generous vegetation. All the rare flowers which people in "the States" rear with such patient care in parlor flower-pots and greenhouses, flourish luxuriantly in the open air there all the year around. Calla lilies, all sorts of geraniums, passion-flowers, moss-roses—I do not know the names of a tenth part of them. I only know that while New-Yorkers are burdened with banks and drifts of snow, Californians are burdened with banks and drifts of flowers, if they only keep their hands off and let them grow. And I have heard that they have also that rarest and most curious of all flowers, the beautiful *Espiritu Santo,* as the Spaniards call it—or flower of the Holy Spirit—though I thought it grew only in Central America—down on the Isthmus. In its cup is the daintiest little facsimile of a dove, as pure as snow. The Spaniards have a superstitious reverence for it. The blossom has been conveyed to the States, submerged in ether; and the bulb has been taken thither also, but every attempt to make it bloom after it arrived, has failed.

I have elsewhere spoken of the endless winter of Mono, California, and but this moment of the eternal spring of San Francisco. Now, if we travel a hundred miles in a straight line, we come to the eternal summer of Sacramento. One never sees summer-clothing or mosquitoes in San Francisco—but they can be found in Sacramento. Not always and unvaryingly, but about one hundred and forty-three months out of twelve years, perhaps. Flowers bloom there, always, the reader can easily believe—people suffer and sweat, and swear, morning, noon, and night, and wear out their stanchest energies fanning themselves. It gets hot there, but if you go down to Fort Yuma you will find it hotter. Fort Yuma is probably the hottest place on earth. The thermometer stays at one hundred and twenty in the shade there all the time—except when it varies and goes higher. It is a U. S. military post, and its occupants get so used to the terrific heat that they suffer without it. There is a tradition (attributed to John Phenix [1]) that a very, very wicked soldier died there, once, and of course, went straight to the hottest corner of perdition—and the next day he *telegraphed back for his blankets.* There is no doubt about the truth of this statement. There can be no doubt about it. I have seen the place where that soldier used to board. In Sacramento it is fiery summer always, and you can gather roses, and eat strawberries and ice-cream, and wear white linen clothes, and pant and perspire, at eight or nine o'clock in the morning, and then take the cars, and at noon put on your furs and your skates, and go skimming over frozen Donner Lake, seven thousand feet above the valley, among snow-banks fifteen feet

[1] It has been purloined by fifty different scribblers who were too poor to invent a fancy but not ashamed to steal one.—M. T.

deep, and in the shadow of grand mountain peaks that lift their frosty crags ten thousand feet above the level of the sea. There is a transition for you! Where will you find another like it in the western hemisphere? And some of us have swept around snow-walled curves of the Pacific Railroad in that vicinity, six thousand feet above the sea, and looked down as the birds do, upon the deathless summer of the Sacramento Valley, with its fruitful fields, its feathery foliage, its silver streams, all slumbering in the mellow haze of its enchanted atmosphere, and all infinitely softened and spiritualized by distance—a dreamy, exquisite glimpse of fairyland, made all the more charming and striking that it was caught through a forbidden gateway of ice and snow, and savage crags and precipices.

It was just after noon, on a bright October day. I was coming down Third Street. The only objects in motion anywhere in sight in that thickly built and populous quarter, were a man in a buggy behind me, and a street-car wending slowly up the cross-street. Otherwise, all was solitude and a Sabbath stillness. As I turned the corner, around a frame house, there was a great rattle and jar, and it occurred to me that here was an item!—no doubt a fight in that house. Before I could turn and seek the door, there came a really terrific shock; the ground seemed to roll under me in waves, interrupted by a violent joggling up and down, and there was a heavy grinding noise as of brick houses rubbing together. I fell up against the frame house and hurt my elbow. I knew what it was, now, and from mere reportorial instinct, nothing else, took out my watch and noted the time of day; at that moment a third and still severer shock came, and as I reeled about on the pavement trying to keep my footing, I saw a sight! The entire front of a tall four-story brick building in Third Street sprung outward like a door and fell sprawling across the street, raising a dust like a great volume of smoke! And here came the buggy—overboard went the man, and in less time than I can tell it the vehicle was distributed in small fragments along three hundred yards of street. One could have fancied that somebody had fired a charge of chair-rounds and rags down the thoroughfare. The street-car had stopped, the horses were rearing and plunging, the passengers were pouring out at both ends, and one fat man had crashed half-way through a glass window on one side of the car, got wedged fast and was squirming and screaming like an impaled madman. Every door of every house, as far as the eye could reach, was vomiting a stream of human beings; and almost before one could execute a wink and begin another, there was a massed multitude of people stretching in endless procession down every street my position commanded. Never was solemn solitude turned into teeming life quicker.

Of the wonders wrought by "the great earthquake," these were all that came under my eye; but the tricks it did, elsewhere, and far and wide over the town, made toothsome gossip for nine days. The destruction of property was trifling—the injury to it was widespread and somewhat serious.

The "curiosities" of the earthquake were simply endless. Gentlemen and ladies who were sick, or were taking a siesta, or had dissipated till a late hour and were making up lost sleep, thronged into the public streets in all sorts of queer apparel, and some without any at all. One woman who had been washing a naked child, ran down the street holding it by the ankles as if it were a dressed turkey. Prominent citizens who were supposed to keep the Sabbath strictly, rushed out of saloons in their shirt-sleeves, with billiard-cues in their hands. Dozens of men with necks swathed in napkins rushed from barber shops, lathered to the eyes or with one cheek clean-shaved and the other still bearing a hairy stubble. Horses broke from stables, and a frightened dog rushed up a short attic ladder and out onto a roof, and when his scare was over had not the nerve to go down again the same way he had gone up. A prominent editor flew down-stairs, in the principal hotel, with nothing on but one brief undergarment—met a chambermaid, and exclaimed:

"Oh, what *shall* I do! Where shall I go!"

She responded with naïve serenity:

"If you have no choice, you might try a clothing store!"

A certain foreign consul's lady was the acknowledged leader of fashion, and every time she appeared in anything new or extraordinary, the ladies in the vicinity made a raid on their husbands' purses and arrayed themselves similarly. One man, who had suffered considerably and growled accordingly, was standing at the window when the shocks came, and the next instant the consul's wife, just out of the bath, fled by with no other apology for clothing than—a bath-towel! The sufferer rose superior to the terrors of the earthquake, and said to his wife:

"Now *that* is something *like!* Get out your towel, my dear!"

The plastering that fell from ceilings in San Francisco that day would have covered several acres of ground. For some days afterward, groups of eying and pointing men stood about many a building, looking at long zigzag cracks that extended from the eaves to the ground. Four feet of the tops of three chimneys on one house were broken square off and turned around in such a way as to completely stop the draught. A crack a hundred feet long gaped open six inches wide in the middle of one street and then shut together again with such force as to ridge up the meeting earth like a slender grave. A lady, sitting in her rocking and quaking parlor, saw the wall part at the ceiling, open and shut twice, like a mouth, and then drop the end of a brick on the floor like a tooth. She was a woman easily disgusted with foolishness, and she arose and went out of there. One lady who was coming down-stairs was astonished to see a bronze Hercules lean forward on its pedestal as if to strike her with its club. They both reached the bottom of the flight at the same time—the woman insensible from the fright. Her child, born some little time afterward, was club-footed. However —on second thought—if the reader sees any coincidence in this, he must do it at his own risk.

The first shock brought down two or three huge organ-pipes in one of the churches. The minister, with uplifted hands, was just closing the services. He glanced up, hesitated, and said:

"However, we will omit the benediction!"—and the next instant there was a vacancy in the atmosphere where he had stood.

After the first shock, an Oakland minister said:

"Keep your seats! There is no better place to die than this—"

And added, after the third:

"But outside is good enough!" He then skipped out at the back door.

Such another destruction of mantel ornaments and toilet bottles as the earthquake created, San Francisco never saw before. There was hardly a girl or a matron in the city but suffered losses of this kind. Suspended pictures were thrown down, but oftener still, by a curious freak of the earthquake's humor, they were whirled completely around with their faces to the wall! There was great difference of opinion, at first, as to the course or direction the earthquake traveled, but water that splashed out of various tanks and buckets settled that. Thousands of people were made so seasick by the rolling and pitching of floors and streets that they were weak and bedridden for hours, and some few for even days afterward. Hardly an individual escaped nausea entirely.

From *Roughing It*, 1872.

9 : Young Days on the River

WHEN I WAS A BOY, there was but one permanent ambition among my comrades in our village on the west bank of the Mississippi River. That was, to be a steamboatman. We had transient ambitions of other sorts, but they were only transient. When a circus came and went, it left us all burning to become clowns; the first negro minstrel show that ever came to our section left us all suffering to try that kind of life; now and then we had a hope that, if we lived and were good, God would permit us to be pirates. These ambitions faded out, each in its turn; but the ambition to be a steamboatman always remained.

Once a day a cheap, gaudy packet arrived upward from St. Louis, and another downward from Keokuk. Before these events, the day was glorious with expectancy; after them, the day was a dead and empty thing. Not only the boys, but the whole village, felt this. After all these years I can picture that old time to myself now, just as it was then: the white town drowsing in the sunshine of a summer's morning; the streets empty, or pretty nearly so; one or two clerks sitting in front of the Water Street stores, with their splint-bottomed chairs tilted back against the walls, chins on breasts, hats slouched over their faces, asleep—with shingle-shavings enough around to show what broke them down; a sow and a litter of pigs loafing along the sidewalk, doing a good business in watermelon rinds and seeds; two or three lonely little freight piles scattered about the "levee"; a pile of "skids" on the slope of the stone-paved wharf, and the fragrant town drunkard asleep in the shadow of them; two or three wood flats at the head of the wharf, but nobody to listen to the peaceful lapping of the wavelets against them; the great Mississippi, the majestic, the magnificent Mississippi, rolling its mile-wide tide along, shining in the sun; the dense forest away on the other side; the "point" above the town, and the "point" below, bounding the river-glimpse and turning it into a sort of sea, and withal a very still and brilliant and lonely one. Presently a film of dark smoke appears above one of those remote "points"; instantly a negro drayman, famous for his quick eye and prodigious voice, lifts up the cry, "S-t-e-a-m-boat a-comin'!" and the scene changes! The town drunkard stirs, the clerks wake up, a furious clatter of drays follows, every house and store pours out a human contribution, and all in a twinkling the dead town is alive and moving. Drays, carts, men, boys, all go hurrying from many quarters to a common center, the wharf. Assembled there, the people fasten their eyes upon the coming boat as upon a wonder they are seeing for the first time. And the boat *is* rather a handsome sight, too. She is long and sharp and trim and pretty; she has two tall, fancy-topped chimneys, with a gilded device of some kind swung between them; a fanciful pilot-house, all glass and "gingerbread," perched on top of the "texas" deck behind them; the paddle-boxes are gorgeous with a picture or with gilded rays above the boat's name; the boiler-deck, the hurricane-deck, and the texas deck are fenced and ornamented with clean white railings; there is a flag gallantly flying from the jack-staff; the furnace doors are open and the fires glaring bravely; the upper decks are black with passengers; the captain stands by the big bell, calm, imposing, the envy of all; great volumes of the blackest smoke are rolling and tumbling out of the chimneys—a husbanded grandeur created with a bit of pitch-pine just before arriving at a town; the crew are grouped on the forecastle; the broad stage is run far out over the port bow, and an envied deck-hand stands picturesquely on the end of it with a coil of rope in his hand; the pent steam is screaming through the gauge-cocks; the captain lifts his hand, a bell rings, the wheels stop; then they turn back, churning the water to foam, and the steamer is at rest. Then such a scramble as there is to get aboard, and to get ashore, and to take in freight and to discharge freight, all at one and the same time; and such a yelling and cursing as the mates facilitate it all with! Ten minutes later the steamer is under way again, with no flag on the jack-staff and no black smoke issuing from the chimneys. After ten more minutes the town is dead again, and the town drunkard asleep by the skids once more.

My father was a justice of the peace, and I supposed he possessed the power of life and death over all men, and could hang anybody that offended him. This was distinction enough for me as a general thing; but the desire to be a steamboatman kept intruding, nevertheless. I first wanted to be a cabin-boy, so that I could come out with a white apron on and shake a table-cloth over the side, where all my old comrades could see me; later I thought I would rather be the deck-hand who stood on the end of the stage-plank with the coil of rope in his hand, because he was particularly conspicuous. But these were only day-dreams—they were too heavenly to be contemplated as real possibilities. By and by one of our boys went away. He was not heard of for a long time. At last he turned up as apprentice engineer or "striker" on a steamboat. This thing shook the bottom out of all my Sunday-school teachings. That boy had been notoriously worldly, and I just the reverse; yet he was exalted to this eminence, and I left in obscurity and misery. There was nothing generous about this fellow in his greatness. He would always manage to have a rusty bolt to scrub while his boat tarried at our town, and he would sit on the inside guard and scrub it, where we all could see him and envy him and loathe him. And whenever his boat was laid up he would come home and swell around the town in his blackest and greasiest clothes, so that nobody could help remembering that he was a steamboatman; and he used all sorts of steamboat technicalities in his talk, as if he were so used to them that he forgot common people could not understand them. He would speak of the "labboard" side of a horse in an easy, natural way that would make one wish he was dead. And he was always talking about "St. Looy" like an old citizen; he would refer casually to occasions when he was "coming down Fourth Street," or when he was "passing by the Planter's House," or when there was a fire and he took a turn on the brakes of "the old Big Missouri"; and then he would go on and lie about how many towns the size of ours were burned down there that day. Two or three of the boys had long been persons of consideration among us because they had been to St. Louis once and had a vague general knowledge of its wonders, but the day of their glory was over now. They lapsed into a humble silence, and learned to disappear when the ruthless "cub"-engineer approached. This fellow had money, too, and hair-oil. Also an ignorant silver watch and a showy brass watch-chain. He wore a leather belt and used no suspenders. If ever a youth was cordially admired and hated by his comrades, this one was. No girl could withstand his charms. He "cut out" every boy in the village. When his boat blew up at last, it diffused a tranquil contentment among us such as we had not known for months. But when he came home the next week, alive, renowned, and appeared in church all battered up and bandaged, a shining hero, stared at and wondered over by everybody, it seemed to us that the partiality of Providence for an undeserving reptile had reached a point where it was open to criticism.

This creature's career could produce but one result, and it speedily followed. Boy after boy managed to get on the river. The minister's son became an engineer. The doctor's and the postmaster's sons became "mud clerks"; the wholesale liquor dealer's son became a barkeeper on a boat; four sons of the chief merchant, and two sons of the county judge, became pilots. Pilot was the grandest position of all. The pilot, even in those days of trivial wages, had a princely salary—from a hundred and fifty to two hundred and fifty dollars a month, and no board to pay. Two months of his wages would pay a preacher's salary for a year. Now some of us were left disconsolate. We could not get on the river—at least our parents would not let us.

So, by and by, I ran away. I said I would never come home again till I was a pilot and could come in glory. But somehow I could not manage it. I went meekly aboard a few of the boats that lay packed together like sardines at the long St. Louis wharf, and humbly inquired for the pilots, but got only a cold shoulder and short words from mates and clerks. I had to make the best of this sort of treatment for the time being, but I had comforting day-dreams of a future when I should be a great and honored pilot, with plenty of money, and could kill some of these mates and clerks and pay for them.

Months afterward the hope within me struggled to a reluctant death, and I found myself without an ambition. But I was ashamed to go home. I was in Cincinnati, and I set to work to map out a new career. I had been reading about the recent exploration of the river Amazon by an expedition sent out by our government. It was said that the expedition, owing to difficulties, had not thoroughly explored a part of the country lying about the headwaters, some four thousand miles from the mouth of the river. It was only about fifteen hundred miles from Cincinnati to New Orleans, where I could doubtless get a ship. I had thirty dollars left; I would go and complete the exploration of the Amazon. This was all the thought I gave to the subject. I never was great in matters of detail. I packed my valise, and took passage on an ancient tub called the *Paul Jones,* for New Orleans. For the sum of sixteen dollars I had the scarred and tarnished splendors of "her" main saloon principally to myself, for she was not a creature to attract the eye of wiser travelers.

When we presently got under way and went poking down the broad Ohio, I became a new being, and the subject of my own admiration. I was a traveler! A word never had tasted so good in my mouth before. I had an exultant sense of being bound for mysterious lands and distant climes which I never have felt in so uplifting a degree since. I was in such a glorified condition that all ignoble feelings departed out of me, and I was able to look down and pity the untraveled with a compassion that had hardly a trace of contempt in it. Still, when we stopped at villages and wood-yards, I could not help lolling carelessly upon the railings of the boiler-deck to enjoy the envy of the country boys on the bank. If they did not seem to discover me, I presently sneezed to attract their attention, or moved to a position where they could not help seeing me. And as soon as I knew they saw me I gaped and stretched, and gave other signs of being mightily bored with traveling.

I kept my hat off all the time, and stayed where the wind and the sun could strike me, because I wanted to get the bronzed and weather-beaten look of an old traveler. Before the second day was half gone I experienced a joy which filled me with the purest gratitude; for I saw that the skin had begun to blister and peel off my face and neck. I wished that the boys and girls at home could see me now.

We reached Louisville in time—at least the neighborhood of it. We stuck hard and fast on the rocks in the middle of the river, and lay there four days. I was now beginning to feel a strong sense of being a part of the boat's family, a sort of infant son to the captain and younger brother to the officers. There is no estimating the pride I took in the grandeur, or the affection that began to swell and grow in me for those people. I could not know how the lordly steamboatman scorns that sort of presumption in a mere landsman. I particularly longed to acquire the least trifle of notice from the big stormy mate, and I was on the alert for an opportunity to do him a service to that end. It came at last. The riotous pow-wow of setting a spar was going on down on the forecastle, and I went down there and stood around in the way—or mostly skipping out of it—till the mate suddenly roared a general order for somebody to bring him a capstan bar. I sprang to his side and said: "Tell me where it is—I'll fetch it!"

If a rag-picker had offered to do a diplomatic service for the Emperor of Russia, the monarch could not have been more astounded than the mate was. He even stopped swearing. He stood and stared down at me. It took him ten seconds to scrape his disjointed remains together again. Then he said impressively: "Well, if this don't beat h——l!" and turned to his work with the air of a man who had been confronted with a problem too abstruse for solution.

I crept away, and courted solitude for the rest of the day. I did not go to dinner; I stayed away from supper until everybody else had finished. I did not feel so much like a member of the boat's family now as before. However, my spirits returned, in instalments, as we pursued our way down the river. I was sorry I hated the mate so, because it was not in (young) human nature not to admire him. He was huge and muscular, his face was bearded and whiskered all over; he had a red woman and a blue woman tattooed on his right arm—one on each side of a blue anchor with a red rope to it; and in the matter of profanity he was sublime. When he was getting out cargo at a landing, I was always where I could see and hear. He felt all the majesty of his great position, and made the world feel it, too. When he gave even the simplest order, he discharged it like a blast of lightning, and sent a long, reverberating peal of profanity thundering after it. I could not help contrasting the way in which the average landsman would give an order with the mate's way of doing it. If the landsman should wish the gangplank moved a foot farther forward, he would probably say: "James, or William, one of you push that plank forward, please"; but put the mate in his place, and he would roar out: "Here, now, start that gang-plank for'ard! Lively, now! *What're* you about! Snatch it! *snatch* it! There! there! Aft again! aft again! Don't you hear me? Dash it to dash! are you going to *sleep* over it! *'Vast* heaving. 'Vast heaving, I tell you! Going to heave it clear astern? WHERE 're you going with that barrel! *for'ard* with it 'fore I make you swallow it, you dash-dash-dash-*dashed* split between a tired mud-turtle and a crippled hearse-horse!"

I wished I could talk like that.

When the soreness of my adventure with the mate had somewhat worn off, I began timidly to make up to the humblest official connected with the boat—the night watchman. He snubbed my advances at first, but I presently ventured to offer him a new chalk pipe, and that softened him. So he allowed me to sit with him by the big bell on the hurricane-deck, and in time he melted into conversation. He could not well have helped it, I hung with such homage on his words and so plainly showed that I felt honored by his notice. He told me the names of dim capes and shadowy islands as we glided by them in the solemnity of the night, under the winking stars, and by and by got to talking about himself. He seemed over-sentimental for a man whose salary was six dollars a week—or rather he might have seemed so to an older person than I. But I drank in his words hungrily, and with a faith that might have moved mountains if it had been applied judiciously. What was it to me that he was soiled and seedy and fragrant with gin? What was it to me that his grammar was bad, his construction worse, and his profanity so void of art that it was an element of weakness rather than strength in his conversation? He was a wronged man, a man who had seen trouble, and that was enough for me. As he mellowed into his plaintive history his tears dripped upon the lantern in his lap, and I cried, too, from sympathy. He said he was the son of an English nobleman—either an earl or an alderman, he could not remember which, but believed was both; his father, the nobleman, loved him, but his mother hated him from the cradle; and so while he was still a little boy he was sent to "one of them old, ancient colleges"—he couldn't remember which; and by and by his father died and his mother seized the property and "shook" him, as he phrased it. After his mother shook him, members of the nobility with whom he was acquainted used their influence to get him the position of "loblolly-boy in a ship"; and from that point my watchman threw off all trammels of date and locality and branched out into a narrative that bristled all along with incredible adventures; a narrative that was so reeking with bloodshed, and so crammed with hair-breadth escapes and the most engaging and unconscious personal villainies, that I sat speechless, enjoying, shuddering, wondering, worshiping.

It was a sore blight to find out afterward that he was a low, vulgar, ignorant, sentimental, half-witted humbug, an untraveled native of the wilds of Illinois, who had absorbed wildcat literature and appropriated its marvels, until in time he had woven odds and ends of the mess into this yarn, and then gone on telling it to fledglings like me, until he had come to believe it himself.

What with lying on the rocks four days at Louisville, and some other delays, the poor old *Paul Jones* fooled away about two weeks in making the voyage from Cincinnati to New Orleans. This gave me a chance to get acquainted with one of the pilots, and he taught me how to steer the boat, and thus made the fascination of river life more potent than ever for me.

It also gave me a chance to get acquainted with a youth who had taken deck passage—more's the pity; for he easily borrowed six dollars of me on a promise to return to the boat and pay it back to me the day after we should arrive. But he probably died or forgot, for he never came. It was doubtless the former, since he had said his parents were wealthy, and he only traveled deck passage because it was cooler.[1]

I soon discovered two things. One was that a vessel would not be likely to sail for the mouth of the Amazon under ten or twelve years; and the other was that the nine or ten dollars still left in my pocket would not suffice for so impossible an exploration as I had planned, even if I could afford to wait for a ship. Therefore it followed that I must contrive a new career. The *Paul Jones* was now bound for St. Louis. I planned a siege against my pilot, and at the end of three hard days he surrendered. He agreed to teach me the Mississippi River from New Orleans to St. Louis for five hundred dollars, payable out of the first wages I should receive after

1 "Deck" passage—*i. e.*, steerage passage.—M. T.

graduating. I entered upon the small enterprise of "learning" twelve or thirteen hundred miles of the great Mississippi River with the easy confidence of my time of life. If I had really known what I was about to require of my faculties, I should not have had the courage to begin. I supposed that all a pilot had to do was to keep his boat in the river, and I did not consider that that could be much of a trick, since it was so wide.

The boat backed out from New Orleans at four in the afternoon, and it was "our watch" until eight. Mr. Bixby, my chief, "straightened her up," plowed her along past the sterns of the other boats that lay at the Levee, and then said, "Here, take her; shave those steamships as close as you'd peel an apple." I took the wheel, and my heartbeat fluttered up into the hundreds; for it seemed to me that we were about to scrape the side off every ship in the line, we were so close. I held my breath and began to claw the boat away from the danger; and I had my own opinion of the pilot who had known no better than to get us into such peril, but I was too wise to express it. In half a minute I had a wide margin of safety intervening between the *Paul Jones* and the ships; and within ten seconds more I was set aside in disgrace, and Mr. Bixby was going into danger again and flaying me alive with abuse of my cowardice. I was stung, but I was obliged to admire the easy confidence with which my chief loafed from side to side of his wheel, and trimmed the ships so closely that disaster seemed ceaselessly imminent. When he had cooled a little he told me that the easy water was close ashore and the current outside, and therefore we must hug the bank, up-stream, to get the benefit of the former, and stay well out, down-stream, to take advantage of the latter. In my own mind I resolved to be a down-stream pilot and leave the up-streaming to people dead to prudence.

Now and then Mr. Bixby called my attention to certain things. Said he, "This is Six-Mile Point." I assented. It was pleasant enough information, but I could not see the bearing of it. I was not conscious that it was a matter of any interest to me. Another time he said, "This is Nine-Mile Point." Later he said, "This is Twelve-Mile Point." They were all about level with the water's edge; they all looked about alike to me; they were monotonously unpicturesque. I hoped Mr. Bixby would change the subject. But no; he would crowd up around a point, hugging the shore with affection, and then say: "The slack water ends here, abreast this bunch of China trees; now we cross over." So he crossed over. He gave me the wheel once or twice, but I had no luck. I either came near chipping off the edge of a sugar-plantation, or I yawed too far from shore, and so dropped back into disgrace again and got abused.

The watch was ended at last, and we took supper and went to bed. At midnight the glare of a lantern shone in my eyes, and the night watchman said:

"Come, turn out!"

And then he left. I could not understand this extraordinary procedure; so I presently gave up trying to, and dozed off to sleep. Pretty soon the watchman was back again, and this time he was gruff. I was annoyed. I said:

"What do you want to come bothering around here in the middle of the night for? Now, as like as not, I'll not get to sleep again to-night."

The watchman said:

"Well, if this ain't good, I'm blessed."

The "off-watch" was just turning in, and I heard some brutal laughter from them, and such remarks as "Hello, watchman! ain't the new cub turned out yet? He's delicate, likely. Give him some sugar in a rag, and send for the chambermaid to sing 'Rock-a-by Baby,' to him."

About this time Mr. Bixby appeared on the scene. Something like a minute later I was climbing the pilot-house steps with some of my clothes on and the rest in my arms. Mr. Bixby was close behind, commenting. Here was something fresh—this thing of getting up in the middle of the night to go to work. It was a detail in piloting that had never occurred to me at all. I knew that boats ran all night, but somehow I had never happened to reflect that somebody had to get up out of a warm bed to run them. I began to fear that piloting was not quite so romantic as I had imagined it was; there was something very real and worklike about this new phase of it.

It was a rather dingy night, although a fair number of stars were out. The big mate was at the wheel, and he had the old tub pointed at a star and was holding her straight up the middle of the river. The shores on either hand were not much more than half a mile apart, but they seemed wonderfully far away and ever so vague and indistinct. The mate said:

"We've got to land at Jones's plantation, sir."

The vengeful spirit in me exulted. I said to myself, "I wish you joy of your job, Mr. Bixby; you'll have a good time finding Mr. Jones's plantation such a night as this; and I hope you never *will* find it as long as you live."

Mr. Bixby said to the mate:

"Upper end of the plantation, or the lower?"

"Upper."

"I can't do it. The stumps there are out of water at this stage. It's no great distance to the lower, and you'll have to get along with that."

"All right, sir. If Jones don't like it, he'll have to lump it, I reckon."

And then the mate left. My exultation began to cool and my wonder to come up. Here was a man who not only proposed to find this plantation on such a night, but to find either end of it you preferred. I dreadfully wanted to ask a question, but I was carrying about as many short answers as my cargo-room would admit of, so I held my peace. All I desired to ask Mr. Bixby was the simple question whether he was ass enough to really imagine he was going to find that plantation on a night when all plantations were exactly alike and all of the same color. But I held in. I used to have fine inspirations of prudence in those days.

Mr. Bixby made for the shore and soon was scraping it, just the same as if it had been daylight. And not only that, but singing:

"Father in heaven, the day is declining," etc.

It seemed to me that I had put my life in the keeping of a peculiarly reckless outcast. Presently he turned on me and said:

"What's the name of the first point above New Orleans?"

I was gratified to be able to answer promptly, and I did. I said I didn't know.

"Don't *know?*"

This manner jolted me. I was down at the foot again, in a moment. But I had to say just what I had said before.

"Well, you're a smart one!" said Mr. Bixby. "What's the name of the *next* point?"

Once more I didn't know.

"Well, this beats anything. Tell me the name of *any* point or place I told you."

I studied awhile and decided that I couldn't.

"Look here! What do you start out from, above Twelve-Mile Point, to cross over?"

"I—I—don't know."

"You—you—don't know?" mimicking my drawling manner of speech. "What *do* you know?"

"I—I—nothing, for certain."

"By the great Cæsar's ghost, I believe you! You're the stupidest dunderhead I ever saw or ever heard of, so help me Moses! The idea of *you* being a pilot—*you!* Why, you don't know enough to pilot a cow down a lane."

Oh, but his wrath was up! He was a nervous man, and he shuffled from one side of his wheel to the other as if the floor was hot. He would boil awhile to himself, and then overflow and scald me again.

"Look here! What do you suppose I told you the names of those points for?"

I tremblingly considered a moment, and then the devil of temptation provoked me to say:

"Well to—to—be entertaining, I thought."

This was a red rag to the bull. He raged and stormed so (he was crossing the river at the time) that I judged it made him blind, because he ran over the steering-oar of a trading-scow. Of course the traders sent up a volley of red-hot profanity. Never was a man so grateful as Mr. Bixby was; because he was brimful, and here were subjects who could *talk back*. He threw open a window, thrust his head out, and such an irruption followed as I never had heard before. The fainter and farther away the scowmen's curses drifted, the higher Mr. Bixby lifted his voice and the weightier his adjectives grew. When he closed the window he was empty. You could have drawn a seine through his system and not caught curses enough to disturb your mother with. Presently he said to me in the gentlest way:

"My boy, you must get a little memorandum-book; and every time I tell you a thing, put it down right away. There's only one way to be a pilot, and that is to get this entire river by heart. You have to know it just like A B C."

That was a dismal revelation to me; for my memory was never loaded with anything but blank cartridges. However, I did not feel discouraged long. I judged that it was best to make some allowances, for doubtless Mr. Bixby was "stretching." Presently he pulled a rope and struck a few strokes on the big bell. The stars were all gone now, and the night was as black as ink. I could hear the wheels churn along the bank, but I was not entirely certain that I could see the shore. The voice of the invisible watchman called up from the hurricane-deck:

"What's this, sir?"

"Jones's plantation."

I said to myself, "I wish I might venture to offer a small bet that it isn't." But I did not chirp. I only waited to see. Mr. Bixby handled the engine-bells, and in due time the boat's nose came to the land, a torch glowed from the forecastle, a man skipped ashore, a darky's voice on the bank said: "Gimme de k'yarpet-bag, Mass' Jones," and the next moment we were standing up the river again, all serene. I reflected deeply awhile, and then said—but not aloud—"Well, the finding of that plantation was the luckiest accident that ever happened; but it couldn't happen again in a hundred years." And I fully believed it *was* an accident, too.

By the time we had gone seven or eight hundred miles up the river, I had learned to be a tolerably plucky up-stream steersman, in daylight; and before we reached St. Louis I had made a trifle of progress in night work, but only a trifle. I had a note-book that fairly bristled with the names of towns, "points," bars, islands, bends, reaches, etc.; but the information was to be found only in the note-book—none of it was in my head. It made my heart ache to think I had only got half of the river set down; for as our watch was four hours off and four hours on, day and night, there was a long four-hour gap in my book for every time I had slept since the voyage began.

My chief was presently hired to go on a big New Orleans boat, and I packed my satchel and went with him. She was a grand affair. When I stood in her pilot-house I was so far above the water that I seemed perched on a mountain; and her decks stretched so far away, fore and aft, below me, that I wondered how I could ever have considered the little *Paul Jones* a large craft. There were other differences, too. The *Paul Jones's* pilot-house was a cheap, dingy, battered rattletrap, cramped for room; but here was a sumptuous glass temple; room enough to have a dance in; showy red and gold window-curtains; an imposing sofa; leather cushions and a back to the high bench where visiting pilots sit, to spin yarns and "look at the river"; bright, fanciful "cuspidores," instead of a broad wooden box filled with sawdust; nice new oilcloth on the floor; a hospitable big stove for winter; a wheel as high as my head, costly with inlaid work; a wire tiller-rope; bright brass knobs for the bells; and a tidy, white-aproned, black "texas-tender," to bring up tarts and ices and coffee during mid-watch, day and night. Now this was "something like"; and so I began to take heart once more to believe that piloting was a romantic sort of occupation after all. The moment we were under way I began to prowl about the great steamer and fill myself with joy. She was as clean and as dainty as a drawing-room; when I looked down her long, gilded saloon, it was like gazing through a splendid tunnel; she had an oil-picture, by some gifted sign-painter, on every stateroom door; she glittered with no end of prism-fringed chandeliers; the clerk's office was elegant, the bar was marvelous, and the barkeeper had been barbered and upholstered at incredible cost. The boiler-deck (*i. e.,* the second story of the boat, so to speak) was as spacious as a church, it seemed to me; so with the forecastle; and there was no pitiful handful of deck-hands, firemen, and roustabouts down there, but a whole battalion of men. The fires were fiercely glaring from a long row of furnaces, and over them were eight large boilers! This was unutterable pomp. The mighty engines—but enough of this. I had never felt so fine before. And when I found that the regiment of natty servants respectfully "sir'd" me, my satisfaction was complete.

From *Life on the Mississippi,* 1883.

10 : *Perplexing Lessons*

AT THE END of what seemed a tedious while, I had managed to pack my head full of islands, towns, bars, "points," and bends; and a curiously inanimate mass of lumber it was, too. However, inasmuch as I could shut my eyes and reel off a good long string of these names without leaving out more than ten miles of river in every fifty, I began to feel that I could take a boat down to New Orleans if I could make her skip those little gaps. But of course my complacency could hardly get start enough to lift my nose a trifle into the air, before Mr. Bixby would think of something to fetch it down again. One day he turned on me suddenly with this settler:

"What is the shape of Walnut Bend?"

He might as well have asked me my grandmother's opinion of protoplasm. I reflected respectfully, and then said I didn't know it had any particular shape. My gun-powdery chief went off with a bang, of course, and then went on loading and firing until he was out of adjectives.

I had learned long ago that he only carried just so many rounds of ammunition, and was sure to subside into a very placable and even remorseful old smooth-bore as soon as they were all gone. That word "old" is merely affectionate; he was not more than thirty-four. I waited. By and by he said:

"My boy, you've got to know the *shape* of the river perfectly. It is all there is left to steer by on a very dark night. Everything else is blotted out and gone. But mind you, it hasn't the same shape in the night that it has in the daytime."

"How on earth am I ever going to learn it, then?"

"How do you follow a hall at home in the dark? Because you know the shape of it. You can't see it."

"Do you mean to say that I've got to know all the million trifling variations of shape in the banks of this interminable river as well as I know the shape of the front hall at home?"

"On my honor, you've got to know them *better* than any man ever did know the shapes of the halls in his own house."

"I wish I was dead!"

"Now I don't want to discourage you, but—"

"Well, pile it on me; I might as well have it now as another time."

"You see, this has got to be learned; there isn't any getting around it. A clear starlight night throws such heavy shadows that, if you didn't know the shape of a shore perfectly, you would claw away from every bunch of timber, because you would take the black shadow of it for a solid cape; and you see you would be getting scared to death every fifteen minutes by the watch. You would be fifty yards from shore all the time when you ought to be within fifty feet of it. You can't see a snag in one of those shadows, but you know exactly where it is, and the shape of the river tells you when you are coming to it. Then there's your pitch-dark night; the river is a very different shape on a pitch-dark night from what it is on a star-light night. All shores seem to be straight lines, then, and mighty dim ones, too; and you'd *run* them for straight lines, only you know better. You boldly drive your boat right into what seems to be a solid, straight wall (you knowing very well that in reality there is a curve there), and that wall falls back and makes way for you. Then there's your gray mist. You take a night when there's one of these grisly, drizzly, gray mists, and then there isn't *any* particular shape to a shore. A gray mist would tangle the head of the oldest man that ever lived. Well, then, different kinds of *moonlight* change the shape of the river in different ways. You see—"

"Oh, don't say any more, please! Have I got to learn the shape of the river according to all these five hundred thousand different ways? If I tried to carry all that cargo in my head it would make me stoop-shouldered."

"*No!* you only learn *the* shape of the river; and you learn it with such absolute certainty that you can always steer by the shape that's *in your head,* and never mind the one that's before your eyes."

"Very well, I'll try it; but, after I have learned it, can I depend on it? Will it keep the same form and not go fooling around?"

Before Mr. Bixby could answer, Mr. W. came in to take the watch, and he said:

"Bixby, you'll have to look out for President's Island, and all that country clear away up above the Old Hen and Chickens. The banks are caving and the shape of the shores changing like everything. Why, you wouldn't know the point above 40. You can go up inside the old sycamore snag, now." [1]

So that question was answered. Here were leagues of shore changing shape. My spirits were down in the mud again. Two things seemed pretty apparent to me. One was, that in order to be a pilot a man had got to learn more than any one man ought to be allowed to know; and the other was, that he must learn it all over again in a different way every twenty-four hours.

That night we had the watch until twelve. Now it was an ancient river custom for the two pilots to chat a bit when the watch changed. While the relieving pilot put on his gloves and lit his cigar, his partner, the retiring pilot, would say something like this:

"I judge the upper bar is making down a little at Hale's Point; had quarter twain with the lower lead and mark twain [2] with the other."

"Yes, I thought it was making down a little, last trip. Meet any boats?"

"Met one abreast the head of 21, but she was away over hugging the bar, and I couldn't make her out entirely. I took her for the *Sunny South*—hadn't any skylights forward of the chimneys."

And so on. And as the relieving pilot took the wheel his partner [3] would mention that we were in such-and-such a bend, and say we were abreast of such-and-such a man's woodyard or plantation. This was courtesy; I supposed it was *necessity*. But Mr. W. came on watch full twelve minutes late on this particular night—a tremendous breach of etiquette; in fact, it is the unpardonable sin among pilots. So Mr. Bixby gave him no greeting whatever, but simply surrendered the wheel and marched out of the pilot-house without a word. I was appalled; it was a villainous night for blackness, we were in a particularly wide and blind part of the river, where there was no shape or substance to anything, and it seemed incredible that Mr. Bixby should have left that poor fellow to kill the boat,

[1] It may not be necessary, but still it can do no harm to explain that "inside" means between the snag and the shore.—M. T.

[2] Two fathoms. Quarter twain is 2¼ fathoms, 13½ feet. Mark three is three fathoms.—M. T.

[3] "Partner" is technical for "the other pilot."—M. T.

trying to find out where he was. But I resolved that I would stand by him anyway. He should find that he was not wholly friendless. So I stood around, and waited to be asked where we were. But Mr. W. plunged on serenely through the solid firmament of black cats that stood for an atmosphere, and never opened his mouth. "Here is a proud devil!" thought I; "here is a limb of Satan that would rather send us all to destruction than put himself under obligations to me, because I am not yet one of the salt of the earth and privileged to snub captains and lord it over everything dead and alive in a steamboat." I presently climbed up on the bench; I did not think it was safe to go to sleep while this lunatic was on watch.

However, I must have gone to sleep in the course of time, because the next thing I was aware of was the fact that day was breaking, Mr. W. gone, and Mr. Bixby at the wheel again. So it was four o'clock and all well—but me; I felt like a skinful of dry bones, and all of them trying to ache at once.

Mr. Bixby asked me what I had stayed up there for. I confessed that it was to do Mr. W. a benevolence—tell him where he was. It took five minutes for the entire preposterousness of the thing to filter into Mr. Bixby's system, and then I judge it filled him nearly up to the chin; because he paid me a compliment—and not much of a one either. He said:

"Well, taking you by and large, you do seem to be more different kinds of an ass than any creature I ever saw before. What did you suppose he wanted to know for?"

I said I thought it might be a convenience to him.

"Convenience! D——nation! Didn't I tell you that a man's got to know the river in the night the same as he'd know his own front hall?"

"Well, I can follow the front hall in the dark if I know it *is* the front hall; but suppose you set me down in the middle of it in the dark and not tell me which hall it is; how am *I* to know?"

"Well, you've *got* to, on the river!"

"All right. Then I'm glad I never said anything to Mr. W."

"I should say so! Why, he'd have slammed you through the window and utterly ruined a hundred dollars' worth of window-sash and stuff."

I was glad this damage had been saved, for it would have made me unpopular with the owners. They always hated anybody who had the name of being careless and injuring things.

I went to work now to learn the shape of the river; and of all the eluding and ungraspable objects that ever I tried to get mind or hands on, that was the chief. I would fasten my eyes upon a sharp, wooded point that projected far into the river some miles ahead of me, and go to laboriously photographing its shape upon my brain; and just as I was beginning to succeed to my satisfaction, we would draw up toward it and the exasperating thing would begin to melt away and fold back into the bank! If there had been a conspicuous dead tree standing upon the very point of the cape, I would find that tree inconspicuously merged into the general forest, and occupying the middle of a straight shore, when I got abreast of it! No prominent hill would stick to its shape long enough for me to make up my mind what its form really was, but it was as dissolving and changeful as if it had been a mountain of butter in the hottest corner of the tropics. Nothing ever had the same shape when I was coming down-stream that it had borne when I went up. I mentioned these little difficulties to Mr. Bixby. He said:

"That's the very main virtue of the thing. If the shapes didn't change every three seconds they wouldn't be of any use. Take this place where we are now, for instance. As long as that hill over yonder is only one hill, I can boom right along the way I'm going; but the moment it splits at the top and forms a V, I know I've got to scratch to starboard in a hurry, or I'll bang this boat's brains out against a rock; and then the moment one of the prongs of the V swings behind the other, I've got to waltz to larboard again, or I'll have a misunderstanding with a snag that would snatch the keelson out of this steamboat as neatly as if it were a sliver in your hand. If that hill didn't change its shape on bad nights there would be an awful steamboat graveyard around here inside of a year."

It was plain that I had got to learn the shape of the river in all the different ways that could be thought of—upside down, wrong end first, inside out, fore-and-aft, and "thort-ships"—and then know what to do on gray nights when it hadn't any shape at all. So I set about it. In the course of time I began to get the best of this knotty lesson, and my self-complacency moved to the front once more. Mr. Bixby was all fixed, and ready to start it to the rear again. He opened on me after this fashion:

"How much water did we have in the middle crossing at Hole-in-the-Wall, trip before last?"

I consider this an outrage. I said:

"Every trip, down and up, the leadsmen are singing through that tangled place for three-quarters of an hour on a stretch. How do you reckon I can remember such a mess as that?"

"My boy, you've got to remember it. You've got to remember the exact spot and the exact marks the boat lay in when we had the shoalest water, in every one of the five hundred shoal places between St. Louis and New Orleans; and you mustn't get the shoal soundings and marks of one trip mixed up with the shoal soundings and marks of another, either, for they're not often twice alike. You must keep them separate."

When I came to myself again, I said:

"When I get so that I can do that, I'll be able to raise the dead, and then I won't have to pilot a steamboat to make a living. I want to retire from this business. I want a slush-bucket and a brush; I'm only fit for a roustabout. I haven't got brains enough to be a pilot; and if I had I wouldn't have strength enough to carry them around, unless I went on crutches."

"Now drop that! When I say I'll learn [1] a man the river, I mean it. And you can depend on it, I'll learn him or kill him."

There was no use in arguing with a person like this. I promptly put such a strain on my memory that by and by even the shoal water and the countless crossing-marks began to stay with me. But the result was just the same. I never could more than get one knotty thing learned before another presented itself. Now I had often seen pilots gazing at the water and pretending to read it as if it were a book; but it was a book that told me nothing. A time came at last, however, when Mr. Bixby seemed to think me far enough advanced to bear a lesson on water-reading. So he began:

"Do you see that long, slanting line on the face of the water? Now, that's a reef. Moreover, it's a bluff reef. There is a solid sand-bar under it that is nearly as straight up and down as the side of a house. There is plenty of water close up to it, but mighty little on top of it. If you were to hit it you would knock the boat's brains out.

[1] "Teach" is not in the river vocabulary.—M. T.

Do you see where the line fringes out at the upper end and begins to fade away?"

"Yes, sir."

"Well, that is a low place; that is the head of the reef. You can climb over there, and not hurt anything. Cross over, now, and follow along close under the reef—easy water there—not much current."

I followed the reef along till I approached the fringed end. Then Mr. Bixby said:

"Now get ready. Wait till I give the word. She won't want to mount the reef; a boat hates shoal water. Stand by—wait—*wait*—keep her well in hand. *Now* cramp her down! Snatch her! snatch her!"

He seized the other side of the wheel and helped to spin it around until it was hard down, and then we held it so. The boat resisted, and refused to answer for a while, and next she came surging to starboard, mounted the reef, and sent a long, angry ridge of water foaming away from her bows.

"Now watch her; watch her like a cat, or she'll get away from you. When she fights strong and the tiller slips a little, in a jerky, greasy sort of way, let up on her a trifle; it is the way she tells you at night that the water is too shoal; but keep edging her up, little by little, toward the point. You are well up on the bar now; there is a bar under every point, because the water that comes down around it forms an eddy and allows the sediment to sink. Do you see those fine lines on the face of the water that branch out like the ribs of a fan? Well, those are little reefs; you want to just miss the ends of them, but run them pretty close. Now look out—look out! Don't you crowd that slick, greasy-looking place; there ain't nine feet there; she won't stand it. She begins to smell it; look sharp, I tell you! Oh, blazes, there you go! Stop the starboard wheel! Quick! Ship up to back! Set her back!"

The engine bells jingled and the engines answered promptly, shooting white columns of steam far aloft out of the 'scape-pipes, but it was too late. The boat had "smelt" the bar in good earnest; the foamy ridges that radiated from her bows suddenly disappeared, a great dead swell came rolling forward, and swept ahead of her, she careened far over to larboard, and went tearing away toward the shore as if she were about scared to death. We were a good mile from where we ought to have been when we finally got the upper hand of her again.

During the afternoon watch the next day, Mr. Bixby asked me if I knew how to run the next few miles. I said:

"Go inside the first snag above the point, outside the next one, start out from the lower end of Higgins's woodyard, make a square crossing, and—"

"That's all right. I'll be back before you close up on the next point."

But he wasn't. He was still below when I rounded it and entered upon a piece of the river which I had some misgivings about. I did not know that he was hiding behind a chimney to see how I would perform. I went gaily along, getting prouder and prouder, for he had never left the boat in my sole charge such a length of time before. I even got to "setting" her and letting the wheel go entirely, while I vaingloriously turned my back and inspected the stern marks and hummed a tune, a sort of easy indifference which I had prodigiously admired in Bixby and other great pilots. Once I inspected rather long, and when I faced to the front again my heart flew into my mouth so suddenly that if I hadn't clapped my teeth together I should have lost it. One of those frightful bluff reefs was stretching its deadly length right across our bows! My head was gone in a moment; I did not know which end I stood on; I gasped and could not get my breath; I spun the wheel down with such rapidity that it wove itself together like a spider's web; the boat answered and turned square away from the reef, but the reef followed her! I fled, but still it followed, still it kept—right across my bows! I never looked to see where I was going, I only fled. The awful crash was imminent. Why didn't that villain come? If I committed the crime of ringing a bell I might get thrown overboard. But better that than kill the boat. So in blind desperation, I started such a rattling "shivaree" down below as never had astounded an engineer in this world before, I fancy. Amidst the frenzy of the bells the engines began to back and fill in a curious way, and my reason forsook its throne—we were about to crash into the woods on the other side of the river. Just then Mr. Bixby stepped calmly into view on the hurricane-deck. My soul went out to him in gratitude. My distress vanished; I would have felt safe on the brink of Niagara with Mr. Bixby on the hurricane-deck. He blandly and sweetly took his toothpick out of his mouth between his fingers, as if it were a cigar—we were just in the act of climbing an overhanging big tree, and the passengers were scudding astern like rats—and lifted up these commands to me ever so gently:

"Stop the starboard! Stop the larboard! Set her back on both!"

The boat hesitated, halted, pressed her nose among the boughs a critical instant, then reluctantly began to back away.

"Stop the larboard! Come ahead on it! Stop the starboard! Come ahead on it! Point her for the bar!"

I sailed away as serenely as a summer's morning. Mr. Bixby came in and said, with mock simplicity:

"When you have a hail, my boy, you ought to tap the big bell three times before you land, so that the engineers can get ready."

I blushed under the sarcasm, and said I hadn't had any hail.

"Ah! Then it was for wood, I suppose. The officer of the watch will tell you when he wants to wood up."

I went on consuming, and said I wasn't after wood.

"Indeed? Why, what could you want over here in the bend, then? Did you ever know of a boat following a bend up-stream at this stage of the river?"

"No, sir—and *I* wasn't trying to follow it. I was getting away from a bluff reef."

"No, it wasn't a bluff reef; there isn't one within three miles of where you were."

"But I saw it. It was as bluff as that one yonder."

"Just about. Run over it!"

"Do you give it as an order?"

"Yes. Run over it!"

"If I don't, I wish I may die."

"All right; I am taking the responsibility."

I was just as anxious to kill the boat, now, as I had been to save it before. I impressed my orders upon my memory, to be used at the inquest, and made a straight break for the reef. As it disappeared under our bows I held my breath; but we slid over it like oil.

"Now, don't you see the difference? It wasn't anything but a *wind* reef. The wind does that."

"So I see. But it is exactly like a bluff reef. How am I ever going to tell them apart?"

"I can't tell you. It is an instinct. By and by you will just naturally *know* one from the other, but you never will be able to explain why or how you know them apart."

It turned out to be true. The face of the water, in time, became a wonderful book—a book that was a dead language to the uneducated passenger, but which told its mind to me without reserve, delivering its most cherished secrets as clearly as if it uttered them with a voice. And it was not a book to be read once and thrown aside, for it had a new story to tell every day. Throughout the long twelve hundred miles there was never a page that was void of interest, never one that you could leave unread without loss, never one that you would want to skip, thinking you could find higher enjoyment in some other thing. There never was so wonderful a book written by man; never one whose interest was so absorbing, so unflagging, so sparklingly renewed with every reperusal. The passenger who could not read it was charmed with a peculiar sort of faint dimple on its surface (on the rare occasions when he did not overlook it altogether); but to the pilot that was an *italicized* passage; indeed, it was more than that, it was a legend of the largest capitals, with a string of shouting exclamation-points at the end of it, for it meant that a wreck or a rock was buried there that could tear the life out of the strongest vessel that ever floated. It is the faintest and simplest expression the water ever makes, and the most hideous to a pilot's eye. In truth, the passenger who could not read this book saw nothing but all manner of pretty pictures in it, painted by the sun and shaded by the clouds, whereas to the trained eye these were not pictures at all, but the grimmest and most dead-earnest of reading-matter.

Now when I had mastered the language of this water, and had come to know every trifling feature that bordered the great river as familiarly as I knew the letters of the alphabet, I had made a valuable acquisition. But I had lost something, too. I had lost something which could never be restored to me while I lived. All the grace, the beauty, the poetry, had gone out of the majestic river! I still kept in mind a certain wonderful sunset which I witnessed when steamboating was new to me. A broad expanse of the river was turned to blood; in the middle distance the red hue brightened into gold, through which a solitary log came floating, black and conspicuous; in one place a long, slanting mark lay sparkling upon the water; in another the surface was broken by boiling, tumbling rings, that were as many-tinted as an opal; where the ruddy flush was faintest, was a smooth spot that was covered with graceful circles and radiating lines, ever so delicately traced; the shore on our left was densely wooded, and the somber shadow that fell from this forest was broken in one place by a long, ruffled trail that shone like silver; and high above the forest wall a clean-stemmed dead tree waved a single leafy bough that glowed like a flame in the unobstructed splendor that was flowing from the sun. There were graceful curves, reflected images, woody heights, soft distances; and over the whole scene, far and near, the dissolving lights drifted steadily, enriching it every passing moment with new marvels of coloring.

I stood like one bewitched. I drank it in, in a speechless rapture. The world was new to me, and I had never seen anything like this at home. But as I have said, a day came when I began to cease from noting the glories and the charms which the moon and the sun and the twilight wrought upon the river's face; another day came when I ceased altogether to note them. Then, if that sunset scene had been repeated, I should have looked upon it without rapture, and should have commented upon it, inwardly, after this fashion: "This sun means that we are going to have wind to-morrow; that floating log means that the river is rising, small thanks to it; that slanting mark on the water refers to a bluff reef which is going to kill somebody's steamboat one of these nights, if it keeps on stretching out like that; those tumbling 'boils' show a dissolving bar and a changing channel there; the lines and circles in the slick water over yonder are a warning that that troublesome place is shoaling up dangerously; that silver streak in the shadow of the forest is the 'break' from a new snag, and he has located himself in the very best place he could have found to fish for steamboats; that tall dead tree, with a single living branch, is not going to last long, and then how is a body ever going to get through this blind place at night without the friendly old landmark?"

No, the romance and beauty were all gone from the river. All the value any feature of it had for me now was the amount of usefulness it could furnish toward compassing the safe piloting of a steamboat. Since those days, I have pitied doctors from my heart. What does the lovely flush in a beauty's cheek mean to a doctor but a "break" that ripples above some deadly disease? Are not all her visible charms sown thick with what are to him the signs and symbols of hidden decay? Does he ever see her beauty at all, or doesn't he simply view her professionally, and comment upon her unwholesome condition all to himself? And doesn't he sometimes wonder whether he has gained most or lost most by learning his trade?

From *Life on the Mississippi,* 1883.

11 : *Rank and Dignity of Piloting*

I HAVE TRIED, by going into the minutiæ of the science of piloting, to carry the reader to a comprehension of what the science consists of; and at the same time I have tried to show him that it is a very curious and wonderful science, too, and very worthy of his attention. If I have seemed to love my subject, it is no surprising thing, for I loved the profession far better than any I have followed since, and I took a measureless pride in it. The reason is plain: a pilot, in those days, was the only unfettered and entirely independent human being that lived in the earth. Kings are but the hampered servants of parliament and the people; parliaments sit in chains forged by their constituency; the editor of a newspaper cannot be independent, but must work with one hand tied behind him by party and patrons, and be content to utter only half or two-thirds of his mind; no clergyman is a free man and may speak the whole truth, regardless of his parish's opinions; writers of all kinds are manacled servants of the public. We write frankly and fearlessly, but then we "modify" before we print. In truth, every man and woman and child has a master, and worries and frets in servitude; but, in the day I write of, the Mississippi pilot had *none*. The captain could stand upon the hurricane-deck, in the pomp of a very brief authority, and give him five or six orders while the vessel backed into the stream, and then the skipper's reign was over. The moment that the boat was under way in the river, she was under the sole and unquestioned control of the pilot. He could do with her exactly as he pleased, run her when and whither he chose, and tie her up to the bank whenever his judgment said that that course was best. His movements were entirely free; he consulted no one, he received commands from nobody, he promptly resented even the merest suggestions. Indeed, the law of the United States forbade him to listen to commands or suggestions, rightly considering that the pilot necessarily knew better how to handle the boat than anybody could tell him. So here was the novelty of a king without a keeper, an absolute monarch who was absolute in sober truth and not by a fiction of words. I have seen a boy of eighteen taking a great steamer serenely into what seemed almost certain destruction, and the aged captain standing mutely by, filled with apprehension but powerless to interfere. His interference, in that particular instance, might have been an excellent thing, but to permit it would have been to establish a most pernicious precedent. It will easily be guessed, considering the pilot's boundless authority, that he was a great personage in the old steamboating days. He was treated with marked courtesy by the captain and with marked deference by all the officers and servants; and this deferential spirit was quickly communicated to the passengers, too. I think pilots were about the only people I ever knew who failed to show, in some degree, embarrassment in the presence of traveling foreign princes. But then, people in one's own grade of life are not usually embarrassing objects.

By long habit, pilots came to put all their wishes in the form of commands. It "gravels" me, to this day, to put my will in the weak shape of a request, instead of launching it in the crisp language of an order.

In those old days, to load a steamboat at St. Louis, take her to New Orleans and back, and discharge cargo, consumed about twenty-five days, on an average. Seven or eight of these days the boat spent at the wharves of St. Louis and New Orleans, and every soul on board was hard at work, except the two pilots; *they* did nothing but play gentleman up-town, and receive the same wages for it as if they had been on duty. The moment the boat touched the wharf at either city they were ashore; and they were not likely to be seen again till the last bell was ringing and everything in readiness for another voyage.

When a captain got hold of a pilot of particularly high reputation, he took pains to keep him. When wages were four hundred dollars a month on the Upper Mississippi, I have known a captain to keep such a pilot in idleness, under full pay, three months at a time, while the river was frozen up. And one must remember that in those cheap times four hundred dollars was a salary of almost inconceivable splendor. Few men on shore got such pay as that, and when they did they were mightily looked up to. When pilots from either end of the river wandered into our small Missouri village, they were sought by the best and the fairest, and treated with exalted respect. Lying in port under wages was a thing which many pilots greatly enjoyed and appreciated; especially if they belonged in the Missouri River in the heyday of that trade (Kansas times), and got nine hundred dollars a trip, which was equivalent to about eighteen hundred dollars a month. Here is a conversation of that day. A chap out of the Illinois River, with a little stern-wheel tub, accosts a couple of ornate and gilded Missouri River pilots:

"Gentlemen, I've got a pretty good trip for the up-country, and shall want you about a month. How much will it be?"

"Eighteen hundred dollars apiece."

"Heavens and earth! You take my boat, let me have your wages, and I'll divide!"

I will remark, in passing, that Mississippi steamboatmen were important in landsmen's eyes (and in their own, too, in a degree) according to the dignity of the boat they were on. For instance, it was a proud thing to be of the crew of such stately craft as the *Aleck Scott* or the *Grand Turk*. Negro firemen, deck-hands, and barbers belonging to those boats were distinguished personages in their grade of life, and they were well aware of that fact, too. A stalwart darky once gave offense at a negro ball in New Orleans by putting on a good many airs. Finally one of the managers bustled up to him and said:

"Who *is* you, anyway? Who *is* you? dat's what *I* wants to know!"

The offender was not disconcerted in the least, but swelled himself up and threw that into his voice which showed that he knew he was not putting on all those airs on a stinted capital.

"Who *is* I? Who *is* I? I let you know mighty quick who I is! I want you niggers to understan' dat I fires de middle do' [1] on de *Aleck Scott!*"

[1] Door.—M. T.

That was sufficient.

The barber of the *Grand Turk* was a spruce young negro, who aired his importance with balmy complacency, and was greatly courted by the circle in which he moved. The young colored population of New Orleans were much given to flirting, at twilight, on the banquettes of the back streets. Somebody saw and heard something like the following, one evening, in one of those localities. A middle-aged negro woman projected her head through a broken pane and shouted (very willing that the neighbors should hear and envy), "You Mary Ann, come in de house dis minute! Stannin' out dah foolin' 'long wid dat low trash, an' heah's de barber off'n de *Gran' Turk* wants to conwerse wid you!"

My reference, a moment ago, to the fact that a pilot's peculiar official position placed him out of the reach of criticism or command, brings Stephen W. naturally to my mind. He was a gifted pilot, a good fellow, a tireless talker, and had both wit and humor in him. He had a most irreverent independence, too, and was deliciously easy-going and comfortable in the presence of age, official dignity, and even the most august wealth. He always had work, he never saved a penny, he was a most persuasive borrower, he was in debt to every pilot on the river, and to the majority of the captains. He could throw a sort of splendor around a bit of harum-scarum, devil-may-care piloting, that made it almost fascinating—but not to everybody. He made a trip with good old Captain Y. once, and was "relieved" from duty when the boat got to New Orleans. Somebody expressed surprise at the discharge. Captain Y. shuddered at the mere mention of Stephen. Then his poor, thin old voice piped out something like this:

"Why, bless me! I wouldn't have such a wild creature on my boat for the world—not for the whole world! He swears, he sings, he whistles, he yells—I never saw such an Injun to yell. All times of the night—it never made any difference to him. He would just yell that way, not for anything in particular, but merely on account of a kind of devilish comfort he got out of it. I never could get into a sound sleep but he would fetch me out of bed, all in a cold sweat, with one of those dreadful war-whoops. A queer being—very queer being; no respect for anything or anybody. Sometimes he called me 'Johnny.' And he kept a fiddle and a cat. He played execrably. This seemed to distress the cat, and so the cat would howl. Nobody could sleep where that man—and his family—was. And reckless? There never was anything like it. Now you may believe it or not, but as sure as I am sitting here, he brought my boat a-tilting down through those awful snags at Chicot under a rattling head of steam, and the wind a-blowing like the very nation, at that! My officers will tell you so. They saw it. And, sir, while he was a-tearing right down through those snags, and I a-shaking in my shoes and praying, I wish I may never speak again if he didn't pucker up his mouth and go to *whistling!* Yes, sir; whistling 'Buffalo gals, can't you come out to-night, can't you come out to-night, can't you come out to-night'; and doing it as calmly as if we were attending a funeral and weren't related to the corpse. And when I remonstrated with him about it, he smiled down on me as if I was his child, and told me to run in the house and try to be good, and not be meddling with my superiors!" [1]

Once a pretty mean captain caught Stephen in New Orleans out of work and as usual out of money. He laid steady siege to Stephen, who was in a very "close place," and finally persuaded him to hire with him at one hundred and twenty-five dollars per month, just half wages, the captain agreeing not to divulge the secret and so bring down the contempt of all the guild upon the poor fellow. But the boat was not more than a day out of New Orleans before Stephen discovered that the captain was boasting of his exploit, and that all the officers had been told. Stephen winced, but said nothing. About the middle of the afternoon the captain stepped out on the hurricane-deck, cast his eye around, and looked a good deal surprised. He glanced inquiringly aloft at Stephen, but Stephen was whistling placidly and attending to business. The captain stood around awhile in evident discomfort, and once or twice seemed about to make a suggestion; but the etiquette of the river taught him to avoid that sort of rashness, and so he managed to hold his peace. He chafed and puzzled a few minutes longer, then retired to his apartments. But soon he was out again, and apparently more perplexed than ever. Presently he ventured to remark, with deference:

[1] Considering a captain's ostentatious but hollow chieftainship, and a pilot's real authority, there was something impudently apt and happy about that way of phrasing it.—M. T.

"Pretty good stage of the river now, ain't it, sir?"

"Well, I should say so! Bank-full *is* a pretty liberal stage."

"Seems to be a good deal of current here."

"Good deal don't describe it! It's worse than a mill-race."

"Isn't it easier in toward shore than it is out here in the middle?"

"Yes, I reckon it is; but a body can't be too careful with a steamboat. It's pretty safe out here; can't strike any bottom here, you can depend on that."

The captain departed, looking rueful enough. At this rate, he would probably die of old age before his boat got to St. Louis. Next day he appeared on deck and again found Stephen faithfully standing up the middle of the river, fighting the whole vast force of the Mississippi, and whistling the same placid tune. This thing was becoming serious. In by the shore was a slower boat clipping along in the easy water and gaining steadily; she began to make for an island chute; Stephen stuck to the middle of the river. Speech was *wrung* from the captain. He said:

"Mr. W., don't that chute cut off a good deal of distance?"

"I think it does, but I don't know."

"Don't know! Well, isn't there water enough in it now to go through?"

"I expect there is, but I am not certain."

"Upon my word this is odd! Why, those pilots on that boat yonder are going to try it. Do you mean to say that you don't know as much as they do?"

"They! Why, *they* are two-hundred-and-fifty-dollar pilots! But don't you be uneasy; I know as much as any man can afford to know for a hundred and twenty-five!"

The captain surrendered.

Five minutes later Stephen was bowling through the chute and showing the rival boat a two-hundred-and-fifty-dollar pair of heels.

From *Life on the Mississippi,* 1883.

12 : *The House Beautiful*

WE TOOK PASSAGE in a Cincinnati boat for New Orleans; or on a Cincinnati boat—either is correct; the former is the Eastern form of putting it, the latter the Western.

Mr. Dickens[1] declined to agree that the Mississippi steamboats were "magnificent," or that they were "floating palaces"—terms which had always been applied to them; terms which did not over-express the admiration with which the people viewed them.

Mr. Dickens's position was unassailable, possibly; the people's position was certainly unassailable. If Mr. Dickens was comparing these boats with the crown jewels; or with the Taj, or with the Matterhorn; or with some other priceless or wonderful thing which he had seen, they were not magnificent—he was right. The people compared them with what *they* had seen; and, thus measured, thus judged, the boats were magnificent—the term was the correct one, it was not at all too strong. The people were as right as was Mr. Dickens. The steamboats were finer than anything on shore. Compared with superior dwelling-houses and first-class hotels in the valley, they were indubitably magnificent, they were "palaces." To a few people living in New Orleans and St. Louis they were not magnificent, perhaps; not palaces; but to the great majority of those populations, and to the entire populations spread over both banks between Baton Rouge and St. Louis, they were palaces; they tallied with the citizen's dream of what magnificence was, and satisfied it.

Every town and village along that vast stretch of double river-frontage had a best dwelling, finest dwelling, mansion—the home of its wealthiest and most conspicuous citizen. It is easy to describe it: large grassy yard, with paling fence painted white—in fair repair; brick walk from gate to door; big, square, two-story "frame" house, painted white and porticoed like a Grecian temple—with this dif-

[1] Charles Dickens, the author.—C. N.

ference, that the imposing fluted columns and Corinthian capitals were a pathetic sham, being made of white pine, and painted; iron knocker; brass door-knob—discolored, for lack of polishing. Within, an uncarpeted hall, of planed boards; opening out of it, a parlor, fifteen feet by fifteen—in some instances five or ten feet larger; ingrain carpet; mahogany center-table; lamp on it, with green-paper shade—standing on a gridiron, so to speak, made of high-colored yarns, by the young ladies of the house, and called a lamp-mat; several books, piled and disposed, with cast-iron exactness, according to an inherited and unchangeable plan; among them, Tupper, much penciled; also, *Friendship's Offering,* and *Affection's Wreath,* with their sappy inanities illustrated in die-away mezzotints; also, Ossian; *Alonzo and Melissa;* maybe *Ivanhoe;* also "Album," full of original "poetry" of the Thou-hast-wounded-the-spirit-that-loved-thee breed; two or three goody-goody works—*Shepherd of Salisbury Plain,* etc.; current number of the chaste and innocuous *Godey's Lady's Book,* with painted fashion-plate of wax-figure women with mouths all alike—lips and eyelids the same size—each five-foot woman with a two-inch wedge sticking from under her dress and letting on to be half of her foot. Polished air-tight stove (new and deadly invention), with pipe passing through a board which closes up the discarded good old fireplace. On each end of the wooden mantel, over the fireplace, a large basket of peaches and other fruits, natural size, all done in plaster, rudely, or in wax, and painted to resemble the originals—which they don't. Over middle of mantel, engraving—"Washington Crossing the Delaware"; on the wall by the door, copy of it done in thunder-and-lightning crewels by one of the young ladies—work of art which would have made Washington hesitate about crossing, if he could have foreseen what advantage was going to be taken of it. Piano—kettle in disguise—with music, bound and unbound, piled on it, and on a stand near by: "Battle of Prague"; "Bird Waltz"; "Arkansas Traveler"; "Rosin the Bow"; "Marseillaise Hymn"; "On a Lone Barren Isle" (St. Helena); "The Last Link Is Broken"; "She Wore a Wreath of Roses the Night When Last We Met"; "Go, Forget Me, Why Should Sorrow o'er That Brow a Shadow Fling"; "Hours That Were to Memory Dearer"; "Long, Long Ago"; "Days of Absence"; "A Life on the Ocean Wave, a Home on the Rolling Deep"; "Bird at Sea"; and spread open on the rack where the plaintive singer has left it, "*Ro*-holl on, silver *moo*-hoon, guide the *trav*el-err on his way," etc. Tilted pensively against the piano, a guitar—guitar capable of playing the Spanish fandango by itself, if you give it a start. Frantic work of art on the wall—pious motto, done on the premises, sometimes in colored yarns, sometimes in faded grasses: progenitor of the "God Bless Our Home" of modern commerce. Framed in black moldings on the wall, other works of art, conceived and committed on the premises, by the young ladies; being grim black-and-white crayons; landscapes, mostly: lake, solitary sailboat, petrified clouds, pregeological trees on shore, anthracite precipice; name of criminal conspicuous in the corner. Lithograph, "Napoleon Crossing the Alps." Lithograph, "The Grave at St. Helena." Steel plates, Trumbull's "Battle of Bunker Hill," and the "Sally from Gibraltar." Copper plates, "Moses Smiting the Rock," and "Return of the Prodigal Son." In big gilt frame, slander of the family in oil: papa holding a book ("Constitution of the United States"); guitar leaning against mamma, blue ribbons fluttering from its neck; the young ladies, as children, in slippers and scalloped pantalettes, one embracing toy horse, the other beguiling kitten with ball of yarn, and both simpering up at mamma, who simpers back. These persons all fresh, raw, and red—apparently skinned. Opposite, in gilt frame, grandpa and grandma, at thirty and twenty-two, stiff, old-fashioned, high-collared, puff-sleeved, glaring pallidly out from a background of solid Egyptian night. Under a glass French clock dome, large bouquet of stiff flowers done in corpsy-white wax. Pyramidal what-not in the corner, the shelves occupied chiefly with bric-à-brac of the period, disposed with an eye to best effect: shell, with the Lord's Prayer carved on it; another shell—of the long-oval sort, narrow, straight orifice, three inches long, running from end to end—portrait of Washington carved on it; not well done; the shell had Washington's mouth, originally—artist should have built to that. These two are memorials of the long-ago bridal trip to New Orleans and the French Market. Other bric-à-brac: Californian "specimens"—quartz, with gold wart adhering; old Guinea-gold locket, with circlet of ancestral hair in it; Indian arrow-heads, of flint; pair of bead moccasins, from uncle who crossed the Plains; three "alum" baskets of various colors—being skeleton-frame of wire, clothed on with cubes of crystallized alum in the rock-candy style—works of art which were achieved by the young ladies; their doubles and duplicates to be found upon all what-nots in the land; convention of desiccated bugs and butterflies pinned to a card; painted toy dog, seated upon bellows attachment—drops its under-jaw and squeaks when pressed upon; sugar-candy rabbit—limbs and features merged together, not strongly defined; pewter presidential-campaign medal; miniature cardboard wood-sawyer, to be attached to the stovepipe and operated by the heat; small Napoleon, done in wax; spread-open daguerreotypes of dim children, parents, cousins, aunts, and friends, in all attitudes but customary ones; no templed portico at back, and manufactured landscape stretching away in the distance—that came in later, with the photograph; all these vague figures lavishly chained and ringed—metal indicated and secured from doubt by stripes and splashes of vivid gold bronze; all of them too much combed, too much fixed up; and all of them uncomfortable in inflexible Sunday clothes of a pattern which the spectator cannot realize could ever have been in fashion; husband and wife generally grouped together—husband sitting, wife standing, with hand on his shoulder—and both preserving, all these fading years, some traceable effect of the daguerreotypist's brisk "Now smile, if you please!" Bracketed over what-not—place of special sacredness—an outrage in watercolor, done by the young niece that came on a visit long ago, and died. Pity, too; for she might have repented of this in time. Horsehair chairs, horsehair sofa which keeps sliding from under you. Window-shades, of oil stuff, with milkmaids and ruined castles stenciled on them in fierce colors. Lambrequins dependent from gaudy boxings of beaten tin, gilded. Bedrooms with rag carpets; bedsteads of the "corded" sort, with a sag in the middle, the cords needing tightening; snuffy feather-bed—not aired often enough; cane-seat chairs, splint-bottomed rocker; looking-glass on wall, school-slate size, veneered frame; inherited bureau; wash-bowl and pitcher, possibly—but not certainly; brass candlestick, tallow candle, snuffers. Nothing else in the room. Not a bathroom in the house; and no visitor likely to come along who has ever seen one.

That was the residence of the principal citizen, all the way from the suburbs of New Orleans to the edge of St. Louis. When he stepped aboard a big fine steamboat, he entered a new and marvelous world: chimney-tops cut to counterfeit a spraying crown of plumes—and maybe painted red; pilot-house, hurricane-deck, boiler-deck guards, all garnished with white wooden filigree-work of fanciful patterns; gilt acorns topping the derricks; gilt deerhorns over the big bell; gaudy symbolical picture on the paddle-box, possibly; big roomy boiler-deck, painted blue, and furnished with Windsor arm-chairs; inside, a far-receding snow-white "cabin"; porcelain knob and oil-picture on every stateroom door; curving patterns of filigree-work touched up with gilding, stretching overhead all down the converging vista; big chandeliers every little way, each an April shower of glittering glass-drops; lovely rainbow-light falling everywhere from the colored glazing of the skylights; the whole a long-drawn, resplendent tunnel, a bewildering and soul-satisfying spectacle! in the ladies' cabin a pink and white Wilton carpet, as soft as mush, and glorified with a ravishing pattern of gigantic flowers. Then the Bridal Chamber—the animal that invented that idea was still alive and unhanged, at that day—Bridal Chamber whose pretentious flummery was necessarily overawing to the now tottering intellect of that hosannahing citizen. Every stateroom had its couple of cozy clean bunks, and perhaps a looking-glass and a snug closet; and sometimes there was even a wash-bowl and pitcher, and part of a towel which could be told from mosquito-netting by an expert—though generally these things were absent, and the shirt-sleeved passengers cleansed themselves at a long row of stationary bowls in the barber shop, where were also public towels, public combs, and public soap.

Take the steamboat which I have just described, and you have her in her highest and finest, and most pleasing, and comfortable, and satisfactory estate. Now cake her over with a layer of ancient and obdurate dirt, and you have the Cincinnati steamer awhile ago referred to. Not all over—only inside; for she was ably officered in all departments except the steward's.

But wash that boat and repaint her, and she would be about the counterpart of the most complimented boat of the old flush times: for the steamboat architecture of the West has undergone no change; neither has steamboat furniture and ornamentation undergone any.

From *Life on the Mississippi,* 1883.

13 : New Orleans

THE APPROACHES TO NEW ORLEANS were familiar; general aspects were unchanged. When one goes flying through London along a railway propped in the air on tall arches, he may inspect miles of upper bedrooms through the open windows, but the lower half of the houses is under his level and out of sight. Similarly, in high-river stage, in the New Orleans region, the water is up to the top of the inclosing levee-rim, the flat country behind it lies low—representing the bottom of a dish—and as the boat swims along, high on the flood, one looks down upon the houses and into the upper windows. There is nothing but that frail breastwork of earth between the people and destruction.

The old brick salt-warehouses clustered at the upper end of the city looked as they had always looked: warehouses which had had a kind of Aladdin's lamp experience, however, since I had seen them; for when the war broke out the proprietor went to bed one night leaving them packed with thousands of sacks of vulgar salt, worth a couple of dollars a sack, and got up in the morning and found his mountain of salt turned into a mountain of gold, so to speak, so suddenly and to so dizzy a height had the war news sent up the price of the article.

The vast reach of plank wharves remained unchanged, and there were as many ships as ever: but the long array of steamboats had vanished; not altogether, of course, but not much of it was left.

The city itself had not changed—to the eye. It had greatly increased in spread and population, but the look of the town was not altered. The dust, waste-paper-littered, was still deep in the streets; the deep troughlike gutters along the curbstones were still half full of reposeful water with a dusty surface; the sidewalks were still—in the sugar and bacon region—encumbered by casks and barrels and hogsheads; the great blocks of austerely plain commercial houses were as dusty-looking as ever.

Canal Street was finer and more attractive and stirring than formerly, with its drifting crowds of people, its several processions of hurrying street-cars, and—toward evening—its broad second-story verandas crowded with gentlemen and ladies clothed according to the latest mode.

Not that there is any "architecture" in Canal Street: to speak in broad, general terms, there is no architecture in New Orleans, except in the cemeteries. It seems a strange thing to say of a wealthy, far-seeing, and energetic city of a quarter of a million inhabitants, but it is true. There is a huge granite United States custom-house—costly enough, genuine enough, but as to decoration it is inferior to a gasometer. It looks like a state prison. But it was built before the war. Architecture in America may be said to have been born since the war. New Orleans, I believe, has had the good luck—and in a sense the bad luck—to have had no great fire in late years. It must be so. If the opposite had been the case, I think one would be able to tell the "burnt district" by the radical improvement in its architecture over the old forms. One can do this in Boston and Chicago. The "burnt district" of Boston was commonplace before the fire; but now there is no commercial district in any city in the world that can surpass it—or perhaps even rival it—in beauty, elegance, and tastefulness.

However, New Orleans has begun—just this moment, as one may say. When completed, the new Cotton Exchange will be a stately and beautiful building: massive, substantial, full of architectural graces; no shams or false pretenses or uglinesses about it anywhere. To the city it will be worth many times its cost, for it will breed its species. What has been lacking hitherto was a model to build toward, something to educate eye and taste: a *suggester,* so to speak.

The city is well outfitted with progressive men—thinking, sagacious, long-headed men. The contrast between the spirit of the city and the city's architecture is like the contrast between waking and sleep. Apparently there is a "boom" in everything but that one dead feature. The water in the gutters used to be stagnant and slimy, and a potent disease-breeder; but the gutters are flushed now two or three times a day by powerful machinery; in many of the gutters the water never stands still, but has a steady current. Other sanitary improvements have been made; and with such effect that New Orleans claims to be (during the long intervals between the occasional yellow-fever assaults) one of the healthiest cities in the Union. There's plenty of ice now for everybody, manufactured in the town. It is a driving place commercially, and has a great river, ocean, and railway business. At the date of our visit it was the best-lighted city in the Union, electrically speaking. The New Orleans electric lights were more numerous than those of New York, and very much better. One had this modified noonday not only in Canal and some neighboring chief streets, but all along a stretch of five miles of river-frontage. There are good clubs in the city now—several of them but recently organized—and inviting modern-style pleasure resorts at West End and Spanish Fort. The telephone is everywhere. One of the most notable advances is in journalism. The newspapers, as I remember them, were not a striking feature. Now they are. Money is spent upon them with a free hand. They get the news, let it cost what it may. The editorial work is not hack-grinding, but literature. As an example of New Orleans journalistic achievement, it may be mentioned that the *Times-Democrat* of August 26, 1882, contained a report of the year's business of the towns of the Mississippi valley, from New Orleans all the way to St. Paul—two thousand miles. That issue of the paper consisted of *forty* pages; seven columns to the page; two hundred and eighty columns in all; fifteen hundred words to the column; an aggregate of four hundred and twenty thousand words. That is to say, not much short of three times as many words as are in this book. One may with sorrow contrast this with the architecture of New Orleans.

I have been speaking of public architecture only. The domestic article in New Orleans is reproachless, notwithstanding it remains as it always was. All the dwellings are of wood—in the American part of the town, I mean—and all have a comfortable look. Those in the wealthy quarter are spacious; painted snow-white usually, and generally have wide verandas, or double verandas, supported by ornamental columns. These mansions stand in the center of large grounds, and rise, garlanded with roses, out of the midst of swelling masses of shining green foliage and many-colored blossoms. No houses could well be in better harmony with their surroundings, or more pleasing to the eye, or more homelike and comfortable-looking.

One even becomes reconciled to the cistern presently; this is a mighty cask, painted green, and sometimes a couple of stories high, which is propped against the house-corner on stilts. There is a mansion-and-brewery suggestion about the combination which seems very incongruous at first. But the people cannot have wells, and so they take rainwater. Neither can they conveniently have cellars or graves,[1] the town being built upon "made" ground; so they do without both, and few of the living complain, and none of the others.

The old French part of New Orleans—anciently the Spanish part—bears no resemblance to the American end of the city: the American end which lies beyond the intervening brick business center. The houses are massed in blocks; are austerely plain and dignified; uniform of pattern, with here and there a departure from it with pleasant effect; all are plastered on the outside, and nearly all have long, iron-railed verandas running along the several stories. Their chief beauty is the deep, warm, varicolored stain with which time and the weather have enriched the plaster. It harmonizes with all the surroundings, and has as natural a look of belonging there as has the flush upon sunset clouds. This charming decoration cannot be successfully imitated; neither is it to be found elsewhere in America.

The iron railings are a specialty, also. The pattern is often exceedingly light and dainty, and airy and graceful—with a large cipher or monogram in the center, a delicate cobweb of baffling, intricate forms, wrought in steel. The ancient railings are handmade, and are now comparatively rare and proportionately valuable. They are become bric-à-brac.

The party had the privilege of idling through this ancient quarter of New Orleans with the South's finest literary genius, the author of *The Grandissimes.* In him the South has found a masterly delineator of its interior life and its history. In truth, I find by experience, that the untrained eye and vacant mind can inspect it and

[1] The Israelites are buried in graves—by permission, I take it, not requirement; but none else, except the destitute, who are buried at public expense. The graves are but three or four feet deep.—M. T.

learn of it and judge of it more clearly and profitably in his books than by personal contact with it.

With Mr. Cable [1] along to see for you, and describe and explain and illuminate, a jog through that old quarter is a vivid pleasure. And you have a vivid *sense* as of unseen or dimly seen things—vivid, and yet fitful and darkling; you glimpse salient features, but lose the fine shades or catch them imperfectly through the vision of the imagination: a case, as it were, of an ignorant, near-sighted stranger traversing the rim of wide, vague horizons of Alps with an inspired and enlightened long-sighted native.

We visited the old St. Louis Hotel, now occupied by municipal offices. There is nothing strikingly remarkable about it; but one can say of it as of the Academy of Music in New York, that if a broom or a shovel has ever been used in it there is no circumstantial evidence to back up the fact. It is curious that cabbages and hay and things do not grow in the Academy of Music; but no doubt it is on account of the interruption of the light by the benches, and the impossibility of hoeing the crop except in the aisles. The fact that the ushers grow their buttonhole bouquets on the premises shows what might be done if they had the right kind of an agricultural head to the establishment.

We visited also the venerable Cathedral, and the pretty square in front of it; the one dim with religious light, the other brilliant with the worldly sort, and lovely with orange trees and blossomy shrubs; then we drove in the hot sun through the wilderness of houses and out onto the wide, dead level beyond, where the villas are, and the waterwheels to drain the town, and the commons populous with cows and children; passing by an old cemetery where we were told lie the ashes of an early pirate; but we took him on trust, and did not visit him. He was a pirate with a tremendous and sanguinary history; and as long as he preserved unspotted, in retirement, the dignity of his name and the grandeur of his ancient calling, homage and reverence were his from high and low; but when at last he descended into politics and became a paltry alderman, the public "shook" him, and turned aside and wept. When he

[1] George Washington Cable. Two years later, in 1884, Mark Twain and Cable "platformed" together—that is, gave readings. Clemens hated the rigors and banalities of lecturing and Cable's presence tranquilized the experience a good deal for him.—C. N.

died, they set up a monument over him; and little by little he has come into respect again; but it is respect for the pirate, not the alderman. To-day the loyal and generous remember only what he was, and charitably forget what he became.

Thence, we drove a few miles across a swamp, along a raised shell road, with a canal on one hand and a dense wood on the other; and here and there, in the distance, a ragged and angular-limbed and moss-bearded cypress-top standing out, clear-cut against the sky, and as quaint of form as the apple trees in Japanese pictures—such was our course and the surroundings of it. There was an occasional alligator swimming comfortably along in the canal, and an occasional picturesque colored person on the bank, flinging his statue-rigid reflection upon the still water and watching for a bite.

And by and by we reached the West End, a collection of hotels of the usual light summer-resort pattern, with broad verandas all around, and the waves of the wide and blue Lake Pontchartrain lapping the thresholds. We had dinner on a ground veranda over the water—the chief dish the renowned fish called pompano, delicious as the less criminal forms of sin.

Thousands of people come by rail and carriage to West End and to Spanish Fort every evening, and dine, listen to the bands, take strolls in the open air under the electric lights, go sailing on the lake, and entertain themselves in various and sundry other ways.

We had opportunities on other days and in other places to test the pompano. Notably, at an editorial dinner at one of the clubs in the city. He was in his last possible perfection there, and justified his fame. In his suite was a tall pyramid of scarlet crayfish—large ones; as large as one's thumb; delicate, palatable, appetizing. Also deviled whitebait; also shrimps of choice quality; and a platter of small soft-shell crabs of a most superior breed. The other dishes were what one might get at Delmonico's or Buckingham Palace; those I have spoken of can be had in similar perfection in New Orleans only, I suppose.

In the West and South they have a new institution—the Broom Brigade. It is composed of young ladies who dress in a uniform costume, and go through the infantry drill, with broom in place of musket. It is a very pretty sight, on private view. When they perform on the stage of a theater, in the blaze of colored fires, it must be a fine and fascinating spectacle. I saw them go through their complex manual with grace, spirit, and admirable precision. I saw them do everything which a human being can possibly do with a broom, except sweep. I did not see them sweep. But I know they could learn. What they have already learned proves that. And if they ever should learn, and should go on the war-path down Tchoupitoulas or some of those other streets around there, those thoroughfares would bear a greatly improved aspect in a very few minutes. But the girls themselves wouldn't; so nothing would be really gained, after all.

The drill was in the Washington Artillery building. In this building we saw many interesting relics of the war. Also a fine oil-painting representing Stonewall Jackson's last interview with General Lee. Both men are on horseback. Jackson has just ridden up, and is accosting Lee. The picture is very valuable, on account of the portraits, which are authentic. But like many another historical picture, it means nothing without its label. And one label will fit it as well as another:

First Interview between Lee and Jackson.
Last Interview between Lee and Jackson.
Jackson Introducing Himself to Lee.
Jackson Accepting Lee's Invitation to Dinner.
Jackson Declining Lee's Invitation to Dinner—with Thanks.
Jackson Apologizing for a Heavy Defeat.
Jackson Reporting a Great Victory.
Jackson Asking Lee for a Match.

It tells *one* story, and a sufficient one; for it says quite plainly and satisfactorily, "Here are Lee and Jackson together." The artist would have made it tell that this is Lee and Jackson's last interview if he could have done it. But he couldn't, for there wasn't any way to do it. A good legible label is usually worth, for information, a ton of significant attitude and expression in a historical picture. In Rome, people with fine sympathetic natures stand up and weep in front of the celebrated "Beatrice Cenci the Day before Her Execution." It shows what a label can do. If they did not know the picture, they would inspect it unmoved, and say, "Young girl with hay fever; young girl with her head in a bag."

I found the half-forgotten Southern intonations and elisions as pleasing to my ear as they had formerly been. A Southerner talks music. At least it is music to me, but then I was born in the South. The educated Southerner has no use for an *r*, except at the beginning of a word. He says "honah," and "dinnah," and "Gove'nuh," and "befo' the waw," and so on. The words may lack charm to the eye, in print, but they have it to the ear. When did the *r* disappear from Southern speech, and how did it come to disappear? The custom of dropping it was not borrowed from the North, nor inherited from England. Many Southerners—most Southerners—put a *y* into occasional words that begin with the *k* sound. For instance, they say Mr. K'yahtah (Carter) and speak of playing k'yahds or of riding in the k'yahs. And they have the pleasant custom—long ago fallen into decay in the North—of frequently employing the respectful "Sir." Instead of the curt Yes, and the abrupt No, they say "Yes, suh"; "No, suh."

But there are some infelicities, such as "like" for "as," and the addition of an "at" where it isn't needed. I heard an educated gentleman say, "Like the flag-officer did." His cook or his butler would have said, "Like the flag-officer done." You hear gentlemen say, "Where have you been at?" And here is the aggravated form—heard a ragged street Arab say it to a comrade: "I was a-ask'n' Tom whah you was a-sett'n' at." The very elect carelessly say "will" when they mean "shall"; and many of them say "I didn't go to do it," meaning "I didn't mean to do it." The Northern word "guess"—imported from England, where it used to be common, and now regarded by satirical Englishmen as a Yankee original—is but little used among Southerners. They say "reckon." They haven't any "doesn't" in their language; they say "don't" instead. The unpolished often use "went" for "gone." It is nearly as bad as the Northern "hadn't ought." This reminds me that a remark of a very peculiar nature was made here in my neighborhood (in the North) a few days ago: "He hadn't ought to have went." How is that? Isn't that a good deal of a triumph? One knows the orders combined in this half-breed's architecture without inquiring: one parent Northern, the other Southern. To-day I heard a schoolmistress ask, "Where is John gone?" This form is so common—so nearly universal, in fact—that if she had used "whither" instead of "where," I think it would have sounded like an affectation.

We picked up one excellent word—a word worth traveling to New Orleans to get; a nice limber, expressive, handy word—"Lagniappe."

They pronounce it lanny-*yap*. It is Spanish—so they said. We discovered it at the head of a column of odds and ends in the *Picayune* the first day; heard twenty people use it the second; inquired what it meant the third; adopted it and got facility in swinging it the fourth. It has a restricted meaning, but I think the people spread it out a little when they choose. It is the equivalent of the thirteenth roll in a "baker's dozen." It is something thrown in, gratis, for good measure. The custom originated in the Spanish quarter of the city. When a child or a servant buys something in a shop—or even the mayor or the governor, for aught I know—he finishes the operation by saying:

"Give me something for lagniappe."

The shopman always responds; gives the child a bit of licorice-root, gives the servant a cheap cigar or a spool of thread, gives the governor—I don't know what he gives the governor; support, likely.

When you are invited to drink—and this does occur now and then in New Orleans—and you say, "What, again?—no, I've had enough," the other party says, "But just this one time more—this is for lagniappe." When the beau perceives that he is stacking his compliments a trifle too high, and sees by the young lady's countenance that the edifice would have been better with the top compliment left off, he puts his "I beg pardon, no harm intended," into the briefer form of "Oh, that's for lagniappe." If the waiter in the restaurant stumbles and spills a gill of coffee down the back of your neck, he says, "F'r lagniappe, sah," and gets you another cup without extra charge.

From *Life on the Mississippi,* 1883.

14 : *Hannibal*

AT SEVEN IN THE MORNING we reached Hannibal, Missouri, where my boyhood was spent. I had had a glimpse of it fifteen years ago, and another glimpse six years earlier, but both were so brief that they hardly counted. The only notion of the town that remained in my mind was the memory of it as I had known it when I first quitted it twenty-nine years ago. That picture of it was still as clear and vivid to me as a photograph. I stepped ashore with the feeling of one who returns out of a dead-and-gone generation. I had a sort of realizing sense of what the Bastille prisoners must have felt when they used to come out and look upon Paris after years of captivity, and note how curiously the familiar and the strange were mixed together before them. I saw the new houses—saw them plainly enough—but they did not affect the older picture in my mind, for through their solid bricks and mortar I saw the vanished houses, which had formerly stood there, with perfect distinctness.

It was Sunday morning, and everybody was abed yet. So I passed through the vacant streets, still seeing the town as it was, and not as it is, and recognizing and metaphorically shaking hands with a hundred familiar objects which no longer exist; and finally climbed Holiday's Hill to get a comprehensive view. The whole town lay spread out below me then, and I could mark and fix every locality, every detail. Naturally, I was a good deal moved. I said, "Many of the people I once knew in this tranquil refuge of my childhood are now in heaven; some, I trust, are in the other place."

The things about me and before me made me feel like a boy again—convinced me that I was a boy again, and that I had simply been dreaming an unusually long dream; but my reflections spoiled all that; for they forced me to say, "I see fifty old houses down yonder, into each of which I could enter and find either a man or a woman who was a baby or unborn when I noticed those houses last, or a grandmother who was a plump young bride at that time."

From this vantage-ground the extensive view up and down the river, and wide over the wooded expanses of Illinois, is very beautiful—one of the most beautiful on the Mississippi, I think; which is a hazardous remark to make, for the eight hundred miles of river between St. Louis and St. Paul afford an unbroken succession of lovely pictures. It may be that my affection for the one in question biases my judgment in its favor; I cannot say as to that. No matter, it was satisfyingly beautiful to me, and it had this advantage over all the other friends whom I was about to greet again: it had suffered no change; it was as young and fresh and comely and gracious as ever it had been; whereas, the faces of the others would be old, and scarred with the campaigns of life, and marked with their griefs and defeats, and would give me no upliftings of spirit.

An old gentleman, out on an early morning walk, came along, and we discussed the weather, and then drifted into other matters. I could not remember his face. He said he had been living here twenty-eight years. So he had come after my time, and I had never seen him before. I asked him various questions; first about a mate of mine in Sunday-school—what became of him?

"He graduated with honor in an Eastern college, wandered off into the world somewhere, succeeded at nothing, passed out of knowledge and memory years ago, and is supposed to have gone to the dogs."

"He was bright, and promised well when he was a boy."

"Yes, but the thing that happened is what became of it all."

I asked after another lad, altogether the brightest in our village school when I was a boy.

"He, too, was graduated with honors, from an Eastern college; but life whipped him in every battle, straight along, and he died in one of the territories, years ago, a defeated man."

I asked after another of the bright boys.

"He is a success, always has been, always will be, I think."

I inquired after a young fellow who came to the town to study for one of the professions when I was a boy.

"He went at something else before he got through—went from medicine to law, or from law to medicine—then to some other new thing; went away for a year, came back with a young wife; fell to drinking, then to gambling behind the door; finally took his wife and two children to her father's, and went off to Mexico; went from bad to worse, and finally died there, without a cent to buy a shroud, and without a friend to attend the funeral."

"Pity, for he was the best-natured and most cheery and hopeful young fellow that ever was."

I named another boy.

"Oh, he is all right. Lives here yet; has a wife and children, and is prospering."

Same verdict concerning other boys.

I named three school-girls.

"The first two live here, are married and have children; the other is long ago dead—never married."

I named, with emotion, one of my early sweethearts.

"She is all right. Been married three times; buried two husbands, divorced from the third, and I hear she is getting ready to marry an old fellow out in Colorado somewhere. She's got children scattered around here and there, most everywheres."

The answer to several other inquiries was brief and simple:

"Killed in the war."

I named another boy.

"Well now, his case *is* curious! There wasn't a human being in this town but knew that that boy was a perfect chucklehead; perfect dummy; just a stupid ass, as you may say. Everybody knew it, and everybody said it. Well, if that very boy isn't the first lawyer in the state of Missouri to-day, I'm a Democrat!"

"Is that so?"

"It's actually so. I'm telling you the truth."

"How do you account for it?"

"Account for it? There ain't any accounting for it, except that if you send a d—d fool to St. Louis, and you don't tell them he's a d—d fool, *they'll* never find it out. There's one thing sure—if I had a d—d fool I should know what to do with him; ship him to St. Louis—it's the noblest market in the world for that kind of property. Well, when you come to look at it all around, and chew at it all around, and chew at it and think it over, *don't* it just bang anything you ever heard of?"

"Well, yes; it does seem to. But don't you think maybe it was the Hannibal people who were mistaken about the boy, and not the St. Louis people?"

"Oh, nonsense! The people here have known him from the very

cradle—they knew him a hundred times better than the St. Louis idiots *could* have known him. No; if you have got any d——d fools that you want to realize on, take my advice—send them to St. Louis."

I mentioned a great number of people whom I had formerly known. Some were dead, some were gone away, some had prospered, some had come to naught; but as regarded a dozen or so of the lot, the answer was comforting:

"Prosperous—live here yet—town littered with their children."

I asked about Miss ——.

"Died in the insane asylum three or four years ago—never was out of it from the time she went in; and was always suffering too; never got a shred of her mind back."

If he spoke the truth, here was a heavy tragedy, indeed. Thirty-six years in a madhouse, that some young fools might have some fun! I was a small boy at the time; and I saw those giddy young ladies come tiptoeing into the room where Miss —— sat reading at midnight by a lamp. The girl at the head of the file wore a shroud and a doughface; she crept behind the victim, touched her on the shoulder, and she looked up and screamed, and then fell into convulsions. She did not recover from the fright, but went mad. In these days it seems incredible that people believed in ghosts so short a time ago. But they did.

After asking after such other folk as I could call to mind, I finally inquired about *myself*.

"Oh, he succeeded well enough—another case of d——d fool. If they'd sent him to St. Louis, he'd have succeeded sooner."

It was with much satisfaction that I recognized the wisdom of having told this candid gentleman, in the beginning, that my name was Smith.

From *Life on the Mississippi,* 1883.

15 : *St. Paul and Minneapolis*

We reached St. Paul, at the head of navigation of the Mississippi, and there our voyage of two thousand miles from New Orleans ended. It is about a ten-day trip by steamer. It can probably be done quicker by rail. I judge so because I know that one may go by rail from St. Louis to Hannibal—a distance of at least a hundred and twenty miles—in seven hours. This is better than walking; unless one is in a hurry.

The season being far advanced when we were in New Orleans, the roses and magnolia blossoms were falling; but here in St. Paul it was the snow. In New Orleans we had caught an occasional withering breath from over a crater, apparently; here in St. Paul we caught a frequent benumbing one from over a glacier, apparently.

I am not trying to astonish by these statistics. No, it is only natural that there should be a sharp difference between climates which lie upon parallels of latitude which are one or two thousand miles apart. I take this position, and I will hold it and maintain it in spite of the newspapers. The newspaper thinks it isn't a natural thing; and once a year, in February, it remarks, with ill-concealed exclamation-points, that while we, away up here, are fighting snow and ice, folks are having new strawberries and peas down South; callas are blooming out-of-doors, and the people are complaining of the warm weather. The newspaper never gets done being surprised about it. It is caught regularly every February. There must be a reason for this; and this reason must be change of hands at the editorial desk. You cannot surprise an individual more than twice with the same marvel—not even with the February miracles of the Southern climate; but if you keep putting new hands at the editorial desk every year or two, and forget to vaccinate them against the annual climatic surprise, that same old thing is going to occur right along. Each year one new hand will have the disease, and be safe from its recurrence; but this does not save the newspaper. No, the newspaper is in as bad case as ever; it will forever have its new hand; and so, it will break out with the strawberry surprise every February as long as it lives. The new hand is curable; the newspaper itself is incurable. An act of Congress—no, Congress could not prohibit the strawberry surprise without questionably stretching its powers. An amendment to the Constitution might fix the thing, and that is probably the best and quickest way to get at it. Under authority of such an amendment, Congress could then pass an act inflicting imprisonment for life for the first offense, and some sort of lingering death for subsequent ones; and this, no doubt, would presently give us a rest. At the same time, the amendment and the resulting act and penalties might easily be made to cover various cognate abuses, such as the Annual-Veteran-who-has-Voted-for-Every-President-from-Washington - down, - and - Walked - to - the - Polls - Yesterday - with-as-Bright-an-Eye-and-as-Firm-a-Step-as-Ever, and ten or eleven other weary yearly marvels of that sort, and of the Oldest-Freemason, and Oldest-Printer, and Oldest-Baptist-Preacher, and Oldest-Alumnus sort, and Three-Children-Born-at-a-Birth sort, and so on, and so on. And then England would take it up and pass a law prohibiting the further use of Sidney Smith's jokes, and appointing a commissioner to construct some new ones. Then life would be a sweet dream of rest and peace, and the nations would cease to long for heaven.

But I wander from my theme. St. Paul is a wonderful town. It is put together in solid blocks of honest brick and stone, and has the air of intending to stay. Its post-office was established thirty-six years ago; and by and by, when the postmaster received a letter, he carried it to Washington, horseback, to inquire what was to be done with it. Such is the legend. Two frame houses were built that year, and several persons were added to the population. A recent number of the leading St. Paul paper, the *Pioneer Press,* gives some statistics which furnish a vivid contrast to that old state of things, to wit: Population, autumn of the present year (1882), 71,000; number of letters handled, first half of the year, 1,209,387; number of houses built during three-quarters of the year, 989; their cost, $3,186,000. The increase of letters over the corresponding six months of last year was fifty per cent. Last year the new buildings added to the city cost above $4,500,000. St. Paul's strength lies in her commerce—I mean his commerce. He is a manufacturing city, of course—all cities of that region are—but he is peculiarly strong in the matter of commerce. Last year his jobbing trade amounted to upward of $52,000,000.

He has a custom-house, and is building a costly capitol to replace the one recently burned—for he is the capital of the state. He has churches without end; and not the cheap poor kind, but the kind that the rich Protestant puts up, the kind that the poor Irish "hired girl" delights to erect. What a passion for building majestic churches the Irish hired girl has! It is a fine thing for our architecture; but too often we enjoy her stately fanes without giving her a grateful thought. In fact, instead of reflecting that "every brick and every stone in this beautiful edifice represents an ache or a pain, and a handful of sweat, and hours of heavy fatigue, contributed by the back and forehead and bones of poverty," it is our habit to forget these things entirely, and merely glorify the mighty temple itself, without vouchsafing one praiseful thought to its humble builder, whose rich heart and withered purse it symbolizes.

This is a land of libraries and schools. St. Paul has three public libraries, and they contain, in the aggregate, some forty thousand books. He has one hundred and sixteen schoolhouses, and pays out more than seventy thousand dollars a year in teachers' salaries.

There is an unusually fine railway-station; so large is it, in fact, that it seemed somewhat overdone, in the matter of size, at first; but at the end of a few months it was perceived that the mistake was distinctly the other way. The error is to be corrected.

The town stands on high ground; it is about seven hundred feet above the sea-level. It is so high that a wide view of river and lowland is offered from its streets.

It is a very wonderful town, indeed, and is not finished yet. All the streets are obstructed with building-material, and this is being compacted into houses as fast as possible, to make room for more—for other people are anxious to build, as soon as they can get the use of the streets to pile up their bricks and stuff in.

How solemn and beautiful is the thought that the earliest pioneer of civilization, the van-leader of civilization, is never the steamboat, never the railroad, never the newspaper, never the Sabbath-school, never the missionary—but always whisky! Such is the case. Look history over; you will see. The missionary comes after the whisky—I mean he arrives after the whisky has arrived; next comes the poor immigrant, with ax and hoe and rifle; next, the trader; next, the miscellaneous rush; next, the gambler, the desperado, the highwayman, and all their kindred in sin of both sexes; and next, the smart chap who has bought up an old grant that covers all the land; this brings the lawyer tribe; the vigilance committee brings the undertaker. All these interests bring the newspaper; the newspaper starts up politics and a railroad; all hands turn to and build a church and a jail—and behold! civilization is established forever in the land. But whisky, you see, was the van-leader in this beneficent work. It always is. It was like a foreigner—and excusable in a foreigner—to be ignorant of this great truth, and wander off into astronomy to borrow a symbol. But if he had been conversant with the facts, he would have said:

Westward the Jug of Empire takes its way.

This great van-leader arrived upon the ground which St. Paul now occupies, in June, 1837. Yes, at that date, Pierre Parrant, a Canadian, built the first cabin, uncorked his jug, and began to sell whisky to the Indians. The result is before us.

All that I have said of the newness, briskness, swift progress, wealth, intelligence, fine and substantial architecture, and general slash and go and energy of St. Paul, will apply to his near neighbor, Minneapolis—with the addition that the latter is the bigger of the two cities.

These extraordinary towns were ten miles apart a few months ago, but were growing so fast that they may possibly be joined now and getting along under a single mayor. At any rate, within five years from now there will be at least such a substantial ligament of buildings stretching between them and uniting them that a stranger will not be able to tell where the one Siamese twin leaves off and the other begins. Combined, they will then number a population of two hundred and fifty thousand, if they continue to grow as they are now growing. Thus, this center of population, at the head of Mississippi navigation, will then begin a rivalry as to numbers with that center of population at the foot of it—New Orleans.

Minneapolis is situated at the falls of St. Anthony, which stretch across the river fifteen hundred feet, and have a fall of eighty-two feet—a water-power which, by art, has been made of inestimable value, businesswise, though somewhat to the damage of the Falls as a spectacle, or as a background against which to get your photograph taken.

Thirty flouring-mills turn out two million barrels of the very choicest of flour every year; twenty saw-mills produce two hundred million feet of lumber annually; then there are woolen-mills, cotton-mills, paper and oil mills; and sash, nail, furniture, barrel, and other factories, without number, so to speak. The great flouring-mills here and at St. Paul use the "new process" and mash the wheat by rolling, instead of grinding it.

Sixteen railroads meet in Minneapolis, and sixty-five passenger-trains arrive and depart daily.

In this place, as in St. Paul, journalism thrives. Here there are three great dailies, ten weeklies, and three monthlies.

There is a university, with four hundred students—and, better still, its good efforts are not confined to enlightening the one sex. There are sixteen public schools, with buildings which cost five hundred thousand dollars; there are six thousand pupils and one hundred and twenty-eight teachers. There are also seventy churches existing, and a lot more projected. The banks aggregate a capital of three million dollars, and the wholesale jobbing trade of the town amounts to fifty million dollars a year. . . .

From *Life on the Mississippi,* 1883.

2 / *Europe*

16 : *Gibraltar*

A WEEK of buffeting a tempestuous and relentless sea;[1] a week of seasickness and deserted cabins; of lonely quarter-decks drenched with spray—spray so ambitious that it even coated the smokestacks thick with a white crust of salt to their very tops; a week of shivering in the shelter of the lifeboats and deck-houses by day, and blowing suffocating "clouds" and boisterously performing at dominoes in the smoking-room at night.

And the last night of the seven was the stormiest of all. There was no thunder, no noise but the pounding blows of the ship, the keen whistling of the gale through the cordage, and the rush of the seething waters. But the vessel climbed aloft as if she would climb to heaven—then paused an instant that seemed a century, and plunged headlong down again, as from a precipice. The sheeted sprays drenched the decks like rain. The blackness of darkness was everywhere. At long intervals a flash of lightning clove it with a quivering line of fire, that revealed a heaving world of water where was nothing before, kindled the dusky cordage to glittering silver, and lit up the faces of the men with a ghastly luster!

Fear drove many on deck that were used to avoiding the night winds and the spray. Some thought the vessel could not live through the night, and it seemed less dreadful to stand out in the midst of the wild tempest and *see* the peril that threatened than to be shut up in the sepulchral cabins, under the dim lamps, and imagine the horrors that were abroad on the ocean. And once out—once where they could see the ship struggling in the strong grasp of the storm—once where they could hear the shriek of the winds, and face the driving spray and look out upon the majestic picture the lightnings disclosed, they were prisoners to a fierce fascination

[1] A week, that is, not out of New York but out of the Azores.—C. N.

they could not resist, and so remained. It was a wild night—and a very, very long one.

Everybody was sent scampering to the deck at seven o'clock this lovely morning of the 30th of June with the glad news that land was in sight! It was a rare thing and a joyful, to see *all* the ship's family abroad once more, albeit the happiness that sat upon every countenance could only partly conceal the ravages which that long siege of storms had wrought there. But dull eyes soon sparkled with pleasure, pallid cheeks flushed again, and frames weakened by sickness gathered new life from the quickening influences of the bright, fresh morning. Yea, and from a still more potent influence: the worn castaways were to see the blessed land again!—and to see it was to bring back that mother-land that was in all their thoughts.

Within the hour we were fairly within the Straits of Gibraltar, the tall yellow-splotched hills of Africa on our right, with their bases veiled in a blue haze and their summits swathed in clouds—the same being according to Scripture, which says that "clouds and darkness are over the land." The words were spoken of this particular portion of Africa, I believe. On our left were the granite-ribbed domes of old Spain. The Strait is only thirteen miles wide in its narrowest part.

At short intervals, along the Spanish shore, were quaint-looking old stone towers—Moorish, we thought—but learned better afterward. In former times the Morocco rascals used to coast along the Spanish Main in their boats till a safe opportunity seemed to present itself, and then dart in and capture a Spanish village, and carry off all the pretty women they could find. It was a pleasant business, and was very popular. The Spaniards built these watch-towers on the hills to enable them to keep a sharper lookout on the Moroccan speculators.

The picture, on the other hand, was very beautiful to eyes weary of the changeless sea, and by and by the ship's company grew wonderfully cheerful. But while we stood admiring the cloud-capped peaks and the lowlands robed in misty gloom, a finer picture burst upon us and chained every eye like a magnet—a stately ship, with canvas piled on canvas till she was one towering mass of bellying sail! She came speeding over the sea like a great bird. Africa and Spain were forgotten. All homage was for the beautiful stranger. While everybody gazed, she swept superbly by and flung the Stars and Stripes to the breeze! Quicker than thought, hats and handkerchiefs flashed in the air, and a cheer went up! She was beautiful before—she was radiant now. Many a one on our decks knew then for the first time how tame a sight his country's flag is at home compared to what it is in a foreign land. To see it is to see a vision of home itself and all its idols, and feel a thrill that would stir a very river of sluggish blood!

We were approaching the famed Pillars of Hercules, and already the African one, "Ape's Hill," a grand old mountain with summit streaked with granite ledges, was in sight. The other, the great Rock of Gibraltar, was yet to come. The ancients considered the Pillars of Hercules the head of navigation and the end of the world. The information the ancients didn't have was very voluminous. Even the prophets wrote book after book and epistle after epistle, yet never once hinted at the existence of a great continent on our side of the water; yet they must have known it was there, I should think.

In a few moments a lonely and enormous mass of rock, standing seemingly in the center of the wide strait and apparently washed on all sides by the sea, swung magnificently into view, and we needed no tedious traveled parrot to tell us it was Gibraltar. There could not be two rocks like that in one kingdom.

The Rock of Gibraltar is about a mile and a half long, I should say, by 1,400 to 1,500 feet high, and a quarter of a mile wide at its base. One side and one end of it come about as straight up out of the sea as the side of a house, the other end is irregular and the other side is a steep slant which an army would find very difficult to climb. At the foot of this slant is the walled town of Gibraltar—or rather the town occupies part of the slant. Everywhere —on hillside, in the precipice, by the sea, on the heights,—everywhere you choose to look, Gibraltar is clad with masonry and bristling with guns. It makes a striking and lively picture, from whatsoever point you contemplate it. It is pushed out into the sea on the end of a flat, narrow strip of land, and is suggestive of a "gob" of mud on the end of a shingle. A few hundred yards of this flat ground at its base belongs to the English, and then, extending across the strip from the Atlantic to the Mediterranean, a distance of a quarter of a mile, comes the "Neutral Ground," a space two or three hundred yards wide, which is free to both parties.

"Are you going through Spain to Paris?" That question was bandied about the ship day and night from Fayal to Gibraltar, and I thought I never could get so tired of hearing any one combination of words again, or more tired of answering, "I don't know."

At the last moment six or seven had sufficient decision of character to make up their minds to go, and did go, and I felt a sense of relief at once—it was forever too late, now, and I could make up my mind at my leisure, not to go. I must have a prodigious quantity of mind; it takes me as much as a week, sometimes, to make it up.

But behold how annoyances repeat themselves. We had no sooner gotten rid of the Spain distress than the Gibraltar guides started another—a tiresome repetition of a legend that had nothing very astonishing about it, even in the first place: "That high hill yonder is called the Queen's Chair; it is because one of the queens of Spain placed her chair there when the French and Spanish troops were besieging Gibraltar, and said she would never move from the spot till the English flag was lowered from the fortresses. If the English hadn't been gallant enough to lower the flag for a few hours one day, she'd have had to break her oath or die up there."

We rode on asses and mules up the steep, narrow streets and entered the subterranean galleries the English have blasted out in the rock. These galleries are like spacious railway tunnels, and at short intervals in them great guns frown out upon sea and town through portholes five or six hundred feet above the ocean. There is a mile or so of this subterranean work, and it must have cost a vast deal of money and labor. The gallery guns command the peninsula and the harbors of both oceans, but they might as well not be there, I should think, for an army could hardly climb the perpendicular wall of the rock anyhow. Those lofty portholes afford superb views of the sea, though. At one place, where a jutting crag was hollowed out into a great chamber whose furniture was huge cannon and whose windows were portholes, a glimpse was caught of a hill not far away, and a soldier said:

"That high hill yonder is called the Queen's Chair; it is because a queen of Spain placed her chair there once, when the French and Spanish troops were besieging Gibraltar, and said she would never move from the spot till the English flag was lowered from the fortresses. If the English hadn't been gallant enough to lower the flag for a few hours one day, she'd have had to break her oath or die up there."

On the topmost pinnacle of Gibraltar we halted a good while, and no doubt the mules were tired. They had a right to be. The military road was good, but rather steep, and there was a good deal of it. The view from the narrow ledge was magnificent; from it vessels seeming like the tiniest little toy boats were turned into noble ships by the telescopes; and other vessels that were fifty miles away, and even sixty, they said, and invisible to the naked eye, could be clearly distinguished through those same telescopes. Below, on one side, we looked down upon an endless mass of batteries, and on the other straight down to the sea.

While I was resting ever so comfortably on a rampart, and cooling my baking head in the delicious breeze, an officious guide belonging to another party came up and said:

"Señor, that high hill yonder is called the Queen's Chair—"

"Sir, I am a helpless orphan in a foreign land. Have pity on me. Don't—now *don't* inflict that most in-FERNAL old legend on me any more today!"

There—I had used strong language, after promising I would never do so again; but the provocation was more than human nature could bear. If you had been bored so, when you had the noble panorama of Spain and Africa and the blue Mediterranean spread abroad at your feet, and wanted to gaze, and enjoy, and surfeit yourself with its beauty in silence, you might have even burst into stronger language than I did.

Gibraltar has stood several protracted sieges, one of them of nearly four years' duration (it failed), and the English only captured it by stratagem. The wonder is that anybody should ever dream of trying so impossible a project as the taking it by assault—and yet it has been tried more than once.

The Moors held the place twelve hundred years ago, and a stanch old castle of theirs of that date still frowns from the middle of the town, with moss-grown battlements and sides well scarred by shots fired in battles and sieges that are forgotten now. A secret chamber, in the rock behind it, was discovered some time ago, which contained a sword of exquisite workmanship, and some quaint old armor of a fashion that antiquaries are not acquainted with, though it is supposed to be Roman. Roman armor and Roman relics, of various kinds, have been found in a cave in the sea extremity of Gibraltar; history says Rome held this part of the country about the Christian era, and these things seem to confirm the statement.

In that cave, also, are found human bones, crusted with a very thick, stony coating, and wise men have ventured to say that those men not only lived before the flood, but as much as ten thousand years before it. It may be true—it looks reasonable enough—but as long as those parties can't vote any more, the matter can be of no great public interest. In this cave, likewise, are found skeletons and fossils of animals that exist in every part of Africa, yet within memory and tradition have never existed in any portion of Spain save this lone peak of Gibraltar! So the theory is that the channel between Gibraltar and Africa was once dry land, and that the low, neutral neck between Gibraltar and the Spanish hills behind it was once ocean, and, of course, that these African animals, being over at Gibraltar (after rock, perhaps—there is plenty there), got closed out when the great change occurred. The hills in Africa, across the channel, are full of apes, and there are now, and always have been, apes on the rock of Gibraltar—but not elsewhere in Spain! The subject is an interesting one.

There is an English garrison at Gibraltar of 6,000 or 7,000 men, and so uniforms of flaming red are plenty; and red and blue, and undress costumes of snowy white, and also the queer uniform of the bare-kneed Highlander; and one sees soft-eyed Spanish girls from San Roque, and veiled Moorish beauties (I suppose they are beauties) from Tarifa, and turbaned, sashed, and trousered Moorish merchants from Fez, and long-robed, bare-legged, ragged Mohammedan vagabonds from Tetouan and Tangier, some brown, some yellow, and some as black as virgin ink—and Jews from all around, in gaberdine, skull-cap, and slippers, just as they are in pictures and theaters, and just as they were three thousand years ago, no doubt. You can easily understand that a tribe (somehow our pilgrims suggest that expression, because they march in a straggling procession through these foreign places with such an Indian-like air of complacency and independence about them) like ours, made up from fifteen or sixteen states of the Union, found enough to stare at in this shifting panorama of fashion to-day.

From *The Innocents Abroad,* 1869.

17 : *Paris*

WHAT EXCELLENT ORDER THEY KEPT about that vast depot! There was no frantic crowding and jostling, no shouting and swearing, and no swaggering intrusion of services by rowdy hackmen. These latter gentry stood outside—stood quietly by their long line of vehicles and said never a word. A kind of hackman-general seemed to have the whole matter of transportation in his hands. He politely received the passengers and ushered them to the kind of conveyance they wanted, and told the driver where to deliver them. There was no "talking back," no dissatisfaction about overcharging, no grumbling about anything. In a little while we were speeding through the streets of Paris, and delightfully recognizing certain names and places with which books had long ago made us familiar. It was like meeting an old friend when we read *"Rue de Rivoli"* on the street corner; we knew the genuine vast palace of the Louvre as well as we knew its picture; when we passed by the Column of July we needed no one to tell us what it was, or to remind us that on its site once stood the grim Bastile, that grave of human hopes and happiness, that dismal prison-house within whose dungeons so many young faces put on the wrinkles of age, so many proud spirits grew humble, so many brave hearts broke.

We secured rooms at the hotel, or rather, we had three beds put into one room, so that we might be together, and then we went out to a restaurant, just after lamp-lighting, and ate a comfortable, satisfactory, lingering dinner. It was a pleasure to eat where everything was so tidy, the food so well cooked, the waiters so polite, and the coming and departing company so mustached, so frisky, so affable, so fearfully and wonderfully Frenchy! All the surroundings were gay and enlivening. Two hundred people sat at little tables on the sidewalk, sipping wine and coffee; the streets were thronged with light vehicles and with joyous pleasure-seekers; there was music in the air, life and action all about us, and a conflagration of gaslight everywhere!

After dinner we felt like seeing such Parisian specialties as we might see without distressing exertion, and so we sauntered through the brilliant streets and looked at the dainty trifles in variety stores and jewelry shops. Occasionally, merely for the pleasure of being cruel, we put unoffending Frenchmen on the rack with questions framed in the incomprehensible jargon of their native language, and while they writhed, we impaled them, we peppered them, we scarified them, with their own vile verbs and participles.

We noticed that in the jewelry stores they had some of the articles marked "gold," and some labeled "imitation." We wondered at this extravagance of honesty, and inquired into the matter. We were informed that inasmuch as most people are not able to tell false gold from the genuine article, the government compels jewelers to have their gold work assayed and stamped officially according to its fineness, and their imitation work duly labeled with the sign of its falsity. They told us the jewelers would not dare to violate this law, and that whatever a stranger bought in one of their stores might be depended upon as being strictly what it was represented to be. Verily, a wonderful land is France!

Then we hunted for a barber shop. From earliest infancy it had been a cherished ambition of mine to be shaved some day in a palatial barber shop of Paris. I wished to recline at full length in a cushioned invalid-chair, with pictures about me, and sumptuous furniture; with frescoed walls and gilded arches above me, and vistas of Corinthian columns stretching far before me, with perfumes of Araby to intoxicate my senses, and the slumbrous drone of distant noises to soothe me to sleep. At the end of an hour I would wake up regretfully and find my face as smooth and as soft as an infant's. Departing, I would lift my hands above that barber's head and say, "Heaven bless you, my son!"

So we searched high and low, for a matter of two hours, but never a barber shop could we see. We saw only wig-making establishments, with shocks of dead and repulsive hair bound upon the heads of painted waxen brigands who stared out from glass boxes upon the passer-by, with their stony eyes, and scared him with the ghostly white of their countenances. We shunned these signs for a time, but finally we concluded that the wig-makers must of necessity be the barbers as well, since we could find no single legitimate representative of the fraternity. We entered and asked, and found that it was even so.

I said I wanted to be shaved. The barber inquired where my room was. I said, never mind where my room was, I wanted to be shaved —there, on the spot. The doctor said he would be shaved also. Then there was an excitement among those two barbers! There was a wild consultation, and afterward a hurrying to and fro and a feverish gathering up of razors from obscure places and a ransacking for soap. Next they took us into a little mean, shabby back room; they got two ordinary sitting-room chairs and placed us in them, with our coats on. My old, old dream of bliss vanished into thin air!

I sat bolt upright, silent, sad, and solemn. One of the wig-making villains lathered my face for ten terrible minutes and finished by plastering a mass of suds into my mouth. I expelled the nasty stuff with a strong English expletive and said, "Foreigner, beware!" Then this outlaw strapped his razor on his boot, hovered over me ominously for six fearful seconds, and then swooped down upon me like the genius of destruction. The first rake of his razor loosened the very hide from my face and lifted me out of the chair. I stormed and raved, and the other boys enjoyed it. Their beards are not strong and thick. Let us draw the curtain over this harrowing scene. Suffice it that I submitted, and went through with the cruel infliction of a shave by a French barber; tears of exquisite agony coursed down my cheeks, now and then, but I survived. Then the incipient assassin held a basin of water under my chin and slopped its contents over my face, and into my bosom, and down the back of my neck, with a mean pretense of washing away the soap and blood. He dried my features with a towel, and was going to comb my hair; but I asked to be excused. I said, with withering irony, that it was sufficient to be skinned—I declined to be scalped.

I went away from there with my handkerchief about my face, and never, never, never desired to dream of palatial Parisian barber shops any more. The truth is, as I believe I have since found out, that they have no barber shops worthy of the name in Paris—and no barbers, either, for that matter. The impostor who does duty as a barber brings his pans and napkins and implements of torture to your residence and deliberately skins you in your private apartments. Ah, I have suffered, suffered, suffered, here in Paris, but never mind—the time is coming when I shall have a dark and bloody revenge. Some day a Parisian barber will come to my room to skin me, and from that day forth that barber will never be heard of more.

At eleven o'clock we alighted upon a sign which manifestly referred to billiards. Joy! We had played billiards in the Azores with balls that were not round, and on an ancient table that was very little smoother than a brick pavement—one of those wretched old things with dead cushions, and with patches in the faded cloth and invisible obstructions that made the balls describe the most astonishing and unsuspected angles and perform feats in the way of unlooked-for and almost impossible "scratches," that were perfectly bewildering. We had played at Gibraltar with balls the size of a walnut, on a table like a public square—and in both instances we achieved far more aggravation than amusement. We expected to fare better here, but we were mistaken. The cushions were a good deal higher than the balls, and as the balls had a fashion of always stopping under the cushions, we accomplished very little in the way of caroms. The cushions were hard and unelastic, and the cues were so crooked that in making a shot you had to allow for the curve or you would infallibly put the "English" on the wrong side of the ball. Dan was to mark while the doctor and I played. At the end of an hour neither of us had made a count, and so Dan was tired of keeping tally with nothing to tally, and we were heated and angry and disgusted. We paid the heavy bill—about six cents—and said we would call around some time when we had a week to spend, and finish the game.

We adjourned to one of those pretty cafés and took supper and tested the wines of the country, as we had been instructed to do, and found them harmless and unexciting. They might have been exciting, however, if we had chosen to drink a sufficiency of them.

To close our first day in Paris cheerfully and pleasantly, we now sought our grand room in the Grand Hotel du Louvre and climbed into our sumptuous bed, to read and smoke—but alas!

It was pitiful,
In a whole city-full,
Gas we had none.

No gas to read by—nothing but dismal candles. It was a shame. We tried to map out excursions for the morrow; we puzzled over French "Guides to Paris"; we talked disjointedly, in a vain endeavor to make head or tail of the wild chaos of the day's sights and experiences; we subsided to indolent smoking; we gaped and yawned, and stretched—then feebly wondered if we were really and truly in renowned Paris, and drifted drowsily away into that vast mysterious void which men call sleep.

We went to see the Cathedral of Notre Dame. We had heard of it before. It surprises me, sometimes, to think how much we *do* know, and how intelligent we are. We recognized the brown old Gothic pile in a moment; it was like the pictures. We stood at a little distance and changed from one point of observation to another, and gazed long at its lofty square towers and its rich front, clustered thick with stony, mutilated saints who had been looking calmly down from their perches for ages. The Patriarch of Jerusalem stood under them in the old days of chivalry and romance, and preached the third Crusade, more than six hundred years ago; and since that day they have stood there and looked quietly down upon the most thrilling scenes, the grandest pageants, the most extraordinary spectacles that have grieved or delighted Paris. These battered and broken-nosed old fellows saw many and many a cavalcade of mail-clad knights come marching home from Holy Land; they heard the bells above them toll the signal for the St. Bartholomew's Massacre, and they saw the slaughter that followed; later, they saw the Reign of Terror, the carnage of the Revolution, the overthrow of a king, the coronation of two Napoleons, the christening of the young prince that lords it over a regiment of servants in the Tuileries to-day—and they may possibly continue to stand there until they see the Napoleon dynasty swept away and the banners of a great Republic floating above its ruins. I wish these old parties could speak. They could tell a tale worth the listening to.

They say that a pagan temple stood where Notre Dame now stands, in the old Roman days, eighteen or twenty centuries ago—remains of it are still preserved in Paris; and that a Christian church took its place about A. D. 300; another took the place of that in A. D. 500; and that the foundations of the present cathedral were laid about A. D. 1100. The ground ought to be measurably sacred by this time, one would think. One portion of this noble old edifice is suggestive of the quaint fashions of ancient times. It was built by Jean Sans-Peur, Duke of Burgundy, to set his conscience at rest—he had assassinated the Duke of Orleans. Alas! Those good old times are gone, when a murderer could wipe the stain from his name and soothe his troubles to sleep simply by getting out his bricks and mortar and building an addition to a church.

The portals of the great western front are bisected by square pillars. They took the central one away, in 1852, on the occasion of thanksgivings for the reinstitution of the Presidential power—but precious soon they had occasion to reconsider that motion and put it back again! And they did.

We loitered through the grand aisles for an hour or two, staring up at the rich stained-glass windows embellished with blue and yellow and crimson saints and martyrs, and trying to admire the numberless great pictures in the chapels, and then we were admitted to the sacristy and shown the magnificent robes which the Pope wore when he crowned Napoleon I.; a wagon-load of solid gold and silver utensils used in the great public processions and ceremonies of the church; some nails of the true cross, a fragment of the cross itself, a part of the crown of thorns. We had already seen a large piece of the true cross in a church in the Azores, but no nails. They showed us likewise the bloody robe which that Archbishop of Paris wore who exposed his sacred person and braved the wrath of the insurgents of 1848, to mount the barricades and hold aloft the olive branch of peace in the hope of stopping the slaughter. His noble effort cost him his life. He was shot dead. They showed us a cast of his face, taken after death, the bullet that killed him, and the two vertebræ in which it lodged. These people have a somewhat singular taste in the matter of relics. Ferguson [1] told us that the silver cross which the good archbishop wore at his girdle was seized and thrown into the Seine, where it lay embedded in the mud for fifteen years, and then an angel appeared to a priest and told him where to dive for it; he *did* dive for it and got it, and now it is there on exhibition at Notre Dame, to be inspected by

1 Mark Twain's nickname for a French guide. He liked the name so well that he applied it to all subsequent guides wherever he went on this first trip abroad.—C. N.

anybody who feels an interest in inanimate objects of miraculous intervention.

Next we went to visit the Morgue, that horrible receptacle for the dead who die mysteriously and leave the manner of their taking off a dismal secret. We stood before a grating and looked through into a room which was hung all about with the clothing of dead men; coarse blouses, water-soaked; the delicate garments of women and children; patrician vestments, flecked and stabbed and stained with red; a hat that was crushed and bloody. On a slanting stone lay a drowned man, naked, swollen, purple; clasping the fragment of a broken bush with a grip which death had so petrified that human strength could not unloose it—mute witness of the last despairing effort to save the life that was doomed beyond all help. A stream of water trickled ceaselessly over the hideous face. We knew that the body and the clothing were there for identification by friends, but still we wondered if anybody could love that repulsive object or grieve for its loss. We grew meditative and wondered if, some forty years ago, when the mother of that ghastly thing was dangling it upon her knee, and kissing it and petting it and displaying it with satisfied pride to the passers-by, a prophetic vision of this dread ending ever flitted through her brain. I half feared that the mother, or the wife or a brother of the dead man might come while we stood there, but nothing of the kind occurred. Men and women came, and some looked eagerly in, and pressed their faces against the bars; others glanced carelessly at the body, and turned away with a disappointed look—people, I thought, who live upon strong excitements, and who attend the exhibitions of the Morgue regularly, just as other people go to see theatrical spectacles every night. When one of these looked in and passed on, I could not help thinking—

"Now this don't afford you any satisfaction—a party with his head shot off is what *you* need."

One night we went to the celebrated Jardin Mabille, but only stayed a little while. We wanted to see some of this kind of Paris life, however, and therefore the next night we went to a similar place of entertainment in a great garden in the suburb of Asnières. We went to the railroad depot, toward evening, and Ferguson got tickets for a second-class carriage. Such a perfect jam of people I have not often seen—but there was no noise, no disorder, no rowdyism. Some of the women and young girls that entered the train we knew to be of the *demi-monde,* but others we were not at all sure about.

The girls and women in our carriage behaved themselves modestly and becomingly all the way out, except that they smoked. When we arrived at the garden in Asnières, we paid a franc or two admission, and entered a place which had flower-beds in it, and grass-plats, and long, curving rows of ornamental shrubbery, with here and there a secluded bower convenient for eating ice-cream in. We moved along the sinuous gravel walks, with the great concourse of girls and young men, and suddenly a domed and filigreed white temple, starred over and over and over again with brilliant gas-jets, burst upon us like a fallen sun. Near by was a large, handsome house with its ample front illuminated in the same way, and above its roof floated the Star-Spangled Banner of America.

"Well!" I said. "How is this?" It nearly took my breath away.

Ferguson said an American—a New-Yorker—kept the place, and was carrying on quite a stirring opposition to the Jardin Mabille.

Crowds, composed of both sexes and nearly all ages, were frisking about the garden or sitting in the open air in front of the flagstaff and the temple, drinking wine and coffee, or smoking. The dancing had not begun yet. Ferguson said there was to be an exhibition. The famous Blondin was going to perform on a tight rope in another part of the garden. We went thither. Here the light was dim, and the masses of people were pretty closely packed together. And now I made a mistake which any donkey might make, but a sensible man never. I committed an error which I find myself repeating every day of my life. Standing right before a young lady, I said:

"Dan,[1] just look at this girl, how beautiful she is!"

"I thank you more for the evident sincerity of the compliment, sir, than for the extraordinary publicity you have given to it!" This in good, pure English.

We took a walk, but my spirits were very, very sadly dampened. I did not feel right comfortable for some time afterward. Why *will* people be so stupid as to suppose themselves the only foreigners among a crowd of ten thousand persons?

[1] Dan Slote, of New York City, Mark Twain's cabin-mate. C. N.

But Blondin came out shortly. He appeared on a stretched cable, far away above the sea of tossing hats and handkerchiefs, and in the glare of the hundreds of rockets that whizzed heavenward by him he looked like a wee insect. He balanced his pole and walked the length of his rope—two or three hundred feet; he came back and got a man and carried him across; he returned to the center and danced a jig; next he performed some gymnastic and balancing feats too perilous to afford a pleasant spectacle; and he finished by fastening to his person a thousand Roman candles, Catherine wheels, serpents and rockets of all manner of brilliant colors, setting them on fire all at once and walking and waltzing across his rope again in a blinding blaze of glory that lit up the garden and the people's faces like a great conflagration at midnight.

The dance had begun, and we adjourned to the temple. Within it was a drinking-saloon; and all around it was a broad circular platform for the dancers. I backed up against the wall of the temple, and waited. Twenty sets formed, the music struck up, and then—I placed my hands before my face for very shame. But I looked through my fingers. They were dancing the renowned "Can-can." A handsome girl in the set before me tripped forward lightly to meet the opposite gentleman—tripped back again, grasped her dresses vigorously on both sides with her hands, raised them pretty high, danced an extraordinary jig that had more activity and exposure about it than any jig I ever saw before, and then, drawing her clothes still higher, she advanced gaily to the center and launched a vicious kick full at her *vis-à-vis* that must infallibly have removed his nose if he had been seven feet high. It was a mercy he was only six.

That is the Can-can. The idea of it is to dance as wildly, as noisily, as furiously as you can; expose yourself as much as possible if you are a woman; and kick as high as you can, no matter which sex you belong to. There is no word of exaggeration in this. Any of the staid, respectable, aged people who were there that night can testify to the truth of that statement. There were a good many such people present. I suppose French morality is not of that strait-laced description which is shocked at trifles.

I moved aside and took a general view of the Can-can. Shouts, laughter, furious music, a bewildering chaos of darting and intermingling forms, stormy jerking and snatching of gay dresses, bobbing heads, flying arms, lightning flashes of white-stockinged calves and dainty slippers in the air, and then a grand final rush, riot, a terrific hubbub, and a wild stampede! Heavens! Nothing like it has been seen on earth since trembling Tam O'Shanter saw the devil and the witches at their orgies that stormy night in "Alloway's auld haunted kirk."

We visited the Louvre, at a time when we had no silk purchases in view, and looked at its miles of paintings by the old masters. Some of them were beautiful, but at the same time they carried such evidences about them of the cringing spirit of those great men that we found small pleasure in examining them. Their nauseous adulation of princely patrons was more prominent to me and chained my attention more surely than the charms of color and expression which are claimed to be in the pictures. Gratitude for kindnesses is well, but it seems to me that some of those artists carried it so far that it ceased to be gratitude, and became worship. If there is a plausible excuse for the worship of men, then by all means let us forgive Rubens and his brethren.

But I will drop the subject, lest I say something about the old masters that might as well be left unsaid.

Of course we drove in the Bois de Boulogne, that limitless park, with its forests, its lakes, its cascades, and its broad avenues. There were thousands upon thousands of vehicles abroad, and the scene was full of life and gaiety. There were very common hacks, with father and mother and all the children in them; conspicuous little open carriages with celebrated ladies of questionable reputation in them; there were Dukes and Duchesses abroad, with gorgeous outriders perched on each of the six horses; there were blue and silver, and green and gold, and pink and black, and all sorts and descriptions of stunning and startling liveries out, and I almost yearned to be a flunkey myself, for the sake of the fine clothes.

But presently the Emperor came along and he outshone them all. He was preceded by a bodyguard of gentlemen on horseback in showy uniforms, his carriage-horses (there appeared to be somewhere in the remote neighborhood of a thousand of them) were bestridden by gallant-looking fellows, also in stylish uniforms, and after the carriage followed another detachment of body-guards. Everybody got out of the way; everybody bowed to the Emperor and his friend the Sultan, and they went by on a swinging trot and disappeared.

I will not describe the Bois de Boulogne. I cannot do it. It is simply a beautiful, cultivated, endless, wonderful wilderness. It is an enchanting place. It is in Paris, now, one may say, but a crumbling old cross in one portion of it reminds one that it was not always so. The cross marks the spot where a celeberated troubadour was waylaid and murdered in the fourteenth century. It was in this park that that fellow with an unpronounceable name made the attempt upon the Russian Czar's life last spring with a pistol. The bullet struck a tree. Ferguson showed us the place. Now in America that interesting tree would be chopped down or forgotten within the next five years, but it will be treasured here. The guides will point it out to visitors for the next eight hundred years, and when it decays and falls down they will put up another there and go on with the same old story just the same.

In Paris we often saw in shop windows the sign, "English Spoken Here," just as one sees in the windows at home the sign, *"Ici on parle français."* We always invaded these places at once—and invariably received the information, framed in faultless French, that the clerk who did the English for the establishment had just gone to dinner and would be back in an hour—would Monsieur buy something? We wondered why those parties happened to take their dinners at such erratic and extraordinary hours, for we never called at a time when an exemplary Christian would be in the least likely to be abroad on such an errand. The truth was, it was a base fraud —a snare to trap the unwary—chaff to catch fledglings with. They had no English-murdering clerk. They trusted to the sign to inveigle foreigners into their lairs, and trusted to their own blandishments to keep them there till they bought something.

We ferreted out another French imposition—a frequent sign to this effect: "ALL MANNER OF AMERICAN DRINKS ARTISTICALLY PREPARED HERE." We procured the services of a gentleman experienced in the nomenclature of the American bar, and moved upon the works of one of these impostors. A bowing, aproned Frenchman skipped forward and said:

"Que voulez les messieurs?" I do not know what *"Que voulez les messieurs?"* means, but such was his remark.

Our General said, "We will take a whisky-straight."

[A stare from the Frenchman.]

"Well, if you don't know what that is, give us a champagne cocktail."

[A stare and a shrug.]

"Well, then, give us a sherry cobbler."

The Frenchman was checkmated. This was all Greek to him.

"Give us a brandy smash!"

The Frenchman began to back away, suspicious of the ominous vigor of the last order—began to back away, shrugging his shoulders and spreading his hands apologetically.

The General followed him up and gained a complete victory. The uneducated foreigner could not even furnish a Santa Cruz Punch, an Eye-Opener, a Stone-Fence, or an Earthquake. It was plain that he was a wicked impostor.

An acquaintance of mine said, the other day, that he was doubtless the only American visitor to the Exposition who had had the high honor of being escorted by the Emperor's body-guard. I said with unobtrusive frankness that I was astonished that such a long-legged, lantern-jawed, unprepossessing-looking specter as he should be singled out for a distinction like that, and asked how it came about. He said he had attended a great military review in the Champ de Mars, some time ago, and while the multitude about him was growing thicker and thicker every moment, he observed an open space inside the railing. He left his carriage and went into it. He was the only person there, and so he had plenty of room, and the situation being central, he could see all the preparations going on about the field. By and by there was a sound of music, and soon the Emperor of the French and the Emperor of Austria, escorted by the famous Cent Gardes, entered the inclosure. They seemed not to observe him, but directly, in response to a sign from the commander of the Guard, a young lieutenant came toward him with a file of his men following, halted, raised his hand and gave the military salute, and then said in a low voice that he was sorry to have to disturb a stranger and a gentleman, but the place was sacred to royalty. Then this New Jersey phantom rose up and bowed and begged pardon, then with the officer beside him, the file of men marching behind him, and with every mark of respect, he was escorted to his carriage by the imperial Cent Gardes! The officer saluted again and fell back, the New Jersey sprite bowed in return and had presence of mind enough to pretend that he had simply called on a matter of private business with those emperors, and so waved them an adieu, and drove from the field!

Imagine a poor Frenchman ignorantly intruding upon a public rostrum sacred to some sixpenny dignitary in America. The police would scare him to death, first, with a storm of their elegant blasphemy, and then pull him to pieces getting him away from there. We are measurably superior to the French in some things, but they are immeasurably our betters in others.

Enough of Paris for the present. We have done our whole duty by it. We have seen the Tuileries, the Napoleon Column, the Madeleine, that wonder of wonders the tomb of Napoleon, all the great churches and museums, libraries, imperial palaces, and sculpture and picture galleries, the Pantheon, Jardin des Plantes, the opera, the circus, the legislative body, the billiard-rooms, the barbers, the grisettes—

Ah, the grisettes! I had almost forgotten. They are another romantic fraud. They were (if you let the books of travel tell it) always so beautiful—so neat and trim, so graceful—so naïve and trusting—so gentle, so winning—so faithful to their shop duties, so irresistible to buyers in their prattling importunity—so devoted to their poverty-stricken students of the Latin Quarter—so light-hearted and happy on their Sunday picnics in the suburbs—and oh, so charmingly, so delightfully immoral!

Stuff! For three or four days I was constantly saying:

"Quick, Ferguson! is that a grisette?"

And he always said "No."

He comprehended, at last, that I wanted to see a grisette. Then he showed me dozens of them. They were like nearly all the Frenchwomen I ever saw—homely. They had large hands, large feet, large mouths; they had pug-noses as a general thing, and mustaches that not even good breeding could overlook; they combed their hair straight back without parting; they were ill-shaped, they were not winning, they were not graceful; I knew by their looks that they ate garlic and onions; and lastly and finally, to my thinking it would be base flattery to call them immoral.

Aroint thee, wench! I sorrow for the vagabond student of the

Latin Quarter now, even more than formerly I envied him. Thus topples to earth another idol of my infancy.

We have seen everything, and to-morrow we go to Versailles. We shall see Paris only for a little while as we come back to take up our line of march for the ship, and so I may as well bid the beautiful city a regretful farewell. We shall travel many thousands of miles after we leave here, and visit many great cities, but we shall find none so enchanting as this.

Some of our party have gone to England, intending to take a roundabout course and rejoin the vessel at Leghorn or Naples, several weeks hence. We came near going to Geneva, but have concluded to return to Marseilles and go up through Italy from Genoa.

I will conclude this chapter with a remark that I am sincerely proud to be able to make—and glad, as well, that my comrades cordially indorse it, to wit: by far the handsomest women we have seen in France were born and reared in America.

I feel, now, like a man who has redeemed a failing reputation and shed luster upon a dimned escutcheon, by a single just deed done at the eleventh hour.

Let the curtain fall, to slow music.

From *The Innocents Abroad,* 1869.

18 : Versailles

VERSAILLES! It is wonderfully beautiful! You gaze, and stare, and try to understand that it is real, that it is on the earth, that it is not the Garden of Eden—but your brain grows giddy, stupefied by the world of beauty around you, and you half believe you are the dupe of an exquisite dream. The scene thrills one like military music! A noble palace, stretching its ornamented front block upon block away, till it seemed that it would never end; a grand promenade before it, whereon the armies of an empire might parade; all about it rainbows of flowers, and colossal statues that were almost numberless, and yet seemed only scattered over the ample space; broad flights of stone steps leading down from the promenade to lower grounds of the park—stairways that whole regiments might stand to arms upon and have room to spare; vast fountains whose great bronze effigies discharged rivers of sparkling water into the air and mingled a hundred curving jets together in forms of matchless beauty; wide grass-carpeted avenues that branched hither and thither in every direction and wandered to seemingly interminable distances, walled all the way on either side with compact ranks of leafy trees whose branches met above and formed arches as faultless and as symmetrical as ever were carved in stone; and here and there were glimpses of sylvan lakes with miniature ships glassed in their surfaces. And everywhere—on the palace steps, and the great promenade, around the fountains, among the trees, and far under the arches of the endless avenues, hundreds and hundreds of people in gay costumes walked or ran or danced, and gave to the fairy picture the life and animation which was all of perfection it could have lacked.

It was worth a pilgrimage to see. Everything is on so gigantic a scale. Nothing is small—nothing is cheap. The statues are all large; the palace is grand; the park covers a fair-sized county; the avenues are interminable. All the distances and all the dimensions about Versailles are vast. I used to think the pictures exaggerated these distances and these dimensions beyond all reason, and that they made Versailles more beautiful than it was possible for any place in the world to be. I know now that the pictures never came up to the subject in any respect, and that no painter could represent Versailles on canvas as beautiful as it is in reality. I used to abuse Louis XIV. for spending two hundred millions of dollars in creating this marvelous park, when bread was so scarce with some of his subjects; but I have forgiven him now. He took a tract of land sixty miles in circumference and set to work to make this park and build this palace and a road to it from Paris. He kept 36,000 men employed daily on it, and the labor was so unhealthy that they used to die and be hauled off by cart-loads every night. The wife of a nobleman of the time speaks of this as an *"inconvenience,"* but naïvely remarks that "it does not seem worthy of attention in the happy state of tranquillity we now enjoy."

I always thought ill of people at home, who trimmed their shrubbery into pyramids and squares and spires and all manner of unnatural shapes, and when I saw the same thing being practised in this great park I began to feel dissatisfied. But I soon saw the idea of the thing and the wisdom of it. They seek the *general* effect. We distort a dozen sickly trees into unaccustomed shapes in a little yard no bigger than a dining-room, and then surely they look absurd enough. But here they take two hundred thousand tall forest trees and set them in a double row; allow no sign of leaf or branch to grow on the trunk lower down than six feet above the ground; from that point the boughs begin to project, and very gradually they extend outward further and further till they meet overhead, and a faultless tunnel of foliage is formed. The arch is mathematically precise. The effect is then very fine. They make trees take fifty different shapes, and so these quaint effects are infinitely varied and picturesque. The trees in no two avenues are shaped alike, and consequently the eye is not fatigued with anything in the nature of monotonous uniformity. I will drop this subject now, leaving it to others to determine how these people manage to make endless ranks of lofty forest trees grow to just a certain thickness of trunk (say a foot and two-thirds); how they make them spring to precisely the same height for miles; how they make them grow so close together; how they compel one huge limb to spring from the same identical spot on each tree and form the main sweep of the arch; and how all these things are kept exactly in the same condition, and in the same exquisite shapeliness and symmetry month after month and year after year—for I have tried to reason out the problem, and have failed.

We walked through the great hall of sculpture and the one hundred and fifty galleries of paintings in the palace of Versailles, and felt that to be in such a place was useless unless one had a whole year at his disposal. These pictures are all battle-scenes, and only one solitary little canvas among them all treats of anything but great French victories. We wandered, also, through the Grand Trianon and the Petit Trianon, those monuments of royal prodigality, and with histories so mournful—filled, as it is, with souvenirs of Napoleon the First, and three dead kings and as many queens. In one sumptuous bed they had all slept in succession, but no one occupies it now. In a large dining-room stood the table at which Louis XIV. and his mistress, Madame Maintenon, and after them

Louis XV., and Pompadour, had sat at their meals naked and unattended—for the table stood upon a trap-door, which descended with it to regions below when it was necessary to replenish its dishes. In a room of the Petit Trianon stood the furniture, just as poor Marie Antoinette left it when the mob came and dragged her and the King to Paris, never to return. Near at hand, in the stables, were prodigious carriages that showed no color but gold—carriages used by former kings of France on state occasions, and never used now save when a kingly head is to be crowned, or an imperial infant christened. And with them were some curious sleighs, whose bodies were shaped like lions, swans, tigers, etc.—vehicles that had once been handsome with pictured designs and fine workmanship, but were dusty and decaying now. They had their history. When Louis XIV. had finished the Grand Trianon, he told Maintenon he had created a Paradise for her, and asked if she could think of anything now to wish for. He said he wished the Trianon to be perfection—nothing less. She said she could think of but one thing—it was summer, and it was balmy France—yet she would like well to sleigh-ride in the leafy avenues of Versailles! The next morning found miles and miles of grassy avenues spread thick with snowy salt and sugar, and a procession of those quaint sleighs waiting to receive the chief concubine of the gayest and most unprincipled court that France has ever seen!

From sumptuous Versailles, with its palaces, its statues, its gardens and its fountains, we journeyed back to Paris and sought its antipodes—the Faubourg St. Antoine. Little, narrow streets; dirty children blockading them; greasy, slovenly women capturing and spanking them; filthy dens on first floors, with rag stores in them (the heaviest business in the Faubourg is the chiffonier's); other filthy dens where whole suits of second and third hand clothing are sold at prices that would ruin any proprietor who did not steal his stock; still other filthy dens where they sold groceries—sold them by the halfpennyworth—five dollars would buy the man out, good will and all. Up these little crooked streets they will murder a man for seven dollars and dump the body in the Seine. And up some other of these streets—most of them, I should say—live lorettes.

All through this Faubourg St. Antoine, misery, poverty, vice, and crime go hand in hand, and the evidences of it stare one in the face from every side. Here the people live who begin the revolutions. Whenever there is anything of that kind to be done, they are always ready. They take as much genuine pleasure in building a barricade as they do in cutting a throat or shoving a friend into the Seine. It is these savage-looking ruffians who storm the splendid halls of the Tuileries, occasionally, and swarm into Versailles when a king is to be called to account.

But they will build no more barricades, they will break no more soldiers' heads with paving-stones. Louis Napoleon has taken care of all that. He is annihilating the crooked streets, and building in their stead noble boulevards as straight as an arrow—avenues which a cannon-ball could traverse from end to end without meeting an obstruction more irresistible than the flesh and bones of men—boulevards whose stately edifices will never afford refuges and plotting-places for starving, discontented revolution-breeders. Five of these great thoroughfares radiate from one ample center—a center which is exceedingly well adapted to the accommodation of heavy artillery. The mobs used to riot there, but they must seek another rallying-place in future. And this ingenious Napoleon paves the streets of his great cities with a smooth, compact composition of asphaltum and sand. No more barricades of flagstones—no more assaulting his Majesty's troops with cobbles. I cannot feel friendly toward my quondam fellow-American, Napoleon III., especially at this time,[1] when in fancy I see his credulous victim, Maximilian, lying stark and stiff in Mexico, and his maniac widow watching eagerly from her French asylum for the form that will never come—but I do admire his nerve, his calm self-reliance, his shrewd good sense.

From *The Innocents Abroad,* 1869.

[1] July, 1867.—M. T.

19 : *Milan*

"DO YOU WIS ZO HAUT CAN BE?"

That was what the guide asked, when we were looking up at the bronze horses on the Arch of Peace. It meant, Do you wish to go up there? I give it as a specimen of guide-English. These are the people that make life a burthen to the tourist. Their tongues are never still. They talk forever and forever, and that is the kind of billingsgate they use. Inspiration itself could hardly comprehend them. If they would only show you a masterpiece of art, or a venerable tomb, or a prison-house, or a battle-field, hallowed by touching memories, or historical reminiscences, or grand traditions, and then step aside and hold still for ten minutes and let you think, it would not be so bad. But they interrupt every dream, every pleasant train of thought, with their tiresome cackling. Sometimes when I have been standing before some cherished old idol of mine that I remembered years and years ago in pictures in the geography at school, I have thought I would give a whole world if the human parrot at my side would suddenly perish where he stood and leave me to gaze, and ponder, and worship.

No, we did not "wis zo haut can be." We wished to go to La Scala, the largest theater in the world, I think they call it. We did so. It was a large place. Seven separate and distinct masses of humanity —six great circles and a monster parquette.

We wished to go to the Ambrosian Library, and we did that also. We saw a manuscript of Virgil, with annotations in the handwriting of Petrarch, the gentleman who loved another man's Laura, and lavished upon her all through life a love which was a clear waste of the raw material. It was sound sentiment, but bad judgment. It brought both parties fame, and created a fountain of commiseration for them in sentimental breasts that is running yet. But who says a word in behalf of poor Mr. Laura? (I do not know his other name.) Who glorifies him? Who bedews him with tears? Who writes poetry about him? Nobody. How do you suppose *he* liked the state of things that has given the world so much pleasure? How did he enjoy having another man following his wife everywhere and making her name a familiar word in every garlic-exterminating mouth in Italy with his sonnets to her pre-empted eyebrows? *They* got fame and sympathy—he got neither. This is a peculiarly felicitous instance of what is called poetical justice. It is all very fine; but it does not chime with my notions of right. It is too one-sided—too ungenerous. Let the world go on fretting about Laura and Petrarch if it will; but as for me, my tears and my lamentations shall be lavished upon the unsung defendant.

We saw also an autograph letter of Lucrezia Borgia, a lady for whom I have always entertained the highest respect, on account of her rare histrionic capabilities, her opulence in solid gold goblets made of gilded wood, her high distinction as an operatic screamer, and the facility with which she could order a sextuple funeral and get the corpses ready for it. We saw one single coarse yellow hair from Lucrezia's head, likewise. It awoke emotions, but we still live. In this same library we saw some drawings by Michael Angelo (these Italians call him Mickel Angelo), and Leonardo da Vinci. (They spell it Vinci and pronounce it Vinchy; foreigners always spell better than they pronounce.) We reserve our opinion of these sketches.

In another building they showed us a fresco representing some lions and other beasts drawing chariots; and they seemed to project so far from the wall that we took them to be sculptures. The artist had shrewdly heightened the delusion by painting dust on the creatures' backs, as if it had fallen there naturally and properly. Smart fellow—if it be smart to deceive strangers.

Elsewhere we saw a huge Roman amphitheater, with its stone seats still in good preservation. Modernized, it is now the scene of more peaceful recreations than the exhibition of a party of wild beasts with Christians for dinner. Part of the time, the Milanese use it for a race-track, and at other seasons they flood it with water and have spirited yachting regattas there. The guide told us these things, and he would hardly try so hazardous an experiment as the telling of a falsehood, when it is all he can do to speak the truth in English without getting the lockjaw.

In another place we were shown a sort of summer arbor, with a fence before it. We saw that was nothing. We looked again, and saw, through the arbor, an endless stretch of garden, and shrubbery, and grassy lawn. We were perfectly willing to go in there and rest, but it could not be done. It was only another delusion—a painting by some ingenious artist with little charity in his heart for tired folk. The deception was perfect. No one could have imagined the park was not real. We even thought we smelled the flowers at first.

We got a carriage at twilight and drove in the shaded avenues with the other nobility, and after dinner we took wine and ices in a fine garden with the great public. The music was excellent, the flowers and shrubbery were pleasant to the eye, the scene vivacious, everybody was genteel and well-behaved, and the ladies were slightly mustached, and handsomely dressed, but very homely.

We adjourned to a café and played billiards an hour, and I made six or seven points by the doctor pocketing his ball, and he made as many by my pocketing my ball. We came near making a carom sometimes, but not the one we were trying to make. The table was of the usual European style—cushions dead and twice as high as the balls; the cues in bad repair. The natives play only a sort of pool on them. We have never seen anybody playing the French three-ball game yet, and I doubt if there is any such game known in France, or that there lives any man mad enough to try to play it on one of those European tables. We had to stop playing, finally, because Dan got to sleeping fifteen minutes between the counts and paying no attention to his marking.

Afterward we walked up and down one of the most popular streets for some time, enjoying other people's comfort and wishing we could export some of it to our restless, driving, vitality-consuming marts at home. Just in this one matter lies the main charm of life in Europe—comfort. In America, we hurry—which is well; but when the day's work is done, we go on thinking of losses and gains, we plan for the morrow, we even carry our business cares to bed with us, and toss and worry over them when we ought to be restoring our racked bodies and brains with sleep. We burn up our energies with these excitements, and either die early or drop into a lean and mean old age at a time of life which they call a man's prime in Europe. When an acre of ground has produced long and well, we let it lie fallow and rest for a season; we take no man clear across the continent in the same coach he started in—the coach is stabled somewhere on the plains and its heated machinery allowed to cool for a few days; when a razor has seen long service and refuses to hold an edge, the barber lays it away for a few weeks, and the edge comes back of its own accord. We bestow thoughtful care upon inanimate objects, but none upon ourselves. What a robust people, what a nation of thinkers we might be, if we would only lay ourselves on the shelf occasionally and renew our edges!

I do envy these Europeans the comfort they take. When the work of the day is done, they forget it. Some of them go, with wife and children, to a beer-hall, and sit quietly and genteelly drinking a mug or two of ale and listening to music; others walk the streets, others drive in the avenues; others assemble in the great ornamental squares in the early evening to enjoy the sight and the fragrance of flowers and to hear the military bands play—no European city being without its fine military music at eventide; and yet others of the populace sit in the open air in front of the refreshment-houses and eat ices and drink mild beverages that could not harm a child. They go to bed moderately early, and sleep well. They are always quiet, always orderly, always cheerful, comfortable, and appreciative of life and its manifold blessings. One never sees a drunken man among them. The change that has come over our little party is surprising. Day by day we lose some of our restlessness and absorb some of the spirit of quietude and ease that is in the tranquil atmosphere about us and in the demeanor of the people. We grow wise apace. We begin to comprehend what life is for.

We have had a bath in Milan, in a public bathhouse. They were going to put all three of us in one bathtub, but we objected. Each of us had an Italian farm on his back. We could have felt affluent if we had been officially surveyed and fenced in. We chose to have three bathtubs, and large ones—tubs suited to the dignity of aristocrats who had real estate, and brought it with them. After we were stripped and had taken the first chilly dash, we discovered that haunting atrocity that has embittered our lives in so many cities and villages of Italy and France—there was no soap. I called. A woman answered, and I barely had time to throw myself against the door—she would have been in, in another second. I said:

"Beware, woman! Go away from here—go away, now, or it will

be the worse for you. I am an unprotected male, but I will preserve my honor at the peril of my life!"

These words must have frightened her, for she scurried away very fast.

Dan's voice rose on the air:

"Oh, bring some soap, why don't you!"

The reply was Italian. Dan resumed:

"Soap, you know—soap. That is what I want—soap. S-o-a-p, soap; s-o-p-e, soap; s-o-u-p, soap. Hurry up! I don't know how you Irish spell it, but I want it. Spell it to suit yourself, but fetch it. I'm freezing."

I heard the doctor say, impressively:

"Dan, how often have we told you that these foreigners cannot understand English? Why will you not depend upon us? Why will you not tell *us* what you want, and let us ask for it in the language of the country? It would save us a great deal of the humiliation your reprehensible ignorance causes us. I will address this person in his mother-tongue: 'Here, cospetto! corpo di Bacco! Sacramento! Solferino!—Soap, you son of a gun!' Dan, if you would let *us* talk for you, you would never expose your ignorant vulgarity."

Even this fluent discharge of Italian did not bring the soap at once, but there was a good reason for it. There was not such an article about the establishment. It is my belief that there never had been. They had to send far up-town, and to several different places before they finally got it, so they said. We had to wait twenty or thirty minutes. The same thing had occurred the evening before, at the hotel. I think I have divined the reason for this state of things at last. The English know how to travel comfortably, and they carry soap with them; other foreigners do not use the article.

At every hotel we stop at we always have to send out for soap, at the last moment, when we are grooming ourselves for dinner, and they put it in the bill along with the candles and other nonsense. In Marseilles they make half the fancy toilet soap we consume in America, but the Marseillaise only have a vague theoretical idea of its use, which they have obtained from books of travel, just as they have acquired an uncertain notion of clean shirts, and the peculiarities of the gorilla, and other curious matters. This reminds me of poor Blucher's note to the landlord in Paris:

PARIS, le 7 Juillet.

Monsieur le Landlord—Sir: *Pourquoi* don't you *mettez* some *savon* in your bed-chambers? *Est-ce que vous pensez* I will steal it? *La nuit passée* you charged me *pour deux chandelles* when I only had one; *hier vous avez* charged me *avec glace* when I had none at all; *tous les jours* you are coming some fresh game or other on me, *mais vous ne pouvez pas* play this *savon* dodge on me twice. *Savon* is a necessary *de la vie* to anybody but a Frenchman, *et je l'aurai hors de cet hôtel* or make trouble. You hear *me. Allons.*

BLUCHER.

I remonstrated against the sending of this note, because it was so mixed up that the landlord would never be able to make head or tail of it; but Blucher said he guessed the old man could read the French of it and average the rest.

Blucher's French is bad enough, but it is not much worse than the English one finds in advertisements all over Italy every day. For instance, observe the printed card of the hotel we shall probably stop at on the shores of Lake Como:

NOTISH

This hotel which the best it is in Italy and most superb, is handsome locate on the best situation of the lake, with the most splendid view near the Villas Melzy, to the King of Belgian, and Serbelloni. This hotel have recently enlarge, do offer all commodities on moderate price, at the strangers gentlemen who whish spend the seasons on the Lake Como.

How is that for a specimen? In the hotel is a handsome little chapel where an English clergyman is employed to preach to such of the guests of the house as hail from England and America, and this fact is also set forth in barbarous English in the same advertisement. Wouldn't you have supposed that the adventurous linguist who framed the card would have known enough to submit it to that clergyman before he sent it to the printer?

Here, in Milan, in an ancient tumble-down ruin of a church, is the mournful wreck of the most celebrated painting in the world—"The Last Supper," by Leonardo da Vinci. We are not infallible judges of pictures, but, of course, we went there to see this wonderful painting, once so beautiful, always so worshiped by masters in art, and forever to be famous in song and story. And the first thing that occurred was the infliction on us of a placard fairly reeking with wretched English. Take a morsel of it:

> Bartholomew (that is the first figure on the left hand side at the spectator), uncertain and doubtful about what he thinks to have heard, and upon which he wants to be assured by himself at Christ and by no others.

Good, isn't it? And then Peter is described as "argumenting in a threatening and angrily condition at Judas Iscariot."

This paragraph recalls the picture. "The Last Supper" is painted on the dilapidated wall of what was a little chapel attached to the main church in ancient times, I suppose. It is battered and scarred in every direction, and stained and discolored by time, and Napoleon's horses kicked the legs off most the disciples when they (the horses, not the disciples) were stabled there more than half a century ago.

I recognized the old picture in a moment—the Saviour with bowed head seated at the center of a long, rough table with scattering fruits and dishes upon it, and six disciples on either side in their long robes, talking to each other—the picture from which all engravings and all copies have been made for three centuries. Perhaps no living man has ever known an attempt to paint the Lord's Supper differently. The world seems to have become settled in the belief, long ago, that it is not possible for human genius to outdo this creation of Da Vinci's. I suppose painters will go on copying it as long as any of the original is left visible to the eye. There were a dozen easels in the room, and as many artists transferring the great picture to their canvases. Fifty proofs of steel engravings and lithographs were scattered around, too. And as usual, I could not help noticing how superior the copies were to the original, that is, to my inexperienced eye. Wherever you find a Raphael, a Rubens, a Michael Angelo, a Caracci, or a Da Vinci (and we see them every day) you find artists copying them, and the copies are always the handsomest. Maybe the originals were handsome when they were new, but they are not now.

This picture is about thirty feet long, and ten or twelve high,

I should think, and the figures are at least life-size. It is one of the largest paintings in Europe.

The colors are dimmed with age; the countenances are scaled and marred, and nearly all expression is gone from them; the hair is a dead blur upon the wall, and there is no life in the eyes. Only the attitudes are certain.

People come here from all parts of the world, and glorify this masterpiece. They stand entranced before it with bated breath and parted lips, and when they speak, it is only in the catchy ejaculations of rapture:

"Oh, wonderful!"

"Such expression!"

"Such grace of attitude!"

"Such dignity!"

"Such faultless drawing!"

"Such matchless coloring!"

"Such feeling!"

"What delicacy of touch!"

"What sublimity of conception!"

"A vision! a vision!"

I only envy these people; I envy them their honest admiration, if it be honest—their delight, if they feel delight. I harbor no animosity toward any of them. But at the same time the thought *will* intrude itself upon me, How can they see what is not visible? What would you think of a man who looked at some decayed, blind, toothless, pock-marked Cleopatra, and said: "What matchless beauty! What soul! What expression!" What would you think of a man who gazed upon a dingy, foggy sunset, and said: "What sublimity! what feeling! what richness of coloring!" What would you think of a man who stared in ecstasy upon a desert of stumps and said: "Oh, my soul, my beating heart, what a noble forest is here!"

You would think that those men had an astonishing talent for seeing things that had already passed away. It was what I thought when I stood before the "Last Supper" and heard men apostrophizing wonders and beauties and perfections which had faded out of the picture and gone, a hundred years before they were born. We can imagine the beauty that was once in an aged face; we can imagine the forest if we see the stumps; but we cannot absolutely *see* these things when they are not there. I am willing to believe that the eye of the practised artist can rest upon the "Last Supper" and renew a luster where only a hint of it is left, supply a tint that has faded away, restore an expression that is gone; patch, and color, and add to the dull canvas until at last its figures shall stand before him aglow with life, the feeling, the freshness, yea, with all the noble beauty that was theirs when first they came from the hand of the master. But *I* cannot work this miracle. Can those other uninspired visitors do it, or do they only happily imagine they do?

After reading so much about it, I am satisfied that the "Last Supper" was a very miracle of art once. But it was three hundred years ago.

It vexes me to hear people talk so glibly of "feeling," "expression," "tone," and those other easily acquired and inexpensive technicalities of art that make such a fine show in conversations concerning pictures. There is not one man in seventy-five hundred that can tell *what* a pictured face is intended to express. There is not one man in five hundred that can go into a court-room and be sure that he will not mistake some harmless innocent of a juryman for the black-hearted assassin on trial. Yet such people talk of "character" and presume to interpret "expression" in pictures. There is an old story that Matthews, the actor, was once lauding the ability of the human face to express the passions and emotions hidden in the breast. He said the countenance could disclose what was passing in the heart plainer than the tongue could.

"Now," he said, "observe my face—what does it express?"

"Despair!"

"Bah, it expresses peaceful resignation! What does *this* express?"

"Rage!"

"Stuff! it means terror! *This!*"

"Imbecility!"

"Fool! It is smothered ferocity! Now *this!*"

"Joy!"

"Oh, perdition! *Any* ass can see it means insanity!"

Expression! People coolly pretend to read it who would think themselves presumptuous if they pretended to interpret the hieroglyphics on the obelisk of Luxor—yet they are fully as competent to do the one thing as the other. I have heard two very intelligent critics speak of Murillo's "Immaculate Conception" (now in the museum at Seville) within the past few days. One said:

"Oh, the Virgin's face is full of the ecstasy of a joy that is complete—that leaves nothing more to be desired on earth!"

The other said:

"Ah, that wonderful face is so humble, so pleading—it says as plainly as words could say it: 'I fear; I tremble; I am unworthy. But Thy will be done; sustain Thou Thy servant!' "

The reader can see the picture in any drawing-room; it can be easily recognized; the Virgin (the only young and really beautiful Virgin that was ever painted by one of the old masters, some of us think) stands in the crescent of the new moon, with a multitude of cherubs hovering about her, and more coming; her hands are crossed upon her breast, and upon her uplifted countenance falls a glory out of the heavens. The reader may amuse himself, if he chooses, in trying to determine which of these gentlemen read the Virgin's "expression" aright, or if either of them did it.

Any one who is acquainted with the old masters will comprehend how much the "Last Supper" is damaged when I say that the spectator cannot really tell, now, whether the disciples are Hebrews or Italians. These ancient painters never succeeded in denationalizing themselves. The Italian artists painted Italian Virgins, the Dutch painted Dutch Virgins, the Virgins of the French painters were Frenchwomen—none of them ever put into the face of the Madonna that indescribable something which proclaims the Jewess, whether you find her in New York, in Constantinople, in Paris, Jerusalem, or in the Empire of Morocco. I saw in the Sandwich Islands, once, a picture, copied by a talented German artist from an engraving in one of the American illustrated papers. It was an allegory, representing Mr. Davis in the act of signing a secession act or some such document. Over him hovered the ghost of Washington in warning attitude, and in the background a troop of shadowy soldiers in Continental uniform were limping with shoeless, bandaged feet through a driving snow-storm. Valley Forge was suggested, of course. The copy seemed accurate, and yet there was a discrepancy somewhere. After a long examination I discovered what it was—the shadowy soldiers were all Germans! Jeff Davis was a German! even the hovering ghost was a German ghost! The artist had unconsciously worked his nationality into the picture. To tell the truth, I am getting a little perplexed about John the Baptist and his portraits. In France I finally grew reconciled to him as a Frenchman;

here he is unquestionably an Italian. What next? Can it be possible that the painters make John the Baptist a Spaniard in Madrid and an Irishman in Dublin?

We took an open barouche and drove two miles out of Milan to "see ze echo," as the guide expressed it. The road was smooth, it was bordered by trees, fields, and grassy meadows, and the soft air was filled with the odor of flowers. Troops of picturesque peasant-girls, coming from work, hooted at us, shouted at us, made all manner of game of us, and entirely delighted me. My long-cherished judgment was confirmed. I always did think those frowsy, romantic, unwashed peasant-girls I had read so much about in poetry were a glaring fraud.

We enjoyed our jaunt. It was an exhilarating relief from tiresome sight-seeing.

We distressed ourselves very little about the astonishing echo the guide talked so much about. We were growing accustomed to encomiums on wonders that too often proved no wonders at all. And so we were most happily disappointed to find in the sequel that the guide had even failed to rise to the magnitude of his subject.

We arrived at a tumble-down old rookery called the Palazzo Simonetti—a massive hewn-stone affair occupied by a family of ragged Italians. A good-looking young girl conducted us to a window on the second floor which looked out on a court walled on three sides by tall buildings. She put her head out at the window and shouted. The echo answered more times than we could count. She took a speaking-trumpet and through it she shouted, sharp and quick, a single

"Ha!" The echo answered:

"Ha————ha! !———ha!——ha!——ha!—ha! ha!h-a-a-a-a!" and finally went off into a rollicking convulsion of the jolliest laughter that could be imagined. It was so joyful, so long-continued, so perfectly cordial and hearty, that everybody was forced to join in. There was no resisting it.

Then the girl took a gun and fired it. We stood ready to count the astonishing clatter of reverberations. We could not say one, two, three, fast enough, but we could dot our note-books with our pencil-points almost rapidly enough to take down a sort of shorthand report of the result. My page revealed the following account. I could not keep up, but I did as well as I could.

I set down fifty-two distinct repetitions, and then the echo got the advantage of me. The doctor set down sixty-four, and thenceforth the echo moved too fast for him, also. After the separate concussions could no longer be noted, the reverberations dwindled to a wild, long-sustained clatter of sounds such as a watchman's rattle produces. It is likely that this is the most remarkable echo in the world.

The doctor, in jest, offered to kiss the young girl, for a franc! The commonest gallantry compelled him to stand by his offer, and so he paid the franc and took the kiss. She was a philosopher. She said a franc was a good thing to have, and she did not care anything for one paltry kiss, because she had a million left. Then our comrade, always a shrewd business man, offered to take the whole cargo at thirty days, but that little financial scheme was a failure.

From *The Innocents Abroad,* 1869.

20 : Venice

THIS VENICE, which was a haughty, invincible, magnificent Republic for nearly fourteen hundred years; whose armies compelled the world's applause whenever and wherever they battled; whose navies well nigh held dominion of the seas, and whose merchant fleets whitened the remotest oceans with their sails and loaded these piers with the products of every clime, is fallen a prey to poverty, neglect and melancholy decay. Six hundred years ago, Venice was the Autocrat of Commerce; her mart was the great commercial center, the distributing-house from whence the enormous trade of the Orient was spread abroad over the Western world. To-day her piers are deserted, her warehouses are empty, her merchant fleets are vanished, her armies and her navies are but memories. Her glory is departed, and with her crumbling grandeur of wharves and palaces about her she sits among her stagnant lagoons, forlorn and beggared, forgotten of the world. She, that in her palmy days commanded the commerce of a hemisphere and made the weal or woe of nations with a beck of her puissant finger, is become the humblest among the peoples of the earth,—a peddler of glass beads for women, and trifling toys and trinkets for school-girls and children.

The venerable Mother of the Republics is scarce a fit subject for flippant speech or the idle gossiping of tourists. It seems a sort of sacrilege to disturb the glamour of old romance that pictures her to us softly from afar off as through a tinted mist, and curtains her ruin and her desolation from our view. One ought, indeed, to turn away from her rags, her poverty, and her humiliation, and think of her only as she was when she sunk the fleets of Charlemagne; when she humbled Frederick Barbarossa or waved her victorious banners above the battlements of Constantinople.

We reached Venice at eight in the evening, and entered a hearse belonging to the Grand Hotel d'Europe. At any rate, it was more like a hearse than anything else, though, to speak by the card, it was a gondola. And this was the storied gondola of Venice!—the fairy boat in which the princely cavaliers of the olden time were wont to cleave the waters of the moonlit canals and look the eloquence of love into the soft eyes of patrician beauties, while the gay gondolier in silken doublet touched his guitar and sang as only gondoliers can sing! This the famed gondola and this the gorgeous gondolier!—the one an inky, rusty old canoe with a sable hearse-body clapped on to the middle of it, and the other a mangy, barefooted gutter-snipe with a portion of his raiment on exhibition which should have been sacred from public scrutiny. Presently, as he turned a corner and shot his hearse into a dismal ditch between two long rows of towering, untenanted buildings, the gay gondolier began to sing, true to the traditions of his race. I stood it a little while. Then I said:

"Now, here, Roderigo Gonzales Michael Angelo, I'm a pilgrim, and I'm a stranger, but I am not going to have my feelings lacerated by any such caterwauling as that. If that goes on, one of us has got to take water. It is enough that my cherished dreams of Venice have been blighted forever as to the romantic gondola and the gorgeous gondolier; this system of destruction shall go no farther; I will accept the hearse, under protest, and you may fly your flag of truce in peace, but here I register a dark and bloody oath that you sha'n't sing. Another yelp, and overboard you go."

I began to feel that the old Venice of song and story had departed forever. But I was too hasty. In a few minutes we swept gracefully out into the Grand Canal, and under the mellow moonlight the Venice of poetry and romance stood revealed. Right from the water's edge rose long lines of stately palaces of marble; gondolas were gliding swiftly hither and thither and disappearing suddenly through unsuspected gates and alleys; ponderous stone bridges threw their shadows athwart the glittering waves. There was life and motion everywhere, and yet everywhere there was a hush, a stealthy sort of stillness, that was suggestive of secret enterprises of bravoes and of lovers; and, clad half in moonbeams and half in mysterious shadows, the grim old mansions of the Republic seemed to have an expression about them of having an eye for just such enterprises as these at that same moment. Music came floating over the waters—Venice was complete.

It was a beautiful picture—very soft and dreamy and beautiful. But what was this Venice to compare with the Venice of midnight? Nothing. There was a fête—a grand fête in honor of some saint who had been instrumental in checking the cholera three hundred years ago, and all Venice was abroad on the water. It was no common affair, for the Venetians did not know how soon they might need the saint's services again, now that the cholera was spreading everywhere. So in one vast space—say a third of a mile wide and two miles long—were collected two thousand gondolas, and every one of them had from two to ten, twenty, and even thirty colored lanterns suspended about it, and from four to a dozen occupants. Just as far as the eye could reach, these painted lights were massed together—like a vast garden of many-colored flowers, except that these blossoms were never still; they were ceaselessly gliding in and out, and mingling together, and seducing you into bewildering attempts to follow their mazy evolutions. Here and there a strong red, green, or blue glare from a rocket that was struggling to get away splendidly illuminated all the boats around it. Every gondola that swam by us, with its crescents and pyramids and circles of colored lamps hung aloft, and lighting up the faces of the young and the sweet-scented and lovely below, was a picture; and the reflections of those lights, so long, so slender, so numberless, so many-colored and so distorted and wrinkled by the waves, was a picture likewise, and one that was enchantingly beautiful. Many and many a party of young ladies and gentlemen had their state gondolas handsomely decorated, and ate supper on board, bringing their swallow-tailed, white-cravatted varlets to wait upon them, and having their tables tricked out as if for a bridal supper. They had brought along the costly globe lamps from their drawing-rooms, and the lace and silken curtains from the same places, I suppose. And they had also brought pianos and guitars, and they played and sang operas, while the plebeian paper-lanterned gondolas from the suburbs and the back alleys crowded around to stare and listen.

There was music everywhere—choruses, string-bands, brass-bands, flutes, everything. I was so surrounded, walled in with music, magnificence, and loveliness, that I became inspired with the spirit of the scene, and sang one tune myself. However, when I observed that the other gondolas had sailed away, and my gondolier was preparing to go overboard, I stopped.

The fête was magnificent. They kept it up the whole night long, and I never enjoyed myself better than I did while it lasted.

What a funny old city this Queen of the Adriatic is! Narrow streets, vast, gloomy marble palaces, black with the corroding damps of centuries, and all partly submerged; no dry land visible anywhere, and no sidewalks worth mentioning; if you want to go to church, to the theater, or to the restaurant, you must call a gondola. It must be a paradise for cripples, for verily a man has no use for legs here.

For a day or two the place looked so like an overflowed Arkansas town, because of its currentless waters laving the very doorsteps of all the houses, and the cluster of boats made fast under the windows, or skimming in and out of the alleys and by-ways, that I could not get rid of the impression that there was nothing the matter here but a spring freshet, and that the river would fall in a few weeks and leave a dirty high-water mark on the houses, and the streets full of mud and rubbish.

In the glare of day, there is little poetry about Venice, but under the charitable moon her stained palaces are white again, their battered sculptures are hidden in shadows, and the old city seems crowned once more with the grandeur that was hers five hundred years ago. It is easy, then, in fancy, to people these silent canals with plumed gallants and fair ladies—with Shylocks in gaberdine and sandals, venturing loans upon the rich argosies of Venetian commerce—with Othellos and Desdemonas, with Iagos and Roderigos—

with noble fleets and victorious legions returning from the wars. In the treacherous sunlight we see Venice decayed, forlorn, poverty-stricken, and commerceless—forgotten and utterly insignificant. But in the moonlight, her fourteen centuries of greatness fling their glories about her, and once more is she the princeliest among the nations of the earth.

> There is a glorious city in the sea;
> The sea is in the broad, the narrow streets,
> Ebbing and flowing; and the salt seaweed
> Clings to the marble of her palaces.
> No track of men, no footsteps to and fro,
> Lead to her gates! The path lies o'er the sea,
> Invisible: and from the land we went,
> As to a floating city—steering in,
> And gliding up her streets, as in a dream,
> So smoothly, silently—by many a dome,
> Mosque-like, and many a stately portico,
> The statues ranged along an azure sky;
> By many a pile, in more than Eastern pride,
> Of old the residence of merchant kings;
> The fronts of some, tho' time had shatter'd them,
> Still glowing with the richest hues of art,
> As tho' the wealth within them had run o'er.

What would one naturally wish to see first in Venice? The Bridge of Sighs, of course—and next the Church and the Great Square of St. Mark, the Bronze Horses, and the famous Lion of St. Mark.

We intended to go to the Bridge of Sighs, but happened into the Ducal Palace first—a building which necessarily figures largely in Venetian poetry and tradition. In the Senate Chamber of the ancient Republic we wearied our eyes with staring at acres of historical paintings by Tintoretto and Paul Veronese, but nothing struck us forcibly except the one thing that strikes *all* strangers forcibly—a black square in the midst of a gallery of portraits. In one long row, around the great hall, were painted the portraits of the doges of Venice (venerable fellows, with flowing white beards, for of the three hundred Senators eligible to the office, the oldest was usually chosen doge), and each had its complimentary inscription attached—till you came to the place that should have had Marino Faliero's picture in it, and that was blank and black—blank, except that it bore a terse inscription, saying that the conspirator had died for his crime. It seemed cruel to keep that pitiless inscription still staring from the walls after the unhappy wretch had been in his grave five hundred years.

At the head of the Giant's Staircase, where Marino Faliero was beheaded, and where the doges were crowned in ancient times, two small slits in the stone wall were pointed out—two harmless, insignificant orifices that would never attract a stranger's attention—yet these were the terrible Lions' Mouths! The heads were gone (knocked off by the French during their occupation of Venice), but these were the throats, down which went the anonymous accusation, thrust in secretly at dead of night by an enemy, that doomed many an innocent man to walk the Bridge of Sighs and descend into the dungeon which none entered and hoped to see the sun again. This was in the old days when the Patricians alone governed Venice—the common herd had no vote and no voice. There were one thousand five hundred Patricians; from these, three hundred Senators were chosen; from the Senators a Doge and a Council of Ten were selected, and by secret ballot the Ten chose from their own number a Council of Three. All these were government spies, then, and every spy was under surveillance himself—men spoke in whispers in Venice, and no man trusted his neighbor—not always his own brother. No man knew who the Council of Three were—not even the Senate, not even the Doge; the members of that dread tribunal met at night in a chamber to themselves, masked, and robed from head to foot in scarlet cloaks, and did not even know each other, unless by voice. It was their duty to judge heinous political crimes, and from their sentence there was no appeal. A nod to the executioner was sufficient. The doomed man was marched down a hall and out at a doorway into the covered Bridge of Sighs, through it and into the dungeon and unto his death. At no time in his transit was he visible to any save his conductor. If a man had an enemy in those old days, the cleverest thing he could do was to slip a note for the Council of Three into the Lion's mouth, saying "This man is plotting against the government." If the awful Three found no proof, ten to one they would drown him anyhow, because he was a deep rascal, since his plots were unsolvable. Masked judges and masked executioners, with unlimited power, and no appeal from their judgments, in that hard, cruel age, were not likely to be lenient with men they suspected yet could not convict.

We walked through the hall of the Council of Ten, and presently entered the infernal den of the Council of Three.

The table around which they had sat was there still, and likewise the stations where the masked inquisitors and executioners formerly stood, frozen, upright and silent, till they received a bloody order, and then, without a word, moved off, like the inexorable machines they were, to carry it out. The frescoes on the walls were startlingly suited to the place. In all the other salons, the halls, the great state chambers of the palace, the walls and ceilings were bright with gilding, rich with elaborate carving, and resplendent with gallant pictures of Venetian victories in war, and Venetian display in foreign courts, and hallowed with portraits of the Virgin, the Saviour of men, and the holy saints that preached the Gospel of Peace upon earth—but here, in dismal contrast, were none but pictures of death and dreadful suffering!—not a living figure but was writhing in torture, not a dead one but was smeared with blood, gashed with wounds, and distorted with the agonies that had taken away its life!

From the palace to the gloomy prison is but a step—one might almost jump across the narrow canal that intervenes. The ponderous stone Bridge of Sighs crosses it at the second story—a bridge that is a covered tunnel—you cannot be seen when you walk in it. It is partitioned lengthwise, and through one compartment walked such as bore light sentences in ancient times, and through the other marched sadly the wretches whom the Three had doomed to lingering misery and utter oblivion in the dungeons, or to sudden and mysterious death. Down below the level of the water, by the light of smoking torches, we were shown the damp, thick-walled cells where many a proud patrician's life was eaten away by the long-drawn miseries of solitary imprisonment—without light, air, books; naked, unshaven, uncombed, covered with vermin; his useless tongue forgetting its office, with none to speak to; the days and nights of his life no longer marked, but merged into one eternal eventless night; far away from all cheerful sounds, buried in the silence of a tomb; forgotten by his helpless friends, and his fate a dark mystery to them forever; losing his own memory at last, and knowing no more who he was or how he came there; devouring the loaf of bread and drinking the water that were thrust into the cell by unseen hands, and troubling his worn spirit no more with hopes and fears and doubts and longings to be free; ceasing to scratch vain prayers and complainings on walls where none, not even himself, could see them, and resigning himself to hopeless apathy, driveling childishness, lunacy! Many and many a sorrowful story like this these stony walls could tell if they could but speak.

In a little narrow corridor, near by, they showed us where many a prisoner, after lying in the dungeons until he was forgotten by all save his persecutors, was brought by masked executioners and garroted, or sewed up in a sack, passed through a little window to a boat, at dead of night, and taken to some remote spot and drowned.

They used to show to visitors the implements of torture wherewith the Three were wont to worm secrets out of the accused—villainous machines for crushing thumbs; the stocks where a prisoner sat immovable while water fell drop by drop upon his head till the torture was more than humanity could bear; and a devilish contrivance of steel, which inclosed a prisoner's head like a shell, and crushed it slowly by means of a screw. It bore the stains of blood that had trickled through its joints long ago, and on one side it had a projection whereon the torturer rested his elbow comfortably and bent down his ear to catch the moanings of the sufferer perishing within.

Of course, we went to see the venerable relic of the ancient glory of Venice, with its pavements worn and broken by the passing feet of a thousand years of plebeians and patricians—The Cathedral of St. Mark. It is built entirely of precious marbles, brought from the Orient—nothing in its composition is domestic. Its hoary traditions make it an object of absorbing interest to even the most careless stranger, and thus far it had interest for me; but no further. I could not go into ecstasies over its coarse mosaics, its unlovely Byzantine architecture, or its five hundred curious interior columns from as many distant quarries. Everything was worn out—every block of stone was smooth and almost shapeless with the polishing hands and shoulders of loungers who devoutly idled here in bygone centuries and have died and gone to the dev—no, simply died, I mean.

Under the altar repose the ashes of St. Mark—and Matthew, Luke, and John, too, for all I know. Venice reveres those relics above all things earthly. For fourteen hundred years St. Mark has been her patron saint. Everything about the city seems to be named after him or so named as to refer to him in some way—so named, or some purchase rigged in some way to scrape a sort of hurrahing acquaintance with him. That seems to be the idea. To be on good terms with St. Mark seems to be the very summit of Venetian ambition. They say St. Mark had a tame lion, and used to travel with him—and everywhere that St. Mark went, the lion was sure to go. It was his protector, his friend, his librarian. And so the Winged Lion of St. Mark, with the open Bible under his paw, is a favorite emblem in the grand old city. It casts its shadow from the most ancient pillar in Venice, in the Grand Square of St. Mark, upon the throngs of free citizens below, and has so done for many a long century. The winged lion is found everywhere—and doubtless here, where the winged lion is, no harm can come.

St. Mark died at Alexandria, in Egypt. He was martyred, I think. However, that has nothing to do with my legend. About the founding of the city of Venice—say four hundred and fifty years after Christ (for Venice is much younger than any other Italian city)—a priest dreamed that an angel told him that until the remains of St. Mark were brought to Venice, the city could never rise to high distinction among the nations; that the body must be captured, brought to the city, and a magnificent church built over it; and that if ever the Venetians allowed the Saint to be removed from his new resting-place, in that day Venice would perish from off the face of the earth. The priest proclaimed his dream, and forthwith Venice set about procuring the corpse of St. Mark. One expedition after another tried and failed, but the project was never abandoned during four hundred years. At last it was secured by stratagem, in the year eight hundred and something. The commander of a Venetian expedition disguised himself, stole the bones, separated them, and packed them in vessels filled with lard. The religion of Mohammed causes its devotees to abhor anything that is in the nature of pork, and so when the Christian was stopped by the officers at the gates of the city, they only glanced once into his precious baskets, then turned up their noses at the unholy lard, and let him go. The bones were buried in the vaults of the grand cathedral, which had been waiting long years to receive them, and thus the safety and the greatness of Venice were secured. And to this day there be those in Venice who believe that if those holy ashes were stolen away, the ancient city would vanish like a dream, and its foundations be buried forever in the unremembering sea.

The Venetian gondola is as free and graceful, in its gliding movement, as a serpent. It is twenty or thirty feet long, and is narrow and deep, like a canoe; its sharp bow and stern sweep upward from the water like the horns of a crescent with the abruptness of the curve slightly modified.

The bow is ornamented with a steel comb with a battle-ax attachment which threatens to cut passing boats in two occasionally, but never does. The gondola is painted black because in the zenith of Venetian magnificence the gondolas became too gorgeous altogether, and the Senate decreed that all such display must cease, and a solemn, unembellished black be substituted. If the truth were known, it would doubtless appear that rich plebeians grew too prominent in their affectation of patrician show on the Grand Canal, and required a wholesome snubbing. Reverence for the hallowed Past and its traditions keeps the dismal fashion in force now that the compulsion exists no longer. So let it remain. It is the color of mourning. Venice mourns. The stern of the boat is decked over and the gondolier stands there. He uses a single oar—a long blade, of course, for he stands nearly erect. A wooden peg, a foot and a half high, with two slight crooks or curves in one side of it and one in the other, projects above the starboard gunwale. Against that peg the gondolier takes a purchase with his oar, changing it at intervals to the other side of the peg or dropping it into another of the crooks, as the steering of the craft may demand—and how in the world he can back and fill, shoot straight ahead, or flirt suddenly around a corner, and make the oar stay in those insignificant notches, is a problem to me and a never-diminishing matter of interest. I am afraid I study the gondolier's marvelous skill more than I do the sculptured palaces we glide among. He cuts a corner so closely, now and then, or misses another gondola by such an imperceptible hair-breadth, that I feel myself "scrooching," as the children say, just as one does when a buggy-wheel grazes his elbow. But he makes all his calculations with the nicest precision, and goes darting in and out among a Broadway confusion of busy craft with the easy confidence of the educated hackman. He never makes a mistake.

Sometimes we go flying down the great canals at such a gait that we can get only the merest glimpses into front doors, and again, in obscure alleys in the suburbs, we put on a solemnity suited to the silence, the mildew, the stagnant waters, the clinging weeds, the deserted houses, and the general lifelessness of the place, and move to the spirit of grave meditation.

The gondolier *is* a picturesque rascal for all he wears no satin harness, no plumed bonnet, no silken tights. His attitude is stately; he is lithe and supple; all his movements are full of grace. When his long canoe, and his fine figure, towering from its high perch on the stern, are cut against the evening sky, they make a picture that is very novel and striking to a foreign eye.

We sit in the cushioned carriage-body of a cabin, with the curtains drawn, and smoke, or read, or look out upon the passing boats, the houses, the bridges, the people, and enjoy ourselves much more than we could in a buggy jolting over our cobblestone pavements at home. This is the gentlest, pleasantest locomotion we have ever known.

But it seems queer—ever so queer—to see a boat doing duty as a private carriage. We see business men come to the front door, step into a gondola, instead of a street-car, and go off down-town to the counting-room.

We see visiting young ladies stand on the stoop, and laugh, and kiss good-by, and flirt their fans and say "Come soon—now *do*—you've been just as mean as ever you can be—mother's dying to see you—and we've moved into the new house, oh, such a love of a place!—so convenient to the post-office and the church, and the Young Men's Christian Association; and we do have such fishing, and such carrying on, and *such* swimming-matches in the back yard—Oh, you *must* come—no distance at all, and if you go down through by St. Mark's and the Bridge of Sighs, and cut through the alley and come up by the church of Santa Maria dei Frari, and into the Grand Canal, there isn't a *bit* of current—now *do* come, Sally Maria—by-by!" and then the little humbug trips down the steps, jumps into the gondola, says, under her breath, "Disagreeable old thing, I hope she *won't!*" goes skimming away, round the corner; and the other girl slams the street door and says, "Well, *that* infliction's over, anyway,—but I suppose I've got to go and see her—tiresome, stuck-up thing!" Human nature appears to be just the same, all over the world. We see the diffident young man, mild of mustache, affluent of hair, indigent of brain, elegant of costume, drive up to *her* father's mansion, tell his hackman to bail out and wait, start fearfully up the steps and meet "the old gentleman" right on the threshold!—hear him ask what street the new British Bank is in—as if *that* were what he came for—and then bounce into his boat and scurry away with his coward heart in his boots!—see him come sneaking around the corner again, directly, with a crack of the curtain open toward the old gentleman's disappearing gondola, and out scampers his Susan with a flock of little Italian endearments fluttering from her lips, and goes to drive with him in the watery avenues down toward the Rialto.

We see the ladies go out shopping, in the most natural way, and flit from street to street and from store to store, just in the good old fashion, except that they leave the gondola, instead of a private carriage, waiting at the curbstone a couple of hours for them—waiting while they make the nice young clerks pull down tons and tons of silks and velvets and moire antiques and those things; and then they buy a paper of pins and go paddling away to confer the rest of their disastrous patronage on some other firm. And they always have their purchases sent home just in the good old way. Human nature is *very* much the same all over the world; and it is *so* like my dear native home to see a Venetian lady go into a store and buy ten cents' worth of blue ribbon and have it sent home in a scow. Ah, it is these little touches of nature that move one to tears in these far-off foreign lands.

We see little girls and boys go out in gondolas with their nurses, for an airing. We see staid families, with prayer-book and beads, enter the gondola dressed in their Sunday best, and float away to church. And at midnight we see the theater break up and discharge its swarm of hilarious youth and beauty; we hear the cries of the hackman-gondoliers, and behold the struggling crowd jump aboard, and the black multitude of boats go skimming down the moonlit avenues; we see them separate here and there, and disappear up divergent streets; we hear the faint sounds of laughter and of shouted farewells floating up out of the distance; and then, the strange pageant being gone, we have lonely stretches of glittering water—of stately buildings—of blotting shadows—of weird stone faces creeping into the moonlight—of deserted bridges—of motionless boats at anchor. And over all broods that mysterious stillness, that stealthy quiet, that befits so well this old dreaming Venice.

We have been pretty much everywhere in our gondola. We have bought beads and photographs in the stores, and wax matches in the Great Square of St. Mark. The last remark suggests a digression. Everybody goes to this vast square in the evening. The military bands play in the center of it and countless couples of ladies and gentlemen promenade up and down on either side, and platoons of them are constantly drifting away toward the old cathedral, and by the venerable column with the Winged Lion of St. Mark on its top, and out to where the boats lie moored; and other platoons are as constantly arriving from the gondolas and joining the great throng. Between the promenaders and the sidewalks are seated hundreds and hundreds of people at small tables, smoking and taking *granita* (a first cousin to ice-cream); on the sidewalks are more employing themselves in the same way. The shops in the first floor of the tall rows of buildings that wall in three sides of the square are brilliantly lighted, the air is filled with music and merry voices, and altogether the scene is as bright and spirited and full of cheerfulness as any man could desire. We enjoy it thoroughly. Very many of the young women are exceedingly pretty and dress with rare good taste. We are gradually and laboriously learning the ill manners of staring them unflinchingly in the face—not because such conduct is agreeable to us, but because it is the custom of the country and they say the girls like it. We wish to learn all the curious, outlandish ways of all the different countries, so that we can "show off" and astonish people when we get home. We wish to excite the envy of our untraveled friends with our strange foreign fashions which we can't shake off. All our passengers are paying strict attention to this thing, with the end in view which I have mentioned. The gentle reader will never, never know what a consummate ass he can become until he goes abroad. I speak now, of course, in the supposition that the gentle reader has not been abroad, and therefore is not already a consummate ass. If the case be otherwise, I beg his pardon and extend to him the cordial hand of fellowship and call him brother. I shall always delight to meet an ass after my own heart when I shall have finished my travels.

On this subject let me remark that there are Americans abroad in Italy who have actually forgotten their mother-tongue in three months—forgot it in France. They cannot even write their address in English in a hotel-register. I append these evidences, which I copied *verbatim* from the register of a hotel in a certain Italian city:

John P. Whitcomb, *États Unis.*

William L. Ainsworth, *travailleur* (he meant traveler, I suppose), *États Unis.*

George P. Morton *et fils, d'Amérique.*

Lloyd B. Williams, *et trois amis, ville de* Boston, *Amérique.*

J. Ellsworth Baker, *tout de suite de France, place de naissance Amérique, destination la Grande Bretagne.*

I love this sort of people. A lady passenger of ours tells of a fellow-citizen of hers who spent eight weeks in Paris and then returned home and addressed his dearest old bosom friend Herbert as Mr. "Er-bare!" He apologized, though, and said, " 'Pon my soul it is aggravating, but I cahn't help it—I have got so used to speaking nothing but French, my dear Erbare—damme there it goes again!—got so used to French pronunciation that I cahn't get rid of it—it is positively annoying, I assure you." This enterprising idiot, whose name was Gordon, allowed himself to be hailed three times in the street before he paid any attention, and then begged a thousand pardons and said he had grown so accustomed to hearing himself addressed as "M'sieu Gor-r-*dong,*" with a roll to the *r,* that he had forgotten the legitimate sound of his name! He wore a rose in his buttonhole; he gave the French salutation—two flips of the hand in front of the face; he called Paris *Pairree* in ordinary English conversation; he carried envelopes bearing foreign postmarks protruding from his breast pocket; he cultivated a mustache and imperial, and did what else he could to suggest to the beholder his pet fancy that he resembled Louis Napoleon—and in a spirit of thankfulness which is entirely unaccountable, considering the slim foundation there was for it, he praised his Maker that he was *as* he was, and went on enjoying his little life just the same as if he really *had* been deliberately designed and erected by the great Architect of the Universe.

Think of our Whitcombs and our Ainsworths and our Williamses writing themselves down in dilapidated French in a foreign hotel-register! We laugh at Englishmen, when we are at home, for sticking so sturdily to their national ways and customs, but we look back upon it from abroad very forgivingly. It is not pleasant to see an American thrusting his nationality forward *obtrusively* in a foreign land, but oh, it is pitiable to see him making of himself a thing that is neither male nor female, neither fish, flesh, nor fowl—a poor, miserable, hermaphrodite Frenchman!

Among a long list of churches, art-galleries, and such things, visited by us in Venice, I shall mention only one—the Church of Santa Maria dei Frari. It is about five hundred years old, I believe, and stands on twelve hundred thousand piles. In it lie the body of Canova and the heart of Titian, under magnificent monuments. Titian died at the age of almost one hundred years. A plague which swept away fifty thousand lives was raging at the time, and there is notable evidence of the reverence in which the great painter was held, in the fact that to him alone the state permitted a public funeral in all that season of terror and death.

In this church, also, is a monument to the doge Foscari, whose name a once resident of Venice, Lord Byron, has made permanently famous.

The monument to the doge Giovanni Pesaro, in this church, is a curiosity in the way of mortuary adornment. It is eighty feet high and is fronted like some fantastic pagan temple. Against it stand four colossal Nubians, as black as night, dressed in white marble garments. The black legs are bare, and through rents in sleeves and breeches, the skin, of shiny black marble, shows. The artist was as ingenious as his funeral designs were absurd. There are two bronze skeletons bearing scrolls, and two great dragons uphold the sarcophagus. On high, amid all this grotesqueness, sits the departed doge.

In the conventual buildings attached to this church are the state archives of Venice. We did not see them, but they are said to number millions of documents. "They are the records of centuries of the most watchful, observant, and suspicious government that ever existed—in which everything was written down and nothing spoken out." They fill nearly three hundred rooms. Among them are manuscripts from the archives of nearly two thousand families, monasteries, and convents. The secret history of Venice for a thousand years is here—its plots, its hidden trials, its assassinations, its commissions of hireling spies and masked bravoes—food, ready to hand, for a world of dark and mysterious romances.

Yes, I think we have seen all of Venice. We have seen, in these old churches, a profusion of costly and elaborate sepulcher ornamentation such as we never dreamt of before. We have stood in the dim religious light of these hoary sanctuaries, in the midst of long ranks of dusty monuments and effigies of the great dead of Venice, until we seemed drifting back, back, back, into the solemn past, and looking upon the scenes and mingling with the peoples of a remote antiquity. We have been in a half-waking sort of dream all the time. I do not know how else to describe the feeling. A part of our being has remained still in the nineteenth century, while another part of it has seemed in some unaccountable way walking among the phantoms of the tenth.

We have seen famous pictures until our eyes are weary with looking at them and refuse to find interest in them any longer. And what wonder, when there are twelve hundred pictures by Palma the Younger in Venice and fifteen hundred by Tintoretto? And behold, there are Titians and the works of other artists in proportion. We have seen Titian's celebrated "Cain and Abel," his "David and Goliah," his "Abraham's Sacrifice." We have seen Tintoretto's monster picture, which is seventy-four feet long and I do not know how many feet high, and thought it a very commodious picture. We have seen pictures of martyrs enough, and saints enough, to regenerate the world. I ought not to confess it, but still, since one has no opportunity in America to acquire a critical judgment in art, and since I could not hope to become educated in it in Europe in a few short weeks, I may therefore as well acknowledge with such apologies as may be due, that to me it seemed that when I had seen one of these martyrs I had seen them all. They all have a marked family resemblance to each other, they dress alike, in coarse monkish robes and sandals, they are all bald-headed, they all stand in about the same attitude, and without exception they are gazing heavenward with countenances which the Ainsworths, the Mortons, and the Williamses, *et fils,* inform me are full of "expression." To me there is nothing tangible about these imaginary portraits, nothing that I can grasp and take a living interest in. If great Titian had only been gifted with prophecy, and had skipped a martyr, and gone over to England and painted a portrait of Shakespeare, even as a youth, which we could all have confidence in now, the world down to the latest generations would have forgiven the lost martyr in the rescued seer. I think posterity could have spared one more martyr for the sake of a great historical picture of Titian's time and painted by his brush—such as Columbus returning in chains from the discovery of a world, for instance. The old masters did paint some Venetian historical pictures, and these we did not tire of looking at, notwithstanding representations of the formal introduction of defunct Doges to the Virgin Mary in regions beyond the clouds clashed rather harshly with the proprieties, it seemed to us.

But, humble as we are, and unpretending, in the matter of art, our researches among the painted monks and martyrs have not been wholly in vain. We have striven hard to learn. We have had some success. We have mastered some things, possibly of trifling import in the eyes of the learned, but to us they give pleasure, and we take as much pride in our little acquirements as do others who have learned far more, and we love to display them full as well. When we see a monk going about with a lion and looking tranquilly up to heaven, we know that that is St. Mark. When we see a monk with a book and pen, looking tranquilly up to heaven, trying to think of a word, we know that that is St. Matthew. When we see a monk sitting on a rock, looking tranquilly up to heaven, with a human skull beside him, and without other baggage, we know that that is St. Jerome. Because we know that he always went flying light in the matter of baggage. When we see a party looking tranquilly up to heaven, unconscious that his body is shot through and through with arrows, we know that that is St. Sebastian. When we see other monks looking tranquilly up to heaven, but having no trade-mark, we always ask who those parties are. We do this because we humbly wish to learn. We have seen thirteen thousand St. Jeromes, and twenty-two thousand St. Marks, and sixteen thousand St. Matthews, and sixty thousand St. Sebastians, and four millions of assorted monks, undesignated, and we feel encouraged to believe that when we have seen some more of these various pictures, and had a larger experience, we shall begin to take an absorbing interest in them like our cultivated countrymen from *Amérique.*

Now it does give me real pain to speak in this almost unappreciative way of the old masters and their martyrs, because good friends of mine in the ship—friends who do thoroughly and conscientiously appreciate them and are in every way competent to discriminate between good pictures and inferior ones—have urged me for my own sake not to make public the fact that I lack this appreciation and this critical discrimination myself. I believe that what I have written and may still write about pictures will give them pain, and I am honestly sorry for it. I even promised that I would hide my uncouth sentiments in my own breast. But alas! I never could keep a promise. I do not blame myself for this weakness, because the fault must lie in my physical organization. It is likely that such a very liberal amount of space was given to the organ which enables me to *make* promises, that the organ which should enable me to keep them was crowded out. But I grieve not. I like no half-way things. I had rather have one faculty nobly developed than two faculties of mere ordinary capacity. I certainly meant to keep that promise, but I find I cannot do it. It is impossible to travel through Italy without speaking of pictures, and can I see them through others' eyes?

If I did not so delight in the grand pictures that are spread before me every day of my life by that monarch of all the old masters, Nature, I should come to believe, sometimes, that I had in me no appreciation of the beautiful, whatsoever.

It seems to me that whenever I glory to think that for once I have discovered an ancient painting that is beautiful and worthy of all praise, the pleasure it gives me is an infallible proof that it is *not* a beautiful picture and not in any wise worthy of commendation. This very thing has occurred more times than I can mention, in Venice. In every single instance the guide has crushed out my swelling enthusiasm with the remark:

"It is nothing—it is of the *Renaissance.*"

I did not know what in the mischief the Renaissance was, and so always I had to simply say:

"Ah! so it is—I had not observed it before."

I could not bear to be ignorant before a cultivated negro, the offspring of a South Carolina slave. But it occurred too often for even my self-complacency, did that exasperating "It is nothing—it is of the *Renaissance.*" I said at last:

"*Who* is this Renaissance? Where did he come from? Who gave him permission to cram the Republic with his execrable daubs?"

We learned, then, that Renaissance was not a man; that *renaissance* was a term used to signify what was at best but an imperfect rejuvenation of art. The guide said that after Titian's time and the time of the other great names we had grown so familiar with, high art declined; then it partially rose again—an inferior sort of painters sprang up, and these shabby pictures were the work of their hands. Then I said, in my heat, that I "wished to goodness high art had declined five hundred years sooner." The Renaissance pictures suit me very well, though sooth to say its school were too much given to painting real men and did not indulge enough in martyrs.

The guide I have spoken of is the only one we have had yet who knew anything. He was born in South Carolina, of slave parents. They came to Venice while he was an infant. He has grown up here. He is well educated. He reads, writes, and speaks English, Italian, Spanish, and French, with perfect facility; is a worshiper of art and thoroughly conversant with it; knows the history of Venice by heart and never tires of talking of her illustrious career. He dressed better than any of us, I think, and is daintily polite. Negroes are deemed as good as white people, in Venice, and so this man feels no desire to go back to his native land. His judgment is correct.

I have had another shave. I was writing in our front room this afternoon and trying hard to keep my attention on my work and refrain from looking out upon the canal. I was resisting the soft influences of the climate as well as I could, and endeavoring to overcome the desire to be indolent and happy. The boys sent for a barber. They asked me if I would be shaved. I reminded them of my tortures in Genoa, Milan, Como; of my declaration that I would suffer no more on Italian soil. I said: "Not any for me, if you please."

I wrote on. The barber began on the doctor. I heard him say:

"Dan, this is the easiest shave I have had since we left the ship."

He said again, presently:

"Why, Dan, a man could go to sleep with this man shaving him."

Dan took the chair. Then he said:

"Why, this is Titian. This is one of the old masters."

I wrote on. Directly Dan said:

"Doctor, it is a perfect luxury. The ship's barber isn't anything to him."

My rough beard was distressing me beyond measure. The barber was rolling up his apparatus. The temptation was too strong. I said:

"Hold on, please. Shave me also."

I sat down in the chair and closed my eyes. The barber soaped my face, and then took his razor and gave me a rake that well-nigh threw me into convulsions. I jumped out of the chair: Dan and the doctor were both wiping blood off their faces and laughing.

I said it was a mean, disgraceful fraud.

They said that the misery of this shave had gone so far beyond anything they had ever experienced before, that they could not bear the idea of losing such a chance of hearing a cordial opinion from me on the subject.

It was shameful. But there was no help for it. The skinning was begun and had to be finished. The tears flowed with every rake, and so did the fervent execrations. The barber grew confused, and brought blood every time. I think the boys enjoyed it better than anything they have seen or heard since they left home.

We have seen the Campanile, and Byron's house, and Balbi's the geographer, and the palaces of all the ancient dukes and doges of Venice, and we have seen their effeminate descendants airing their nobility in fashionable French attire in the Grand Square of St. Mark, and eating ices and drinking cheap wines, instead of wearing gallant coats of mail and destroying fleets and armies as their great ancestors did in the days of Venetian glory. We have seen no bravoes with poisoned stilettoes, no masks, no wild carnival; but we have seen the ancient pride of Venice, the grim Bronze Horses that figure in a thousand legends. Venice may well cherish them, for they are the only horses she ever had. It is said there are hundreds of people in this curious city who never have seen a living horse in their lives. It is entirely true, no doubt.

And so, having satisfied ourselves, we depart tomorrow, and leave the venerable Queen of the Republics to summon her vanished ships, and marshal her shadowy armies, and know again in dreams the pride of her old renown.

From *The Innocents Abroad,* 1869.

21 : *Florence*

FLORENCE PLEASED US FOR A WHILE. I think we appreciated the great figure of David in the grand square, and the sculptured group they call the Rape of the Sabines. We wandered through the endless collections of paintings and statues of the Pitti and Uffizzi galleries, of course. I make that statement in self-defense; there let it stop. I could not rest under the imputation that I visited Florence and did not traverse its weary miles of picture-galleries. We tried indolently to recollect something about the Guelphs and Ghibelines and the other historical cut-throats whose quarrels and assassinations make up so large a share of Florentine history, but the subject was not attractive. We had been robbed of all the fine mountain scenery on our little journey by a system of railroading that had three miles of tunnel to a hundred yards of daylight, and we were not inclined to be sociable with Florence. We had seen the spot, outside the city somewhere, where these people had allowed the bones of Galileo to rest in unconsecrated ground for an age because his great discovery that the world turned around was regarded as a damning heresy by the church; and we know that long after the world had accepted his theory and raised his name high in the list of its great men, they had still let him rot there. That we had lived to see his dust in honored sepulture in the Church of Santa Croce we owed to a society of *literati,* and not to Florence or her rulers. We saw Dante's tomb in that church, also, but we were glad to know that his body was not in it; that the ungrateful city that had exiled him and persecuted him would give much to have it there, but need not hope to ever secure that high honor to herself. Medicis are good enough for Florence. Let her plant Medicis and build grand monuments over them to testify how gratefully she was wont to lick the hand that scourged her.

Magnanimous Florence! Her jewelry marts are filled with artists in mosaic. Florentine mosaics are the choicest in all the world. Florence loves to have that said. Florence is proud of it. Florence would foster this specialty of hers. She is grateful to the artists that bring to her this high credit and fill her coffers with foreign money, and so she encourages them with pensions. With pensions! Think of the lavishness of it. She knows that people who piece together the beautiful trifles die early, because the labor is so confining, and so exhausting to hand and brain, and so she has decreed that all these people who reach the age of sixty shall have a pension after that! I have not heard that any of them have called for their dividends yet. One man did fight along till he was sixty, and started after his pension, but it appeared that there had been a mistake of a year in his family record, and so he gave it up and died. These artists will take particles of stone or glass no larger than a mustard seed, and piece them together on a sleeve-button or a shirt-stud, so smoothly and with such nice adjustment of the delicate shades of color the pieces bear, as to form a pygmy rose with stem, thorn, leaves, petals complete, and all as softly and as truthfully tinted as though Nature had builded it herself. They will counterfeit a fly, or a high-toned bug, or the ruined Coliseum, within the cramped circle of a breastpin, and do it so deftly and so neatly that any man might think a master painted it.

I saw a little table in the great mosaic school in Florence—a little trifle of a center-table—whose top was made of some sort of precious polished stone, and in the stone was inlaid the figure of a flute, with bell-mouth and a mazy complication of keys. No painting in the world could have been softer or richer; no shading out of one tint into another could have been more perfect; no work of art of any kind could have been more faultless than this flute, and yet to count the multitude of little fragments of stone of which they swore it was formed would bankrupt any man's arithmetic! I do not think one could have seen where two particles joined each other with eyes of ordinary shrewdness. Certainly *we* could detect no such blemish. This table top cost the labor of one man for ten long years, so they said, and it was for sale for thirty-five thousand dollars.

We went to the Church of Santa Croce, from time to time, in Florence, to weep over the tombs of Michael Angelo, Raphael, and Machiavelli (I suppose they are buried there, but it may be that they reside elsewhere and rent their tombs to other parties—such being the fashion in Italy), and between times we used to go and stand on the bridges and admire the Arno. It is popular to admire the Arno. It is a great historical creek with four feet in the channel and some scows floating around. It would be a very plausible river if they would pump some water into it. They all call it a river, and they honestly think it *is* a river, do these dark and bloody Florentines. They even help out the delusion by building bridges over it. I do not see why they are too good to wade.

How the fatigues and annoyances of travel fill one with bitter prejudices sometimes! I might enter Florence under happier auspices a month hence and find it all beautiful, all attractive. But I do not care to think of it now, at all, nor of its roomy shops filled to the ceiling with snowy marble and alabaster copies of all the celebrated sculptures in Europe—copies so enchanting to the eye that I wonder how they can really be shaped like the dingy petrified nightmares they are the portraits of. I got lost in Florence at nine o'clock, one night, and stayed lost in that labyrinth of narrow streets and long rows of vast buildings that look all alike, until toward three o'clock in the morning. It was a pleasant night and at first there were a good many people abroad, and there were cheerful lights about. Later, I grew accustomed to prowling about mysterious drifts and tunnels and astonishing and interesting myself with coming around corners expecting to find the hotel staring me in the face, and not finding it doing anything of the kind. Later still, I felt tired. I soon felt remarkably tired. But there was no one abroad, now—not even a policeman. I walked till I was out of all patience, and very hot and thirsty. At last, somewhere after one o'clock, I came unexpectedly to one of the city gates. I knew then that I was very far from the hotel. The soldiers thought I wanted to leave the city, and they sprang up and barred the way with their muskets. I said:

"Hotel d'Europe!"

It was all the Italian I knew, and I was not certain whether that was Italian or French. The soldiers looked stupidly at each other and at me, and shook their heads and took me into custody. I said I wanted to go home. They did not understand me. They took me into the guardhouse and searched me, but they found no sedition on me. They found a small piece of soap (we carry soap with us now), and I made them a present of it, seeing that they regarded it as a curiosity. I continued to say Hotel d'Europe, and they continued to shake their heads, until at last a young soldier nodding in the corner roused up and said something. He said he knew where the hotel was, I suppose, for the officer of the guard sent him away with me. We walked a hundred or a hundred and fifty miles, it appeared to me, and then *he* got lost. He turned this way and that, and finally gave it up and signified that he was going to spend the remainder of the morning trying to find the city gate again. At that moment it struck me that there was something familiar about the house over the way. It was the hotel!

It was a happy thing for me that there happened to be a soldier there that knew even as much as he did; for they say that the policy of the government is to change the soldiery from one place to another constantly and from country to city, so that they cannot become acquainted with the people and grow lax in their duties and enter into plots and conspiracies with friends. My experiences of Florence were chiefly unpleasant. I will change the subject.

From *The Innocents Abroad,* 1869.

22 : *Italy*

THERE ARE A GOOD MANY THINGS about this Italy which I do not understand—and more especially I cannot understand how a bankrupt government can have such palatial railroad depots and such marvels of turnpikes. Why, these latter are as hard as adamant, as straight as a line, as smooth as a floor, and as white as snow. When it is too dark to see any other object, one can still see the white turnpikes of France and Italy; and they are clean enough to eat from, without a table-cloth. And yet no tolls are charged.

As for the railways—we have none like them. The cars slide as smoothly along as if they were on runners. The depots are vast palaces of cut marble, with stately colonnades of the same royal stone traversing them from end to end, and with ample walls and ceilings richly decorated with frescoes. The lofty gateways are graced with statues, and the broad floors are all laid in polished flags of marble.

These things win me more than Italy's hundred galleries of priceless art treasures, because I can understand the one and am not competent to appreciate the other. In the turnpikes, the railways, the depots, and the new boulevards of uniform houses in Florence and other cities here, I see the genius of Louis Napoleon, or rather, I see the works of that statesman imitated. But Louis has taken care that in France there shall be a foundation for these improvements—money. He has always the wherewithal to back up his projects; they strengthen France and never weaken her. Her material prosperity is genuine. But here the case is different. This country is bankrupt. There is no real foundation for these great works. The prosperity they would seem to indicate is a pretense. There is no money in the treasury, and so they enfeeble her instead of strengthening. Italy has achieved the dearest wish of her heart and become an independent state—and in so doing she has drawn an elephant in the political lottery. She has nothing to feed it on. Inexperienced in government, she plunged into all manner of useless expenditure, and swamped her treasury almost in a day. She squandered millions of francs on a navy which she did not need, and the first time she took her new toy into action she got it knocked higher than Gilderoy's kite—to use the language of the Pilgrims.

But it is an ill wind that blows nobody good. A year ago, when Italy saw utter ruin staring her in the face and her greenbacks hardly worth the paper they were printed on, her Parliament ventured upon a *coup de main* that would have appalled the stoutest of her statesmen under less desperate circumstances. They, in a manner, confiscated the domains of the Church! This in priest-ridden Italy! This in a land which has groped in the midnight of priestly superstition for sixteen hundred years! It was a rare good fortune for Italy, the stress of weather that drove her to break from this prison-house.

They do not call it *confiscating* the church property. That would sound too harshly yet. But it amounts to that. There are thousands of churches in Italy, each with untold millions of treasures stored away in its closets, and each with its battalion of priests to be supported. And then there are the estates of the Church—league on league of the richest lands and the noblest forests in all Italy—all yielding immense revenues to the Church, and none paying a cent in taxes to the state. In some great districts the Church owns *all* the property—lands, water-courses, woods, mills and factories. They buy, they sell, they manufacture, and since they pay no taxes, who can hope to compete with them!

Well, the government has seized all this in effect, and will yet seize it in rigid and unpoetical reality, no doubt. Something must be done to feed a starving treasury, and there is no other resource in all Italy—none but the riches of the Church. So the government intends to take to itself a great portion of the revenues arising from priestly farms, factories, etc., and also intends to take possession of the churches and carry them on, after its own fashion and upon its own responsibility. In a few instances it will leave the establishments of great pet churches undisturbed, but in all others only a handful of priests will be retained to preach and pray, a few will be pensioned, and the balance turned adrift.

Pray glance at some of these churches and their embellishments, and see whether the government is doing a righteous thing or not. In Venice, to-day, a city of a hundred thousand inhabitants, there are twelve hundred priests. Heaven only knows how many there were before the Parliament reduced their numbers. There was the great Jesuit Church. Under the old régime it required sixty priests to engineer it—the government does it with five now, and the others are discharged from service. All about that church wretchedness and poverty abound. At its door a dozen hats and bonnets were doffed to us, as many heads were humbly bowed, and as many hands extended, appealing for pennies—appealing with foreign words we could not understand, but appealing mutely, with sad eyes, and sunken cheeks, and ragged raiment, that no words were needed to translate. Then we passed within the great doors, and it seemed that the riches of the world were before us! Huge columns carved out of single masses of marble, and inlaid from top to bottom with a hundred intricate figures wrought in costly verde antique; pulpits of the same rich materials, whose draperies hung down in many a pictured fold, the stony fabric counterfeiting the delicate work of the loom; the grand altar brilliant with polished facings and balustrades of oriental agate, jasper, verde antique, and other precious stones, whose names, even, we seldom hear—and slabs of priceless lapis lazuli lavished everywhere as recklessly as if the church had owned a quarry of it. In the midst of all this magnificence, the solid gold and silver furniture of the altar seemed cheap and trivial. Even the floors and ceilings cost a princely fortune.

Now, where is the use of allowing all those riches to lie idle, while half of that community hardly know, from day to day, how they are going to keep body and soul together? And, where is the wisdom in permitting hundreds upon hundreds of millions of francs to be locked up in the useless trumpery of churches all over Italy, and the people ground to death with taxation to uphold a perishing government?

As far as I can see, Italy, for fifteen hundred years, has turned all her energies, all her finances, and all her industry to the building up of a vast array of wonderful church edifices, and starving half her citizens to accomplish it. She is to-day one vast museum of magnificence and misery. All the churches in an ordinary American city put together could hardly buy the jeweled frippery in one of her hundred cathedrals. And for every beggar in America, Italy can show a hundred—and rags and vermin to match. It is the wretchedest, princeliest land on earth.

Look at the grand Duomo of Florence—a vast pile that has been sapping the purses of her citizens for five hundred years, and is not nearly finished yet. Like all other men, I fell down and worshiped it, but when the filthy beggars swarmed around me the contrast was too striking, too suggestive, and I said, "Oh, sons of classic Italy, *is* the spirit of enterprise, of self-reliance, of noble endeavor, utterly dead within ye? Curse your indolent worthlessness, why don't you rob your church?"

Three hundred happy, comfortable priests are employed in that cathedral.

And now that my temper is up, I may as well go on and abuse everybody I can think of. They have a grand mausoleum in Florence, which they built to bury our Lord and Saviour and the Medici family in. It sounds blasphemous, but it is true, and here they *act* blasphemy. The dead and damned Medicis who cruelly tyrannized over Florence and were her curse for over two hundred years, are salted away in a circle of costly vaults, and in their midst the Holy Sepulcher was to have been set up. The expedition sent to Jerusalem to seize it got into trouble and could not accomplish the burglary, and so the center of the mausoleum is vacant now. They say the entire mausoleum was intended for the Holy Sepulcher, and was only turned into a family burying-place after the Jerusalem expedition failed—but you will excuse me. Some of those Medicis would have smuggled themselves in sure. What *they* had not the effrontery to do, was not worth doing. Why, they had their trivial, forgotten exploits on land and sea pictured out in grand frescoes (as did also the ancient doges of Venice) with the Saviour and the Virgin throwing bouquets to them out of the clouds, and the Deity himself applauding from his throne in Heaven! And who painted these things? Why, Titian, Tintoretto, Paul Veronese, Raphael—none other than the world's idols, the "old masters."

Andrea del Sarto glorified his princes in pictures that must save them forever from the oblivion they merited, and they let him starve. Served him right. Raphael pictured such infernal villains as Catherine and Marie de Medici seated in heaven and conversing familiarly with the Virgin Mary and the angels (to say nothing of higher personages), and yet my friends abuse me because I am a little prejudiced against the old masters—because I fail sometimes to see the beauty that is in their productions. I cannot help but see it, now and then, but I keep on protesting against the groveling spirit that could persuade those masters to prostitute their noble talents to the adulation of such monsters as the French, Venetian, and Florentine princes of two and three hundred years ago, all the same.

I am told that the old masters had to do these shameful things for bread, the princes and potentates being the only patrons of art. If a grandly gifted man may drag his pride and his manhood in the dirt for bread rather than starve with the nobility that is in him untainted, the excuse is a valid one. It would excuse theft in Washingtons and Wellingtons, and unchastity in women as well.

But, somehow, I cannot keep that Medici mausoleum out of my memory. It is as large as a church; its pavement is rich enough for the pavement of a king's palace; its great dome is gorgeous with frescoes; its walls are made of—what? Marble?—plaster?—wood?—paper?—No. Red porphyry—verde antique—jasper—oriental agate—alabaster—mother-of-pearl—chalcedony—red coral—lapis lazuli! All the vast walls are made wholly of these precious stones, worked in and in and in together in elaborate patterns and figures, and polished till they glow like great mirrors with the pictured splendors reflected from the dome overhead. And before a statue of one of those dead Medicis reposes a crown that blazes with diamonds and emeralds enough to buy a ship of the line, almost. These are the things the government has its evil eye upon, and a happy thing it will be for Italy when they melt away in the public treasury.

And now— However, another beggar approaches. I will go out and destroy him, and then come back and write another chapter of vituperation.

Having eaten the friendless orphan—having driven away his comrades—having grown calm and reflective at length—I now feel in a kindlier mood. I feel that after talking so freely about the priests and the churches, justice demands that if I know anything good about either I ought to say it. I *have* heard of many things that redound to the credit of the priesthood, but the most notable matter that occurs to me now is the devotion one of the mendicant orders showed during the prevalence of the cholera last year. I speak of the Dominican friars—men who wear a coarse, heavy brown robe and a cowl, in this hot climate, and go barefoot. They live on alms altogether, I believe. They must unquestionably love their religion, to suffer so much for it. When the cholera was raging in Naples; when the people were dying by hundreds and hundreds every day; when every concern for the public welfare was swallowed up in selfish private interest, and every citizen made the taking care of himself his sole object, these men banded themselves together and went about nursing the sick and burying the dead. Their noble efforts cost many of them their lives. They laid them down cheerfully, and well they might. Creeds mathematically precise, and hair-splitting niceties of doctrine, are absolutely necessary for the salvation of some kinds of souls, but surely the charity, the purity, the unselfishness that are in the hearts of men like these would save their souls though they were bankrupt in the true religion—which is ours.

One of these fat barefooted rascals came here to Civita Vecchia with us in the little French steamer. There were only half a dozen of us in the cabin. He belonged in the steerage. He was the life of the ship, the bloody-minded son of the Inquisition! He and the leader of the marine band of a French man-of-war played on the piano and sang opera turn about; they sang duets together; they rigged impromptu theatrical costumes and gave us extravagant farces and pantomimes. We got along first-rate with the friar, and were excessively conversational, albeit he could not understand what we said, and certainly he never uttered a word that we could guess the meaning of.

This Civita Vecchia is the finest nest of dirt, vermin, and ignorance we have found yet, except that African perdition they call Tangier, which is just like it. The people here live in alleys two yards wide, which have a smell about them which is peculiar but not entertaining. It is well the alleys are not wider, because they hold as much smell now as a person can stand, and, of course, if they were wider they would hold more, and then the people would die. These alleys are paved with stone, and carpeted with deceased cats, and decayed rags, and decomposed vegetable tops, and remnants of old boots, all soaked with dish-water, and the people sit around on stools and enjoy it. They are indolent, as a general thing, and yet have few pastimes. They work two or three hours at a time, but not hard, and then they knock off and catch flies. This does not require any talent, because they only have to grab —if they do not get the one they are after, they get another. It is all the same to them. They have no partialities. Whichever one they get is the one they want.

They have other kinds of insects, but it does not make them arrogant. They are very quiet, unpretending people. They have more of these kind of things than other communities, but they do not boast.

They are very uncleanly—these people—in face, in person, and dress. When they see anybody with a clean shirt on, it arouses their scorn. The women wash clothes, half the day, at the public tanks in the streets, but they are probably somebody else's. Or maybe they keep one set to wear and another to wash; because they never put on any that have ever been washed. When they get done washing, they sit in the alleys and nurse their cubs. They nurse one ash-cat at a time, and the others scratch their backs against the door-post and are happy.

All this country belongs to the Papal states. They do not appear to have any schools here, and only one billiard-table. Their education is at a very low stage. One portion of the men go into the military, another into the priesthood, and the rest into the shoemaking business.

They keep up the passport system here, but so they do in Turkey. This shows that the Papal states are as far advanced as Turkey. This fact will be alone sufficient to silence the tongues of malignant calumniators. I had to get my passport *viséd* for Rome in Florence, and then they would not let me come ashore here until a policeman had examined it on the wharf and sent me a permit. They did not even dare to let me take my passport in my hands for twelve hours, I looked so formidable. They judged it best to let me cool down. They thought I wanted to take the town, likely. Little did they know me. I wouldn't have it. They examined my baggage at the depot. They took one of my ablest jokes and read it over carefully twice and then read it backward. But it was too deep for them. They passed it around, and everybody speculated on it awhile, but it mastered them all.

It was no common joke. At length a veteran officer spelled it over deliberately and shook his head three or four times and said that, in his opinion, it was seditious. That was the first time I felt alarmed. I immediately said I would explain the document, and they crowded around. And so I explained and explained and explained, and they took notes of all I said, but the more I explained the more they could not understand it, and when they desisted at last, I could not even understand it myself. They said they believed it was an incendiary document, leveled at the government. I declared solemnly that it was not, but they only shook their heads and would not be satisfied. Then they consulted a good while; and finally they confiscated it. I was very sorry for this, because I had worked a long time on that joke, and took a good deal of pride in it, and now I suppose I shall never see it any more. I suppose it will be sent up and filed away among the criminal archives of Rome, and will always be regarded as a mysterious infernal machine which would have blown up like a mine and scattered the good Pope all around, but for a miraculous providential interference. And I suppose that all the time I am in Rome the police will dog me about from place to place because they think I am a dangerous character.

It is fearfully hot in Civita Vecchia. The streets are made very narrow and the houses built very solid and heavy and high, as a protection against the heat. This is the first Italian town I have seen which does not appear to have a patron saint. I suppose no saint but the one that went up in the chariot of fire could stand the climate.

There is nothing here to see. They have not even a cathedral, with eleven tons of solid silver archbishops in the back room; and they do not show you any moldy buildings that are seven thousand years old; nor any smoke-dried old fire-screens which are *chef d'œuvres* of Rubens or Simpson, or Titian or Ferguson, or any of those parties; and they haven't any bottled fragments of saints, and not even a nail from the true cross. We are going to Rome. There is nothing to see here.

From *The Innocents Abroad,* 1869.

23 : *Rome*

OF COURSE we have been to the monster Church of St. Peter, frequently. I knew its dimensions. I knew it was a prodigious structure. I knew it was just about the length of the capitol at Washington—say seven hundred and thirty feet. I knew it was three hundred and sixty-four feet wide, and consequently wider than the capitol. I knew that the cross on the top of the dome of the church was four hundred and thirty-eight feet above the ground, and therefore about a hundred or maybe a hundred and twenty-five feet higher than the dome of the capitol. Thus I had one gauge. I wished to come as near forming a correct idea of how it was going to look as possible; I had a curiosity to see how much I would err. I erred considerably. St. Peter's did not look nearly so large as the capitol, and certainly not a twentieth part as beautiful, from the outside.

When we reached the door, and stood fairly within the church, it was impossible to comprehend that it was a *very* large building. I had to *cipher* a comprehension of it. I had to ransack my memory for some more similes. St. Peter's is bulky. Its height and size would represent two of the Washington capitol set one on top of the other —if the capitol were wider; or two blocks or two blocks and a half of ordinary buildings set one on top of the other. St. Peter's *was* that large, but it could and would not look so. The trouble was that everything in it and about it was on such a scale of uniform vastness that there were no contrasts to judge by—none but the people, and I had not noticed them. They were insects. The statues of children holding vases of holy water were immense, according to the tables of figures, but so was everything else around them. The mosaic pictures in the dome were huge, and were made of thousands and thousands of cubes of glass as large as the end of my little finger, but those pictures looked smooth, and gaudy of color, and in good proportion to the dome. Evidently they would not answer to measure by. Away down toward the far end of the church (I thought it was really clear at the far end, but discovered afterward that it was in the center, under the dome) stood the thing they call the *baldacchino*—a great bronze pyramidal framework like that which upholds a mosquito-bar. It only looked like a considerably magnified bedstead—nothing more. Yet I knew it was a good deal more than half as high as Niagara Falls. It was overshadowed by a dome so mighty that its own height was snubbed. The four great square piers or pillars that stand equidistant from each other in the church, and support the roof, I could not work up to their real dimensions by any method of comparison. I knew that the faces of each were about the width of a very large dwelling-house front (fifty or sixty feet), and that they were twice as high as an ordinary three-story dwelling, but still they looked small. I tried all the different ways I could think of to compel myself to understand how large St. Peter's was, but with small success. The mosaic portrait of an Apostle who was writing with a pen six feet long seemed only an ordinary Apostle.

But the people attracted my attention after a while. To stand in the door of St. Peter's and look at men down toward its further extremity, two blocks away, has a diminishing effect on them; surrounded by the prodigious pictures and statues, and lost in the vast spaces, they look very much smaller than they would if they stood two blocks away in the open air. I "averaged" a man as he passed me and watched him as he drifted far down by the *baldacchino* and beyond—watched him dwindle to an insignificant school-boy, and then, in the midst of the silent throng of human pygmies gliding about him, I lost him. The church had lately been decorated, on the occasion of a great ceremony in honor of St. Peter, and men were engaged now in removing the flowers and gilt paper from the walls and pillars. As no ladders could reach the great heights, the men swung themselves down from balustrades and the capitals of pilasters by ropes, to do this work. The upper gallery which encircles the inner sweep of the dome is two hundred and forty feet above the floor of the church—very few steeples in America could reach up to it. Visitors always go up there to look down into the church because one gets the best idea of some of the heights and distances from that point. While we stood on the floor one of the workmen swung loose from that gallery at the end of a long rope. I had not supposed, before, that a man *could* look so much like a spider. He was insignificant in size, and his rope seemed only a thread. Seeing that he took up so little space, I could believe the story, then, that ten thousand troops went to St. Peter's once to hear mass, and their commanding officer came afterward, and not finding them, supposed they had not yet arrived. But they were in the church, nevertheless—they were in one of the transepts. Nearly fifty thousand persons assembled in St. Peter's to hear the publishing of the dogma of the Immaculate Conception. It is estimated that the floor of the church affords standing-room for—for a large number of people; I have forgotten the exact figures. But it is no matter—it is near enough.

They have twelve small pillars, in St. Peter's, which came from Solomon's Temple. They have, also—which was far more interesting to me—a piece of the true cross, and some nails, and a part of the crown of thorns.

Of course, we ascended to the summit of the dome, and, of course, we also went up into the gilt copper ball which is above it. There was room there for a dozen persons, with a little crowding, and it was as close and hot as an oven. Some of those people who are so fond of writing their names in prominent places had been there before us—a million or two, I should think. From the dome of St. Peter's one can see every notable object in Rome, from the Castle of St. Angelo to the Coliseum. He can discern the seven hills upon which Rome is built. He can see the Tiber, and the locality of the bridge which Horatius kept "in the brave days of old" when Lars Porsena attempted to cross it with his invading host. He can see the spot where the Horatii and the Curiatii fought their famous battle. He can see the broad green Campagna, stretching away toward the mountains, with its scattered arches and broken aqueducts of the olden time, so picturesque in their gray ruin, and so daintily festooned with vines. He can see the Alban Mountains, the Apennines, the Sabine Hills, and the blue Mediterranean. He can see a panorama that is varied, extensive, beautiful to the eye, and more illustrious in history than any other in Europe. About his feet is spread the remnant of a city that once had a population of four million souls; and among its massed edifices stand the ruins of temples, columns, and triumphal arches that knew the Cæsars, and the noonday of Roman splendor; and close by them, in unimpaired strength, is a drain of arched and heavy masonry that belonged to that older city which stood here before Romulus and Remus were born or Rome thought of. The Appian Way is here yet, and looking much as it did, perhaps, when the triumphal processions of the emperors moved over it in other days bringing fettered princes from the confines of the earth. We cannot see the long array of chariots and mail-clad men laden with the spoils of conquest, but we can imagine the pageant, after a fashion. We look out upon many objects of interest from the dome of St. Peter's; and last of all, almost at our feet, our eyes rest upon the building which was once the Inquisition. How times changed, between the older ages and the new! Some seventeen or eighteen centuries ago, the ignorant men of Rome were wont to put Christians in the arena of the Coliseum yonder, and turn the wild beasts in upon them for a show. It was for a lesson as well. It was to teach the people to abhor and fear the new doctrine the followers of Christ were teaching. The beasts tore the victims limb from limb and made poor mangled corpses of them in the twinkling of an eye. But when the Christians came into power, when the holy Mother Church became mistress of the barbarians, she taught them the error of their ways by no such means. No, she put them in this pleasant Inquisition and pointed to the Blessed Redeemer, who was so gentle and so merciful toward all men, and they urged the barbarians to love him; and they did all they could to persuade them to love and honor him—first by twisting their thumbs out of joint with a screw; then by nipping their flesh with pincers—red-hot ones, because they are the most comfortable in cold weather; then by skinning them alive a little, and finally by roasting them in public. They always convinced those barbarians. The true religion, properly administered, as the good Mother Church used to administer it, is very, very soothing. It is wonderfully persuasive, also. There is a great difference between feeding parties to wild beasts and stirring up their finer feelings in an Inquisition. One is the system of degraded barbarians, the other of enlightened, civilized people. It is a great pity the playful Inquisition is no more.

I prefer not to describe St. Peter's. It has been done before. The ashes of Peter, the disciple of the Saviour, repose in a crypt under the *baldacchino*. We stood reverently in that place; so did we also in the Mamertine Prison, where he was confined, where he converted the soldiers, and where tradition says he caused a spring of water to flow in order that he might baptize them. But when they showed us the print of Peter's face in the hard stone of the prison wall and said he made that by falling up against it, we doubted. And when, also, the monk at the Church of San Sebastian showed us a paving-stone with two great footprints in it and said that Peter's feet made those, we lacked confidence again. Such things do not impress one. The monk said that angels came and liberated Peter from prison by night, and he started away from Rome by the Appian Way. The Saviour met him and told him to go back, which he did. Peter left those footprints in the stone upon which he stood at the time. It was not stated how it was ever discovered whose footprints they were, seeing the interview occurred secretly and at night. The print of the face in the prison was that of a man of common size; the footprints were those of a man ten or twelve feet high. The discrepancy confirmed our unbelief.

We necessarily visited the Forum, where Cæsar was assassinated, and also the Tarpeian Rock. We saw the Dying Gladiator at the Capitol, and I think that even we appreciated that wonder of art; as much, perhaps, as we did that fearful story wrought in marble, in the Vatican—the Laocoön. And then the Coliseum.

Everybody knows the picture of the Coliseum; everybody recognizes at once that "looped and windowed" band-box with a side bitten out. Being rather isolated, it shows to better advantage than any other of the monuments of ancient Rome. Even the beautiful Pantheon, whose pagan altars uphold the cross now, and whose

Venus, tricked out in consecrated gimcracks, does reluctant duty as a Virgin Mary to-day, is built about with shabby houses and its stateliness sadly marred. But the monarch of all European ruins, the Coliseum, maintains that reserve and that royal seclusion which is proper to majesty. Weeds and flowers spring from its massy arches and its circling seats, and vines hang their fringes from its lofty walls. An impressive silence broods over the monstrous structure where such multitudes of men and women were wont to assemble in other days. The butterflies have taken the places of the queens of fashion and beauty of eighteen centuries ago, and the lizards sun themselves in the sacred seat of the emperor. More vividly than all the written histories, the Coliseum tells the story of Rome's grandeur and Rome's decay. It is the worthiest type of both that exists. Moving about the Rome of to-day, we might find it hard to believe in her old magnificence and her millions of population; but with this stubborn evidence before us that she was obliged to have a theater with sitting-room for eighty thousand persons and standing-room for twenty thousand more, to accommodate such of her citizens as required amusement, we find belief less difficult. The Coliseum is over one thousand six hundred feet long, seven hundred and fifty wide, and one hundred and sixty-five high. Its shape is oval.

In America we make convicts useful at the same time that we punish them for their crimes. We farm them out and compel them to earn money for the state by making barrels and building roads. Thus we combine business with retribution, and all things are lovely. But in ancient Rome they combined religious duty with pleasure. Since it was necessary that the new sect called Christians should be exterminated, the people judged it wise to make this work profitable to the state at the same time, and entertaining to the public. In addition to the gladiatorial combats and other shows, they sometimes threw members of the hated sect into the arena of the Coliseum and turned wild beasts in upon them. It is estimated that seventy-thousand Christians suffered martyrdom in this place. This has made the Coliseum holy ground, in the eyes of the followers of the Saviour. And well it might; for if the chain that bound a saint, and the footprints a saint has left upon a stone he chanced to stand upon, be holy, surely the spot where a man gave up his life for his faith is holy.

Seventeen or eighteen centuries ago this Coliseum was *the* theater of Rome, and Rome was mistress of the world. Splendid pageants were exhibited here, in the presence of the emperor, the great ministers of state, the nobles, and vast audiences of citizens of smaller consequence. Gladiators fought with gladiators and at times with warrior prisoners from many a distant land. It was *the* theater of Rome—of the world—and the man of fashion who could not let fall in a casual and unintentional manner something about "my private box at the Coliseum" could not move in the first circles. When the clothing-store merchant wished to consume the corner-grocery man with envy, he bought reserved seats in the front row and let the thing be known. When the irresistible dry-goods clerk wished to blight and destroy, according to his native instinct, he got himself up regardless of expense and took some other fellow's young lady to the Coliseum, and then accented the affront by cramming her with ice-cream between the acts, or by approaching the cage and stirring up the martyrs with his whalebone cane for her edification. The Roman swell was in his true element only when he stood up against a pillar and fingered his mustache unconscious of the ladies; when he viewed the bloody combats through an opera-glass two inches long; when he excited the envy of provincials by criticisms which showed that he had been to the Coliseum many and many a time and was long ago over the novelty of it; when he turned away with a yawn at last and said:

"*He* a star! handles his sword like an apprentice brigand! he'll do for the country, maybe, but he don't answer for the metropolis!"

Glad was the contraband that had a seat in the pit at the Saturday matinée, and happy the Roman street boy who ate his peanuts and guyed the gladiators from the dizzy gallery.

For me was reserved the high honor of discovering among the rubbish of the ruined Coliseum the only playbill of that establishment now extant. There was a suggestive smell of mint-drops about it still, a corner of it had evidently been chewed, and on the margin, in choice Latin, these words were written in a delicate female hand:

> Meet me on the Tarpeian Rock to-morrow evening, dear, at sharp seven. Mother will be absent on a visit to her friends in the Sabine Hills. CLAUDIA.

Ah, where is that lucky youth to-day, and where the little hand that wrote those dainty lines? Dust and ashes these seventeen hundred years:

Thus reads the bill:

ROMAN COLISEUM.

UNPARALLELED ATTRACTION!

NEW PROPERTIES! NEW LIONS! NEW GLADIATORS!

Engagement of the renowned

MARCUS MARCELLUS VALERIAN!

FOR SIX NIGHTS ONLY!

The management beg leave to offer to the public an entertainment surpassing in magnificence anything that has heretofore been attempted on any stage. No expense has been spared to make the opening season one which shall be worthy the generous patronage which the management feel sure will crown their efforts. The management beg leave to state that they have succeeded in securing the services of a

GALAXY OF TALENT!

such as has not been beheld in Rome before.

The performance will commence this evening with a

GRAND BROADSWORD COMBAT!

between two young and promising amateurs and a celebrated Parthian gladiator who has just arrived a prisoner from the Camp of Verus.

This will be followed by a grand moral

BATTLE-AX ENGAGEMENT!

between the renowned Valerian (with one hand tied behind him) and two gigantic savages from Britain.

After which the renowned Valerian (if he survive) will fight with the broadsword,

LEFT HANDED!

against six Sophomores and a Freshman from the Gladiatorial College!

A long series of brilliant engagements will follow, in which the finest talent of the Empire will take part.

After which the celebrated Infant Prodigy known as

"THE YOUNG ACHILLES,"

will engage four tiger whelps in combat, armed with no other weapon than his little spear!

The whole to conclude with a chaste and elegant

GENERAL SLAUGHTER!

In which thirteen African Lions and twenty-two Barbarian Prisoners will war with each other until all are exterminated.

BOX OFFICE NOW OPEN.

Dress Circle One Dollar; Children and Servants half price.

An efficient police force will be on hand to preserve order and keep the wild beasts from leaping the railings and discommoding the audience.

Doors open at 7; performance begins at 8.

POSITIVELY NO FREE LIST.

Diodorus Job Press.

It was as singular as it was gratifying that I was also so fortunate as to find among the rubbish of the arena a stained and mutilated copy of the *Roman Daily Battle-Ax,* containing a critique upon this very performance. It comes to hand too late by many centuries to rank as news, and therefore I translate and publish it simply to show how very little the general style and phraseology of dramatic criticism has altered in the ages that have dragged their slow length along since the carriers laid this one damp and fresh before their Roman patrons:

THE OPENING SEASON.—COLISEUM.—Notwithstanding the inclemency of the weather, quite a respectable number of the rank and fashion of the city assembled last night to witness the debut upon metropolitan boards of the young tragedian who has of late been winning such golden opinions in the amphitheaters of the provinces. Some sixty thousand persons were present, and but for the fact that the streets were almost impassable, it is fair to presume that the house would have been full. His august Majesty, the Emperor Aurelius, occupied the imperial box, and was the cynosure of all eyes. Many illustrious nobles and generals of the Empire graced the occasion with their presence, and not the least among them was the young patrician lieutenant whose laurels, won in the ranks of the "Thundering Legion," are still so green upon his brow. The cheer which greeted his entrance was heard beyond the Tiber!

The late repairs and decorations add both to the comeliness and the comfort of the Coliseum. The new cushions are a great improvement upon the hard marble seats we have been so long accustomed to. The present management deserve well of the public. They have restored to the Coliseum the gilding, the rich upholstery, and the uniform magnificence which old Coliseum frequenters tell us Rome was so proud of fifty years ago.

The opening scene last night—the broadsword combat between two young amateurs and a famous Parthian gladiator who was sent here a prisoner—was very fine. The elder of the two young gentlemen handled his weapon with a grace that marked the possession of extraordinary talent. His feint of thrusting, followed instantly by a happily delivered blow which unhelmeted the Parthian, was received with hearty applause. He was not thoroughly up in the backhanded stroke, but it was very gratifying to his numerous friends to know that in time, practice would have overcome this defect. However, he was killed. His sisters, who were present, expressed considerable regret. His mother left the Coliseum. The other youth maintained the contest with such spirit as to call forth enthusiastic bursts of applause. When at last he fell a corpse, his aged mother ran screaming, with hair disheveled and tears streaming from her eyes, and swooned away just as her hands were clutching at the railings of the arena. She was promptly removed by the police. Under the circumstances the woman's conduct was pardonable, perhaps, but we suggest that such exhibitions interfere with the decorum which should be preserved during the performances, and are highly improper in the presence of the Emperor. The Parthian prisoner fought bravely and well; and well he might, for he was fighting for both life and liberty. His wife and children were there to nerve his arm with their love, and to remind him of the old home he should see again if he conquered. When his second assailant fell, the woman clasped her children to her breast and wept for joy. But it was only a transient happiness. The captive staggered toward her and she saw that the liberty he had earned was earned too late. He was wounded unto death. Thus the first act closed in a manner which was entirely satisfactory. The manager was called before the curtain and returned his thanks for the honor done him, in a speech which was replete with wit and humor, and closed by hoping that his humble efforts to afford cheerful and instructive entertainment would continue to meet with the approbation of the Roman public.

The star now appeared, and was received with vociferous applause and the simultaneous waving of sixty thousand handkerchiefs. Marcus Marcellus Valerian (stage-name—his real name is Smith) is a splendid specimen of physical development, and an artist of rare merit. His management of the battle-ax is wonderful. His gaiety and his playfulness are irresistible, in his comic parts, and yet they are inferior to his sublime conceptions in the grave realm of tragedy. When his ax was describing fiery circles about the heads of the bewildered barbarians, in exact time with his springing body and his prancing legs, the audience gave way to uncontrollable bursts of laughter; but when the back of his weapon broke the skull of one and almost in the same instant its edge clove the other's body in twain, the howl of enthusiastic applause that shook the building was the acknowledgment of a critical assemblage that he was a master of the noblest department of his profession. If he has a fault (and we are sorry to even intimate that he has), it is that of glancing at the audience, in the midst of the most exciting moments of the performance, as if seeking admiration. The pausing in a fight to bow when bouquets are thrown to him is also in bad taste. In the great left-handed combat he appeared to be looking at the audience half the time, instead of carving his adversaries; and when he had slain all the sophomores and was dallying with the freshman, he stooped and snatched a bouquet as it fell, and offered it to his adversary at a time when a blow was descending which promised favorably to be his death-warrant. Such levity is proper enough in the provinces, we make no doubt, but it ill suits the dignity of the metropolis. We trust our young friend will take these remarks in good part, for we mean them solely for his benefit. All who know us are aware that although we are at times justly severe upon tigers and martyrs, we never intentionally offend gladiators.

The Infant Prodigy performed wonders. He overcame his four tiger whelps with ease, and with no other hurt than the loss of a portion of his scalp. The General Slaughter was rendered with a faithfulness to details which reflects the highest credit upon the late participants in it.

Upon the whole, last night's performances shed honor not only upon the management but upon the city that encourages and sustains such wholesome and instructive entertainments. We would simply suggest that the practice of vulgar young boys in the gallery of shying peanuts and paper pellets at the tigers, and saying "Hi-yi!" and manifesting approbation or dissatisfaction by such observations as "Bully for the lion!" "Go it, Gladdy!" "Boots!" "Speech!" "Take a walk around the block!" and so on, are extremely reprehensible, when the Emperor is present, and ought to be stopped by the police. Several times last night when the supernumeraries entered the arena to drag out the bodies, the young ruffians in the gallery shouted,

"Supe! supe!" and also, "Oh, what a coat!" and "Why don't you pad them shanks?" and made use of various other remarks expressive of derision. These things are very annoying to the audience.

A matinee for the little folks is promised for this afternoon, on which occasion several martyrs will be eaten by the tigers. The regular performance will continue every night till further notice. Material change of program every evening. Benefit of Valerian, Tuesday, 29, if he lives.

I used to worship the mighty genius of Michael Angelo—that man who was great in poetry, painting, sculpture, architecture—great in everything he undertook. But I do not want Michael Angelo for breakfast—for luncheon—for dinner—for tea—for supper—for between meals. I like a change, occasionally. In Genoa, he designed everything; in Milan he or his pupils designed everything; he designed the Lake of Como; in Padua, Verona, Venice, Bologna, who did we ever hear of, from guides but Michael Angelo? In Florence, he painted everything, designed everything, nearly, and what he did not design he used to sit on a favorite stone and look at, and they showed us the stone. In Pisa he designed everything but the old shot-tower, and they would have attributed that to him if it had not been so awfully out of the perpendicular. He designed the piers of Leghorn and the custom-house regulations of Civita Vecchia. But, here—here it is frightful. He designed St. Peter's; he designed the Pope; he designed the Pantheon, the uniform of the Pope's soldiers, the Tiber, the Vatican, the Coliseum, the Capitol, the Tarpeian Rock, the Barberini Palace, St. John Lateran, the Campagna, the Appian Way, the Seven Hills, the Baths of Caracalla, the Claudian Aqueduct, the Cloaca Maxima—the eternal bore designed the Eternal City, and unless all men and books do lie, he painted everything in it! Dan said the other day to the guide, "Enough, enough, enough! Say no more! Lump the whole thing! say that the Creator made Italy from designs by Michael Angelo!"

I never felt so fervently thankful, so soothed, so tranquil, so filled with a blessed peace, as I did yesterday when I learned that Michael Angelo was dead. . . .

In this place I may as well jot down a chapter concerning those necessary nuisances, European guides. Many a man has wished in his heart he could do without his guide; but knowing he could not, has wished he could get some amusement out of him as a remuneration for the affliction of his society. We accomplished this latter matter, and if our experience can be made useful to others they are welcome to it.

Guides know about enough English to tangle everything up so that a man can make neither head nor tail of it. They know their story by heart—the history of every statue, painting, cathedral, or other wonder they show you. They know it and tell it as a parrot would—and if you interrupt, and throw them off the track, they have to go back and begin over again. All their lives long, they are employed in showing strange things to foreigners and listening to their bursts of admiration. It is human nature to take delight in exciting admiration. It is what prompts children to say "smart" things, and do absurd ones, and in other ways "show off" when company is present. It is what makes gossips turn out in rain and storm to go and be the first to tell a startling bit of news. Think, then, what a passion it becomes with a guide, whose privilege it is, every day, to show to strangers wonders that throw them into perfect ecstasies of admiration! He gets so that he could not by any possibility live in a soberer atmosphere. After we discovered this, we *never* went into ecstasies any more—we never admired anything—we never showed any but impassible faces and stupid indifference in the presence of the sublimest wonders a guide had to display. We had found their weak point. We have made good use of it ever since. We have made some of those people savage at times, but we have never lost our own serenity.

The doctor asks the questions, generally, because he can keep his countenance, and look more like an inspired idiot, and throw more imbecility into the tone of his voice than any man that lives. It comes natural to him.

The guides in Genoa are delighted to secure an American party, because Americans so much wonder, and deal so much in sentiment and emotion before any relic of Columbus. Our guide there fidgeted about as if he had swallowed a spring mattress. He was full of animation—full of impatience. He said:

"Come wis me, genteelmen!—come! I show you ze letter-writing by Christopher Colombo!—write it himself!—write it wis his own hand!—come!"

He took us to the municipal palace. After much impressive fumbling of keys and opening of locks, the stained and aged document was spread before us. The guide's eyes sparkled. He danced about us and tapped the parchment with his finger:

"What I tell you, genteelmen! Is it not so? See! handwriting Christopher Colombo!—write it himself!"

We looked indifferent—unconcerned. The doctor examined the document very deliberately, during a painful pause. Then he said, without any show of interest:

"Ah—Ferguson—what—what did you say was the name of the party who wrote this?"

"Christopher Colombo! ze great Christopher Colombo!"

Another deliberate examination.

"Ah—did he write it himself, or—or how?"

"He write it himself!—Christopher Colombo! he's own handwriting, write by himself!"

Then the doctor laid the document down and said:

"Why, I have seen boys in America only fourteen years old that could write better than that."

"But zis is ze great Christo—"

"I don't care who it is! It's the worst writing I ever saw. Now you mustn't think you can impose on us because we are strangers. We are not fools, by a good deal. If you have got any specimens of penmanship of real merit, trot them out!—and if you haven't, drive on!"

We drove on. The guide was considerably shaken up, but he made one more venture. He had something which he thought would overcome us. He said:

"Ah, genteelmen, you come wis me! I show you beautiful, oh, magnificent bust Christopher Colombo!—splendid, grand, magnificent!"

He brought us before the beautiful bust—for it *was* beautiful—and sprang back and struck an attitude:

"Ah, look, genteelmen!—beautiful, grand,—bust Christopher Colombo!—beautiful bust, beautiful pedestal!"

The doctor put up his eyeglass—procured for such occasions:

"Ah—what did you say this gentleman's name was?"

"Christopher Colombo!—ze great Christopher Colombo!"

"Christopher Colombo—the great Christopher Colombo. Well, what did *he* do?"

"Discover America!—discover America, oh, ze devil!"

"Discover America. No—that statement will hardly wash. We are just from America ourselves. We heard nothing about it. Christopher Colombo—pleasant name—is—is he dead?"

"Oh, *corpo di Baccho!*—three hundred year!"

"What did he die of?"

"I do not know!—I cannot tell."

"Smallpox, think?"

"I do not know, genteelmen!—I do not know *what* he die of!"

"Measles, likely?"

"Maybe—maybe—I do *not* know—I think he die of somethings."

"Parents living?"

"Im-posseeble!"

"Ah—which is the bust and which is the pedestal?"

"Santa Maria!—*zis* ze bust!—*zis* ze pedestal!"

"Ah, I see, I see—happy combination—very happy combination, indeed. Is—is this the first time this gentleman was ever on a bust?"

That joke was lost on the foreigner—guides cannot master the subtleties of the American joke.

We have made it interesting for this Roman guide. Yesterday we spent three or four hours in the Vatican again, that wonderful world of curiosities. We came very near expressing interest, sometimes—even admiration—it was very hard to keep from it. We succeeded though. Nobody else ever did, in the Vatican museums. The guide was bewildered—nonplussed. He walked his legs off, nearly, hunting up extraordinary things, and exhausted all his ingenuity on us, but it was a failure; we never showed any interest in anything. He had reserved what he considered to be his greatest wonder till the last—a royal Egyptian mummy, the best-preserved in the world, perhaps. He took us there. He felt so sure, this time, that some of his old enthusiasm came back to him:

"See, genteelmen!—Mummy! Mummy!"

The eyeglass came up as calmly, as deliberately as ever.

"Ah—Ferguson—what did I understand you to say the gentleman's name was?"

"Name?—he got no name!—Mummy!—'Gyptian mummy!"

"Yes, yes. Born here?"

"No! *'Gyptian* mummy!"

"Ah, just so. Frenchman, I presume?"

"No!—*not* Frenchman, not Roman!—Born in Egypta!"

"Born in Egypta. Never heard of Egypta before. Foreign locality, likely. Mummy—mummy. How calm he is—how self-possessed. Is, ah—is he dead?"

"Oh, *sacré bleu,* been dead three thousan' year!"

The doctor turned on him savagely:

"Here, now, what do you mean by such conduct as this! Playing us for Chinamen because we are strangers and trying to learn! Trying to impose your vile second-hand carcasses on *us!*—thunder and lightning, I've a notion to—to—if you've got a nice *fresh* corpse, fetch him out!—or, by George, we'll brain you!"

We make it exceedingly interesting for this Frenchman. However, he has paid us back, partly, without knowing it. He came to the hotel this morning to ask if we were up, and he endeavored as well as he could to describe us, so that the landlord would know which persons he meant. He finished with the casual remark that we were lunatics. The observation was so innocent and so honest that it amounted to a very good thing for a guide to say.

There is one remark (already mentioned) which never yet has failed to disgust these guides. We use it always, when we can think of nothing else to say. After they have exhausted their enthusiasm pointing out to us and praising the beauties of some ancient bronze image or broken-legged statue, we look at it stupidly and in silence for five, ten, fifteen minutes—as long as we can hold out, in fact—and then ask:

"Is—is he dead?"

That conquers the serenest of them. It is not what they are looking for—especially a new guide. Our Roman Ferguson is the most patient, unsuspecting, long-suffering subject we have had yet. We shall be sorry to part with him. We have enjoyed his society very much. We trust he has enjoyed ours, but we are harassed with doubts.

We have been in the catacombs. It was like going down into a very deep cellar, only it was a cellar which had no end to it. The narrow passages are roughly hewn in the rock, and on each hand, as you pass along, the hollowed shelves are carved out, from three to fourteen deep; each held a corpse once. There are names, and Christian symbols, and prayers, or sentences expressive of Christian hopes, carved upon nearly every sarcophagus. The dates belong away back in the dawn of the Christian era, of course. Here, in these holes in the ground, the first Christians sometimes burrowed to escape persecution. They crawled out at night to get food, but remained under cover in the daytime. The priest told us that St. Sebastian lived underground for some time while he was being hunted; he went out one day, and the soldiery discovered and shot him to death with arrows. Five or six of the early Popes—those who reigned about sixteen hundred years ago—held their papal courts and advised with their clergy in the bowels of the earth. During seventeen years—from A. D. 235 to A. D. 252—the Popes did not appear above ground. Four were raised to the great office during that period. Four years apiece, or thereabouts. It is very suggestive of the unhealthiness of underground graveyards as places of residence. One Pope afterward spent his entire pontificate in the catacombs—eight years. Another was discovered in them and murdered in the episcopal chair. There was no satisfaction in being a Pope in those days. There were too many annoyances. There are one hundred and sixty catacombs under Rome, each with its maze of narrow passages crossing and recrossing each other and each passage walled to the top with scooped graves its entire length. A careful estimate makes the length of the passages of all the catacombs combined foot up nine hundred miles, and their graves number seven millions. We did not go through all the passages of all the catacombs. We were very anxious to do it, and made the necessary arrangements, but our too limited time obliged us to give up the idea. So we only groped through the dismal labyrinth of St. Calixtus, under the Church of St. Sebastian. In the various catacombs are small chapels rudely hewn in the stones, and here the early Christians often held their religious services by dim, ghostly lights. Think of mass and a sermon away down in those tangled caverns under ground!

In the catacombs were buried St. Cecilia, St. Agnes, and several other of the most celebrated of the saints. In the catacombs of St. Calixtus, St. Bridget used to remain long hours in holy contemplation, and St. Charles Borromeo was wont to spend whole nights in prayer there. It was also the scene of a very marvelous thing.

> Here the heart of St. Philip Neri was so inflamed with divine love as to burst his ribs.

I find that grave statement in a book published in New York, in 1858, and written by "Rev. William H. Neligan, LL.D., M.A., Trinity College, Dublin; Member of the Archæological Society of

Great Britain." Therefore, I believe it. Otherwise, I could not. Under other circumstances I should have felt a curiosity to know what Philip had for dinner.

This author puts my credulity on its mettle every now and then. He tells of one St. Joseph Calasanctius whose house in Rome he visited; he visited only the house—the priest has been dead two hundred years. He says the Virgin Mary appeared to this saint. Then he continues:

> His tongue and his heart, which were found after nearly a century to be whole, when the body was disinterred before his canonization, are still preserved in a glass case, and after two centuries the heart is still whole. When the French troops came to Rome, and when Pius VII was carried away prisoner, blood dripped from it.

To read that in a book written by a monk far back in the Middle Ages, would surprise no one; it would sound natural and proper; but when it is seriously stated in the middle of the nineteenth century, by a man of finished education, an LL.D., M.A., and archæological magnate, it sounds strangely enough. Still, I would gladly change my unbelief for Neligan's faith, and let him make the conditions as hard as he pleased.

The old gentleman's undoubting, unquestioning simplicity has a rare freshness about it in these matter-of-fact railroading and telegraphing days.

From *The Innocents Abroad,* 1869.

24 : Naples and Vicinity

THE SHIP IS LYING HERE in the harbor of Naples—quarantined. She has been here several days and will remain several more. We that came by rail from Rome have escaped this misfortune. Of course no one is allowed to go on board the ship, or come ashore from her. She is a prison, now. The passengers probably spend the long, blazing days looking out from under the awnings at Vesuvius and the beautiful city—and in swearing. Think of ten days of this sort of pastime!—We go out every day in a boat and request them to come ashore. It soothes them. We lie ten steps from the ship and tell them how splendid the city is; and how much better the hotel fare is here than anywhere else in Europe; and how cool it is; and what frozen continents of ice-cream there are; and what a time we are having cavorting about the country and sailing to the islands in the Bay. This tranquilizes them.

ASCENT OF VESUVIUS

I shall remember our trip to Vesuvius for many a day—partly because of its sight-seeing experiences, but chiefly on account of the fatigue of the journey. Two or three of us had been resting ourselves among the tranquil and beautiful scenery of the island of Ischia, eighteen miles out in the harbor, for two days; we called it "resting," but I do not remember now what the resting consisted of, for when we got back to Naples we had not slept for forty-eight hours. We were just about to go to bed early in the evening, and catch up on some of the sleep we had lost, when we heard of this Vesuvius expedition. There were to be eight of us in the party, and we were to leave Naples at midnight. We laid in some provisions for the trip, engaged carriages to take us to Annunciation, and then moved about the city, to keep awake, till twelve. We got away punctually, and in the course of an hour and a half arrived at the town of Annunciation. Annunciation is the very last place under the sun. In other towns in Italy, the people lie around quietly and wait for you to ask them a question or do some overt act that can be charged for—but in Annunciation they have lost even that fragment of delicacy; they seize a lady's shawl from a chair and hand it to her and charge a penny; they open a carriage door, and charge for it—shut it when you get out, and charge for it; they help you to take off a duster—two cents; brush your clothes and make them worse than they were before—two cents; smile upon you—two cents; bow, with a lickspittle smirk, hat in hand—two cents; they volunteer all information, such as that the mules will arrive presently—two cents—warm day, sir—two cents—take you four hours to make the ascent—two cents. And so they go.

They crowd you—infest you—swarm about you, and sweat and smell offensively, and look sneaking and mean, and obsequious. There is no office too degrading for them to perform, for money. I have had no opportunity to find out anything about the upper classes by my own observation, but from what I hear said about them I judge that what they lack in one or two of the bad traits the *canaille* have they make up in one or two others that are worse. How the people beg!—many of them very well dressed, too.

I said I knew nothing against the upper classes by personal observation. I must recall it! I had forgotten. What I saw their bravest and their fairest do last night, the lowest multitude that could be scraped up out of the purlieus of Christendom would blush to do, I think. They assembled by hundreds, and even thousands, in the great Theater of San Carlo, to do—what? Why, simply, to make fun of an old woman—to deride, to hiss, to jeer at an actress they once worshiped, but whose beauty is faded now and whose voice has lost its former richness. Everybody spoke of the rare sport there was to be. They said the theater would be crammed, because Frezzolini was going to sing. It was said she could not sing well, now, but then the people liked to see her, anyhow. And so we went. And every time the woman sang they hissed and laughed—the whole magnificent house—and as soon as she left the stage they called her on again with applause. Once or twice she was encored five and six times in succession, and received with hisses when she appeared, and discharged with hisses and laughter when she had finished—then instantly encored and insulted again! And how the high-born knaves enjoyed it! White-kidded gentlemen and ladies laughed till the tears came, and clapped their hands in very ecstasy when that unhappy old woman would come meekly out for the sixth time, with uncomplaining patience, to meet a storm of hisses! It was the cruelest exhibition—the most wanton, the most unfeeling. The singer would have conquered an audience of American rowdies by her brave, unflinching tranquillity (for she answered encore after encore, and smiled and bowed pleasantly, and sang the best she possibly could, and went bowing off, through all the jeers and hisses, without ever losing countenance or temper): and surely in any other land than Italy her sex and her helplessness must have been an ample protection to her—she could have needed no other. Think what a multitude of small souls were crowded into that theater last night. If the manager could have filled his theater with Neapolitan souls alone, without the bodies, he could not have cleared less than ninety millions of dollars. What traits of character must a man have to enable him to help three thousand miscreants to hiss, and jeer, and laugh at one friendless old woman, and shamefully humiliate her? He must have *all* the vile, mean traits there are. My observation persuades me (I do not like to venture beyond my own personal observation) that the upper classes of Naples possess those traits of character. Otherwise they may be very good people; I cannot say.

ASCENT OF VESUVIUS—CONTINUED

In this city of Naples, they believe in and support one of the wretchedest of all the religious impostures one can find in Italy—the miraculous liquefaction of the blood of St. Januarius. Twice a year the priests assemble all the people at the Cathedral, and get out this vial of clotted blood and let them see it slowly dissolve and become liquid—and every day for eight days this dismal farce is repeated while the priests go among the crowd and collect money for the exhibition. The first day, the blood liquefies in forty-seven minutes—the church is crammed, then, and time must be allowed the collectors to get around: after that it liquefies a little quicker and a little quicker, every day, as the houses grow smaller, till on the eighth day, with only a few dozen present to see the miracle, it liquefies in four minutes.

And here, also, they used to have a grand procession, of priests, citizens, soldiers, sailors, and the high dignitaries of the City Government, once a year, to shave the head of a made-up Madonna—a stuffed and painted image, like a milliner's dummy—whose hair miraculously grew and restored itself every twelve months. They still kept up this shaving procession as late as four or five years ago. It was a source of great profit to the church that possessed the remarkable effigy, and the ceremony of the public barbering of her was always carried out with the greatest possible éclat and display—the more the better, because the more excitement there was about it the larger the crowds it drew and the heavier the revenues it produced—but at last a day came when the Pope and his servants were unpopular in Naples, and the City Government stopped the Madonna's annual show.

There we have two specimens of these Neapolitans—two of the

silliest possible frauds, which half the population religiously and faithfully believed, and the other half either believed also or else said nothing about, and thus lent themselves to the support of the imposture. I am very well satisfied to think the whole population believed in those poor, cheap miracles—a people who want two cents every time they bow to you, and who abuse a woman, are capable of it, I think.

ASCENT OF VESUVIUS—CONTINUED

These Neapolitans always ask four times as much money as they intend to take, but if you give them what they first demand, they feel ashamed of themselves for aiming so low, and immediately ask more. When money is to be paid and received, there is always some vehement jawing and gesticulating about it. One cannot buy and pay for two cents' worth of clams without trouble and a quarrel. One "course," in a two-horse carriage, costs a franc—that is law—but the hackman always demands more, on some pretense or other, and if he gets it he makes a new demand. It is said that a stranger took a one-horse carriage for a course—tariff, half a franc. He gave the man five francs, by way of experiment. He demanded more, and received another franc. Again he demanded more, and got a franc—demanded more, and it was refused. He grew vehement—was again refused, and became noisy. The stranger said, "Well, give me the seven francs again, and I will see what I can do"—and when he got them, he handed the hackman half a franc, and he immediately asked for two cents to buy a drink with. It may be thought that I am prejudiced. Perhaps I am. I would be ashamed of myself if I were not.

ASCENT OF VESUVIUS—CONTINUED

Well, as I was saying, we got our mules and horses, after an hour and a half of bargaining with the population of Annunciation, and started sleepily up the mountain, with a vagrant at each mule's tail who pretended to be driving the brute along, but was really holding on and getting himself dragged up instead. I made slow headway at first, but I began to get dissatisfied at the idea of paying my minion five francs to hold my mule back by the tail and keep him from going up the hill, and so I discharged him.

We had one magnificent picture of Naples from a high point on the mountainside. We saw nothing but the gas-lamps, of course—two-thirds of a circle, skirting the great Bay—a necklace of diamonds glinting up through the darkness from the remote distance—less brilliant than the stars overhead, but more softly, richly beautiful—and over all the great city the lights crossed and recrossed each other in many and many a sparkling line and curve. And back of the town, far around and abroad over the miles of level campagna, were scattered rows, and circles, and clusters of lights, all glowing like so many gems, and marking where a score of villages were sleeping. About this time, the fellow who was hanging on to the tail of the horse in front of me and practising all sorts of unnecessary cruelty upon the animal, got kicked some fourteen rods, and this incident, together with the fairy spectacle of the lights far in the distance, made me serenely happy, and I was glad I started to Vesuvius.

ASCENT OF VESUVIUS—CONTINUED

This subject will be excellent matter for a chapter, and to-morrow or next day I will write it.

ASCENT OF VESUVIUS—CONTINUED

"See Naples and die." Well, I do not know that one would necessarily die after merely seeing it, but to attempt to live there might turn out a little differently. To see Naples as we saw it in the early dawn from far up on the side of Vesuvius, is to see a picture of wonderful beauty. At that distance its dingy buildings looked white—and so, rank on rank of balconies, windows, and roofs, they piled themselves up from the blue ocean till the colossal castle of St. Elmo topped the grand white pyramid and gave the picture symmetry, emphasis, and completeness. And when its lilies turned to roses—when it blushed under the sun's first kiss—it was beautiful beyond all description. One might well say, then, "See Naples and die." The frame of the picture was charming, itself. In front, the smooth sea—a vast mosaic of many colors; the lofty island swimming in a dreamy haze in the distance; at our end of the city the stately double peak of Vesuvius, and its strong black ribs and seams of lava stretching down to the limitless level campagna—a green carpet that enchants the eye and leads it on and on, past clusters of trees, and isolated houses, and snowy villages, until it shreds out in a fringe of mist and general vagueness far away. It is from the Hermitage, there on the side of Vesuvius, that one should "see Naples and die."

But do not go within the walls and look at it in detail. That takes away some of the romance of the thing. The people are filthy in their habits, and this makes filthy streets and breeds disagreeable sights and smells. There never was a community so prejudiced against the cholera as these Neapolitans are. But they have good reason to be. The cholera generally vanquishes a Neapolitan when it seizes him, because, you understand, before the doctor can dig through the dirt and get at the disease the man dies. The upper classes take a sea-bath every day, and are pretty decent.

The streets are generally about wide enough for one wagon, and how they do swarm with people! It is Broadway repeated in every street, in every court, in every alley! Such masses, such throngs, such multitudes of hurrying, bustling, struggling humanity! We never saw the like of it, hardly even in New York, I think. There are seldom any sidewalks, and when there are, they are not often wide enough to pass a man on without caroming on him. So everybody walks in the street—and where the street is wide enough, carriages are forever dashing along. Why a thousand people are not run over and crippled every day is a mystery that no man can solve.

But if there is an eighth wonder in the world, it must be the dwelling-houses of Naples. I honestly believe a good majority of them are a hundred feet high! And the solid brick walls are seven feet through. You go up nine flights of stairs before you get to the "first" floor. No, not nine, but there or thereabouts. There is a little bird-cage of an iron railing in front of every window clear away up, up, up, among the eternal clouds, where the roof is, and there is always somebody looking out of every window—people of ordinary size looking out from the first floor, people a shade smaller from the second, people that look a little smaller yet from the third—and from thence upward they grow smaller and smaller by a regularly graduated diminution, till the folks in the topmost windows seem more like birds in an uncommonly tall martin-box than anything else. The perspective of one of these narrow cracks of streets, with its rows of tall houses stretching away till they come together in the distance like railway-tracks; its clothes-lines crossing over at all altitudes and waving their bannered raggedness over the swarms of people below; and the white-dressed women perched in balcony railings all the way from the pavement up to the heavens—a perspective like that is really worth going into Neapolitan details to see.

ASCENT OF VESUVIUS—CONTINUED

Naples, with its immediate suburbs, contains six hundred and twenty-five thousand inhabitants, but I am satisfied it covers no more ground than an American city of one hundred and fifty thousand. It reaches up into the air infinitely higher than three American cities, though, and there is where the secret of it lies. I will observe here, in passing, that the contrasts between opulence and poverty, and magnificence and misery, are more frequent and more striking in Naples than in Paris even. One must go to the Bois de Boulogne to see fashionable dressing, splendid equipages, and stunning liveries, and to the Faubourg St. Antoine to see vice, misery, hunger, rags, dirt—but in the thoroughfares of Naples these things are all mixed together. Naked boys of nine years and the fancy-dressed children of luxury; shreds and tatters, and brilliant uniforms; jackass carts and state carriages; beggars, princes, and bishops, jostle each other in every street. At six o'clock every evening, all Naples turns out to drive on the Riviera di Chiaja (whatever that may mean); and for two hours one may stand there and see the motliest and the worst-mixed procession go by that ever eyes beheld. Princes (there are more princes than policemen in Naples—the city is infested with them)—princes who live up seven flights of stairs and don't own any principalities, will keep a carriage and go hungry; and clerks, mechanics, milliners, and strumpets will go without their dinners and squander the money on a hack-ride in the Chiaja; the ragtag and rubbish of the city stack themselves up, to the number of twenty or thirty, on a rickety little go-cart hauled by a donkey not much bigger than a cat, and *they* drive in the Chiaja; dukes and bankers, in sumptuous carriages and with gorgeous drivers and footmen, turn out, also, and so the furious procession goes. For two hours rank and wealth, and obscurity and poverty, clatter along side by side in the wild procession, and then go home serene, happy, covered with glory!

I was looking at a magnificent marble staircase in the King's palace, the other day, which, it was said, cost five million francs, and I suppose it did cost half a million, maybe. I felt as if it must be a fine thing to live in a country where there was such comfort and such luxury as this. And then I stepped out musing, and almost walked over a vagabond who was eating his dinner on the curbstone—a piece of bread and a bunch of grapes. When I found that this mustang was clerking in a fruit establishment (he had the establishment along with him in a basket), at two cents a day, and that he had no palace at home where he lived, I lost some of my enthusiasm concerning the happiness of living in Italy.

This naturally suggests to me a thought about wages here. Lieutenants in the army get about a dollar a day, and common soldiers a couple of cents. I only know one clerk—he gets four dollars a month. Printers get six dollars and a half a month, but I have heard of a foreman who gets thirteen. To be growing suddenly and violently rich, as this man is, naturally makes him a bloated aristocrat. The airs he puts on are insufferable.

And, speaking of wages, reminds me of prices of merchandise. In Paris you pay twelve dollars a dozen for Jouvin's best kid gloves; gloves of about as good quality sell here at three or four dollars a dozen. You pay five and six dollars apiece for fine linen shirts in Paris; here and in Leghorn you pay two and a half. In Marseilles you pay forty dollars for a first-class dress-coat made by a good tailor, but in Leghorn you can get a full-dress suit for the same money. Here you get handsome business suits at from ten to twenty dollars, and in Leghorn you can get an overcoat for fifteen dollars that would cost you seventy in New York. Fine kid boots are worth eight dollars in Marseilles and four dollars here. Lyons velvets rank higher in America than those of Genoa. Yet the bulk of Lyons velvets you buy in the States are made in Genoa and imported into Lyons, where they receive the Lyons stamp and are then exported to America. You can buy enough velvet in Genoa for twenty-five dollars to make a five-hundred-dollar cloak in New York—so the ladies tell me. Of course, these things bring me back, by a natural and easy transition, to the

ASCENT OF VESUVIUS—CONTINUED

And thus the wonderful Blue Grotto is suggested to me. It is situated on the island of Capri, twenty-two miles from Naples. We chartered a little steamer and went out there. Of course, the police boarded us and put us through a health examination, and inquired into our politics, before they would let us land. The airs these little insect governments put on are in the last degree ridiculous. They even put a policeman on board of our boat to keep an eye on us as long as we were in the Capri dominions. They thought we wanted to steal the grotto, I suppose. It was worth stealing. The entrance to the cave is four feet high and four feet wide, and is in the face of a lofty perpendicular cliff—the sea-wall. You enter in small boats—and a tight squeeze it is, too. You cannot go in at all when the tide is up. Once within, you find yourself in an arched cavern about one hundred and sixty feet long, one hundred and twenty wide, and about seventy high. How deep it is no man knows. It goes down to the bottom of the ocean. The waters of this placid subterranean lake are the brightest, loveliest blue that can be imagined. They are as transparent as plate-glass, and their coloring would shame the richest sky that ever bent over Italy. No tint could be more ravishing, no luster more superb. Throw a stone into the water, and the myriad of tiny bubbles that are created flash out a brilliant glare like blue theatrical fires. Dip an oar, and its blade turns to splendid frosted silver, tinted with blue. Let a man jump in, and instantly he is cased in an armor more gorgeous than ever kingly Crusader wore.

Then we went to Ischia, but I had already been to that island and tired myself to death "resting" a couple of days and studying human villainy, with the landlord of the Grande Sentinelle for a model. So we went to Procida, and from thence to Pozzuoli, where St. Paul landed after he sailed from Samos. I landed at precisely the same spot where St. Paul landed, and so did Dan and the others. It was a remarkable coincidence. St. Paul preached to these people seven days before he started to Rome.

Nero's Baths, the ruins of Baiæ, the Temple of Serapis; Cumæ, where the Cumæan Sibyl interpreted the oracles, the Lake Agnano, with its ancient submerged city still visible far down in its depths—these and a hundred other points of interest we examined with critical imbecility, but the Grotto of the Dog claimed our chief attention, because we had heard and read so much about it. Everybody has written about the Grotto del Cane and its poisonous vapors, from Pliny down to Smith, and every tourist has held a dog over its floor by the legs to test the capabilities of the place. The dog dies in a minute and a half—a chicken instantly. As a general thing, strangers who crawl in there to sleep do not get up until they are called. And then they don't, either. The stranger that ventures to sleep there takes a permanent contract. I longed to see this grotto. I resolved to take a dog and hold him myself; suffocate him a little, and time him; suffocate him some more, and then finish him. We reached the grotto about three in the afternoon, and proceeded at once to make the experiments. But now, an important difficulty presented itself. We had no dog.

ASCENT OF VESUVIUS—CONTINUED

At the Hermitage we were about fifteen or eighteen hundred feet above the sea, and thus far a portion of the ascent had been pretty abrupt. For the next two miles the road was a mixture—sometimes the ascent was abrupt and sometimes it was not; but one characteristic it possessed all the time, without failure—without modification—it was all uncompromisingly and unspeakably infamous. It was a rough, narrow trail, and led over an old lava-flow—a black ocean which was tumbled into a thousand fantastic shapes—a wild chaos of ruin, desolation, and barrenness—a wilderness of billowy upheavals, of furious whirlpools, of miniature mountains rent asunder—of gnarled and knotted, wrinkled and twisted masses of blackness that mimicked branching roots, great vines, trunks of trees, all interlaced and mingled together; and all these weird shapes, all this turbulent panorama, all this stormy, far-stretching waste of blackness, with its thrilling suggestiveness of life, of action, of boiling, surging, furious motion, was petrified!—all stricken dead and cold in the instant of its maddest rioting!—fettered, paralyzed, and left to glower at heaven in impotent rage forevermore!

Finally we stood in a level, narrow valley (a valley that had been created by the terrific march of some old-time eruption) and on either hand towered the two steep peaks of Vesuvius. The one we had to climb—the one that contains the active volcano—seemed about eight hundred or one thousand feet high, and looked almost too straight-up-and-down for any man to climb, and certainly no mule could climb it with a man on his back. Four of these native pirates will carry you to the top in a sedan-chair, if you wish it, but suppose they were to slip and let you fall—is it likely that you would ever stop rolling? Not this side of eternity, perhaps. We left the mules, sharpened our finger-nails, and began the ascent I have been writing about so long, at twenty minutes to six in the morning. The path led straight up a rugged sweep of loose chunks of pumice-stone, and for about every two steps forward we took, we slid back one. It was so excessively steep that we had to stop, every fifty or sixty steps, and rest a moment. To see our comrades, we had to look very nearly straight up at those above us, and very nearly straight down at those below. We stood on the summit at last—it had taken an hour and fifteen minutes to make the trip.

What we saw there was simply a circular crater—a circular ditch, if you please—about two hundred feet deep, and four or five hundred feet wide, whose inner wall was about half a mile in circumference. In the center of the great circus-ring thus formed was a torn and ragged upheaval a hundred feet high, all snowed over with a sulphur crust of many and many a brilliant and beautiful color, and the ditch inclosed this like the moat of a castle, or surrounded it as a little river does a little island, if the simile is gaudy in the extreme—all mingled together in the richest confusion were red, blue, brown, black, yellow, white—I do not know that there was a color, or shade of a color, or combination of colors, unrepresented—and when the sun burst through the morning mists and fired this tinted magnificence, it topped imperial Vesuvius like a jeweled crown!

The crater itself—the ditch—was not so variegated in coloring, but yet, in its softness, richness, and unpretentious elegance, it was more charming, more fascinating to the eye. There was nothing "loud" about its well-bred and well-dressed look. Beautiful? One could stand and look down upon it for a week without getting tired of it. It had the semblance of a pleasant meadow, whose slender grasses and whose velvety mosses were frosted with a shining dust, and tinted with palest green that deepened gradually to the darkest hue of the orange leaf, and deepened yet again into gravest brown, then faded into orange, then into brightest gold, and culminated in the delicate pink of a new-blown rose. Where portions of the meadow had sunk, and where other portions had been broken up like an ice-flow, the cavernous openings of the one, and the ragged upturned edges exposed by the other, were hung with a lacework of soft-tinted crystals of sulphur that changed their deformities into quaint shapes and figures that were full of grace and beauty.

The walls of the ditch were brilliant with yellow banks of sulphur and with lava and pumice-stone of many colors. No fire was visible anywhere, but gusts of sulphurous steam issued silently and invisibly from a thousand little cracks and fissures in the crater, and were wafted to our noses with every breeze. But so long as we kept our nostrils buried in our handkerchiefs, there was small danger of suffocation.

Some of the boys thrust long slips of paper down into holes and set them on fire, and so achieved the glory of lighting their cigars by the flames of Vesuvius, and others cooked eggs over fissures in the rocks and were happy.

The view from the summit would have been superb but for the fact that the sun could only pierce the mists at long intervals. Thus the glimpses we had of the grand panorama below were only fitful and unsatisfactory.

THE DESCENT

The descent of the mountain was a labor of only four minutes. Instead of stalking down the rugged path we ascended, we chose one which was bedded knee-deep in loose ashes, and plowed our way with prodigious strides that would almost have shamed the performance of him of the seven-league boots.

The Vesuvius of to-day is a very poor affair compared to the mighty volcano of Kilauea, in the Sandwich Islands, but I am glad I visited it. It was well worth it.

It is said that during one of the grand eruptions of Vesuvius it discharged massy rocks weighing many tons a thousand feet into the air, its vast jets of smoke and steam ascended thirty miles toward the firmament, and clouds of its ashes were wafted abroad and fell upon the decks of ships seven hundred and fifty miles at sea! I will take the ashes at a moderate distance, if any one will take the thirty miles of smoke, but I do not feel able to take a commanding interest in the whole story by myself.

From *The Innocents Abroad,* 1869.

25 : *Athens*

WE ARRIVED, AND ENTERED the ancient harbor of the Piræus at last. We dropped anchor within half a mile of the village. Away off, across the undulating Plain of Attica, could be seen a little square-topped hill with a something on it, which our glasses soon discovered to be the ruined edifices of the citadel of the Athenians, and most prominent among them loomed the venerable Parthenon. So exquisitely clear and pure is this wonderful atmosphere that every column of the noble structure was discernible through the telescope, and even the smaller ruins about it assumed some semblance of shape. This at a distance of five or six miles. In the valley, near the Acropolis (the square-topped hill before spoken of), Athens itself could be vaguely made out with an ordinary lorgnette. Everybody was anxious to get ashore and visit these classic localities as quickly as possible. No land we had yet seen had aroused such universal interest among the passengers.

But bad news came. The commandant of the Piræus came in his boat, and said we must either depart or else get outside the harbor and remain imprisoned in our ship, under rigid quarantine, for eleven days! So we took up the anchor and moved outside, to lie a dozen hours or so, taking in supplies, and then sail for Constantinople. It was the bitterest disappointment we had yet experienced. To lie a whole day in sight of the Acropolis, and yet be obliged to go away without visiting Athens! Disappointment was hardly a strong enough word to describe the circumstances.

All hands were on deck, all the afternoon, with books and maps and glasses, trying to determine which "narrow rocky ridge" was the Areopagus, which sloping hill the Pnyx, which elevation the Museum Hill, and so on. And we got things confused. Discussion became heated, and party spirit ran high. Church-members were gazing with emotion upon a hill which they said was the one St. Paul preached from, and another faction claimed that that hill was

Hymettus, and another that it was Pentelicon! After all the trouble, we could be certain of only one thing—the square-topped hill was the Acropolis, and the grand ruin that crowned it was the Parthenon, whose picture we knew in infancy in the school-books.

We inquired of everybody who came near the ship, whether there were guards in the Piræus, whether they were strict, what the chances were of capture should any of us slip ashore, and in case any of us made the venture and were caught, what would be probably done to us? The answers were discouraging: There was a strong guard or police force; the Piræus was a small town, and any stranger seen in it would surely attract attention—capture would be certain. The commandant said the punishment would be "heavy"; when asked "How heavy?" he said it would be "very severe"—that was all we could get out of him.

At eleven o'clock at night, when most of the ship's company were abed, four of us stole softly ashore in a small boat, a clouded moon favoring the enterprise, and started two and two, and far apart, over a low hill, intending to go clear around the Piræus, out of the range of its police. Picking our way so stealthily over that rocky, nettle-grown eminence, made me feel a good deal as if I were on my way somewhere to steal something. My immediate comrade and I talked in an undertone about quarantine laws and their penalties, but we found nothing cheering in the subject. I was posted. Only a few days before, I was talking with our captain, and he mentioned the case of a man who swam ashore from a quarantined ship somewhere, and got imprisoned six months for it; and when he was in Genoa a few years ago, a captain of a quarantined ship went in his boat to a departing ship, which was already outside of the harbor, and put a letter on board to be taken to his family, and the authorities imprisoned him three months for it, and then conducted him and his ship fairly to sea, and warned him never to show himself in that port again while he lived. This kind of conversation did no good, further than to give a sort of dismal interest to our quarantine-breaking expedition, and so we dropped it. We made the entire circuit of the town without seeing anybody but one man, who stared at us curiously, but said nothing, and a dozen persons asleep on the ground before their doors, whom we walked among and never woke—but we woke up dogs enough, in all conscience—we always had one or two barking at our heels, and several times we had as many as ten and twelve at once. They made such a preposterous din that persons aboard our ship said they could tell how we were progressing for a long time, and where we were, by the barking of the dogs. The clouded moon still favored us. When we had made the whole circuit, and were passing among the houses on the further side of the town, the moon came out splendidly, but we no longer feared the light. As we approached a well, near a house, to get a drink, the owner merely glanced at us and went within. He left the quiet, slumbering town at our mercy. I record it here proudly, that we didn't do anything to it.

Seeing no road, we took a tall hill to the left of the distant Acropolis for a mark, and steered straight for it over all obstructions, and over a little rougher piece of country than exists anywhere else outside of the state of Nevada, perhaps. Part of the way it was covered with small, loose stones—we trod on six at a time, and they all rolled. Another part of it was dry, loose, newly plowed ground. Still another part of it was a long stretch of low grape vines, which were tanglesome and troublesome, and which we took to be brambles. The Attic Plain, barring the grape vines, was a barren, desolate, unpoetical waste—I wonder what it was in Greece's Age of Glory, five hundred years before Christ?

In the neighborhood of one o'clock in the morning, when we were heated with fast walking and parched with thirst, Denny exclaimed, "Why, these weeds are grape vines!" and in five minutes we had a score of bunches of large, white, delicious grapes, and were reaching down for more when a dark shape rose mysteriously up out of the shadows beside us and said "Ho!" And so we left.

In ten minutes more we struck into a beautiful road, and unlike some others we had stumbled upon at intervals, it led in the right direction. We followed it. It was broad and smooth and white —handsome and in perfect repair, and shaded on both sides for a mile or so with single ranks of trees, and also with luxuriant vineyards. Twice we entered and stole grapes, and the second time somebody shouted at us from some invisible place. Whereupon we left again. We speculated in grapes no more on that side of Athens.

Shortly we came upon an ancient stone aqueduct, built upon arches, and from that time forth we had ruins all about us—we were approaching our journey's end. We could not see the Acropolis now or the high hill, either, and I wanted to follow the road till we were abreast of them, but the others overruled me, and we toiled laboriously up the stony hill immediately in our front—and from its summit saw another—climbed it and saw another! It was an hour of exhausting work. Soon we came upon a row of open graves, cut in the solid rock— (for a while one of them served Socrates for a prison) —we passed around the shoulder of the hill, and the citadel, in all its ruined magnificence, burst upon us! We hurried across the ravine and up a winding road, and stood on the old Acropolis, with the prodigious walls of the citadel towering above our heads. We did not stop to inspect their massive blocks of marble, or measure their height, or guess at their extraordinary thickness, but passed at once through a great arched passage like a railway-tunnel, and went straight to the gate that leads to the ancient temples. It was locked! So, after all, it seemed that we were not to see the great Parthenon face to face. We sat down and held a council of war. Result: The gate was only a flimsy structure of wood—we would break it down. It seemed like desecration, but then we had traveled far, and our necessities were urgent. We could not hunt up guides and keepers —we must be on the ship before daylight. So we argued. This was all very fine, but when we came to break the gate, we could not do it. We moved around an angle of the wall and found a low bastion—eight feet high without—ten or twelve within. Denny prepared to scale it, and we got ready to follow. By dint of hard scrambling he finally straddled the top, but some loose stones crumbled away and fell with a crash into the court within. There was instantly a banging of doors and a shout. Denny dropped from the wall in a twinkling, and we retreated in disorder to the gate. Xerxes took that mighty citadel four hundred and eighty years before Christ, when his five millions of soldiers and camp-followers followed him to Greece, and if we four Americans could have remained unmolested five minutes longer, we would have taken it too.

The garrison had turned out—four Greeks. We clamored at the gate, and they admitted us. [Bribery and corruption.]

We crossed a large court, entered a great door, and stood upon a pavement of purest white marble, deeply worn by footprints. Before us, in the flooding moonlight, rose the noblest ruins we had ever looked upon—the Propylæa; a small temple of Minerva; the Temple of Hercules, and the grand Parthenon. [We got these names from the Greek guide, who didn't seem to know more than seven men ought to know.] These edifices were all built of the whitest Pentelic marble, but have a pinkish stain upon them now. Where any part is broken, however, the fracture looks like fine loaf-sugar. Six caryatides, or marble women, clad in flowing robes, support the portico of the Temple of Hercules, but the porticoes and colonnades of the other structures are formed of massive Doric and Ionic pillars, whose flutings and capitals are still measurably perfect, notwithstanding the centuries that have gone over them and the sieges they have suffered. The Parthenon, originally, was two hundred and twenty-six feet long, one hundred wide, and seventy high, and had two rows of great columns, eight in each, at either end, and single rows of seventeen each down the sides, and was one of the most graceful and beautiful edifices ever erected.

Most of the Parthenon's imposing columns are still standing, but the roof is gone. It was a perfect building two hundred and fifty years ago, when a shell dropped into the Venetian magazine stored here, and the explosion which followed wrecked and unroofed it. I remember but little about the Parthenon, and I have put in one or two facts and figures for the use of other people with short memories. Got them from the guide-book.

As we wandered thoughtfully down the marble-paved length of this stately temple, the scene about us was strangely impressive. Here and there, in lavish profusion, were gleaming white statues of men and women, propped against blocks of marble, some of them armless, some without legs, others headless—but all looking mournful in the moonlight, and startlingly human! They rose up and confronted the midnight intruder on every side—they stared at him with stony eyes from unlooked-for nooks and recesses; they peered at him over fragmentary heaps far down the desolate corridors; they barred his way in the midst of the broad forum, and solemnly pointed with handless arms the way from the sacred fane; and through the roofless temple the moon looked down, and banded the floor and darkened the scattered fragments and broken statues with the slanting shadows of the columns.

What a world of ruined sculpture was about us! Set up in rows—stacked up in piles—scattered broadcast over the wide area of the Acropolis—were hundreds of crippled statues of all sizes and of the most exquisite workmanship; and vast fragments of marble that once belonged to the entablatures, covered with bas-reliefs representing battles and sieges, ships of war with three and four tiers of oars, pageants and processions—everything one could think of. History says that the temples of the Acropolis were filled with the noblest works of Praxiteles and Phidias, and of many a great master in sculpture besides—and surely these elegant fragments attest it.

We walked out into the grass-grown, fragment-strewn court beyond the Parthenon. It startled us, every now and then, to see a stony white face stare suddenly up at us out of the grass with its dead eyes. The place seemed alive with ghosts. I half expected to see the Athenian heroes of twenty centuries ago glide out of the shadows and steal into the old temple they knew so well and regarded with such boundless pride.

The full moon was riding high in the cloudless heavens now. We sauntered carelessly and unthinkingly to the edge of the lofty battlements of the citadel, and looked down—a vision! And such a vision! Athens by moonlight! The prophet that thought the splendors of the New Jerusalem were revealed to him, surely saw this instead. It lay in the level plain right under our feet—all spread abroad like a picture—and we looked down upon it as we might have looked from a balloon. We saw no semblance of a street, but every house, every window, every clinging vine, every projection, was as distinct and sharply marked as if the time were noonday; and yet there was no glare, no glitter, nothing harsh or repulsive—the noiseless city was flooded with the mellowest light that ever streamed from the moon, and seemed like some living creature wrapped in peaceful slumber. On its further side was a little temple, whose delicate pillars and ornate front glowed with a rich luster that chained the eye like a spell; and nearer by, the palace of the king reared its creamy walls out of the midst of a great garden of shrubbery that was flecked all over with a random shower of amber lights—a spray of golden sparks that lost their brightness in the glory of the moon, and glinted softly upon the sea of dark foliage like the pallid stars of the milky way. Overhead the stately columns, majestic still in their ruin—underfoot the dreaming city—in the distance the silver sea—not on the broad earth is there another picture half so beautiful!

As we turned and moved again through the temple, I wished that the illustrious men who had sat in it in the remote ages could visit it again and reveal themselves to our curious eyes—Plato, Aristotle, Demosthenes, Socrates, Phocion, Pythagoras, Euclid, Pindar, Xenophon, Herodotus, Praxiteles and Phidias, Zeuxis the painter. What a constellation of celebrated names! But more than all, I wished that old Diogenes, groping so patiently with his lantern, searching so zealously for one solitary honest man in all the world, might meander along and stumble on our party. I ought not to say it, maybe, but still I suppose he would have put out his light.

We left the Parthenon to keep its watch over old Athens, as it had kept it for twenty-three hundred years, and went and stood outside the walls of the citadel. In the distance was the ancient, but still almost perfect, Temple of Theseus, and close by, looking to the West, was the Bema, from whence Demosthenes thundered his philippics and fired the wavering patriotism of his countrymen. To the right was Mars Hill, where the Areopagus sat in ancient times, and where St. Paul defined his position, and below was the market-place where he "disputed daily" with the gossip-loving Athenians. We climbed the stone steps St. Paul ascended, and stood in the square-cut place he stood in, and tried to recollect the Bible account of the matter—but for certain reasons, I could not recall the words. I have found them since:

> Now while Paul waited for them at Athens, his spirit was stirred in him, when he saw the city wholly given up to idolatry.
>
> Therefore disputed he in the synagogue with the Jews, and with the devout persons, and in the market daily with them that met with him.
>
> . . . .
>
> And they took him and brought him unto Areopagus, saying, May we know what this new doctrine whereof thou speakest is?
>
> . . . .
>
> Then Paul stood in the midst of Mars hill, and said, Ye men of Athens, I perceive that in all things ye are too superstitious:
>
> For as I passed by and beheld your devotions, I found an altar with this inscription: TO THE UNKNOWN GOD. Whom, therefore, ye ignorantly worship, him declare I unto you.—*Acts,* ch. xvii.

It occurred to us, after a while, that if we wanted to get home before daylight betrayed us, we had better be moving. So we hurried away. When far on our road, we had a parting view of the Parthenon, with the moonlight streaming through its open colonnades and touching its capitals with silver. As it looked then, solemn, grand, and beautiful, it will always remain in our memories.

As we marched along, we began to get over our fears, and ceased to care much about quarantine scouts or anybody else. We grew bold and reckless; and once, in a sudden burst of courage, I even threw a stone at a dog. It was a pleasant reflection, though, that I did not hit him, because his master might just possibly have been a policeman. Inspired by this happy failure, my valor became utterly uncontrollable, and at intervals I absolutely whistled, though on a moderate key. But boldness breeds boldness, and shortly I plunged into a vineyard, in the full light of the moon, and captured a gallon of superb grapes, not even minding the presence of a peasant who rode by on a mule. Denny and Birch followed my example. Now I had grapes enough for a dozen, but then Jackson was all swollen up with courage, too, and he was obliged to enter a vineyard presently. The first bunch he seized brought trouble. A frowsy, bearded brigand sprang into the road with a shout, and flourished a musket in the light of the moon! We sidled toward the Piræus—not running, you understand, but only advancing with celerity. The brigand shouted again, but still we advanced. It was getting late, and we had no time to fool away on every ass that wanted to drivel Greek platitudes to us. We would just as soon have talked with him as not if we had not been in a hurry. Presently Denny said, "Those fellows are following us!"

We turned, and, sure enough, there they were—three fantastic pirates armed with guns. We slackened our pace to let them come up, and in the mean time I got out my cargo of grapes and dropped them firmly but reluctantly into the shadows by the wayside. But I was not afraid. I only felt that it was not right to steal grapes. And all the more so when the owner was around—and not only around, but with his friends around also. The villains came up and searched a bundle Dr. Birch had in his hand, and scowled upon him when they found it had nothing in it but some holy rocks from Mars Hill, and these were not contraband. They evidently suspected him of playing some wretched fraud upon them, and seemed half inclined to scalp the party. But finally they dismissed us with a warning, couched in excellent Greek, I suppose, and dropped tranquilly in our wake. When they had gone three hundred yards they stopped, and we went on rejoiced. But behold, another armed rascal came out of the shadows and took their place, and followed us two hundred yards. Then he delivered us over to another miscreant, who emerged from some mysterious place, and he in turn to another! For a mile and a half our rear was guarded all the while by armed men. I never traveled in so much state before in all my life.

It was a good while after that before we ventured to steal any more grapes, and when we did we stirred up another troublesome brigand, and then we ceased all further speculation in that line. I suppose that fellow that rode by on the mule posted all the sentinels, from Athens to the Piræus, about us.

Every field on that long route was watched by an armed sentinel, some of whom had fallen asleep, no doubt, but were on hand, nevertheless. This shows what sort of a country modern Attica is—a community of questionable characters. These men were not there to guard their possessions against strangers, but against each other; for strangers seldom visit Athens and the Piræus, and when they do, they go in daylight, and can buy all the grapes they want for a trifle. The modern inhabitants are confiscators and falsifiers of high repute, if gossip speaks truly concerning them, and I freely believe it does.

Just as the earliest tinges of the dawn flushed the eastern sky and turned the pillared Parthenon to a broken harp hung in the pearly horizon, we closed our thirteenth mile of weary, roundabout marching, and emerged upon the seashore abreast the ships, with our usual escort of fifteen hundred Piræan dogs howling at our heels. We hailed a boat that was two or three hundred yards from shore, and discovered in a moment that it was a police-boat on the lookout for any quarantine-breakers that might chance to be abroad. So we dodged—we were used to that by this time—and when the scouts reached the spot we had so lately occupied, we were absent. They cruised along the shore, but in the wrong direction, and shortly our own boat issued from the gloom and took us aboard. They had heard our signal on the ship. We rowed noiselessly away, and before the police-boat came in sight again, we were safe at home once more.

Four more of our passengers were anxious to visit Athens, and started half an hour after we returned; but they had not been ashore five minutes till the police discovered and chased them so hotly that they barely escaped to their boat again, and that was all. They pursued the enterprise no further.

We set sail for Constantinople to-day, but some of us little care for that. We have seen all there was to see in the old city that had its birth sixteen hundred years before Christ was born, and was an old town before the foundations of Troy were laid—and saw it in its most attractive aspect. Wherefore, why should *we* worry?

Two other passengers ran the blockade successfully last night. So we learned this morning. They slipped away so quietly that they were not missed from the ship for several hours. They had the hardihood to march into the Piræus in the early dusk and hire a carriage. They ran some danger of adding two or three months' imprisonment to the other novelties of their Holy Land Pleasure Excursion. I admire "cheek." [1] But they went and came safely, and never walked a step.

From *The Innocents Abroad,* 1869.

26 : Constantinople

WE DROPPED ANCHOR IN THE MOUTH OF THE GOLDEN HORN at daylight in the morning. Only three or four of us were up to see the great Ottoman capital. The passengers do not turn out at unseasonable hours, as they used to, to get the earliest possible glimpse of strange foreign cities. They are well over that. If we were lying in sight of the Pyramids of Egypt, they would not come on deck until after breakfast, nowadays.

The Golden Horn is a narrow arm of the sea, which branches from the Bosporus (a sort of broad river which connects the Marmora and Black Seas), and, curving around, divides the city in the middle. Galata and Pera are on one side of the Bosporus, and the Golden Horn; Stamboul (ancient Byzantium) is upon the other. On the other bank of the Bosporus is Scutari and other suburbs of Constantinople. This great city contains a million inhabitants, but so narrow are its streets, and so crowded together are its houses,

[1] Quotation from the Pilgrims.—M. T.

that it does not cover much more than half as much ground as New York City. Seen from the anchorage or from a mile or so up the Bosporus, it is by far the handsomest city we have seen. Its dense array of houses swells upward from the water's edge, and spreads over the domes of many hills; and the gardens that peep out here and there, the great globes of the mosques, and the countless minarets that meet the eye everywhere, invest the metropolis with the quaint Oriental aspect one dreams of when he reads books of Eastern travel. Constantinople makes a noble picture.

But its attractiveness begins and ends with its picturesqueness. From the time one starts ashore till he gets back again, he execrates it. The boat he goes in is admirably miscalculated for the service it is built for. It is handsomely and neatly fitted up, but no man could handle it well in the turbulent currents that sweep down the Bosporus from the Black Sea, and few men could row it satisfactorily even in still water. It is a long, light canoe (caique), large at one end and tapering to a knife-blade at the other. They make that long sharp end the bow, and you can imagine how these boiling currents spin it about. It has two oars, and sometimes four, and no rudder. You start to go to a given point and you run in fifty different directions before you get there. First one oar is backing water, and then the other; it is seldom that both are going ahead at once. This kind of boating is calculated to drive an impatient man mad in a week. The boatmen are the awkwardest, the stupidest, and the most unscientific on earth, without question.

Ashore, it was—well, it was an eternal circus. People were thicker than bees, in those narrow streets, and the men were dressed in all the outrageous, outlandish, idolatrous, extravagant, thunder-and-lightning costumes that ever a tailor with the delirium tremens and seven devils could conceive of. There was no freak in dress too crazy to be indulged in; no absurdity too absurd to be tolerated; no frenzy in ragged diabolism too fantastic to be attempted. No two men were dressed alike. It was a wild masquerade of all imaginable costumes—every struggling throng in every street was a dissolving view of stunning contrasts. Some patriarchs wore awful turbans, but the grand mass of the infidel horde wore the fiery red skull-cap they call a fez. All the remainder of the raiment they indulged in was utterly indescribable.

The shops here are mere coops, mere boxes, bathrooms, closets—

anything you please to call them—on the first floor. The Turks sit cross-legged in them, and work and trade and smoke long pipes, and smell like—like Turks. That covers the ground. Crowding the narrow streets in front of them are beggars, who beg forever, yet never collect anything; and wonderful cripples, distorted out of all semblance of humanity, almost; vagabonds driving laden asses; porters carrying dry-goods boxes as large as cottages on their backs; peddlers of grapes, hot corn, pumpkin seeds, and a hundred other things, yelling like fiends; and sleeping happily, comfortably, serenely, among the hurrying feet, are the famed dogs of Constantinople; drifting noiselessly about are squads of Turkish women, draped from chin to feet in flowing robes, and with snowy veils bound about their heads, that disclose only the eyes and a vague, shadowy notion of their features. Seen moving about, far away in the dim, arched aisles of the Great Bazar, they look as the shrouded dead must have looked when they walked forth from their graves amid the storms and thunders and earthquakes that burst upon Calvary that awful night of the Crucifixion. A street in Constantinople is a picture which one ought to see once—not oftener.

And then there was the goose-rancher—a fellow who drove a hundred geese before him about the city, and tried to sell them. He had a pole ten feet long, with a crook in the end of it, and occasionally a goose would branch out from the flock and make a lively break around the corner, with wings half lifted and neck stretched to its utmost. Did the goose-merchant get excited? No. He took his pole and reached after that goose with unspeakable *sang froid*—took a hitch round his neck, and "yanked" him back to his place in the flock without an effort. He steered his geese with that stick as easily as another man would steer a yawl. A few hours afterward we saw him sitting on a stone at a corner, in the midst of the turmoil, sound asleep in the sun, with his geese squatting around him, or dodging out of the way of asses and men. We came by again, within the hour, and he was taking account of stock, to see whether any of his flock had strayed or been stolen. The way he did it was unique. He put the end of his stick within six or eight inches of a stone wall, and made the geese march in single file between it and the wall. He counted them as they went by. There was no dodging that arrangement.

If you want dwarfs—I mean just a few dwarfs for a curiosity—

go to Genoa. If you wish to buy them by the gross, for retail, go to Milan. There are plenty of dwarfs all over Italy, but it did seem to me that in Milan the crop was luxuriant. If you would see a fair average style of assorted cripples, go to Naples, or travel through the Roman states. But if you would see the very heart and home of cripples and human monsters, both, go straight to Constantinople. A beggar in Naples who can show a foot which has all run into one horrible toe, with one shapeless nail on it, has a fortune—but such an exhibition as that would not provoke any notice in Constantinople. The man would starve. Who would pay any attention to attractions like his among the rare monsters that throng the bridges of the Golden Horn and display their deformities in the gutters of Stamboul? Oh, wretched impostor! How could he stand against the three-legged woman, and the man with his eye in his cheek? How would he blush in presence of the man with fingers on his elbow? Where would he hide himself when the dwarf with seven fingers on each hand, no upper lip, and his under-jaw gone, came down in his majesty? Bismillah! The cripples of Europe are a delusion and a fraud. The truly gifted flourish only in the byways of Pera and Stamboul.

That three-legged woman lay on the bridge, with her stock in trade so disposed as to command the most striking effect—one natural leg, and two long, slender, twisted ones with feet on them like somebody else's forearm. Then there was a man further along who had no eyes, and whose face was the color of a fly-blown beefsteak, and wrinkled and twisted like a lava-flow—and verily so tumbled and distorted were his features that no man could tell the wart that served him for a nose from his cheekbones. In Stamboul was a man with a prodigious head, an uncommonly long body, legs eight inches long, and feet like snow-shoes. He traveled on those feet and his hands, and was as sway-backed as if the Colossus of Rhodes had been riding him. Ah, a beggar has to have exceedingly good points to make a living in Constantinople. A blue-faced man, who had nothing to offer except that he had been blown up in a mine, would be regarded as a rank impostor, and a mere damaged soldier on crutches would never make a cent. It would pay him to get a piece of his head taken off, and cultivate a wen like a carpet-sack.

The Mosque of St. Sophia is the chief lion of Constantinople. You must get a firman and hurry there the first thing. We did that. We did not get a firman, but we took along four or five francs apiece, which is much the same thing.

I do not think much of the Mosque of St. Sophia. I suppose I lack appreciation. We will let it go at that. It is the rustiest old barn in heathendom. I believe all the interest that attaches to it comes from the fact that it was built for a Christian church and then turned into a mosque, without much alteration, by the Mohammedan conquerors of the land. They made me take off my boots and walk into the place in my stocking feet. I caught cold, and got myself so stuck up with a complication of gums, slime, and general corruption, that I wore out more than two thousand pair of boot-jacks getting my boots off that night, and even then some Christian hide peeled off with them. I abate not a single boot-jack.

St. Sophia is a colossal church, thirteen or fourteen hundred years old, and unsightly enough to be very, very much older. Its immense dome is said to be more wonderful than St. Peter's, but its dirt is much more wonderful than its dome, though they never mention it. The church has a hundred and seventy pillars in it, each a single piece, and all of costly marbles of various kinds, but they came from ancient temples at Baalbec, Heliopolis, Athens, and Ephesus, and are battered, ugly, and repulsive. They were a thousand years old when this church was new, and then the contrast must have been ghastly—if Justinian's architects did not trim them any. The inside of the dome is figured all over with a monstrous inscription in Turkish characters, wrought in gold mosaic, that looks as glaring as a circus bill; the pavements and the marble balustrades are all battered and dirty; the perspective is marred everywhere by a web of ropes that depend from the dizzy height of the dome, and suspend countless dingy, coarse oil-lamps, and ostrich eggs, six or seven feet above the floor. Squatting and sitting in groups, here and there and far and near, were ragged Turks reading books, hearing sermons, or receiving lessons like children, and in fifty places were more of the same sort bowing and straightening up, bowing again and getting down to kiss the earth, muttering prayers the while, and keeping up their gymnastics till they ought to have been tired, if they were not.

Everywhere was dirt and dust and dinginess and gloom; everywhere were signs of a hoary antiquity, but with nothing touching or beautiful about it; everywhere were those groups of fantastic pagans; overhead the gaudy mosaics and the web of lamp-ropes—nowhere was there anything to win one's love or challenge his admiration.

The people who go into ecstasies over St. Sophia must surely get them out of the guide-book (where every church is spoken of as being "considered by good judges to be the most marvelous structure, in many respects, that the world has ever seen"). Or else they are those old connoisseurs from the wilds of New Jersey who laboriously learn the difference between a fresco and a fire-plug, and from that day forward feel privileged to void their critical bathos on painting, sculpture, and architecture forevermore.

We visited the Dancing Dervishes. There were twenty-one of them. They wore a long, light-colored loose robe that hung to their heels. Each in his turn went up to the priest (they were all within a large circular railing) and bowed profoundly and then went spinning away deliriously and took his appointed place in the circle, and continued to spin. When all had spun themselves to their places, they were about five or six feet apart—and so situated, the entire circle of spinning pagans spun itself three separate times around the room. It took twenty-five minutes to do it. They spun on the left foot, and kept themselves going by passing the right rapidly before it and digging it against the waxed floor. Some of them made incredible "time." Most of them spun around forty times in a minute, and one artist averaged about sixty-one times a minute, and kept it up during the whole twenty-five. His robe filled with air and stood out all around him like a balloon.

They made no noise of any kind, and most of them tilted their heads back and closed their eyes, entranced with a sort of devotional ecstasy. There was a rude kind of music, part of the time, but the musicians were not visible. None but spinners were allowed within the circle. A man had to either spin or stay outside. It was about as barbarous an exhibition as we have witnessed yet. Then sick persons came and lay down, and beside them women laid their sick children (one a babe at the breast), and the patriarch of the Dervishes walked upon their bodies. He was supposed to cure their diseases by trampling upon their breasts or backs or standing on the back of their necks. This is well enough for a people who think all their affairs are made or marred by viewless spirits of the air—by giants, gnomes, and genii—and who still believe, to this day, all the wild tales in the Arabian Nights. Even so an intelligent missionary tells me.

We visited the Thousand and One Columns. I do not know what it was originally intended for, but they said it was built for a reservoir. It is situated in the center of Constantinople. You go down a flight of stone steps in the middle of a barren place, and there you are. You are forty feet underground, and in the midst of a perfect wilderness of tall, slender, granite columns, of Byzantine architecture. Stand where you would, or change your position as often as you pleased, you were always a center from which radiated a dozen long archways and colonnades that lost themselves in distance and the somber twilight of the place. This old dried-up reservoir is occupied by a few ghostly silk-spinners now, and one of them showed me a cross cut high up in one of the pillars. I suppose he meant me to understand that the institution was there before the Turkish occupation, and I thought he made a remark to that effect; but he must have had an impediment in his speech, for I did not understand him.

We took off our shoes and went into the marble mausoleum of the Sultan Mahmoud, the neatest piece of architecture, inside, that I have seen lately. Mahmoud's tomb was covered with a black velvet pall, which was elaborately embroidered with silver; it stood within a fancy silver railing; at the side and corners were silver candlesticks that would weigh more than a hundred pounds, and they supported candles as large as a man's leg; on the top of the sarcophagus was a fez, with a handsome diamond ornament upon it, which an attendant said cost a hundred thousand pounds, and lied like a Turk when he said it. Mahmoud's whole family were comfortably planted around him.

We went to the Great Bazar in Stamboul, of course, and I shall not describe it further than to say it is a monstrous hive of little shops—thousands, I should say—all under one roof, and cut up into innumerable little blocks by narrow streets which are arched overhead. One street is devoted to a particular kind of merchandise, another to another, and so on. When you wish to buy a pair of shoes you have the swing of the whole street—you do not have to walk yourself down hunting stores in different localities. It is the same with silks, antiquities, shawls, etc. The place is crowded with people all the time, and as the gay-colored Eastern fabrics are lavishly displayed before every shop, the Great Bazar of Stamboul is one of the sights that are worth seeing. It is full of life, and stir, and business, dirt, beggars, asses, yelling peddlers, porters, dervishes, high-born Turkish female shoppers, Greeks, and weird-looking and weirdly dressed Mohammedans from the mountains and the far provinces—and the only solitary thing one does not smell when he is in the Great Bazar, is something which smells good.

I shall never want another Turkish lunch. The cooking apparatus was in a little lunch-room, near the bazar, and it was all open to the street. The cook was slovenly, and so was the table, and it had no cloth on it. The fellow took a mass of sausage-meat and coated it round a wire and laid it on a charcoal fire to cook. When it was done, he laid it aside and a dog walked sadly in and nipped it. He smelt it first, and probably recognized the remains of a friend. The cook took it away from him and laid it before us. Jack said, "I pass"—he plays euchre sometimes—and we all passed in turn. Then the cook baked a broad, flat, wheaten cake, greased it well with the sausage, and started toward us with it. It dropped in the dirt, and he picked it up and polished it on his breeches, and laid it before us. Jack said, "I pass." We all passed. He put some eggs in a frying-pan, and stood pensively prying slabs of meat from between his teeth with a fork. Then he used the fork to turn the eggs with—and brought them along. Jack said "Pass again." All followed suit. We did not know what to do, and so we ordered a new ration of sausage. The cook got out his wire, apportioned a proper amount of sausage-meat, spat on his hands, and fell to work! This time, with one accord, we all passed out. We paid and left. That is all I learned about Turkish lunches. A Turkish lunch is good, no doubt, but it has its little drawbacks.

When I think how I have been swindled by books of Oriental travel, I want a tourist for breakfast. For years and years I have dreamed of the wonders of the Turkish bath; for years and years I have promised myself that I would yet enjoy one. Many and many a time, in fancy, I have lain in the marble bath, and breathed the slumbrous fragrance of Eastern spices that filled the air; then passed through a weird and complicated system of pulling and hauling and drenching and scrubbing, by a gang of naked savages who loomed vast and vaguely through the steaming mists, like demons;

then rested for a while on a divan fit for a king; then passed through another complex ordeal, and one more fearful than the first; and, finally, swathed in soft fabrics, been conveyed to a princely saloon and laid on a bed of eiderdown, where eunuchs, gorgeous of costume, fanned me while I drowsed and dreamed, or contentedly gazed at the rich hangings of the apartment, the soft carpets, the sumptuous furniture, the pictures, and drank delicious coffee, smoked the soothing narghili, and dropped, at the last, into tranquil repose, lulled by sensuous odors from unseen censers, by the gentle influence of the narghili's Persian tobacco, and by the music of fountains that counterfeited the pattering of summer rain.

That was the picture, just as I got it from incendiary books of travel. It was a poor, miserable imposture. The reality is no more like it than the Five Points are like the Garden of Eden. They received me in a great court, paved with marble slabs; around it were broad galleries, one above another, carpeted with seedy matting, railed with unpainted balustrades, and furnished with huge rickety chairs, cushioned with rusty old mattresses, indented with impressions left by the forms of nine successive generations of men who had reposed upon them. The place was vast, naked, dreary; its court a barn, its galleries stalls for human horses. The cadaverous, half-nude varlets that served in the establishment had nothing of poetry in their appearance, nothing of romance, nothing of Oriental splendor. They shed no entrancing odors—just the contrary. Their hungry eyes and their lank forms continually suggested one glaring, unsentimental fact—they wanted what they term in California "a square meal."

I went into one of the racks and undressed. An unclean starveling wrapped a gaudy table-cloth about his loins, and hung a white rag over my shoulders. If I had had a tub then, it would have come natural to me to take in washing. I was then conducted down-stairs into the wet, slippery court, and the first things that attracted my attention were my heels. My fall excited no comment. They expected it, no doubt. It belonged in the list of softening, sensuous influences peculiar to this home of Eastern luxury. It was softening enough, certainly, but its application was not happy. They now gave me a pair of wooden clogs—benches in miniature, with leather straps over them to confine my feet (which they would have done, only I do not wear No. 13's). These things dangled uncomfortably by the straps when I lifted up my feet, and came down in awkward and unexpected places when I put them on the floor again, and sometimes turned sideways and wrenched my ankles out of joint. However, it was all Oriental luxury, and I did what I could to enjoy it.

They put me in another part of the barn and laid me on a stuffy sort of pallet, which was not made of cloth of gold, or Persian shawls, but was merely the unpretending sort of thing I have seen in the negro quarters of Arkansas. There was nothing whatever in this dim marble prison but five more of these biers. It was a very solemn place. I expected that the spiced odors of Araby were going to steal over my senses, now, but they did not. A copper-colored skeleton, with a rag around him, brought me a glass decanter of water, with a lighted tobacco pipe in the top of it, and a pliant stem a yard long, with a brass mouthpiece to it.

It was the famous "narghili" of the East—the thing the Grand Turk smokes in the pictures. This began to look like luxury. I took one blast at it, and it was sufficient; the smoke went in a great volume down into my stomach, my lungs, even into the uttermost parts of my frame. I exploded one mighty cough, and it was as if Vesuvius had let go. For the next five minutes I smoked at every pore, like a frame house that is on fire on the inside. Not any more narghili for me. The smoke had a vile taste, and the taste of a thousand infidel tongues that remained on that brass mouthpiece was viler still. I was getting discouraged. Whenever, hereafter, I see the cross-legged Grand Turk smoking his narghili, in pretended bliss, on the outside of a paper of Connecticut tobacco, I shall know him for the shameless humbug he is.

This prison was filled with hot air. When I had got warmed up sufficiently to prepare me for a still warmer temperature, they took me where it was—into a marble room, wet, slippery, and steamy, and laid me out on a raised platform in the center. It was very warm. Presently my man sat me down by a tank of hot water, drenched me well, gloved his hand with a coarse mitten, and began to polish me all over with it. I began to smell disagreeably. The more he polished the worse I smelt. It was alarming. I said to him:

"I perceive that I am pretty far gone. It is plain that I ought to be buried without any unnecessary delay. Perhaps you had better go after my friends at once, because the weather is warm, and I cannot 'keep' long."

He went on scrubbing, and paid no attention. I soon saw that he was reducing my size. He bore hard on his mitten, and from under it rolled little cylinders, like macaroni. It could not be dirt, for it was too white. He pared me down in this way for a long time. Finally I said:

"It is a tedious process. It will take hours to trim me to the size you want me; I will wait; go and borrow a jack-plane."

He paid no attention at all.

After a while he brought a basin, some soap, and something that seemed to be the tail of a horse. He made up a prodigious quantity of soap-suds, deluged me with them from head to foot, without warning me to shut my eyes, and then swabbed me viciously with the horse-tail. Then he left me there, a snowy statue of lather, and went away. When I got tired of waiting I went and hunted him up. He was propped against the wall, in another room, asleep. I woke him. He was not disconcerted. He took me back and flooded me with hot water, then turbaned my head, swathed me with dry table-cloths, and conducted me to a latticed chicken-coop in one of the galleries, and pointed to one of those Arkansas beds. I mounted it, and vaguely expected the odors of Araby again. They did not come.

The blank, unornamented coop had nothing about it of that oriental voluptuousness one reads of so much. It was more suggestive of the county hospital than anything else. The skinny servitor brought a narghili, and I got him to take it out again without wasting any time about it. Then he brought the world-renowned Turkish coffee that poets have sung so rapturously for many generations, and I seized upon it as the last hope that was left of my old dreams of Eastern luxury. It was another fraud. Of all the unchristian beverages that ever passed my lips, Turkish coffee is the worst. The cup is small, it is smeared with grounds; the coffee is black, thick, unsavory of smell, and execrable in taste. The bottom of the cup has a muddy sediment in it half an inch deep. This goes down your throat, and portions of it lodge by the way, and produce a tickling aggravation that keeps you barking and coughing for an hour.

Here endeth my experience of the celebrated Turkish bath, and here also endeth my dream of the bliss the mortal revels in who passes through it. It is a malignant swindle. The man who enjoys it is qualified to enjoy anything that is repulsive to sight or sense, and he that can invest it with a charm of poetry is able to do the same with anything else in the world that is tedious, and wretched, and dismal, and nasty.

From *The Innocents Abroad,* 1869.

27 : *Sebastopol*

RUINED POMPEII IS IN GOOD CONDITION compared to Sebastopol. Here, you may look in whatsoever direction you please, and your eye encounters scarcely anything but ruin, ruin, ruin!—fragments of houses, crumbled walls, torn and ragged hills, devastation everywhere! It is as if a mighty earthquake had spent all its terrible forces upon this one little spot. For eighteen long months the storms of war beat upon the helpless town, and left it at last the saddest wreck that ever the sun has looked upon. Not one solitary house escaped unscathed—not one remained habitable, even. Such utter and complete ruin one could hardly conceive of. The houses had all been solid, dressed-stone structures; most of them were plowed through and through by cannon-balls—unroofed and sliced down from eaves to foundation—and now a row of them, half a mile long, looks merely like an endless procession of battered chimneys. No semblance of a house remains in such as these. Some of the larger buildings had corners knocked off; pillars cut in two; cornices smashed; holes driven straight through the walls. Many of these holes are as round and as cleanly cut as if they had been made with an auger. Others are half pierced through, and the clean impression is there in the rock, as smooth and as shapely as if it were done in putty. Here and there a ball still sticks in a wall, and from it iron tears trickle down and discolor the stone.

The battle-fields were pretty close together. The Malakoff tower is on a hill which is right in the edge of the town. The Redan was within rifle-shot of the Malakoff; Inkerman was a mile away; and Balaklava removed but an hour's ride. The French trenches, by which they approached and invested the Malakoff, were carried so close under its sloping sides that one might have stood by the Russian guns and tossed a stone into them. Repeatedly, during three terrible days, they swarmed up the little Malakoff hill, and were beaten back with terrible slaughter. Finally, they captured the place, and drove the Russians out, who then tried to retreat into the town, but the English had taken the Redan, and shut them off with a wall of flame; there was nothing for them to do but go back and retake the Malakoff or die under its guns. They did go back; they took the Malakoff and retook it two or three times, but their desperate valor could not avail, and they had to give up at last.

These fearful fields, where such tempests of death used to rage, are peaceful enough now; no sound is heard, hardly a living thing moves about them, they are lonely and silent—their desolation is complete.

There was nothing else to do, and so everybody went to hunting relics. They have stocked the ship with them. They brought them from the Malakoff, from the Redan, Inkerman, Balaklava—everywhere. They have brought cannon-balls, broken ramrods, fragments of shell—iron enough to freight a sloop. Some have even brought bones—brought them laboriously from great distances, and were grieved to hear the surgeon pronounce them only bones of mules and oxen. I knew Blucher would not lose an opportunity like this. He brought a sack full on board and was going for another. I prevailed upon him not to go. He has already turned his stateroom into a museum of worthless trumpery, which he has gathered up in his travels. He is labeling his trophies, now. I picked up one a while ago, and found it marked "Fragment of a Russian General." I carried it out to get a better light upon it—it was nothing but a couple of teeth and part of the jawbone of a horse. I said with some asperity:

"Fragment of a Russian General! This is absurd. Are you never going to learn any sense?"

He only said: "Go slow—the old woman won't know any different." [His aunt.]

This person gathers mementoes with a perfect recklessness, nowadays; mixes them all up together, and then serenely labels them without any regard to truth, propriety, or even plausibility. I have found him breaking a stone in two, and labeling half of it "Chunk busted from the pulpit of Demosthenes," and the other half "Dornick from the Tomb of Abelard and Heloise." I have known him to gather up a handful of pebbles by the roadside, and bring them on board ship and label them as coming from twenty celebrated localities five hundred miles apart. I remonstrate against these outrages upon reason and truth, of course, but it does no good. I get the same tranquil, unanswerable reply every time:

"It don't signify—the old woman won't know any different."

Ever since we three or four fortunate ones made the midnight trip to Athens, it has afforded him genuine satisfaction to give everybody in the ship a pebble from the Mars Hill where St. Paul preached. He got all those pebbles on the seashore, abreast the ship, but professes to have gathered them from one of our party. However, it is not of any use for me to expose the deception—it affords him pleasure, and does no harm to anybody. He says he never expects to run out of mementoes of St. Paul as long as he is in reach of a sandbank. Well, he is no worse than others. I notice that all travelers supply deficiencies in their collections in the same way. I shall never have any confidence in such things again while I live.

From *The Innocents Abroad,* 1869.

28 : Odessa

ODESSA IS ABOUT TWENTY HOURS' RUN from Sebastopol, and is the most northerly port in the Black Sea. We came here to get coal, principally. The city has a population of one hundred and thirty-three thousand, and is growing faster than any other small city out of America. It is a free port, and is the great grain mart of this particular part of the world. Its roadstead is full of ships. Engineers are at work, now, turning the open roadstead into a spacious artificial harbor. It is to be almost inclosed by massive stone piers, one of which will extend into the sea over three thousand feet in a straight line.

I have not felt so much at home for a long time as I did when I "raised the hill" and stood in Odessa for the first time. It looked just like an American city; fine, broad streets, and straight as well; low houses (two or three stories), wide, neat, and free from any quaintness of architectural ornamentation; locust trees bordering the sidewalks (they call them acacias); a stirring, business look about the streets and the stores; fast walkers; a familiar *new* look about the houses and everything; yea, and a driving and smothering cloud of dust that was so like a message from our own dear native land that we could hardly refrain from shedding a few grateful tears and execrations in the old time-honored American way. Look up the street or down the street, this way or that way, we saw only America! There was not one thing to remind us that we were in Russia. We walked for some little distance, reveling in this home vision, and then we came upon a church and a hack-driver, and presto! the illusion vanished! The church had a slender-spired dome that rounded inward at its base, and looked like a turnip turned upside down, and the hackman seemed to be dressed in a long petticoat without any hoops. These things were essentially foreign, and so were the carriages—but everybody knows about these things, and there is no occasion for my describing them.

We were only to stay here a day and a night and take in coal; we consulted the guide-books and were rejoiced to know that there were no sights in Odessa to see; and so we had one good, untrammeled holiday on our hands, with nothing to do but idle about the city and enjoy ourselves. We sauntered through the markets and criticized the fearful and wonderful costumes from the back country; examined the populace as far as eyes could do it; and closed the entertainment with an ice-cream debauch. We do not get ice-cream everywhere, and so, when we do, we are apt to dissipate to excess. We never cared anything about ice-cream at home, but we look upon it with a sort of idolatry now that it is so scarce in these red-hot climates of the East.

We only found two pieces of statuary, and this was another blessing. One was a bronze image of the Duc de Richelieu, grandnephew of the splendid Cardinal. It stood in a spacious, handsome promenade, overlooking the sea, and from its base a vast flight of stone steps led down to the harbor—two hundred of them, fifty feet long, and a wide landing at the bottom of every twenty. It is a noble staircase, and from a distance the people toiling up it looked like insects. I mention this statue and this stairway because they have their story. Richelieu founded Odessa—watched over it with paternal care—labored with a fertile brain and a wise understanding for its best interests—spent his fortune freely to the same end—endowed it with a sound prosperity, and one which will yet make it one of the great cities of the Old World—built this noble stairway with money from his own private purse—and— Well, the people for whom he had done so much let him walk down these same steps, one day, unattended, old, poor, without a second coat to his back; and when, years afterward, he died in Sebastopol in poverty and neglect, they called a meeting, subscribed liberally, and immediately erected this tasteful monument to his memory, and named a great street after him. It reminds me of what Robert Burns's mother said when they erected a stately monument to his memory: "Ah, Robbie, ye asked them for bread and they hae gi'en ye a stane."

The people of Odessa have warmly recommended us to go and call on the Emperor, as did the Sebastopolians. They have telegraphed his Majesty, and he has signified his willingness to grant us an audience. So we are getting up the anchors and preparing to sail to his watering-place. What a scratching around there will be now! what a holding of important meetings and appointing of solemn committees!—and what a furbishing up of claw-hammer coats and white silk neckties! As this fearful ordeal we are about to pass through pictures itself to my fancy in all its dread sublimity, I begin to feel my fierce desire to converse with a genuine Emperor cooling down and passing away. What am I to do with my hands? What am I to do with my feet? What in the world am I to do with myself?

From *The Innocents Abroad,* 1869.

29 : *Yalta and the Emperor*

We anchored here at Yalta, Russia, two or three days ago. To me the place was a vision of the Sierras. The tall, gray mountains that back it, their sides bristling with pines—cloven with ravines—here and there a hoary rock towering into view—long, straight streaks sweeping down from the summit to the sea, marking the passage of some avalanche of former times—all these were as like what one sees in the Sierras as if the one were a portrait of the other. The little village of Yalta nestles at the foot of an amphitheater which slopes backward and upward to the wall of hills, and looks as if it might have sunk quietly down to its present position from a higher elevation. This depression is covered with the great parks and gardens of noblemen, and through the mass of green foliage the bright colors of their palaces bud out here and there like flowers. It is a beautiful spot.

We had the United States consul on board—the Odessa consul. We assembled in the cabin and commanded him to tell us what we must do to be saved, and tell us quickly. He made a speech. The first thing he said fell like a blight on every hopeful spirit; he had never seen a court reception. (Three groans for the consul.) But he said he had seen receptions at the Governor-General's in Odessa, and had often listened to people's experiences of receptions at the Russian and other courts, and believed he knew very well what sort of ordeal we were about to essay. (Hope budded again.) He said we were many; the summer-place was small—a mere mansion; doubtless we should be received in summer fashion—in the garden; we would stand in a row, all the gentlemen in swallow-tail coats, white kids, and white neckties, and the ladies in light-colored silks, or something of that kind; at the proper moment—12 meridian—the Emperor, attended by his suite arrayed in splendid uniforms, would appear and walk slowly along the line, bowing to some, and saying two or three words to others. At the moment his Majesty appeared, a universal, delighted, enthusiastic smile ought to break out like a rash among the passengers—a smile of love, of gratification, of admiration—and with one accord, the party must begin to bow—not obsequiously, but respectfully, and with dignity; at the end of fifteen minutes the Emperor would go in the house, and we could run along home again. We felt immensely relieved. It seemed, in a manner, easy. There was not a man in the party but believed that with a little practice he could stand in a row, especially if there were others along; there was not a man but believed he could bow without tripping on his coat-tail and breaking his neck; in a word, we came to believe we were equal to any item in the performance except that complicated smile. The consul also said we ought to draft a little address to the Emperor, and present it to one of his aides-de-camp, who would forward it to him at the proper time. Therefore, five gentlemen were appointed to prepare the document, and the fifty others went sadly smiling about the ship—practising. During the next twelve hours we had the general appearance, somehow, of being at a funeral, where everybody was sorry the death had occurred, but glad it was over—where everybody was smiling, and yet broken-hearted.

A committee went ashore to wait on his Excellency, the Governor-General, and learn our fate. At the end of three hours of boding suspense, they came back and said the Emperor would receive us at noon the next day—would send carriages for us—would hear the address in person. The Grand Duke Michael had sent to invite us to his palace also. Any man could see that there was an intention here to show that Russia's friendship for America was so genuine as to render even her private citizens objects worthy of kindly attentions.

At the appointed hour we drove out three miles and assembled in the handsome garden in front of the Emperor's palace.

We formed a circle under the trees before the door, for there was no one room in the house able to accommodate our threescore persons comfortably, and in a few minutes the imperial family came out, bowing and smiling, and stood in our midst. A number of great dignitaries of the empire, in undress uniforms, came with them. With every bow, his Majesty said a word of welcome. I copy these speeches. There is character in them—Russian character—which is politeness itself, and the genuine article. The French are polite, but it is often mere ceremonious politeness. A Russian imbues his polite things with a heartiness, both of phrase and expression, that compels belief in their sincerity. As I was saying, the Czar punctuated his speeches with bows:

"Good morning—I am glad to see you—I am gratified—I am delighted—I am happy to receive you!"

All took off their hats, and the consul inflicted the address on him. He bore it with unflinching fortitude; then took the rusty-looking document and handed it to some great officer or other, to be filed away among the archives of Russia—in the stove. He thanked us for the address, and said he was very much pleased to see us, especially as such friendly relations existed between Russia and the United States. The Empress said the Americans were favorites in Russia, and she hoped the Russians were similarly regarded in America. These were all the speeches that were made, and I recommend them to parties who present policemen with gold watches, as models of brevity and point. After this the Empress went and talked sociably (for an Empress) with various ladies around the circle; several gentlemen entered into a disjointed general conversation with the Emperor; the Dukes and Princes, Admirals and Maids of Honor dropped into free-and-easy chat with first one and then another of our party, and whoever chose stepped forward and spoke with the modest little Grand Duchess Marie, the Czar's daughter. She is fourteen years old, light-haired, blue-eyed, unassuming, and pretty. Everybody talks English.

The Emperor wore a cap, frock-coat, and pantaloons, all of some kind of plain white drilling—cotton or linen—and sported no jewelry or any insignia whatever of rank. No costume could be less ostentatious. He is very tall and spare, and a determined-looking man, though a very pleasant-looking one, nevertheless. It is easy to see that he is kind and affectionate. There is something very noble in his expression when his cap is off. There is none of that cunning in his eye that all of us noticed in Louis Napoleon's.

The Empress and the little Grand Duchess wore simple suits of foulard (or foulard silk, I don't know which is proper), with a small blue spot in it; the dresses were trimmed with blue; both ladies wore broad blue sashes about their waists; linen collars and clerical ties of muslin; low-crowned straw hats trimmed with blue velvet; parasols and flesh-colored gloves. The Grand Duchess had no heels on her shoes. I do not know this of my own knowledge, but one of our ladies told me so. I was not looking at her shoes. I was glad to observe that she wore her own hair, plaited in thick braids against the back of her head, instead of the uncomely thing they call a waterfall, which is about as much like a waterfall as a canvas-covered ham is like a cataract. Taking the kind expression that is in the Emperor's face and the gentleness that is in his young daughter's into consideration, I wondered if it would not tax the Czar's firmness to the utmost to condemn a supplicating wretch to misery in the wastes of Siberia if she pleaded for him. Every time their eyes met, I saw more and more what a tremendous power that weak, diffident school-girl could wield if she chose to do it. Many and many a time she might rule the Autocrat of Russia, whose lightest word is law to seventy millions of human beings! She was only a girl, and she looked like a thousand others I have seen, but never a girl provoked such a novel and peculiar interest in me before. A strange, new sensation is a rare thing in this humdrum life, and I had it here. There was nothing stale or worn out about the thoughts and feelings the situation and the circumstances created. It seemed strange—stranger than I can tell—to think that the central figure in the cluster of men and women, chatting here under the trees like the most ordinary individual in the land, was a man who could open his lips and ships would fly through the waves, locomotives would speed over the plains, couriers would hurry from village to village, a hundred telegraphs would flash the word to the four corners of an empire that stretches its vast proportions over a seventh part of the habitable globe, and a countless multitude of men would spring to do his bidding. I had a sort of vague desire to examine his hands and see if they were of flesh and blood, like other men's. Here was a man who could do this wonderful thing, and yet if I chose I could knock him down. The case was plain, but it seemed preposterous, nevertheless—as preposterous as trying to knock down a mountain or wipe out a continent. If this man sprained his ankle, a million miles of telegraph would carry the news over mountains—valleys—uninhabited deserts—under the trackless sea—and ten thousand newspapers would prate of it; if he were grievously ill, all the nations would know it before the sun rose again; if he dropped lifeless where he stood, his fall might shake the thrones of half a world! If I could have stolen his coat, I would have done it. When I meet a man like that, I want something to remember him by.

As a general thing, we have been shown through palaces by some plush-legged, filigreed flunky or other, who charged a franc for it; but after talking with the company half an hour, the Emperor of Russia and his family conducted us all through their mansion themselves. They made no charge. They seemed to take a real pleasure in it.

We spent half an hour idling through the palace, admiring the cozy apartments and the rich but eminently homelike appointments of the place, and then the imperial family bade our party a kind good-by, and proceeded to count the spoons.

An invitation was extended to us to visit the palace of the eldest son, the Crown Prince of Russia, which was near at hand. The young man was absent, but the Dukes and Countesses and Princes went over the premises with us as leisurely as was the case at the Emperor's, and conversation continued as lively as ever.

It was a little after one o'clock now. We drove to the Grand Duke Michael's, a mile away, in response to his invitation, previously given.

We arrived in twenty minutes from the Emperor's. It is a lovely place. The beautiful palace nestles among the grand old groves of the park, the park sits in the lap of the picturesque crags and hills, and both look out upon the breezy ocean. In the park are rustic seats, here and there, in secluded nooks that are dark with shade; there are rivulets of crystal water; there are lakelets, with inviting, grassy banks; there are glimpses of sparkling cascades through openings in the wilderness of foliage; there are streams of clear water gushing from mimic knots on the trunks of forest trees; there are miniature marble temples perched upon gray old crags; there are airy lookouts whence one may gaze upon a broad expanse of landscape and ocean. The palace is modeled after the choicest forms of Grecian architecture, and its wide colonnades surround a central court that is banked with rare flowers that fill the place with their fragrance, and in their midst springs a fountain that cools the summer air, and may possibly breed mosquitoes, but I do not think it does.

The Grand Duke and his Duchess came out, and the presentation ceremonies were as simple as they had been at the Emperor's. In a few minutes, conversation was under way, as before. The Empress appeared in the veranda, and the little Grand Duchess came out into the crowd. They had beaten us there. In a few minutes, the Emperor came himself on horseback. It was very pleasant. You can appreciate it if you have ever visited royalty and felt occasionally that possibly you might be wearing out your welcome—though as a general thing, I believe, royalty is not scrupulous about discharging you when it is done with you.

The Grand Duke is the third brother of the Emperor, is about thirty-seven years old, perhaps, and is the princeliest figure in Russia. He is even taller than the Czar, as straight as an Indian, and bears himself like one of those gorgeous knights we read about in romances of the Crusades. He looks like a great-hearted fellow who would pitch an enemy into the river in a moment, and then jump in and risk his life fishing him out again. The stories they tell of him show him to be of a brave and generous nature. He must have been desirous of proving that Americans were welcome guests in the imperial palaces of Russia, because he rode all the way to Yalta and escorted our procession to the Emperor's himself, and kept his aides scurrying about, clearing the road and offering assistance wherever it could be needed. We were rather familiar with him then, because we did not know who he was. We recognized him now, and appreciated the friendly spirit that prompted him to do us a favor that any other Grand Duke in the world would have doubtless declined to do. He had plenty of servitors whom he could have sent, but he chose to attend to the matter himself.

The Grand Duke was dressed in the handsome and showy uniform of a Cossack officer. The Grand Duchess had on a white alpaca robe, with the seams and gores trimmed with black barb lace, and a little gray hat with a feather of the same color. She is young, rather pretty, modest and unpretending, and full of winning politeness.

Our party walked all through the house, and then the nobility escorted them all over the grounds, and finally brought them back to the palace about half past two o'clock to breakfast. They called it breakfast, but we would have called it luncheon. It consisted of two kinds of wine; tea, bread, cheese, and cold meats, and was served on the center-tables in the reception-room and the verandas

—anywhere that was convenient; there was no ceremony. It was a sort of picnic. I had heard before that we were to breakfast there, but Blucher said he believed Baker's boy had suggested it to his Imperial Highness. I think not—though it would be like him. Baker's boy is the famine-breeder of the ship. He is always hungry. They say he goes about the staterooms when the passengers are out, and eats up all the soap. And they say he eats oakum. They say he will eat anything he can get between meals, but he prefers oakum. He does not like oakum for dinner, but he likes it for a lunch, at odd hours, or anything that way. It makes him very disagreeable, because it makes his breath bad, and keeps his teeth all stuck up with tar. Baker's boy may have suggested the breakfast, but I hope he did not. It went off well, anyhow. The illustrious host moved about from place to place, and helped to destroy the provisions and keep the conversation lively, and the Grand Duchess talked with the veranda parties and such as had satisfied their appetites and straggled out from the reception-room.

The Grand Duke's tea was delicious. They give one a lemon to squeeze into it, or iced milk, if he prefers it. The former is best. This tea is brought overland from China. It injures the article to transport it by sea.

When it was time to go, we bade our distinguished hosts good-by, and they retired happy and contented to their apartments to count *their* spoons.

We had spent the best part of half a day in the home of royalty, and had been as cheerful and comfortable all the time as we could have been in the ship. I would as soon have thought of being cheerful in Abraham's bosom as in the palace of an Emperor. I supposed that Emperors were terrible people. I thought they never did anything but wear magnificent crowns and red velvet dressing-gowns with dabs of wool sewed on them in spots, and sit on thrones and scowl at the flunkies and the people in the parquette, and order Dukes and Duchesses off to execution. I find, however, that when one is so fortunate as to get behind the scenes and see them at home and in the privacy of their firesides, they are strangely like common mortals. They are pleasanter to look upon then than they are in their theatrical aspect. It seems to come as natural to them to dress and act like other people as it is to put a friend's cedar pencil in your pocket when you are done using it. But I can never have any confidence in the tinsel kings of the theater after this. It will be a great loss. I used to take such a thrilling pleasure in them. But, hereafter, I will turn me sadly away and say:

"This does not answer—this isn't the style of king that *I* am acquainted with."

When they swagger around the stage in jeweled crowns and splendid robes, I shall feel bound to observe that all the Emperors that ever *I* was personally acquainted with wore the commonest sort of clothes, and did not swagger. And when they come on the stage attended by a vast body-guard of supes in helmets and tin breastplates, it will be my duty as well as my pleasure to inform the ignorant that no crowned head of my acquaintance has a soldier anywhere about his house or his person.

Possibly it may be thought that our party tarried too long, or did other improper things, but such was not the case. The company felt that they were occupying an unusually responsible position—they were representing the people of America, not the government—and therefore they were careful to do their best to perform their high mission with credit.

On the other hand, the Imperial families, no doubt, considered that in entertaining us they were more especially entertaining the people of America than they could by showering attentions on a whole platoon of ministers plenipotentiary; and therefore they gave to the event its fullest significance, as an expression of good will and friendly feeling toward the entire country. We took the kindnesses we received as attentions thus directed, of course, and not to ourselves as a party. That we felt a personal pride in being received as the representatives of a nation, we do not deny; that we felt a national pride in the warm cordiality of that reception, cannot be doubted.

Our poet has been rigidly suppressed, from the time we let go the anchor. When it was announced that we were going to visit the Emperor of Russia, the fountains of his great deep were broken up, and he rained ineffable bosh for four-and-twenty hours. Our original anxiety as to what we were going to do with ourselves, was suddenly transformed into anxiety about what we were going to do with our poet. The problem was solved at last. Two alternatives were offered him—he must either swear a dreadful oath that he would not issue a line of his poetry while he was in the Czar's dominions, or else remain under guard on board the ship until we were safe at Constantinople again. He fought the dilemma long, but yielded at last. It was a great deliverance. Perhaps the savage reader would like a specimen of his style. I do not mean this term to be offensive. I only use it because "the gentle reader" has been used so often that any change from it cannot but be refreshing:

> Save us and sanctify us, and finally, then,
> See good provisions we enjoy while we journey to Jerusa*lem.*
> For so man proposes, which it is most true,
> And time will wait for none, nor for us too.

The sea has been unusually rough all day. However, we have had a lively time of it, anyhow. We have had quite a run of visitors. The Governor-General came, and we received him with a salute of nine guns. He brought his family with him. I observed that carpets were spread from the pierhead to his carriage for him to walk on, though I have seen him walk there without any carpet when he was not on business. I thought maybe he had what the accidental insurance people might call an extra-hazardous polish ("policy"—joke, but not above mediocrity) on his boots, and wished to protect them, but I examined and could not see that they were blacked any better than usual. It may have been that he had forgotten his carpet before, but he did not have it with him, anyhow. He was an exceedingly pleasant old gentleman; we all liked him, especially Blucher. When he went away, Blucher invited him to come again and fetch his carpet along.

Prince Dolgorouki and a Grand Admiral or two, whom we had seen yesterday at the reception, came on board also. I was a little distant with these parties, at first, because when I have been visiting Emperors I do not like to be too familiar with people I only know by reputation, and whose moral characters and standing in society I cannot be thoroughly acquainted with. I judged it best to be a little offish, at first. I said to myself, Princes and Counts and Grand Admirals are very well, but they are not Emperors, and one cannot be too particular about whom he associates with.

Baron Wrangel came, also. He used to be a Russian Ambassador at Washington. I told him I had an uncle who fell down a shaft and broke himself in two, as much as a year before that. That was a falsehood, but then I was not going to let any man eclipse me on surprising adventures, merely for the want of a little invention. The Baron is a fine man, and is said to stand high in the Emperor's confidence and esteem.

Baron Ungern-Sternberg, a boisterous, whole-souled old nobleman, came with the rest. He is a man of progress and enterprise—a representative man of the age. He is the Chief Director of the railway system of Russia—a sort of railroad king. In his line he is making things move along in this country. He has traveled extensively in America. He says he has tried convict labor on his railroads, and with perfect success. He says the convicts work well, and are quiet and peaceable. He observed that he employs nearly ten thousand of them now. This appeared to be another call on my resources. I was equal to the emergency. I said we had eighty thousand convicts employed on the railways in America—all of them under sentence of death for murder in the first degree. That closed *him* out. We had General Todleben (the famous defender of Sebastopol, during the siege), and many inferior army and also navy officers, and a number of unofficial Russian ladies and gentlemen. Naturally, a champagne luncheon was in order, and was accomplished without loss of life. Toasts and jokes were discharged freely, but no speeches were made save one thanking the Emperor and the Grand Duke, through the Governor-General, for our hospitable reception, and one by the Governor-General in reply, in which he returned the Emperor's thanks for the speech, etc.

We returned to Constantinople, and after a day or two spent in exhausting marches about the city and voyages up the Golden Horn in *caiques,* we steamed away again. We passed through the Sea of Marmora and the Dardanelles, and steered for a new land—a new one to us, at least—Asia. We had as yet only acquired a bowing acquaintance with it, through pleasure excursions to Scutari and the regions round about.

We passed between Lemnos and Mytilene, and saw them as we had seen Elba and the Balearic Isles—mere bulky shapes, with the softening mists of distance upon them—whales in a fog, as it were. Then we held our course southward, and began to "read up" celebrated Smyrna.

At all hours of the day and night the sailors in the forecastle amused themselves and aggravated us by burlesquing our visit to royalty. The opening paragraph of our Address to the Emperor was framed as follows:

"We are a handful of private citizens of America, traveling simply for recreation—and unostentatiously, as becomes our unofficial state—and, therefore, we have no excuse to tender for presenting ourselves before your Majesty, save the desire of offering our grateful acknowledgments to the lord of a realm which, through good and through evil report, has been the steadfast friend of the land we love so well."

The third cook, crowned with a resplendent tin basin and wrapped royally in a table-cloth mottled with grease-spots and coffee-stains, and bearing a scepter that looked strangely like a belaying pin, walked upon a dilapidated carpet and perched himself on the capstan, careless of the flying spray; his tarred and weather-beaten Chamberlains, Dukes, and Lord High Admirals surrounded him, arrayed in all the pomp that spare tarpaulins and remnants of old sails could furnish. Then the visiting "watch below," transformed into graceless ladies and uncouth pilgrims, by rude travesties upon waterfalls, hoop-skirts, white kid gloves, and swallow-tail coats, moved solemnly up the companionway, and bowing low, began a system of complicated and extraordinary smiling which few monarchs could look upon and live. Then the mock consul, a slush-plastered deck-sweep, drew out a soiled fragment of paper and proceeded to read, laboriously:

"To his Imperial Majesty, Alexander II., Emperor of Russia:

"We are a handful of private citizens of America, traveling simply for recreation—and unostentatiously, as becomes our unofficial state—and, therefore, we have no excuse to tender for presenting ourselves before your Majesty—"

The Emperor—"Then what the devil did you come for?"

—"Save the desire of offering our grateful acknowledgments to the lord of a realm which—"

The Emperor—"Oh, d—n the Address!—read it to the police. Chamberlain, take these people over to my brother, the Grand Duke's, and give them a square meal. Adieu! I am happy—I am gratified—I am delighted—I am bored. Adieu, adieu—vamose the ranch! The First Groom of the Palace will proceed to count the portable articles of value belonging to the premises."

The farce then closed, to be repeated again with every change of the watches, and embellished with new and still more extravagant inventions of pomp and conversation.

At all times of the day and night the phraseology of that tiresome address fell upon our ears. Grimy sailors came down out of the foretop placidly announcing themselves as "a handful of private citizens of America, *traveling simply for recreation* and unostentatiously," etc.; the coal-passers moved to their duties in the profound depths of the ship, explaining the blackness of their faces and their uncouthness of dress, with the reminder that *they* were "a handful of private citizens, traveling simply for recreation," etc., and when the cry rang through the vessel at midnight: "EIGHT BELLS!—LARBOARD WATCH, TURN OUT!" the larboard watch came gaping and stretching out of their den, with the everlasting formula: "Aye, aye, sir! We are a handful of private citizens of America, traveling simply for recreation, and unostentatiously, as becomes our unofficial state!"

As I was a member of the committee, and helped to frame the Address, these sarcasms came home to me. I never heard a sailor proclaiming himself as a handful of American citizens traveling for recreation, but I wished he might trip and fall overboard, and so reduce his handful by one individual, at least. I never was so tired of any one phrase as the sailors made me of the opening sentence of the Address to the Emperor of Russia.

From *The Innocents Abroad,* 1869.

30 : Heidelberg

HEIDELBERG LIES AT THE MOUTH of a narrow gorge—a gorge the shape of a shepherd's crook; if one looks up it he perceives that it is about straight, for a mile and a half, then makes a sharp curve to the right and disappears. This gorge—along whose bottom pours the swift Neckar,—is confined between (or cloven through) a couple of long, steep ridges, a thousand feet high and densely wooded clear to their summits, with the exception of one section which has been shaved and put under cultivation. These ridges are chopped off at the mouth of the gorge and form two bold and conspicuous headlands, with Heidelberg nestling between them; from their bases spreads away the vast dim expanse of the Rhine valley, and into this expanse the Neckar goes wandering in shining curves and is presently lost to view.

Now if one turns and looks up the gorge once more, he will see the Schloss Hotel on the right, perched on a precipice overlooking the Neckar—a precipice which is so sumptuously cushioned and draped with foliage that no glimpse of the rock appears. The building seems very airily situated. It has the appearance of being on a shelf half way up the wooded mountain side; and as it is remote and isolated, and very white, it makes a strong mark against the lofty leafy rampart at its back.

This hotel had a feature which was a decided novelty, and one which might be adopted with advantage by any house which is perched in a commanding situation. This feature may be described as a series of glass-inclosed parlors *clinging to the outside of the house,* one against each and every bed-chamber and drawing-room. They are like long, narrow, high-ceiled bird-cages hung against the building. My room was a corner room, and had two of these things, a north one and a west one.

From the north cage one looks up the Neckar gorge; from the west one he looks down it. This last affords the most extensive view, and it is one of the loveliest that can be imagined, too. Out of a billowy upheaval of vivid green foliage, a rifle-shot removed, rises the huge ruin of Heidelberg Castle, with empty window arches, ivy-mailed battlements, moldering towers—the Lear of inanimate nature—deserted, discrowned, beaten by the storms, but royal still, and beautiful. It is a fine sight to see the evening sunlight suddenly strike the leafy declivity at the Castle's base and dash up it and drench it as with a luminous spray, while the adjacent groves are in deep shadows.

Behind the Castle swells a great dome-shaped hill, forest-clad, and beyond that a nobler and loftier one. The Castle looks down upon the compact brown-roofed town; and from the town two picturesque old bridges span the river. Now the view broadens; through the gateway of the sentinel headlands you gaze out over the wide Rhine plain, which stretches away, softly and richly tinted, grows gradually and dreamily indistinct, and finally melts imperceptibly into the remote horizon.

I have never enjoyed a view which had such a serene and satisfying charm about it as this one gives.

The first night we were there, we went to bed and to sleep early; but I awoke at the end of two or three hours, and lay a comfortable while listening to the soothing patter of the rain against the balcony windows. I took it to be rain, but it turned out to be only the murmur of the restless Neckar, tumbling over her dikes and dams far below, in the gorge. I got up and went into the west balcony and saw a wonderful sight. Away down on the level, under the black mass of the Castle, the town lay, stretched along the river, its intricate cobweb of streets jeweled with twinkling lights; there were rows of lights on the bridges; these flung lances of light upon the water, in the black shadows of the arches; and away at the extremity of all this fairy spectacle blinked and glowed a massed multitude of gas jets which seemed to cover acres of ground; it was as if all the diamonds in the world had been spread out there. I did not know before, that a half mile of sextuple railway tracks could be made such an adornment.

One thinks Heidelberg by day—with its surroundings—is the last possibility of the beautiful: but when he sees Heidelberg by night, a fallen Milky Way, with that glittering railway constellation pinned to the border, he requires time to consider upon the verdict.

One never tires of poking about in the dense woods that clothe all these lofty Neckar hills to their tops. The great deeps of a boundless forest have a beguiling and impressive charm in any country; but German legends and fairy tales have given these an added charm. They have peopled all that region with gnomes, and dwarfs, and all sorts of mysterious and uncanny creatures. At the time I am writing of, I had been reading so much of this literature that sometimes I was not sure but I was beginning to believe in the gnomes and fairies as realities.

One afternoon I got lost in the woods about a mile from the hotel, and presently fell into a train of dreamy thought about animals which talk, and kobolds, and enchanted folk, and the rest of the pleasant legendary stuff; and so, by stimulating my fancy, I finally got to imagining I glimpsed small flitting shapes here and there down the columned aisles of the forest. It was a place which was peculiarly meet for the occasion. It was a pine wood, with so thick and soft a carpet of brown needles that one's footfall made no more sound than if he were treading on wool; the tree-trunks were as round and straight and smooth as pillars, and stood close together; they were bare of branches to a point about twenty-five feet above ground, and from there upward so thick with boughs that not a ray of sunlight could pierce through. The world was bright with sunshine outside, but a deep and mellow twilight reigned in there, and also a silence so profound that I seemed to hear my own breathings.

When I had stood ten minutes, thinking and imagining, and getting my spirit in tune with the place, and in the right mood to enjoy the supernatural, a raven suddenly uttered a horse croak over my head. It made me start; and then I was angry because I started. I looked up, and the creature was sitting on a limb right over me, looking down at me. I felt something of the same sense of humiliation and injury which one feels when he finds that a human stranger has been clandestinely inspecting him in his privacy and mentally commenting upon him. I eyed the raven, and the raven eyed me. Nothing was said during some seconds. Then the bird stepped a little way along his limb to get a better point of observation, lifted his wings, stuck his head far down below his shoulders toward me, and croaked again—a croak with a distinctly insulting expression about it. If he had spoken in English he could not have said any more plainly than he did say in raven, "Well, what do *you* want here?" I felt as foolish as if I had been caught in some mean act by a responsible being, and reproved for it. However, I made no reply; I would not bandy words with a raven. The adversary waited a while, with his shoulders still lifted, his head thrust down between them, and his keen bright eye fixed on me; then he threw out two or three more insults, which I could not understand, further than that I knew a portion of them consisted of language not used in church.

I still made no reply. Now the adversary raised his head and called. There was an answering croak from a little distance in the wood,—evidently a croak of inquiry. The adversary explained with enthusiasm, and the other raven dropped everything and came. The two sat side by side on the limb and discussed me as freely and offensively as two great naturalists might discuss a new kind of bug.

The thing became more and more embarrassing. They called in another friend. This was too much. I saw that they had the advantage of me, and so I concluded to get out of the scrape by walking out of it. They enjoyed my defeat as much as any low white people could have done. They craned their necks and laughed at me (for a raven *can* laugh, just like a man), they squalled insulting remarks after me as long as they could see me. They were nothing but ravens—I knew that,—what they thought about me could be a matter of no consequence,—and yet when even a raven shouts after you, "What a hat!" "Oh, pull down your vest!" and that sort of thing, it hurts you and humiliates you, and there is no getting around it with fine reasoning and pretty arguments.

From *A Tramp Abroad,* 1880.

31 : Dueling

ONE DAY IN THE INTEREST OF SCIENCE my agent obtained permission to bring me to the students' dueling place. We crossed the river and drove up the bank a few hundred yards, then turned to the left, entered a narrow alley, followed it a hundred yards and arrived at a two-story public house; we were acquainted with its outside aspect, for it was visible from the hotel. We went up stairs and passed into a large whitewashed apartment which was perhaps fifty feet long by thirty feet wide and twenty or twenty-five high. It was a well-lighted place. There was no carpet. Across one end and down both sides of the room extended a row of tables, and at these some fifty or seventy-five students were sitting.

Some of them were sipping wine, others were playing cards, others chess, other groups were chatting together, and many were smoking cigarettes while they waited for the coming duels. Nearly all of them wore colored caps; there were white caps, green caps, blue caps, red caps, and bright yellow ones; so, all the five corps were present in strong force. In the windows at the vacant end of the room stood six or eight long, narrow-bladed swords with large protecting guards for the hand, and outside was a man at work sharpening others on a grindstone. He understood his business; for when a sword left his hand one could shave himself with it.

It was observable that the young gentlemen neither bowed to nor spoke with students whose caps differed in color from their own. This did not mean hostility, but only an armed neutrality. It was considered that a person could strike harder in the duel, and with a more earnest interest, if he had never been in a condition of comradeship with his antagonist; therefore, comradeship between the corps was not permitted. At intervals the presidents of the five corps have a cold official intercourse with each other, but nothing further. For example, when the regular dueling day of one of the corps approaches, its president calls for volunteers from among the membership to offer battle; three or more respond,—but there must not be less than three; the president lays their names before the other presidents, with the request that they furnish antagonists for these challengers from among their corps. This is promptly done. It chanced that the present occasion was the battle day of the Red Cap Corps. They were the challengers, and certain caps of other colors had volunteered to meet them. The students fight duels in the room which I have described, *two days in every week during seven and a half or eight months in every year.* This custom has continued in Germany two hundred and fifty years.

To return to my narrative. A student in a white cap met us and introduced us to six or eight friends of his who also wore white caps, and while we stood conversing, two strange-looking figures were led in from another room. They were students panoplied for the duel. They were bareheaded; their eyes were protected by iron goggles which projected an inch or more, the leather straps of which bound their ears flat against their heads; their necks were wound around and around with thick wrappings which a sword could not cut through; from chin to ankle they were padded thoroughly against injury; their arms were bandaged and re-bandaged, layer upon layer, until they looked like solid black logs. These weird apparitions had been handsome youths, clad in fashionable attire, fifteen minutes before, but now they did not resemble any beings one ever sees unless in nightmares. They strode along, with their arms projecting straight out from their bodies; they did not hold them out themselves, but fellow students walked beside them and gave the needed support.

There was a rush for the vacant end of the room, now, and we followed and got good places. The combatants were placed face to face, each with several members of his own corps about him to assist; two seconds, well padded, and with swords in their hands, took near stations; a student belonging to neither of the opposing corps placed himself in a good position to umpire the combat; another student stood by with a watch and a memorandum-book to keep record of the time and the number and nature of the wounds; a gray-haired surgeon was present with his lint, his bandages, and his instruments. After a moment's pause the duelists saluted the umpire respectfully, then one after another the several officials stepped forward, gracefully removed their caps and saluted him also, and returned to their places. Everything was ready now; students stood crowded together in the foreground, and others stood behind them on chairs and tables. Every face was turned toward the center of attraction.

The combatants were watching each other with alert eyes; a perfect stillness, a breathless interest reigned. I felt that I was going to see some wary work. But not so. The instant the word was given, the two apparitions sprang forward and began to rain blows down upon each other with such lightning rapidity that I could not quite tell whether I saw the swords or only the flashes they made in the air; the rattling din of these blows, as they struck steel or paddings was something wonderfully stirring, and they were struck with such terrific force that I could not understand why the opposing sword was not beaten down under the assault. Presently, in the midst of the sword-flashes, I saw a handful of hair skip into the air as if it had lain loose on the victim's head and a breath of wind had puffed it suddenly away.

The seconds cried "Halt!" and knocked up the combatants' swords with their own. The duelists sat down; a student-official stepped forward, examined the wounded head and touched the place with a sponge once or twice; the surgeon came and turned back the hair from the wound—and revealed a crimson gash two or three inches long, and proceeded to bind an oval piece of leather and a bunch of lint over it; the tally-keeper stepped up and tallied one for the opposition in his book.

Then the duelists took position again; a small stream of blood was flowing down the side of the injured man's head, and over his shoulder and down his body to the floor, but he did not seem to mind this. The word was given, and they plunged at each other as fiercely as before; once more the blows rained and rattled and flashed; every few moments the quick-eyed seconds would notice that a sword was bent—then they called "Halt!" struck up the contending weapons, and an assisting student straightened the bent one.

The wonderful turmoil went on—presently a bright spark sprung from a blade, and that blade, broken in several pieces, sent one of its fragments flying to the ceiling. A new sword was provided, and the fight proceeded. The exercise was tremendous, of course, and in time the fighters began to show great fatigue. They were allowed to rest a moment, every little while; they got other rests by wounding each other, for then they could sit down while the doctor applied the lint and bandages. The law is that the battle must continue fifteen minutes if the men can hold out; and as the pauses do not count, this duel was protracted to twenty or thirty minutes, I judged. At last it was decided that the men were too much wearied to do battle longer. They were led away drenched with crimson from head to foot. That was a good fight, but it could not count, partly because it did not last the lawful fifteen minutes (of actual fighting), and partly because neither man was disabled by his wounds. It was a drawn battle, and corps law requires that drawn battles shall be re-fought as soon as the adversaries are well of their hurts.

During the conflict, I had talked a little, now and then, with a young gentleman of the White Cap corps, and he had mentioned that he was to fight next,—and had also pointed out his challenger, a young gentleman who was leaning against the opposite wall smoking a cigarette and restfully observing the duel then in progress.

My acquaintanceship with a party to the coming contest had the effect of giving me a kind of personal interest in it; I naturally wished he might win, and it was the reverse of pleasant to learn that he probably would not, because, although he was a notable swordsman, the challenger was held to be his superior.

The duel presently began and in the same furious way which had marked the previous one. I stood close by, but could not tell which blows told and which did not, they fell and vanished so like flashes of light. They all seemed to tell; the swords always bent over the opponents' heads, from the forehead back over the crown, and seemed to touch, all the way; but it was not so,—a protecting blade, invisible to me, was always interposed between. At the end of ten seconds each man had struck twelve or fifteen blows, and warded off twelve or fifteen, and no harm done; then a sword became disabled, and a short rest followed whilst a new one was brought. Early in the next round the White Corps student got an ugly wound on the side of his head and gave his opponent one like it. In the third round the latter received another bad wound in the head, and the former had his under-lip divided. After that, the White Corps student gave many severe wounds, but got none of consequence in return. At the end of five minutes from the beginning of the duel the surgeon stopped it; the challenging party had suffered such injuries that any addition to them might be dangerous. These injuries were a fearful spectacle, but are better left undescribed. So, against expectation, my acquaintance was the victor.

The third duel was brief and bloody. The surgeon stopped it when he saw that one of the men had received such bad wounds that he could not fight longer without endangering his life.

The fourth duel was a tremendous encounter; but at the end of five or six minutes the surgeon interfered once more: another man so severely hurt as to render it unsafe to add to his harms. I watched this engagement as I had watched the others,—with rapt interest and strong excitement, and with a shrink and a shudder for every blow that laid open a cheek or a forehead; and a conscious paling of my face when I occasionally saw a wound of a yet more shocking nature inflicted. My eyes were upon the loser of this duel when he got his last and vanquishing wound,—it was in his face and it carried away his—but no matter, I must not enter into details. I had but a glance, and then turned quickly away, but I would not have been looking at all if I had known what was coming. No, that is probably not true; one thinks he would not look if he knew what was coming, but the interest and the excitement are so powerful that they would doubtless conquer all other feelings; and so, under the fierce exhilaration of the clashing steel, he would yield and look, after all. Sometimes spectators of these duels faint,—and it does seem a very reasonable thing to do, too.

Both parties to this fourth duel were badly hurt; so much so that the surgeon was at work upon them nearly or quite an hour,—a fact which is suggestive. But this waiting interval was not wasted in idleness by the assembled students. It was past noon; therefore they ordered their landlord, down stairs, to send up hot beefsteaks, chickens, and such things, and these they ate, sitting comfortably at the several tables, whilst they chatted, disputed and laughed. The door to the surgeon's room stood open, meantime, but the cutting, sewing, splicing, and bandaging going on in there in plain view did not seem to disturb anyone's appetite. I went in and saw the surgeon labor awhile, but could not enjoy it; it was much less trying to see the wounds given and received than to see them mended; the stir and turmoil, and the music of the steel, were wanting here,—one's nerves were wrung by this grisly spectacle, whilst the duel's compensating pleasurable thrill was lacking.

Finally the doctor finished, and the men who were to fight the closing battle of the day came forth. A good many dinners were not completed, yet, but no matter, they could be eaten cold, after the battle; therefore everybody crowded forward to see. This was not a love duel, but a "satisfaction" affair. These two students had quarreled, and were here to settle it. They did not belong to any of the corps, but they were furnished with weapons and armor, and permitted to fight here by the five corps as a courtesy. Evidently these two young men were unfamiliar with the dueling ceremonies, though they were not unfamiliar with the sword. When they were placed in position they thought it was time to begin,—and they did begin, too, and with a most impetuous energy, without waiting for anybody to give the word. This vastly amused the spectators, and even broke down their studied and courtly gravity and surprised them into laughter. Of course the seconds struck up the swords and started the duel over again. At the word, the deluge of blows began, but before long the surgeon once more interfered,—for the only reason which ever permits him to interfere,—and the day's war was over. It was now two in the afternoon, and I had been present since half past nine in the morning. The field of battle was indeed a red one by this time; but some sawdust soon righted that. There had been one duel before I arrived. In it one of the men received many injuries, while the other one escaped without a scratch.

I had seen the heads and faces of ten youths gashed in every direction by the keen two-edged blades, and yet had not seen a victim wince, nor heard a moan, or detected any fleeting expression which confessed the sharp pain the hurts were inflicting. This was good fortitude, indeed. Such endurance is to be expected in savages and prize fighters, for they are born and educated to it; but to find it in such perfection in these gently-bred and kindly-natured young fellows is matter for surprise. It was not merely under the excitement of the sword-play that this fortitude was shown; it was shown in the surgeon's room where an uninspiring quiet reigned, and where there was no audience. The doctor's manipulations brought out neither grimaces nor moans. And in the fights it was observable that these lads hacked and slashed with the same tremendous spirit, after they were covered with streaming wounds, which they had shown in the beginning.

The world in general looks upon the college duels as very farcical affairs; true, but considering that the college duel is fought by boys; that the swords are real swords; and that the head and face are exposed, it seems to me that it is a farce which has quite a grave side to it. People laugh at it mainly because they think the student is so covered up with armor that he cannot be hurt. But it is not so; his eyes and ears are protected, but the rest of his face and head are bare. He cannot only be badly wounded, but his life is in danger; and he would sometimes lose it but for the interference of the surgeon. It is not intended that his life shall be endangered. Fatal accidents are possible, however. For instance, the student's sword may break, and the end of it fly up behind his antagonist's ear and cut an artery which could not be reached if the sword remained whole. This has happened, sometimes, and death has resulted on the spot. Formerly the student's armpits were not protected,—and at that time the swords were pointed, whereas they are blunt, now; so an artery in the armpit was sometimes cut, and death followed. Then in the days of sharp-pointed swords, a spectator was an occasional victim,—the end of a broken sword flew five or ten feet and buried itself in his neck or his heart, and death ensued instantly. The student duels in Germany occasion two or three deaths every year, now, but this arises only from the carelessness of the wounded men; they eat or drink imprudently, or commit excesses in the way of over-exertion; inflammation sets in and gets such a headway that it cannot be arrested. Indeed, there is blood and pain and danger enough about the college duel to entitle it to a considerable degree of respect.

All the customs, all the laws, all the details, pertaining to the student duel are quaint and naïve. The grave, precise, and courtly ceremony with which the thing is conducted, invests it with a sort of antique charm.

This dignity, and these knightly graces suggest the tournament, not the prize fight. The laws are as curious as they are strict. For instance, the duelist may step forward from the line he is placed upon, if he chooses, but never back of it. If he steps back of it, or even leans back, it is considered that he did it to avoid a blow or contrive an advantage; so he is dismissed from his corps in disgrace. It would seem but natural to step from under a descending sword unconsciously, and against one's will and intent—yet this unconsciousness is not allowed. Again: if under the sudden anguish of a wound the receiver of it makes a grimace, he falls some degrees in the estimation of his fellows; his corps are ashamed of him: they call him "hare foot," which is the German equivalent for chicken-hearted.

From *A Tramp Abroad,* 1880.

32 : Mannheim

ONE DAY WE TOOK THE TRAIN and went down to Mannheim to see King Lear played in German. It was a mistake. We sat in our seats three whole hours and never understood anything but the thunder and lightning; and even that was reversed to suit German ideas, for the thunder came first and the lightning followed after.

The behavior of the audience was perfect. There were no rustlings, or whisperings, or other little disturbances; each act was listened to in silence, and the applauding was done after the curtain was down. The doors opened at half past four, the play began promptly at half past five, and within two minutes afterward all who were coming were in their seats, and quiet reigned. A German gentleman in the train had said that a Shakespearian play was an appreciated treat in Germany and that we should find the house filled. It was true; all the six tiers were filled, and remained so to the end—which suggested that it is not only balcony people who like Shakespeare in Germany, but those of the pit and the gallery, too.

Another time, we went to Mannheim and attended a shivaree,—otherwise an opera,—the one called Lohengrin. The banging and slamming and booming and crashing were something beyond belief. The racking and pitiless pain of it remains stored up in my memory alongside the memory of the time that I had my teeth fixed. There were circumstances which made it necessary for me to stay through the four hours to the end, and I stayed; but the recollection of that long, dragging, relentless season of suffering is indestructible. To have to endure it in silence, and sitting still, made it all the harder. I was in a railed compartment with eight or ten strangers, of the two sexes, and this compelled repression; yet at times the pain was so exquisite that I could hardly keep the tears back. At those times, as the howlings and wailings and shriekings of the singers, and the ragings and roarings and explosions of the vast orchestra rose higher and higher, and wilder and wilder, and fiercer and fiercer, I could have cried if I had been alone. Those strangers would not have been surprised to see a man do such a thing who was being gradually skinned, but they would have marveled at it here, and made remarks about it no doubt, whereas there was nothing in the present case which was an advantage over being skinned. There was a wait of half an hour at the end of the first act, and I could have gone out and rested during that time, but I could not trust myself to do it, for I felt that I should desert and stay out. There was another wait of half an hour toward nine o'clock, but I had gone through so much by that time that I had no spirit left, and so had no desire but to be let alone.

I do not wish to suggest that the rest of the people there were like me, for, indeed, they were not. Whether it was that they naturally liked that noise, or whether it was that they had learned to like it by getting used to it, I did not at that time know; but they did like it,—this was plain enough. While it was going on they sat and looked as rapt and grateful as cats do when one strokes their backs; and whenever the curtain fell they rose to their feet, in one solid mighty multitude, and the air was snowed thick with waving handkerchiefs, and hurricanes of applause swept the place. This was not comprehensible to me. Of course, there were many people there who were not under compulsion to stay; yet the tiers were as full at the close as they had been at the beginning. This showed that the people liked it.

It was a curious sort of a play. In the matter of costumes and scenery it was fine and showy enough; but there was not much action. That is to say, there was not much really done, it was only talked about; and always violently. It was what one might call a narrative play. Everybody had a narrative and a grievance, and none were reasonable about it, but all in an offensive and ungovernable state. There was little of that sort of customary thing where the tenor and the soprano stand down by the footlights, warbling, with blended voices, and keep holding out their arms toward each other and drawing them back and spreading both hands over first one breast and then the other with a shake and a pressure,—no, it was every rioter for himself and no blending. Each sang his indictive narrative in turn, accompanied by the whole orchestra of sixty instruments, and when this had continued for some time, and one was hoping they might come to an understanding and modify the noise, a great chorus composed entirely of maniacs would suddenly break forth, and then during two minutes, and sometimes three, I lived over again all that I had suffered the time the orphan asylum burned down.

We only had one brief little season of heaven and heaven's sweet ecstasy and peace during all this long and diligent and acrimonious reproduction of the other place. This was while a gorgeous procession of people marched around and around, in the third act, and sang the Wedding Chorus. To my untutored ear that was music,—almost divine music. While my seared soul was steeped in the healing balm of those gracious sounds, it seemed to me that I could almost re-suffer the torments which had gone before, in order to be so healed again. There is where the deep ingenuity of the operatic idea is betrayed. It deals so largely in pain that its scattered delights are prodigiously augmented by the contrasts. A pretty air in an opera is prettier there than it could be anywhere else, I suppose, just as an honest man in politics shines more than he would elsewhere.

I have since found out that there is nothing the Germans like so much as an opera. They like it, not in a mild and moderate way, but with their whole hearts. This is a legitimate result of habit and education. Our nation will like the opera, too, by and by, no doubt. One in fifty of those who attend our operas likes it already, perhaps, but I think a good many of the other forty-nine go in order to learn to like it, and the rest in order to be able to talk knowingly about it. The latter usually hum the airs while they are being sung, so that their neighbors may perceive that they have been to operas before. The funerals of these do not occur often enough.

A gentle, old-maidish person and a sweet young girl of seventeen sat right in front of us that night at the Mannheim opera. These people talked, between the acts, and I understood them, though I understood nothing that was uttered on the distant stage. At first they were guarded in their talk, but after they had heard my agent and me conversing in English they dropped their reserve and I picked up many of their little confidences; no, I mean many of *her* little confidences,—meaning the elder party,—for the young girl only listened, and gave assenting nods, but never said a word. How pretty she was, and how sweet she was! I wished she would speak. But evidently she was absorbed in her own thoughts, her own young-girl dreams, and found a dearer pleasure in silence. But she was not dreaming sleepy dreams,—no, she was awake, alive, alert, she could not sit still a moment. She was an enchanting study. Her gown was of a soft white silky stuff that clung to her round young figure like a fish's skin, and it was rippled over with the gracefullest little fringy films of lace; she had deep, tender eyes, with long, curved lashes; and she had peachy cheeks, and a dimpled chin, and such a dear little dewy rosebud of a mouth; and she was so dove-like, so pure, and so gracious, so sweet and bewitching. For long hours I did mightily wish she would speak. And at last she did; the red lips parted, and out leaped her thought,—and with such a guileless and pretty enthusiasm, too: "Auntie, I just *know* I've got five hundred fleas on me!"

That was probably over the average. Yes, it must have been very much over the average. The average at that time in the Grand Duchy of Baden was forty-five to a young person (when alone), according to the official estimate of the home secretary for that year; the average for older people was shifty and indeterminable, for whenever a wholesome young girl came into the presence of her elders she immediately lowered their average and raised her own. She became a sort of contribution-box. This dear young thing in the theater had been sitting there unconsciously taking up a collection. Many a skinny old being in our neighborhood was the happier and the restfuller for her coming.

In that large audience, that night, there were eight very conspicuous people. These were ladies who had their hats or bonnets on. What a blessed thing it would be if a lady could make herself conspicuous in our theaters by wearing her hat. It is not usual in Europe to allow ladies and gentlemen to take bonnets, hats, overcoats, canes, or umbrellas into the auditorium, but in Mannheim this rule was not enforced because the audiences were largely made up of people from a distance, and among these were always a few timid ladies who were afraid that if they had to go into an anteroom to get their things when the play was over, they would miss their train. But the great mass of those who came from a distance always ran the risk and took the chances, preferring the loss of the train to a breach of good manners and the discomfort of being unpleasantly conspicuous during a stretch of three or four hours.

From *A Tramp Abroad,* 1880.

33 : Baden-Baden

BADEN-BADEN SITS IN THE LAP OF THE HILLS, and the natural and artificial beauties of the surroundings are combined effectively and charmingly. The level strip of ground which stretches through and beyond the town is laid out in handsome pleasure grounds, shaded by noble trees and adorned at intervals with lofty and sparkling fountain-jets. Thrice a day a fine band makes music in the public promenade before the Conversation-House, and in the afternoon and evenings that locality is populous with fashionably-dressed people of both sexes, who march back and forth past the great music-stand and look very much bored, though they make a show of feeling otherwise. It seems like a rather aimless and stupid existence. A good many of these people are there for a real purpose, however; they are racked with rheumatism, and they are there to stew it out in the hot baths. These invalids looked melancholy enough, limping about on their canes and crutches, and apparently brooding over all sorts of cheerless things. People say that Germany, with her damp stone houses, is the home of rheumatism. If that is so, Providence must have foreseen that it would be so, and therefore filled the land with these healing baths. Perhaps no other country is so generously supplied with medicinal springs as Germany. Some of these baths are good for one ailment, some for another; and again, peculiar ailments are conquered by combining the individual virtues of several different baths. For instance, for some forms of disease, the patient drinks the native hot water of Baden-Baden, with a spoonful of salt from the Carlsbad springs dissolved in it. That is not a dose to be forgotten right away.

They don't *sell* this hot water; no, you go into the great Trinkhalle, and stand around, first on one foot and then on the other, while two or three young girls sit pottering at some sort of lady-like sewing work in your neighborhood and can't seem to see you, —polite as three-dollar clerks in government offices.

By and by one of these rises painfully, and "stretches";—stretches fists and body heavenward till she raises her heels from the floor, at the same time refreshing herself with a yawn of such comprehensiveness that the bulk of her face disappears behind her upper lip and one is able to see how she is constructed inside,—then she slowly closes her cavern, brings down her fists and her heels, comes languidly forward, contemplates you contemptuously, draws you a glass of hot water and sets it down where you can get it by reaching for it. You take it and say:

"How much?"—and she returns you, with elaborate indifference, a beggar's answer:

"Nach Beliebe" (what you please).

This thing of using the common beggar's trick and the common beggar's shibboleth to put you on your liberality when you were expecting a simple straight-forward commercial transaction, adds a little to your prospering sense of irritation. You ignore her reply, and ask again:

"How much?"

—and she calmly, indifferently, repeats:

"Nach Beliebe."

You are getting angry, but you are trying not to show it; you resolve to keep on asking your question till she changes her answer, or at least her annoyingly indifferent manner. Therefore, if your case be like mine, you two fools stand there, and without perceptible emotion of any kind, or any emphasis on any syllable, you look blandly into each other's eyes, and hold the following idiotic conversation:

"How much?"

"Nach Beliebe."

"How much?"

"Nach Beliebe."

"How much?"

"Nach Beliebe."

"How much?"

"Nach Beliebe."

"How much?"

"Nach Beliebe."

"How much?"

"Nach Beliebe."

I do not know what another person would have done, but at this point I gave it up; that cast-iron indifference, that tranquil contemptuousness, conquered me, and I struck my colors. Now I knew she was used to receiving about a penny from many people who care nothing about the opinions of scullery maids, and about tuppence from moral cowards; but I laid a silver twenty-five cent piece within her reach and tried to shrivel her up with this sarcastic speech:

"If it isn't enough, will you stoop sufficiently from your official dignity to say so?"

She did not shrivel. Without deigning to look at me at all, she languidly lifted the coin and bit it!—to see if it was good. Then she turned her back and placidly waddled to her former roost again, tossing the money into an open till as she went along. She was victor to the last, you see.

I have enlarged upon the ways of this girl because they are typical; her manners are the manners of a goodly number of the Baden-Baden shopkeepers. The shopkeeper there swindles you if he can, and insults you whether he succeeds in swindling you or not. The keepers of baths also take great and patient pains to insult you. The frowsy woman who sat at the desk in the lobby of the great Friederichsbad and sold bath tickets, not only insulted me twice every day, with rigid fidelity to her great trust, but she took trouble enough to cheat me out of a shilling, one day, to have fairly entitled her to ten. Baden-Baden's splendid gamblers are gone, only her microscopic knaves remain.

An English gentleman who had been living there several years, said:

"If you could disguise your nationality, you would not find any insolence here. These shopkeepers detest the English and despise the Americans; they are rude to both, more especially to ladies of your nationality and mine. If these go shopping without a gentleman or a man servant, they are tolerably sure to be subjected to petty insolences,—insolences of manner and tone, rather than word, though words that are hard to bear are not always wanting. I know of an instance where a shopkeeper tossed a coin back to an American lady with the remark, snappishly uttered, 'We don't take French money here.' And I know of a case where an English lady said to one of these shopkeepers, 'Don't you think you ask too much for this article?' and he replied with the question, 'Do you think you are obliged to buy it?' However, these people are not impolite to Russians or Germans. And as to rank, they worship that, for they have long been used to generals and nobles. If you wish to see to what abysses servility can descend, present yourself before a Baden-Baden shopkeeper in the character of a Russian prince."

It is an inane town, filled with sham, and petty fraud, and snobbery, but the baths are good. I spoke with many people, and they were all agreed in that. I had had twinges of rheumatism unceasingly during three years, but the last one departed after a fortnight's bathing there, and I have never had one since. I fully believe I left my rheumatism in Baden-Baden. Baden-Baden is welcome to it. It was little, but it was all I had to give. I would have preferred to leave something that was catching, but it was not in my power.

There are several hot springs there, and during two thousand years they have poured forth a never diminishing abundance of the healing water. This water is conducted in pipes to the numerous bath-houses, and is reduced to an endurable temperature by the addition of cold water. The new Friederichsbad is a very large and beautiful building, and in it one may have any sort of bath that has ever been invented, and with all the additions of herbs and drugs that his ailment may need or that the physician of the establishment may consider a useful thing to put into the water. You go there, enter the great door, get a bow graduated to your style and clothes from the gorgeous portier, and a bath ticket and an insult from the frowsy woman for a quarter; she strikes a bell and a serving man conducts you down a long hall and shuts you into a commodious room which has a washstand, a mirror, a bootjack, and a sofa in it, and there you undress at your leisure.

The room is divided by a great curtain; you draw this curtain aside, and find a large white marble bathtub, with its rim sunk to the level of the floor, and with three wide marble steps leading down into it. This tub is full of water which is as clear as crystal, and is tempered to 28 degrees Réaumur (about 95 degrees Fahrenheit). Sunk into the floor, by the tub, is a covered copper box which contains some warm towels and a sheet. You look fully as white as an angel when you are stretched out in that limpid bath. You remain in it ten minutes, the first time, and afterward increase the duration from day to day, till you reach twenty-five or thirty minutes. There you stop. The appointments of the place are so luxurious, the benefit so marked, the price so moderate, and the insults so sure, that you very soon find yourself adoring the Friederichsbad and infesting it.

We had a plain, simple, unpretending, good hotel, in Baden-Baden,—the Hôtel de France,—and alongside my room I had a giggling, cackling, chattering family who always went to bed just two hours after me and always got up just two hours ahead of me. But that is common in German hotels; the people generally go to bed long after eleven and get up long before eight. The partitions convey sound like a drum-head, and everybody knows it; but no matter, a German family who are all kindness and consideration in the daytime make apparently no effort to moderate their noises for your benefit at night. They will sing, laugh, and talk loudly, and bang furniture around in the most pitiless way. If you knock on your wall appealingly, they will quiet down and discuss the matter softly amongst themselves for a moment,—then, like the mice, they fall to persecuting you again, and as vigorously as before. They keep cruelly late and early hours, for such noisy folk.

Of course, when one begins to find fault with foreign people's ways, he is very likely to get a reminder to look nearer home, before he gets far with it. I open my note-book to see if I can find some more information of a valuable nature about Baden-Baden, and the first thing I fall upon is this:

Baden-Baden (no date). Lot of vociferous Americans at breakfast this morning. Talking *at* everybody, while pretending to talk among themselves. On their first travels, manifestly. Showing off. The usual signs,—airy, easy-going references to grand distances and foreign places. "Well, *good*-bye, old fellow,—if I don't run across you in Italy, you hunt me up in London before you sail."

The next item which I find in my note-book is this one:

"The fact that a band of 6,000 Indians are now murdering our frontiersmen at their impudent leisure, and that we are only able to send 1,200 soldiers against them, is utilized here to discourage emigration to America. The common people think the Indians are in New Jersey."

This is a new and peculiar argument against keeping our army down to a ridiculous figure in the matter of numbers. It is rather a striking one, too. I have not distorted the truth in saying that the facts in the above item, about the army and the Indians, are made use of to discourage emigration to America. That the common people should be rather foggy in their geography, and foggy as to the location of the Indians, is matter for amusement, maybe, but not of surprise.

There is an interesting old cemetery in Baden-Baden, and we spent several pleasant hours in wandering through it and spelling out the inscriptions on the aged tombstones. Apparently after a man has lain there a century or two, and has had a good many people buried on top of him, it is considered that his tombstone is not needed by him any longer. I judge so from the fact that hundreds of old gravestones have been removed from the graves and placed against the inner walls of the cemetery. What artists they had in the old times! They chiseled angels and cherubs and devils and skeletons on the tombstones in the most lavish and generous way,—as to supply,—but curiously grotesque and outlandish as to form. It is not always easy to tell which of the figures belong among the blest and which of them among the opposite party. But there was an inscription, in French, on one of those old stones, which was quaint and pretty, and was plainly not the work of any other than a poet. It was to this effect:

HERE
REPOSES IN GOD,
CAROLINE DE CLERY,
A RELIGIEUSE OF ST. DENIS,
AGED 83 YEARS,—AND BLIND.
THE LIGHT WAS RESTORED TO HER
IN BADEN THE 5TH OF JANUARY,
1839.

We made several excursions on foot to the neighboring villages, over winding and beautiful roads and through enchanting woodland scenery. The woods and roads were similar to those at Heidelberg, but not so bewitching. I suppose that roads and woods which are up to the Heidelberg mark are rare in the world.

Once we wandered clear away to La Favorita Palace, which is several miles from Baden-Baden. The grounds about the palace were fine; the palace was a curiosity. It was built by a Margravine in 1725, and remains as she left it at her death. We wandered through a great many of its rooms, and they all had striking peculiarities of decoration. For instance, the walls of one room were pretty completely covered with small pictures of the Margravine in all conceivable varieties of fanciful costumes, some of them male.

The walls of another room were covered with grotesquely and elaborately figured hand-wrought tapestry. The musty ancient beds remained in the chambers, and their quilts and curtains and canopies were decorated with curious hand-work, and the walls and ceilings frescoed with historical and mythological scenes in glaring colors. There was enough crazy and rotten rubbish in the building to make the true brick-a-bracker green with envy. A painting in the dining hall verged upon the indelicate,—but then the Margravine was herself a trifle indelicate.

It is in every way a wildly and picturesquely decorated house, and brimful of interest as a reflection of the character and tastes of that rude bygone time.

In the grounds, a few rods from the palace, stands the Margravine's chapel, just as she left it,—a coarse wooden structure, wholly barren of ornament. It is said that the Margravine would give herself up to debauchery and exceedingly fast living for several months at a time, and then retire to this miserable wooden den and spend a few months in repenting and getting ready for another good time. She was a devoted Catholic, and was perhaps quite a model sort of a Christian as Christians went then, in high life.

Tradition says she spent the last two years of her life in the strange den I have been speaking of, after having indulged herself in one final, triumphant, and satisfying spree. She shut herself up there, without company, and without even a servant, and so abjured and forsook the world. In her little bit of a kitchen she did her own cooking; she wore a hair shirt next the skin, and castigated herself with whips,—these aids to grace are exhibited there yet. She prayed and told her beads, in another little room, before a waxen Virgin niched in a little box against the wall; she bedded herself like a slave.

In another small room is an unpainted wooden table, and behind it sit half-life-size waxen figures of the Holy Family, made by the very worst artist that ever lived, perhaps, and clothed in gaudy, flimsy drapery.[1] The Margravine used to bring her meals to this table and *dine with the Holy Family.* What an idea that was! What a grisly spectacle it must have been! Imagine it: Those rigid, shock-headed figures, with corpsy complexions and fishy glass eyes, occupying one side of the table in the constrained attitudes and dead fixedness that distinguish all men that are born of wax, and this wrinkled, smouldering old fire-eater occupying the other side, mumbling her prayers and munching her sausages in the ghostly stillness and shadowy indistinctness of a winter twilight. It makes one feel crawly even to think of it.

In this sordid place, and clothed, bedded, and fed like a pauper, this strange princess lived and worshiped during two years, and in it she died. Two or three hundred years ago, this would have made the poor den holy ground; and the church would have set up a miracle-factory there and made plenty of money out of it. The den could be moved into some portions of France and made a good property even now.

From *A Tramp Abroad,* 1880.

[1] The Saviour was represented as a lad of about 15 years of age. This figure had lost one eye.—M. T.

34 : Lucerne

NEXT MORNING WE LEFT IN THE TRAIN for Switzerland, and reached Lucerne about ten o'clock at night. The first discovery I made was that the beauty of the lake had not been exaggerated. . . .

Lucerne is a charming place. It begins at the water's edge, with a fringe of hotels, and scrambles up and spreads itself over two or three sharp hills in a crowded, disorderly, but picturesque way, offering to the eye a heaped-up confusion of red roofs, quaint gables, dormer windows, toothpick steeples, with here and there a bit of ancient embattled wall bending itself over the ridges, worm fashion, and here and there an old square tower of heavy masonry. And also here and there a town clock with only one hand,—a hand which stretches straight across the dial and has no joint in it; such a clock helps out the picture, but you cannot tell the time of day by it. Between the curving line of hotels and the lake is a broad avenue with lamps and a double rank of low shade trees. The lake front is walled with masonry like a pier, and has a railing, to keep people from walking overboard. All day long the vehicles dash along the avenue, and nurses, children and tourists sit in the shade of the trees, or lean on the railing and watch the schools of fishes darting about in the clear water, or gaze out over the lake at the stately border of snow-hooded mountain peaks. Little pleasure-steamers, black with people, are coming and going all the time; and everywhere one sees young girls and young men paddling about in fanciful row boats, or skimming along by the help of sails when there is any wind. The front rooms of the hotels have little railed balconies, where one may take his private luncheon in calm, cool comfort and look down upon this busy and pretty scene and enjoy it without having to do any of the work connected with it.

Most of the people, both male and female, are in walking costume, and carry alpenstocks. Evidently, it is not considered safe to go about in Switzerland, even in town, without an alpenstock. If the tourist forgets and comes down to breakfast without his alpenstock he goes back and gets it, and stands it up in the corner. When his touring in Switzerland is finished, he does not throw that broomstick away, but lugs it home with him, to the far corners of the earth, although this costs him more trouble and bother than a baby or a courier could. You see, the alpenstock is his trophy; his name is burned upon it; and if he has climbed a hill, or jumped a brook, or traversed a brickyard with it, he has the names of those places burned upon it, too. Thus it is his regimental flag, so to speak, and bears the record of his achievements. It is worth three francs when he buys it, but a bonanza could not purchase it after his great deeds have been inscribed upon it. There are artisans all about Switzerland whose trade it is to burn these things upon the alpenstock of the tourist. And observe, a man is respected in Switzerland according to his alpenstock. I found I could get no attention there, while I carried an unbranded one. However, branding is not expensive, so I soon remedied that. The effect upon the next detachment of tourists was very marked. I felt repaid for my trouble.

The Hofkirche is celebrated for its organ concerts. All summer long the tourists flock to that church about six o'clock in the evening, and pay their franc, and listen to the noise. They don't stay to hear all of it, but get up and tramp out over the sounding stone floor, meeting late comers who tramp in in a sounding and vigorous way. This tramping back and forth is kept up nearly all the time, and is accented by the continuous slamming of the door, and the coughing and barking and sneezing of the crowd. Meantime, the big organ is booming and crashing and thundering away, doing its best to prove that it is the biggest and loudest organ in Europe, and that a tight little box of a church is the most favorable place to average and appreciate its powers in. It is true, there were some soft and merciful passages occasionally, but the tramp-tramp of the tourists only allowed one to get fitful glimpses of them, so to speak. Then right away the organist would let go another avalanche.

The commerce of Lucerne consists mainly in gimcrackery of the souvenir sort; the shops are packed with Alpine crystals, photographs of scenery, and wooden and ivory carvings. I will not conceal the fact that miniature figures of the Lion of Lucerne are to be had in them. Millions of them. But they are libels upon him, every one of them. There is a subtle something about the majestic pathos of the original which the copyist cannot get. Even the sun fails to get it; both the photographer and the carver give you a dying lion, and that is all. The shape is right, the attitude is right, the proportions are right, but that indescribable something which makes the Lion of Lucerne the most mournful and moving piece of stone in the world, is wanting.

The Lion lies in his lair in the perpendicular face of a low cliff,—for he is carved from the living rock of the cliff. His size is colossal, his attitude is noble. His head is bowed, the broken spear is sticking in his shoulder, his protecting paw rests upon the lilies of France. Vines hang down the cliff and wave in the wind, and a clear stream trickles from above and empties into a pond at the base, and in the smooth surface of the pond the lion is mirrored, among the water lilies.

Around about are green trees and grass. The place is a sheltered, reposeful, woodland nook, remote from noise and stir and confusion,—and all this is fitting, for lions do die in such places, and not on granite pedestals in public squares fenced with fancy iron railings. The Lion of Lucerne would be impressive anywhere, but nowhere so impressive as where he is. . . .

We did not buy any wooden images of the Lion, nor any ivory or ebony or marble or chalk or sugar or chocolate ones, or even any photographic slanders of him. The truth is, these copies were so common, so universal, in the shops and everywhere, that they presently became as intolerable to the wearied eye as the latest popular melody usually becomes to the harassed ear. In Lucerne, too, the wood carvings of other sorts, which had been so pleasant to look upon when one saw them occasionally at home, soon began to fatigue us. We grew very tired of seeing wooden quails and chickens picking and strutting around clock-faces, and still more tired of seeing wooden images of the alleged chamois skipping about wooden rocks, or lying upon them in family groups, or peering alertly up from behind them. The first day, I would have bought a hundred and fifty of these clocks if I had had the money,—and I did buy three,—but on the third day the disease had run its course, I had convalesced, and was in the market once more,—trying to sell. However, I had no luck; which was just as well, for the things will be pretty enough, no doubt, when I get them home.

For years my pet aversion had been the cuckoo clock; now here I was, at last, right in the creature's home; so wherever I went that distressing "*hoo*'hoo! *hoo*'hoo! *hoo*'hoo!" was always in my ears. For a nervous man, this was a fine state of things. Some sounds are hatefuller than others, but no sound is quite so inane, and silly, and aggravating as the "*hoo*'hoo" of a cuckoo clock, I think. I bought one, and am carrying it home to a certain person; for I have always said that if the opportunity ever happened, I would do that man an ill turn. What I meant, was, that I would break one of his legs, or something of that sort; but in Lucerne I instantly saw that I could impair his mind. That would be more lasting, and more satisfactory every way. So I bought the cuckoo clock; and if I ever get home with it, he is "my meat," as they say in the mines. I thought of another candidate,—a book reviewer whom I could name if I wanted to,—but after thinking it over, I didn't buy him a clock. I couldn't injure his mind.

From *A Tramp Abroad,* 1880.

35 : A Young American in Europe

CLOSE BY THE LION OF LUCERNE is what they call the "Glacier Garden,"—and it is the only one in the world. It is on high ground. Four or five years ago, some workmen who were digging foundations for a house came upon this interesting relic of a long departed age. Scientific men perceived in it a confirmation of their theories concerning the glacial period; so through their persuasions the little tract of ground was bought and permanently protected against being built upon. The soil was removed, and there lay the rasped and guttered track which the ancient glacier had made as it moved along upon its slow and tedious journey. This track was perforated by huge pot-shaped holes in the bed-rock, formed by the furious washing-around in them of bowlders by the turbulent torrent which flows beneath all glaciers. These huge round bowlders still remain in the holes; they and the walls of the holes are worn smooth by the long continued chafing which they gave each other in those old days. It took a mighty force to churn these big lumps of stone around in that vigorous way. The neighboring country had a very different shape, at that time—the valleys have risen up and become hills, since, and the hills have become valleys. The bowlders discovered in the pots had traveled a great distance, for there is no rock like them nearer than the distant Rhone Glacier.

For some days we were content to enjoy looking at the blue lake Lucerne and at the piled-up masses of snow mountains that border it all around—an enticing spectacle, this last, for there is a strange and fascinating beauty and charm about a majestic snow-peak with the sun blazing upon it or the moonlight softly enriching it,—but finally we concluded to try a bit of excursioning around on a steam-boat, and a dash on foot at the Rigi. Very well, we had a delightful trip to Fluelen, on a breezy, sunny day. Everybody sat on the upper deck, on benches, under an awning; everybody talked, laughed, and exclaimed at the wonderful scenery; in truth, a trip on that lake is almost the perfection of pleasuring. The mountains were a never-ceasing marvel. Sometimes they rose straight up out of the lake, and towered aloft and overshadowed our pigmy steamer with their prodigious bulk in the most impressive way. Not snow-clad mountains, these, yet they climbed high enough toward the sky to meet the clouds and veil their foreheads in them. They were not barren and repulsive, but clothed in green, and restful and pleasant to the eye. And they were so almost straight-up-and-down, sometimes, that one could not imagine a man being able to keep his footing upon such a surface, yet there are paths, and the Swiss people go up and down them every day.

Sometimes one of these monster precipices had the slight inclination of the huge ship houses in dockyards,—then high aloft, toward the sky, it took a little stronger inclination, like that of a mansard roof,—and perched on this dizzy mansard one's eye detected little things like martin boxes, and presently perceived that these were the dwellings of peasants,—an airy place for a home, truly. And suppose a peasant should walk in his sleep, or his child should fall out of the front yard?—the friends would have a tedious long journey down out of those cloud-heights before they found the remains. And yet those far-away homes looked ever so seductive, they were so remote from the troubled world, they dozed in such an atmosphere of peace and dreams,—surely no one who had learned to live up there would ever want to live on a meaner level.

We swept through the prettiest little curving arms of the lake, among these colossal green walls, enjoying new delights, always, as the stately panorama unfolded itself before us and re-rolled and hid itself behind us; and now and then we had the thrilling surprise of bursting suddenly upon a tremendous white mass like the distant and dominating Jungfrau, or some kindred giant, looming head and shoulders above a tumbled waste of lesser Alps.

Once, while I was hungrily taking in one of these surprises, and doing my best to get all I possibly could of it while it should last, I was interrupted by a young and care-free voice:

"You're an American, I think,—so'm I."

He was about eighteen, or possibly nineteen; slender and of medium height; open, frank, happy face; a restless but independent eye; a snub nose, which had the air of drawing back with a decent reserve from the silky new-born moustache below it until it should be introduced; a loosely-hung jaw, calculated to work easily in the sockets. He wore a low-crowned, narrow-brimmed straw hat, with a broad blue ribbon around it which had a white anchor enbroidered on it in front; nobby short-tailed coat, pantaloons, vest, all trim and neat and up with the fashion; red-striped stockings, very low-quarter patent-leather shoes, tied with black ribbon; blue ribbon around his neck, wide-open collar; tiny diamond studs; wrinkleless kids; projecting cuffs, fastened with large oxydized silver sleeve-buttons, bearing the device of a dog's face,—English pug. He carried a slim cane, surmounted with an English pug's head with red glass eyes. Under his arm he carried a German grammar,—Otto's. His hair was short, straight, and smooth, and presently when he turned his head a moment, I saw that it was nicely parted behind. He took a cigarette out of a dainty box, stuck it into a meerschaum-holder which he carried in a morocco case, and reached for my cigar. While he was lighting, I said:

"Yes,—I am an American."

"I knew it—I can always tell them. What ship did you come over in?"

"Holsatia."

"We came in the *Batavia*—Cunard, you know. What kind of a passage did you have?"

"Tolerably rough."

"So did we. Captain said he'd hardly ever seen it rougher. Where are you from?"

"New England."

"So'm I. I'm from New Bloomfield. Anybody with you?"

"Yes,—a friend."

"Our whole family's along. It's awful slow, going around alone,—don't you think so?"

"Rather slow."

"Ever been over here before?"

"Yes."

"I haven't. My first trip. But we've been all around—Paris and everywhere. I'm to enter Harvard next year. Studying German all the time, now. Can't enter till I know German. I know considerable French,—I get along pretty well in Paris, or anywhere where they speak French. What hotel are you stopping at?"

"Schweitzerhof."

"No! is that so? I never see you in the reception room. I go to the reception room a good deal of the time, because there's so many Americans there. I make lots of acquaintances. I know an American as soon as I see him—and so I speak to him and make his acquaintance. I like to be always making acquaintances—don't you?"

"Lord, yes!"

"You see it breaks up a trip like this, first rate. I never get bored on a trip like this, if I can make acquaintances and have somebody to talk to. But I think a trip like this would be an awful bore, if a body couldn't find anybody to get acquainted with and talk to on a trip like this. I'm fond of talking, ain't you?"

"Passionately."

"Have you felt bored, on this trip?"

"Not all the time, part of it."

"That's it!—you see you ought to go around and get acquainted, and talk. That's my way. That's the way I always do,—I just go 'round, 'round, 'round, and talk, talk, talk,—I never get bored. You been up the Rigi yet?"

"No."

"Going?"

"I think so."

"What hotel you going to stop at?"

"I don't know. Is there more than one?"

"Three. You stop at the Schreiber—you'll find it full of Americans. What ship did you say you came over in?"

"City of Antwerp."

"German, I guess. You going to Geneva?"

"Yes."

"What hotel you going to stop at?"

"Hotel de l'Écu de Génève."

"Don't you do it! No Americans there! You stop at one of those big hotels over the bridge,—they're packed full of Americans."

"But I want to practice my Arabic."

"Good gracious, do you speak Arabic?"

"Yes,—well enough to get along."

"Why, hang it, you won't get along in Geneva,—*they* don't speak Arabic, they speak French. What hotel are you stopping at here?"

"Hotel Pension-Beaurivage."

"Sho, you ought to stop at the Schweitzerhof. Didn't you know the Schweitzerhof was the best hotel in Switzerland?—look at your Baedeker."

"Yes, I know,—but I had an idea there warn't any Americans there."

"No Americans! Why, bless your soul, it's just alive with them! I'm in the great reception room most all the time. I make lots of acquaintances there. Not as many as I did at first, because now only the new ones stop in there,—the others go right along through. Where are you from?"

"Arkansaw."

"Is that so? I'm from New England,—New Bloomfield's my town when I'm at home. I'm having a mighty good time to-day, ain't you?"

"Divine."

"That's what I call it. I like this knocking around, loose and easy, and making acquaintances and talking. I know an American, soon as I see him; so I go and speak to him and make his acquaintance. I ain't ever bored, on a trip like this, if I can make new acquaintances and talk. I'm awful fond of talking when I can get hold of the right kind of a person, ain't you?"

"I prefer it to any other dissipation."

"That's my notion, too. Now some people like to take a book and sit down and read, and read, and read, or moon around yawping at the lake or these mountains and things, but that ain't my way; no, sir, if they like it, let 'em do it, I don't object; but as for me, talking's what *I* like. You been up the Rigi?"

"Yes."

"What hotel did you stop at?"

"Schreiber."

"That's the place!—I stopped there too. *Full* of Americans, *wasn't* it? It always is,—always is. That's what they say. Everybody says that. What ship did you come over in?"

"Ville de Paris."

"French, I reckon. What kind of a passage did . . . excuse me a minute, there's some Americans I haven't seen before."

And away he went. He went uninjured, too,—I had the murderous impulse to harpoon him in the back with my alpenstock, but as I raised the weapon the disposition left me; I found I hadn't the heart to kill him, he was such a joyous, innocent, good-natured numbskull.

Half an hour later I was sitting on a bench inspecting, with strong interest, a noble monolith which we were skimming by,—a monolith not shaped by man, but by Nature's free great hand,—a massy pyramidal rock eighty feet high, devised by Nature ten million years ago against the day when a man worthy of it should need it for his monument. The time came at last, and now this grand remembrancer bears Schiller's name in huge letters upon its face. Curiously enough, this rock was not degraded or defiled in any way. It is said that two years ago a stranger let himself down from the top of it with ropes and pulleys, and painted all over it, in blue letters bigger than those in Schiller's name, these words:

"TRY SOZODONT;"
"BUY SUN STOVE POLISH;"
"HELMBOLD'S BUCHU;"
"TRY BENZALINE FOR THE BLOOD."

He was captured, and it turned out that he was an American. Upon his trial the judge said to him:

"You are from a land where any insolent that wants to is privileged to profane and insult Nature, and, through her, Nature's God, if by so doing he can put a sordid penny in his pocket. But here the case is different. Because you are a foreigner and ignorant,

I will make your sentence light; if you were a native I would deal strenuously with you. Hear and obey:—You will immediately remove every trace of your offensive work from the Schiller monument; you pay a fine of ten thousand francs; you will suffer two years' imprisonment at hard labor; you will then be horsewhipped, tarred and feathered, deprived of your ears, ridden on a rail to the confines of the canton, and banished forever. The severer penalties are omitted in your case,—not as a grace to you, but to that great republic which had the misfortune to give you birth."

The steamer's benches were ranged back to back across the deck. My back hair was mingling innocently with the back hair of a couple of ladies. Presently they were addressed by some one and I overheard this conversation:

"You are Americans, I think? So'm I."

"Yes,—we are Americans."

"I knew it,—I can always tell them. What ship did you come over in?"

"City of Chester."

"Oh, yes,—Inman line. We came in the *Batavia,*—Cunard, you know. What kind of a passage did you have?"

"Pretty fair."

"That was luck. We had it awful rough. Captain said he'd hardly ever seen it rougher. Where are you from?"

"New Jersey."

"So'm I. No—I didn't mean that; I'm from New England. New Bloomfield's my place. These your children?—belong to both of you?"

"Only to one of us; they are mine; my friend is not married."

"Single, I reckon? So'm I. Are you two ladies traveling alone?"

"No,—my husband is with us."

"Our whole family's along. It's awful slow, going around alone,—don't you think so?"

"I suppose it must be."

"Hi, there's Mount Pilatus coming in sight again. Named after Pontius Pilate, you know, that shot the apple off of William Tell's head. Guide-book tells all about it, they say. I didn't read it—an American told me. I don't read when I'm knocking around like this, having a good time. Did you ever see the chapel where William Tell used to preach?"

"I did not know he ever preached there."

"Oh, yes, he did. That American told me so. He don't ever shut up his guide-book. He knows more about this lake than the fishes in it. Besides, they *call* it 'Tell's Chapel'—you know that yourself. You ever been over here before?"

"Yes."

"I haven't. It's my first trip. But we've been all around,—Paris and everywhere. I'm to enter Harvard next year. Studying German all the time now. Can't enter till I know German. This book's Otto's grammar. It's a mighty good book to get the *ich habe gehabt haben's* out of. But I don't really study when I'm knocking around this way. If the notion takes me, I just run over my little old *ich habe gehabt, du hast gehabt, er hat gehabt, wir haben gehabt, ihr haben gehabt, sie haben gehabt,*—kind of 'Now-I-lay-me-down-to-sleep' fashion, you know, and after that, maybe I don't buckle to it again for three days. It's awful undermining to the intellect, German is; you want to take it in small doses, or first you know your brains all run together, and you feel them sloshing around in your head same as so much drawn butter. But French is different; *French* ain't anything. I ain't any more afraid of French than a tramp's afraid of pie; I can rattle off my little *j'ai, tu as, il a,* and the rest of it, just as easy as a-b-c. I get along pretty well in Paris, or anywhere where they speak French. What hotel you stopping at?"

"The Schweitzerhof."

"No! is that so? I never see you in the big reception room. I go in there a good deal of the time, because there's so many Americans there. I make lots of acquaintances. You been up the Rigi yet?"

"No."

"Going?"

"We think of it."

"What hotel you going to stop at?"

"I don't know."

"Well, then, you stop at the Schreiber,—it's full of Americans. What ship did you come over in?"

"City of Chester."

"Oh, yes, I remember I asked you that before. But I always ask everybody what ship they came over in, and so sometimes I forget and ask again. You going to Geneva?"

"Yes."

"What hotel you going to stop at?"

"We expect to stop in a pension."

"I don't hardly believe you'll like that; there's very few Americans in the pensions. What hotel are you stopping at here?"

"The Schweitzerhof."

"Oh, yes, I asked you that before, too. But I always ask everybody what hotel they're stopping at, and so I've got my head all mixed up with hotels. But it makes talk, and I love to talk. It refreshes me up so,—don't it you,—on a trip like this?"

"Yes,—sometimes."

"Well, it does me, too. As long as I'm talking I never feel bored,—ain't that the way with you?"

"Yes—generally. But there are exceptions to the rule."

"Oh, of course. *I* don't care to talk to everybody, *myself*. If a person starts in to jabber-jabber-jabber about scenery, and history, and pictures, and all sorts of tiresome things, I get the fan-tods mighty soon. I say 'Well, I must be going now,—hope I'll see you again'—and then I take a walk. Where you from?"

"New Jersey."

"Why, bother it all, I asked you *that* before, too. Have you seen the Lion of Lucerne?"

"Not yet."

"Nor I, either. But the man who told me about Mount Pilatus says it's one of the things to see. It's twenty-eight feet long. It don't seem reasonable, but he said so, anyway. He saw it yesterday; said it was dying, then, so I reckon it's dead by this time. But that ain't any matter, of course they'll stuff it. Did you say the children are yours,—or *hers?*"

"Mine."

"Oh, so you did. Are you going up the . . . no, I asked you that. What ship . . . no, I asked you that, too. What hotel are you . . . no, you told me that. Let me see . . . um . . . Oh, what kind of a voy . . . no, we've been over that ground, too. Um . . . um . . . well, I believe that is all. *Bonjour*—I am very glad to have made your acquaintance, ladies. *Guten Tag.*"

From *A Tramp Abroad,* 1880.

36 : *Geneva*

We spent a few pleasant restful days at Geneva, that delightful city where accurate time-pieces are made for all the rest of the world, but whose own clocks never give the correct time of day by any accident.

Geneva is filled with pretty little shops, and the shops are filled with the most enticing gimcrackery, but if one enters one of these places he is at once pounced upon, and followed up, and so persecuted to buy this, that, and the other thing, that he is very grateful to get out again, and is not at all apt to repeat his experiment. The shopkeepers of the smaller sort, in Geneva, are as troublesome and persistent as are the salesmen of that monster hive in Paris, the Grands Magasins du Louvre—an establishment where ill-mannered pestering, pursuing, and insistence have been reduced to a science.

In Geneva, prices in the smaller shops are very elastic—that is another bad feature. I was looking in at a window at a very pretty string of beads, suitable for a child. I was only admiring them; I had no use for them; I hardly ever wear beads. The shopwoman came out and offered them to me for thirty-five francs. I said it was cheap, but I did not need them.

"Ah, but monsieur, they are so beautiful!"

I confessed it, but said they were not suitable for one of my age and simplicity of character. She darted in and brought them out and tried to force them into my hands, saying:

"Ah, but only see how lovely they are! Surely monsieur will take them; monsieur shall have them for thirty francs. There, I have said it—it is a loss, but one must live."

I dropped my hands, and tried to move her to respect my unprotected situation. But no, she dangled the beads in the sun before my face, exclaiming, "Ah, monsieur *cannot* resist them!" She hung them on my coat button, folded her hands resignedly, and said: "Gone,—and for thirty francs, the lovely things—it is incredible!—but the good God will sanctify the sacrifice to me."

I removed them gently, returning them, and walked away, shaking my head and smiling a smile of silly embarrassment while the passers-by halted to observe. The woman leaned out of her door, shook the beads, and screamed after me:

"Monsieur shall have them for twenty-eight!"

I shook my head.

"Twenty-seven! It is a cruel loss, it is ruin—but take them, only take them."

I still retreated, still wagging my head.

"Mon Dieu, they shall even go for twenty-six! There, I have said it. Come!"

I wagged another negative. A nurse and a little English girl had been near me, and were following me, now. The shopwoman ran to the nurse, thrust the beads into her hands, and said:

"Monsieur shall have them for twenty-five! Take them to the hotel—he shall send me the money to-morrow—next day—when he likes." Then to the child: "When thy father sends me the money, come thou also, my angel, and thou shalt have something oh so pretty!"

I was thus providentially saved. The nurse refused the beads squarely and firmly, and that ended the matter.

The "sights" of Geneva are not numerous. I made one attempt to hunt up the houses once inhabited by those two disagreeable people, Rousseau and Calvin, but had no success. Then I concluded to go home. I found it was easier to propose to do that than to do it; for that town is a bewildering place. I got lost in a tangle of narrow and crooked streets, and stayed lost for an hour or two. Finally I found a street which looked somewhat familiar, and said to myself, "Now I am at home, I judge." But I was wrong; this was "*Hell* street." Presently I found another place which had a familiar look, and said to myself, "Now I am at home, sure." It was another error. This was "*Purgatory* street." After a little I said, "*Now* I've got the right place, anyway . . . no, this is '*Paradise* street'; I'm further from home than I was in the beginning." Those were queer names—Calvin was the author of them, likely. "Hell" and "Purgatory" fitted those two streets like a glove, but the "Paradise" appeared to be sarcastic.

From *A Tramp Abroad,* 1880.

37 : *Dining in Europe*

In Venice we had a luxury which very seldom fell to our lot on the Continent—a home dinner with a private family. If one could always stop with private families, when traveling, Europe would have a charm which it now lacks. As it is, one must live in the hotels, of course, and that is a sorrowful business. A man accustomed to American food and American domestic cookery would not starve to death suddenly in Europe; but I think he would gradually waste away, and eventually die.

He would have to do without his accustomed morning meal. That is too formidable a change altogether; he would necessarily suffer from it. He could get the shadow, the sham, the base counterfeit of that meal; but that would do him no good, and money could not buy the reality.

To particularize: the average American's simplest and commonest form of breakfast consists of coffee and beefsteak; well, in Europe, coffee is an unknown beverage. You can get what the European hotel-keeper thinks is coffee, but it resembles the real thing as hypocrisy resembles holiness. It is a feeble, characterless, uninspiring sort of stuff, and almost as undrinkable as if it had been made in an American hotel. The milk used for it is what the French call "Christian" milk,—milk which has been baptized.

After a few months' acquaintance with European "coffee," one's mind weakens, and his faith with it, and he begins to wonder if the rich beverage of home, with its clotted layer of yellow cream on top of it, is not a mere dream, after all, and a thing which never existed.

Next comes the European bread,—fair enough, good enough, after a fashion, but cold; cold and tough, and unsympathetic; and never any change, never any variety,—always the same tiresome thing.

Next, the butter,—the sham and tasteless butter; no salt in it, and made of goodness knows what.

Then there is the beefsteak. They have it in Europe, but they don't know how to cook it. Neither will they cut it right. It comes on the table in a small, round, pewter platter. It lies in the center of this platter, in a bordering bed of grease-soaked potatoes; it is the size, shape, and thickness of a man's hand with the thumb and fingers cut off. It is a little overdone, is rather dry, it tastes pretty insipidly, it rouses no enthusiasm.

Imagine a poor exile contemplating that inert thing; and imagine an angel suddenly sweeping down out of a better land and setting before him a mighty porterhouse steak an inch and a half thick, hot and sputtering from the griddle; dusted with fragrant pepper; enriched with little melting bits of butter of the most unimpeachable freshness and genuineness; the precious juices of the meat trickling out and joining the gravy, archipelagoed with mushrooms; a township or two of tender, yellowish fat gracing an outlying district of this ample county of beefsteak; the long white bone which divides the sirloin from the tenderloin still in its place; and imagine that the angel also adds a great cup of American home-made coffee, with the cream a-froth on top, some real butter, firm and yellow and fresh, some smoking-hot biscuits, a plate of hot buckwheat cakes, with transparent syrup,—could words describe the gratitude of this exile?

The European dinner is better than the European breakfast, but it has its faults and inferiorities; it does not satisfy. He comes to the table eager and hungry; he swallows his soup,—there is an undefinable lack about it somewhere; thinks the fish is going to be the thing he wants,—eats it and isn't sure; thinks the next dish is perhaps the one that will hit the hungry place,—tries it, and is conscious that there was a something wanting about it, also. And thus he goes on, from dish to dish, like a boy after a butterfly which just misses getting caught every time it alights, but somehow doesn't get caught after all; and at the end the exile and the boy have fared about alike; the one is full, but grievously unsatisfied, the other has had plenty of exercise, plenty of interest, and a fine lot of hopes, but he hasn't got any butterfly. There is here and there an American who will say he can remember rising from a European table d'hôte perfectly satisfied; but we must not overlook the fact that there is also here and there an American who will lie.

The number of dishes is sufficient; but then it is such a monotonous variety of *unstriking* dishes. It is an inane dead level of "fair-to-middling." There is nothing to *accent* it. Perhaps if the roast of mutton or of beef,—a big, generous one,—were brought on the table and carved in full view of the client, that might give the right sense of earnestness and reality to the thing; but they don't do that, they pass the sliced meat around on a dish, and so you are perfectly calm, it does not stir you in the least. Now a vast roast turkey, stretched on the broad of his back, with his heels in the air and the rich juices oozing from his fat sides . . . but I may as well stop there, for they would not know how to cook him. They can't even cook a chicken respectably; and as for carving it, they do that with a hatchet.

This is about the customary table d'hôte bill in summer:

Soup (characterless).

Fish—sole, salmon, or whiting—usually tolerably good.

Roast—mutton or beef—tasteless—and some last year's potatoes.

A pâte, or some other made dish—usually good—"considering."

One vegetable—brought on in state, and all alone—usually insipid lentils, or string beans, or indifferent asparagus.

Roast chicken, as tasteless as paper.

Lettuce-salad—tolerably good.

Decayed strawberries or cherries.

Sometimes the apricots and figs are fresh, but this is no advantage, as these fruits are of no account anyway.

The grapes are generally good, and sometimes there is a tolerably good peach, by mistake.

The variations of the above bill are trifling. After a fortnight one discovers that the variations are only apparent, not real; in the third week you get what you had the first, and in the fourth week you get what you had the second. Three or four months of this weary sameness will kill the robustest appetite.

It has now been many months, at the present writing, since I have had a nourishing meal, but I shall soon have one,—a modest, private affair, all to myself. I have selected a few dishes, and made out a little bill of fare, which will go home in the steamer that precedes me, and be hot when I arrive—as follows:

Radishes. Baked apples, with cream.
Fried oysters; stewed oysters. Frogs.
American coffee, with real cream.
American butter.
Fried chicken, Southern style.
Porter-house steak.
Saratoga potatoes.
Broiled chicken, American style.
Hot biscuits, Southern style.
Hot wheat-bread, Southern style.
Hot buckwheat cakes.
American toast. Clear maple syrup.
Virginia bacon, broiled.
Blue points, on the half shell.
Cherry-stone clams.
San Francisco mussels, steamed.
Oyster soup. Clam soup.
Philadelphia Terrapin soup.
Oysters roasted in shell – Northern style.
Soft-shell crabs. Connecticut shad.
Baltimore perch.
Brook trout, from Sierra Nevadas.
Lake trout, from Tahoe.
Sheephead and croakers from New Orleans.
Black bass from the Mississippi.
American roast beef.
Roast turkey, Thanksgiving style.
Cranberry sauce. Celery.
Roast wild turkey. Woodcock.
Canvasback-duck, from Baltimore.
Prairie hens, from Illinois.
Missouri partridges, broiled.
'Possum. Coon.
Boston bacon and beans.
Bacon and greens, Southern style.
Hominy. Boiled onions. Turnips.
Pumpkin. Squash. Asparagus.
Butter Beans. Sweet potatoes.
Lettuce. Succotash. String beans.
Mashed potatoes. Catsup.
Boiled potatoes, in their skins.
New potatoes, minus the skins.
Early rose potatoes, roasted in the ashes, Southern style, served hot.
Sliced tomatoes, with sugar or vinegar. Stewed tomatoes.
Green corn, cut from the ear and served with butter and pepper.
Green corn, on the ear.
Hot corn-pone, with chitlings, Southern style.
Hot hoe-cake, Southern style.
Hot egg-bread, Southern style.
Hot light-bread, Southern style.
Buttermilk. Iced sweet milk.
Apple dumplings, with real cream.
Apple pie. Apple fritters.
Apple puffs, Southern style.
Peach cobbler, Southern style.
Peach pie. American mince pie.
Pumpkin pie. Squash pie.
All sorts of American pastry.

From *A Tramp Abroad,* 1880.

3 / *Asia*

38 : *Ephesus*

THIS HAS BEEN A STIRRING DAY. The superintendent of the railway put a train at our disposal, and did us the further kindness of accompanying us to Ephesus and giving to us his watchful care. We brought sixty scarcely perceptible donkeys in the freight-cars, for we had much ground to go over. We have seen some of the most grotesque costumes, along the line of the railroad, that can be imagined. I am glad that no possible combination of words could describe them, for I might then be foolish enough to attempt it.

At ancient Ayassalook, in the midst of a forbidding desert, we came upon long lines of ruined aqueducts, and other remnants of architectural grandeur, that told us plainly enough we were nearing what had been a metropolis once. We left the train and mounted the donkeys, along with our invited guests—pleasant young gentlemen from the officers' list of an American man-of-war.

The little donkeys had saddles upon them which were made very high in order that the rider's feet might not drag the ground. The preventative did not work well in the cases of our tallest pilgrims, however. There were no bridles—nothing but a single rope, tied to the bit. It was purely ornamental, for the donkey cared nothing for it. If he were drifting to starboard, you might put your helm down hard the other way, if it were any satisfaction to you to do it, but he would continue to drift to starboard all the same. There was only one process which could be depended on, and that was to get down and lift his rear around until his head pointed in the right direction, or take him under your arm and carry him to a part of the road which he could not get out of without climbing. The sun flamed down as hot as a furnace, and neck-scarfs, veils, and umbrellas seemed hardly any protection; they served only to make the long procession look more than ever fantastic—for be it known the ladies were all riding astride because they could not stay on the shapeless saddles sidewise, the men were perspiring and out of temper, their feet were banging against the rocks, the donkeys were capering in every direction but the right one and being belabored with clubs for it, and every now and then a broad umbrella would suddenly go down out of the cavalcade, announcing to all that one more pilgrim had bitten the dust. It was a wilder picture than those solitudes had seen for many a day. No donkeys ever existed that were as hard to navigate as these, I think, or that had so many vile, exasperating instincts. Occasionally, we grew so tired and breathless with fighting them that we had to desist—and immediately the donkey would come down to a deliberate walk. This, with the fatigue, and the sun, would put a man asleep; and as soon as the man was asleep, the donkey would lie down. My donkey shall never see his boyhood's home again. He has lain down once too often. He must die.

We all stood in the vast theater of ancient Ephesus—the stone-benched amphitheater, I mean—and had our picture taken. We looked as proper there as we would look anywhere, I suppose. We do not embellish the general desolation of a desert much. We add what dignity we can to a stately ruin with our green umbrellas and jackasses, but it is little. However, we mean well.

I wish to say a brief word of the aspect of Ephesus.

On a high, steep hill, toward the sea, is a gray ruin of ponderous blocks of marble, wherein, tradition says, St. Paul was imprisoned eighteen centuries ago. From these old walls you have the finest view of the desolate scene where once stood Ephesus, the proudest city of ancient times, and whose Temple of Diana was so noble in design and so exquisite of workmanship, that it ranked high in the list of the Seven Wonders of the World.

Behind you is the sea; in front is a level green valley (a marsh, in fact), extending far away among the mountains; to the right of the front view is the old citadel of Ayassalook, on a high hill; the ruined mosque of the Sultan Selim stands near it in the plain (this is built over the grave of St. John, and was formerly a Christian church); further toward you is the hill of Prion, around whose front is clustered all that remains of the ruins of Ephesus that still stand; divided from it by a narrow valley is the long, rocky, rugged mountain of Coressus. The scene is a pretty one, and yet desolate—for in that wide plain no man can live, and in it is no human habitation. But for the crumbling arches and monstrous piers and broken walls that rise from the foot of the hill of Prion, one could not believe that in this place once stood a city whose renown is older than tradition itself. It is incredible to reflect that things as familiar all over the world to-day as household words belong in the history and in the shadowy legends of this silent, mournful solitude. We speak of Apollo and of Diana—they were born here; of the metamorphosis of Syrinx into a reed—it was done here; of the great god Pan—he dwelt in the caves of this hill of Coressus; of the Amazons—this was their best-prized home; of Bacchus and Hercules—both fought the warlike women here; of the Cyclops—they laid the ponderous marble blocks of some of the ruins yonder; of Homer—this was one of his many birthplaces; of Cimon of Athens; of Alcibiades, Lysander, Agesilaus—they visited here; so did Alexander the Great; so did Hannibal and Antiochus, Scipio, Lucullus, and Sylla; Brutus, Cassius, Pompey, Cicero, and Augustus; Antony was a judge in this place, and left his seat in the open court, while the advocates were speaking, to run after Cleopatra, who passed the door; from this city these two sailed on pleasure excursions, in galleys with silver oars and perfumed sails, and with companies of beautiful girls to serve them, and actors and musicians to amuse them; in days that seem almost modern, so remote are they from the early history of this city, Paul the Apostle preached the new religion here, and so did John, and here it is supposed the former was pitted against wild beasts, for in I Corinthians, xv:32, he says:

> If after the manner of men I have fought with beasts at Ephesus [etc.]

when many men still lived who had seen the Christ; here Mary Magdalen died, and here the Virgin Mary ended her days with John, albeit Rome has since judged it best to locate her grave elsewhere; six or seven hundred years ago—almost yesterday, as it were—troops of mail-clad Crusaders thronged the streets; and to come down to trifles, we speak of meandering streams, and find a new interest in a common word when we discover that the crooked river Meander, in yonder valley, gave it to our dictionary. It makes me feel as old as these dreary hills to look down upon these moss-hung ruins, this historic desolation. One may read the Scriptures and believe, but he cannot go and stand yonder in the ruined theater and in imagination people it again with the vanished multitudes who mobbed Paul's comrades there and shouted, with one voice, "Great is Diana of the Ephesians!" The idea of a shout in such a solitude as this almost makes one shudder.

It was a wonderful city, this Ephesus. Go where you will about these broad plains, you find the most exquisitely sculptured marble fragments scattered thick among the dust and weeds; and protruding from the ground, or lying prone upon it, are beautiful fluted columns of porphyry and all precious marbles; and at every step you find elegantly carved capitals and massive bases, and polished tablets engraved with Greek inscriptions. It is a world of precious relics, a wilderness of marred and mutilated gems. And yet what are these things to the wonders that lie buried here under the ground? At Constantinople, at Pisa, in the cities of Spain, are great mosques and cathedrals, whose grandest columns came from the temples and palaces of Ephesus, and yet one has only to scratch the ground here to match them. We shall never know what magnificence is, until this imperial city is laid bare to the sun.

The finest piece of sculpture we have yet seen and the one that impressed us most (for we do not know much about art and cannot easily work up ourselves into ecstasies over it), is one that lies in this old theater of Ephesus which St. Paul's riot has made so celebrated. It is only the headless body of a man, clad in a coat of mail, with a Medusa head upon the breastplate, but we feel persuaded that such dignity and such majesty were never thrown into a form of stone before.

What builders they were, these men of antiquity! The massive arches of some of these ruins rest upon piers that are fifteen feet square and built entirely of solid blocks of marble, some of which are as large as a Saratoga trunk, and some the size of a boarding-house sofa. They are not shells or shafts of stone filled inside with rubbish, but the whole pier is a mass of solid masonry. Vast arches, that may have been the gates of the city, are built in the same way. They have braved the storms and sieges of three thousand years, and have been shaken by many an earthquake, but still they stand. When they dig alongside of them, they find ranges of ponderous masonry that are as perfect in every detail as they were the day those old Cyclopean giants finished them. An English company is going to excavate Ephesus—and then!

From *The Innocents Abroad,* 1869.

39 : *Damascus*

As THE GLARE OF DAY MELLOWED into twilight, we looked down upon a picture which is celebrated all over the world. I think I have read about four hundred times that when Mohammed was a simple camel-driver he reached this point and looked down upon Damascus for the first time, and then made a certain renowned remark. He said man could enter only one paradise; he preferred to go to the one above. So he sat down there and feasted his eyes upon the earthly paradise of Damascus, and then went away without entering its gates. They have erected a tower on the hill to mark the spot where he stood.

Damascus *is* beautiful from the mountain. It is beautiful even to foreigners accustomed to luxuriant vegetation, and I can easily understand how unspeakably beautiful it must be to eyes that are only used to the God-forsaken barrenness and desolation of Syria. I should think a Syrian would go wild with ecstasy when such a picture bursts upon him for the first time.

From his high perch, one sees before him and below him a wall of dreary mountains, shorn of vegetation, glaring fiercely in the sun; it fences in a level desert of yellow sand, smooth as velvet and threaded far away with fine lines that stand for roads, and dotted with creeping mites we know are camel-trains and journeying men; right in the midst of the desert is spread a billowy expanse of green foliage; and nestling in its heart sits the great white city, like an island of pearls and opals gleaming out of a sea of emeralds. This is the picture you see spread far below you, with distance to soften it, the sun to glorify it, strong contrasts to heighten the effects, and over it and about it a drowsing air of repose to spiritualize it and make it seem rather a beautiful estray from the mysterious worlds we visit in dreams than a substantial tenant of our coarse, dull globe. And when you think of the leagues of blighted, blasted, sandy, rocky, sunburnt, ugly, dreary, infamous country you have ridden over to get here, you think it is the most beautiful, beautiful picture that ever human eyes rested upon in all the broad universe! If I were to go to Damascus again, I would camp on Mohammed's hill about a week, and then go away. There is no need to go inside the walls. The Prophet was wise without knowing it when he decided not to go down into the paradise of Damascus.

There is an honored old tradition that the immense garden which Damascus stands in was the Garden of Eden, and modern writers have gathered up many chapters of evidence tending to show that it really was the Garden of Eden, and that the rivers Pharpar and Abana are the "two rivers" that watered Adam's Paradise. It may be so, but it is not paradise now, and one would be as happy outside of it as he would be likely to be within. It is so crooked and cramped and dirty that one cannot realize that he is in the splendid city he saw from the hilltop. The gardens are hidden by high mud-walls, and the paradise is become a very sink of pollution and uncomeliness. Damascus has plenty of clear, pure water in it, though, and this is enough, of itself, to make an Arab think it beautiful and blessed. Water is scarce in blistered Syria. We run railways by our large cities in America; in Syria they curve the roads so as to make them run by the meager little puddles they call "fountains," and which are not found oftener on a journey than every four hours. But the "rivers" of Pharpar and Abana of Scripture (mere creeks) run through Damascus, and so every house and every garden have their sparkling fountains and rivulets of water. With her forest of foliage and her abundance of water, Damascus must be a wonder of wonders to the Bedouin from the deserts. Damascus is simply an oasis—that is what it is. For four thousand years its waters have not gone dry or its fertility failed. Now we can understand why the city has existed so long. It could not die. So long as its waters remain to it away out there in the midst of that howling desert, so long will Damascus live to bless the sight of the tired and thirsty wayfarer.

> Though old as history itself, thou art fresh as the breath of spring, blooming as thine own rose-bud, and fragrant as thine own orange flower, O Damascus, pearl of the East!

Damascus dates back anterior to the days of Abraham, and is the oldest city in the world. It was founded by Uz, the grandson of Noah. "The early history of Damascus is shrouded in the mists of a hoary antiquity." Leave the matters written of in the first eleven chapters of the Old Testament out, and no recorded event has occurred in the world but Damascus was in existence to receive the news of it. Go back as far as you will into the vague past, there was always a Damascus. In the writings of every century for more than four thousand years, its name has been mentioned and its praises sung. To Damascus, years are only moments, decades are only flitting trifles of time. She measures time, not by days and months and years, but by the empires she has seen rise and prosper and crumble to ruin. She is a type of immortality. She saw the foundations of Baalbec, and Thebes, and Ephesus laid; she saw these villages grow into mighty cities, and amaze the world with their grandeur—and she has lived to see them desolate, deserted, and given over to the owls and the bats. She saw the Israelitish empire exalted, and she saw it annihilated. She saw Greece rise, and flourish two thousand years, and die. In her old age she saw Rome built; she saw it overshadow the world with its power; she saw it perish. The few hundreds of years of Genoese and Venetian might and splendor were, to grave old Damascus, only a trifling scintillation hardly worth remembering. Damascus has seen all that has ever occurred on earth, and still she lives. She has looked upon the dry bones of a thousand empires, and will see the tombs of a thousand more before she dies. Though another claims the name, old Damascus is by right the Eternal City.

We reached the city gates just at sundown. They do say that one can get into any walled city of Syria, after night, for bucksheesh, except Damascus. But Damascus, with its four thousand years of respectability in the world, has many old fogy notions. There are no street-lamps there, and the law compels all who go abroad at night to carry lanterns, just as was the case in old days, when heroes and heroines of the Arabian Nights walked the streets of Damascus, or flew away toward Bagdad on enchanted carpets.

It was fairly dark a few minutes after we got within the wall, and we rode long distances through wonderfully crooked streets, eight to ten feet wide, and shut in on either side by the high mud-walls of the gardens. At last we got to where lanterns could be seen flitting about here and there, and knew we were in the midst of the curious old city. In a little narrow street, crowded with our pack-mules and with a swarm of uncouth Arabs, we alighted, and through a kind of a hole in the wall entered the hotel. We stood in a great flagged court, with flowers and citron trees about us, and a huge tank in the center that was receiving the waters of many pipes. We crossed the court and entered the rooms prepared to receive four of us. In a large marble-paved recess between the two rooms was a tank of clear, cool water, which was kept running over all the time by the streams that were pouring into it from half a dozen pipes. Nothing in this scorching, desolate land could look so refreshing as this pure water flashing in the lamplight; nothing could look so beautiful, nothing could sound so delicious as this mimic rain to ears long unaccustomed to sounds of such a nature. Our rooms were large, comfortably furnished, and even had their floors clothed with soft, cheerful-tinted carpets. It was a pleasant thing to see a carpet again, for if there is anything drearier than the tomblike, stone-paved parlors and bedrooms of Europe and Asia, I do not know what it is. They make one think of the grave all the time. A very broad, gaily caparisoned divan, some twelve or fourteen feet long, extended across one side of each room, and opposite were single beds with spring mattresses. There were great looking-glasses and marble-top tables. All this luxury was as grateful to systems and senses worn out with an exhausting day's travel, as it was unexpected—for one cannot tell what to expect in a Turkish city of even a quarter of a million inhabitants.

I do not know, but I think they used that tank between the rooms to draw drinking-water from; that did not occur to me, however, until I had dipped my baking head far down into its cool depths. I thought of it then, and, superb as the bath was, I was sorry I had taken it, and was about to go and explain to the landlord. But a finely curled and scented poodle dog frisked up and nipped the calf of my leg just then, and before I had time to think I had soused him to the bottom of the tank, and when I saw a servant coming with a pitcher I went off and left the pup trying to climb out and not succeeding very well. Satisfied revenge was all I needed to make me perfectly happy, and when I walked in to supper that first night in Damascus I was in that condition. We lay on those divans a long time, after supper, smoking narghilis and long-stemmed chibouks, and talking about the dreadful ride of the day, and I knew then what I had sometimes known before—that it is worth while to get tired out, because one so enjoys resting afterward.

In the morning we sent for donkeys. It is worthy of note that we had to *send* for these things. I said Damascus was an old fossil, and she is. Anywhere else we would have been assailed by a clamorous army of donkey-drivers, guides, peddlers, and beggars—but in Damascus they so hate the very sight of a foreign Christian that they want no intercourse whatever with him; only a year or two ago, his person was not always safe in Damascus streets. It is the most fanatical Mohammedan purgatory out of Arabia. Where you see one green turban of a Hadji elsewhere (the honored sign that my lord has made the pilgrimage to Mecca), I think you will see a dozen in Damascus. The Damascenes are the ugliest, wickedest looking villains we have seen. All the veiled women we had seen yet, nearly, left their eyes exposed, but numbers of these in Damascus completely hid the face under a close-drawn black veil that made the woman look like a mummy. If ever we caught an eye exposed it was quickly hidden from our contaminating Christian vision; the beggars actually passed us by without demanding bucksheesh; the merchants in the bazars did not hold up their goods and cry out eagerly, "Hey, John!" or "Look this, Howajji!" On the contrary, they only scowled at us and said never a word.

The narrow streets swarmed like a hive with men and women in strange Oriental costumes, and our small donkeys knocked them right and left as we plowed through them, urged on by the merciless donkey-boys. These persecutors run after the animals, shouting and goading them for hours together; they keep the donkey in a gallop always, yet never get tired themselves or fall behind. The donkeys fell down and spilt us over their heads occasionally, but there was nothing for it but to mount and hurry on again. We were banged against sharp corners, loaded porters, camels, and citizens generally; and we were so taken up with looking out for collisions and casualties that we had no chance to look about us at all. We rode half through the city and through the famous "street which is called Straight" without seeing anything, hardly. Our bones were nearly knocked out of joint, we were wild with excitement, and our sides ached with the jolting we had suffered. I do not like riding in the Damascus street-cars.

We were on our way to the reputed houses of Judas and Ananias. About eighteen or nineteen hundred years ago, Saul, a native of Tarsus, was particularly bitter against the new sect called Christians, and he left Jerusalem and started across the country on a furious crusade against them. He went forth "breathing threatenings and slaughter against the disciples of the Lord."

> And as he journeyed, he came near Damascus, and suddenly there shined round about him a light from heaven:
>
> And he fell to the earth and heard a voice saying unto him, Saul, Saul, why persecutest thou me?
>
> And when he knew that it was Jesus that spoke to him he trembled, and was astonished, and said, Lord, what wilt thou have me to do?

He was told to arise and go into the ancient city and one would tell him what to do. In the meantime his soldiers stood speechless and awe-stricken, for they heard the mysterious voice but saw no man. Saul rose up and found that that fierce supernatural light had destroyed his sight, and he was blind, so "they led him by the hand and brought him to Damascus." He was converted.

Paul lay three days blind, in the house of Judas, and during that time he neither ate nor drank.

There came a voice to a citizen of Damascus, named Ananias, saying, "Arise, and go into the street which is called Straight, and inquire at the house of Judas, for one called Saul, of Tarsus; for behold, he prayeth."

Ananias did not wish to go at first, for he had heard of Saul before, and he had his doubts about that style of a "chosen vessel" to preach the gospel of peace. However, in obedience to orders, he went into the "street called Straight" (how he ever found his way into it, and after he did, how he ever found his way out of it again, are mysteries only to be accounted for by the fact that he was acting under Divine inspiration). He found Paul and restored him, and ordained him a preacher; and from this old house we had hunted up in the street which is miscalled Straight, he had started out on that bold missionary career which he prosecuted till his death.

It was not the house of the disciple who sold the Master for thirty pieces of silver. I make this explanation in justice to Judas, who was a far different sort of man from the person just referred to. A very different style of man, and lived in a very good house. It is a pity we do not know more about him.

I have given, in the above paragraphs, some more information for people who will not read Bible history until they are defrauded into it by some such method as this. I hope that no friend of progress and education will obstruct or interfere with my peculiar mission.

The street called Straight is straighter than a corkscrew, but not as straight as a rainbow. St. Luke is careful not to commit himself; he does not say it is the street which *is* straight, but the "street which is *called* Straight." It is a fine piece of irony; it is the only facetious remark in the Bible, I believe. We traversed the street called Straight a good way, and then turned off and called at the reputed house of Ananias. There is small question that a part of the original house is there still; it is an old room twelve or fifteen feet underground, and its masonry is evidently ancient. If Ananias did not live there in St. Paul's time, somebody else did, which is just as well. I took a drink out of Ananias's well, and, singularly enough, the water was just as fresh as if the well had been dug yesterday.

We went out toward the north end of the city to see the place where the disciples let Paul down over the Damascus wall at dead of night—for he preached Christ so fearlessly in Damascus that the people sought to kill him, just as they would to-day for the same offense, and he had to escape and flee to Jerusalem.

Then we called at the tomb of Mohammed's children and at a tomb which purported to be that of St. George who killed the dragon, and so on out to the hollow place under a rock where Paul hid during his flight till his pursuers gave him up; and up to the mausoleum of the five thousand Christians who were massacred in Damascus in 1861 by the Turks. They say those narrow streets ran blood for several days, and that men, women, and children were butchered indiscriminately and left to rot by hundreds all through the Christian quarter; they say, further, that the stench was dreadful. All the Christians who could get away fled from the city, and the Mohammedans would not defile their hands by burying the "infidel dogs." The thirst for blood extended to the high lands of Hermon and Anti-Lebanon, and in a short time twenty-five thousand more Christians were massacred and their possessions laid waste. How they hate a Christian in Damascus!—and pretty much all over Turkeydom as well. And how they will pay for it when Russia turns her guns upon them again!

It is soothing to the heart to abuse England and France for interposing to save the Ottoman Empire from the destruction it has so richly deserved for a thousand years. It hurts my vanity to see these pagans refuse to eat of food that has been cooked for us; or to eat from a dish we have eaten from; or to drink from a goatskin which we have polluted with our Christian lips, except by filtering the water through a rag which they put over the mouth of it or through a sponge! I never disliked a Chinaman as I do these degraded Turks and Arabs, and, when Russia is ready to war with them again, I hope England and France will not find it good breeding or good judgment to interfere.

In Damascus they think there are no such rivers in all the world as their little Abana and Pharpar. The Damascenes have always thought that way. In II Kings, chapter v, Naaman boasts extravagantly about them. That was three thousand years ago. He says: "Are not Abana and Pharpar, rivers of Damascus, better than all the waters of Israel? May I not wash in them and be clean?" But some of my readers have forgotten who Naaman was, long ago. Naaman was the commander of the Syrian armies. He was the favorite of the king and lived in great state. "He was a mighty man of valor, but he was a leper." Strangely enough, the house they point out to you now as his has been turned into a leper hospital, and the inmates expose their horrid deformities and hold up their hands and beg for buck-sheesh when a stranger enters.

One cannot appreciate the horror of this disease until he looks upon it in all its ghastliness in Naaman's ancient dwelling in Damascus. Bones all twisted out of shape, great knots protruding from face and body, joints decaying and dropping away—horrible!

From *The Innocents Abroad,* 1869.

40 : *Nazareth*

We descended from Mount Tabor, crossed a deep ravine, and followed a hilly, rocky road to Nazareth—distant two hours. All distances in the East are measured by hours, not miles. A good horse will walk three miles an hour over nearly any kind of a road; therefore, an hour here always stands for three miles. This method of computation is bothersome and annoying; and until one gets thoroughly accustomed to it, it carries no intelligence to his mind until he has stopped and translated the pagan hours into Christian miles, just as people do with the spoken words of a foreign language they are acquainted with, but not familiarly enough to catch the meaning in a moment. Distances traveled by human feet are also estimated by hours and minutes, though I do not know what the base of the calculation is. In Constantinople you ask, "How far is it to the Consulate?" and they answer, "About ten minutes." "How far is it to the Lloyds' Agency?" "Quarter of an hour." "How far is it to the lower bridge?" "Four minutes." I cannot be positive about it, but I think that there, when a man orders a pair of pantaloons, he says he wants them a quarter of a minute in the legs and nine seconds around the waist.

Two hours from Tabor to Nazareth—and as it was an uncommonly narrow, crooked trail, we necessarily met all the canal-trains and jackass-caravans between Jericho and Jacksonville in that particular place and nowhere else. The donkeys do not matter so much, because they are so small that you can jump your horse over them if he is an animal of spirit, but a camel is not jumpable. A camel is as tall as any ordinary dwelling-house in Syria—which is to say a camel is from one to two, and sometimes nearly three feet taller than a good-sized man. In this part of the country his load is oftenest in the shape of colossal sacks—one on each side. He and his cargo take up as much room as a carriage. Think of meeting this style of obstruction in a narrow trail. The camel would not turn out for a king. He stalks serenely along, bringing his cushioned stilts forward with the long, regular swing of a pendulum, and whatever is in the way must get out of the way peaceably, or be wiped out forcibly by the bulky sacks. It was a tiresome ride to us, and perfectly exhausting to the horses. We were compelled to jump over upward of eighteen hundred donkeys, and only one person in the party was unseated less than sixty times by the camels. This seems like a powerful statement, but the poet has said, "Things are not what they seem." I cannot think of anything now more certain to make one shudder, than to have a soft-footed camel sneak up behind him and touch him on the ear with its cold, flabby under-lip. A camel did this for one of the boys, who was drooping over his saddle in a brown-study. He glanced up and saw the majestic apparition hovering above him, and made frantic efforts to get out of the way, but the camel reached out and bit him on the shoulder before he accomplished it. This was the only pleasant incident of the journey.

At Nazareth we camped in an olive grove near the Virgin Mary's fountain, and that wonderful Arab "guard" came to collect some bucksheesh for his "services" in following us from Tiberias and warding off invisible dangers with the terrors of his armament. The dragoman had paid his master, but that counted as nothing—if you hire a man to sneeze for you here, and another man chooses to help him, you have got to pay both. They do nothing whatever without pay. How it must have surprised these people to hear the way of salvation offered to them *"without money and without price."* If the manners, the people, or the customs of this country have changed since the Saviour's time, the figures and metaphors of the Bible are not the evidences to prove it by.

We entered the great Latin Convent which is built over the traditional dwelling-place of the Holy Family. We went down a flight of fifteen steps below the ground-level, and stood in a small chapel tricked out with tapestry hangings, silver lamps, and oil-paintings. A spot marked by a cross, in the marble floor, under the altar, was exhibited as the place made forever holy by the feet of the Virgin when she stood up to receive the message of the angel. So simple, so unpretending a locality, to be the scene of so mighty an event! The very scene of the Annunciation—an event which has been commemorated by splendid shrines and august temples all over the civilized world, and one which the princes of art have made it their loftiest ambition to picture worthily on their canvas; a spot whose history is familiar to the very children of every house, and city, and obscure hamlet of the furthest lands of Christendom; a spot which myriads of men would toil across the breadth of a world to see, would consider it a priceless privilege to look upon. It was easy to think these thoughts. But it was not easy to bring myself up to the magnitude of the situation. I could sit off several thousand miles and imagine the angel appearing, with shadowy wings and lustrous countenance, and note the glory that streamed downward upon the Virgin's head while the message from the Throne of God fell upon her ears—any one can do that, beyond the ocean, but few can do it here. I saw the little recess from which the angel stepped, but could not fill its void. The angels that I know are creatures of unstable fancy—they will not fit in niches of substantial stone. Imagination labors best in distant fields. I doubt if any man can stand in the Grotto of the Annunciation and people with the phantom images of his mind its too tangible walls of stone.

They showed us a broken granite pillar, depending from the roof, which they said was hacked in two by the Moslem conquerors of Nazareth, in the vain hope of pulling down the sanctuary. But the pillar remained miraculously suspended in the air, and, unsupported itself, supported then and still supports the roof. By dividing this statement up among eight, it was found not difficult to believe it.

These gifted Latin monks never do anything by halves. If they were to show you the Brazen Serpent that was elevated in the wilderness, you could depend upon it that they had on hand the pole it was elevated on also, and even the hole it stood in. They have got the "Grotto" of the Annunciation here; and just as convenient to it as one's throat is to his mouth, they have also the Virgin's Kitchen, and even her sitting-room, where she and Joseph watched the infant Saviour play with Hebrew toys eighteen hundred years ago. All under one roof, and all clean, spacious, comfortable "grottoes." It seems curious that personages intimately connected with the Holy Family always lived in grottoes—in Nazareth, in Bethlehem, in imperial Ephesus—and yet nobody else in their day and generation thought of doing anything of the kind. If they ever did, their grottoes are all gone, and I suppose we ought to wonder at the peculiar marvel of the preservation of these I speak of. When the Virgin fled from Herod's wrath, she hid in a grotto in Bethlehem, and the same is there to this day. The slaughter of the innocents in Bethlehem was done in a grotto; the Saviour was born in a grotto—both are shown to pilgrims yet. It is exceedingly strange that these tremendous events all happened in grottoes—and exceedingly fortunate, likewise, because the strongest houses must crumble to ruin in time, but a grotto in the living rock will last forever. It is an imposture—this grotto stuff—but it is one that all men ought to thank the Catholics for. Wherever they ferret out a lost locality made holy by some Scriptural event, they straightway build a massive—almost imperishable—church there, and preserve the memory of that locality for the gratification of future generations. If it had been left to Protestants to do this most worthy work, we would not even know where Jerusalem is to-day, and the man who could go and put his finger on Nazareth would be too wise for this world. The world owes the Catholics its good will even for the happy rascality of hewing out these bogus grottoes in the rock; for it is infinitely more satisfactory to look at a grotto, where people have faithfully believed for centuries that the Virgin once lived, than to have to imagine a dwelling-place for her somewhere, anywhere, nowhere, loose and at large all over this town of Nazareth. There is too large a scope of country. The imagination cannot work. There is no one particular spot to chain your eye, rivet your interest, and make you think. The memory of the Pilgrims cannot perish while Plymouth Rock remains to us. The old monks are wise. They know how to drive a stake through a pleasant tradition that will hold it to its place forever.

We visited the places where Jesus worked for fifteen years as a carpenter, and where he attempted to teach in the synagogue and was driven out by a mob. Catholic chapels stand upon these sites and protect the little fragments of the ancient walls which remain. Our pilgrims broke off specimens. We visited, also, a new chapel, in the midst of the town, which is built around a boulder some twelve feet long by four feet thick; the priests discovered, a few years ago, that the disciples had sat upon this rock to rest once, when they had walked up from Capernaum. They hastened to preserve the relic. Relics are very good property. Travelers are expected to pay for seeing them, and they do it cheerfully. We like the idea. One's conscience can never be the worse for the knowledge that he has paid his way like a man. Our pilgrims would have liked very well to get out their lampblack and stencil-plates and paint their names on that rock, together with the names of the villages they hail from in America, but the priests permit nothing of that kind. To speak the strict truth, however, our party seldom offend in that way, though we have men in the ship who never lose an opportunity to do it. Our pilgrims' chief sin is their lust for "specimens." I suppose that by this time they know the dimensions of that rock to an inch, and its weight to a ton; and I do not hesitate to charge that they will go back there to-night and try to carry it off.

This "Fountain of the Virgin" is the one which tradition says Mary used to get water from, twenty times a day, when she was a girl, and bear it away in a jar upon her head. The water streams through faucets in the face of a wall of ancient masonry which stands removed from the houses of the village. The young girls of Nazareth still collect about it by the dozen and keep up a riotous laughter and skylarking. The Nazarene girls are homely. Some of them have large, lustrous eyes, but none of them have pretty faces. These girls wear a single garment, usually, and it is loose, shapeless, of undecided color; it is generally out of repair, too. They wear, from crown to jaw, curious strings of old coins, after the manner of the belles of Tiberias, and brass jewelry upon their wrists and in their ears. They wear no shoes and stockings. They are the most human girls we have found in the country yet, and the best natured. But there is no question that these picturesque maidens sadly lack comeliness.

A pilgrim—the "Enthusiast"—said: "See that tall, graceful girl! look at the Madonna-like beauty of her countenance."

Another pilgrim came along presently and said: "Observe that tall, graceful girl; what queenly Madonna-like graciousness of beauty is in her countenance."

I said: "She is not tall, she is short; she is not beautiful, she is homely; she is graceful enough, I grant, but she is rather boisterous."

The third and last pilgrim moved by, before long, and he said: "Ah, what a tall, graceful girl! what Madonna-like gracefulness of queenly beauty!"

The verdicts were all in. It was time, now, to look up the authorities for all these opinions. I found this paragraph, which follows. Written by whom? Wm. C. Grimes:

> After we were in the saddle, we rode down to the spring to have a last look at the women of Nazareth, who were, as a class, much the prettiest that we had seen in the East. As we approached the crowd a tall girl of nineteen advanced toward Miriam and offered her a cup of water. Her movement was graceful and queenly. We exclaimed on the spot at the Madonna-like beauty of her countenance. Whitely was suddenly thirsty, and begged for water, and drank it slowly, with his eyes over the top of the cup, fixed on her large black eyes, which gazed on him quite as curiously as he on her. Then Moreright wanted water. She gave it to him and he managed to spill it so as to ask for another cup, and by the time she came to me she saw through the operation; her eyes were full of fun as she looked at me. I laughed outright, and she joined me in as gay a shout as ever country maiden in old Orange County. I wished for a picture of her. A Madonna, whose face was a portrait of that beautiful Nazareth girl, would be a "thing of beauty" and "a joy forever."

That is the kind of gruel which has been served out from Palestine for ages. Commend me to Fenimore Cooper to find beauty in the Indians, and to Grimes to find it in the Arabs. Arab men are often fine-looking, but Arab women are not. We can all believe that the Virgin Mary was beautiful; it is not natural to think otherwise; but does it follow that it is our duty to find beauty in these present women of Nazareth?

I love to quote from Grimes, because he is so dramatic. And because he is so romantic. And because he seems to care but little whether he tells the truth or not, so he scares the reader or excites his envy or his admiration.

He went through this peaceful land with one hand forever on his revolver, and the other on his pocket-handkerchief. Always, when he was not on the point of crying over a holy place, he was on the point of killing an Arab. More surprising things happened to him in Palestine than ever happened to any traveler here or elsewhere since Munchausen died.

From *The Innocents Abroad,* 1869.

41 : *Jerusalem*

At last, away in the middle of the day, ancient bits of wall and crumbling arches began to line the way—we toiled up one more hill, and every pilgrim and every sinner swung his hat on high! Jerusalem!

Perched on its eternal hills, white and domed and solid, massed together and hooped with high gray walls, the venerable city gleamed in the sun. So small! Why, it was no larger than an American village of four thousand inhabitants, and no larger than an ordinary Syrian city of thirty thousand. Jerusalem numbers only fourteen thousand people.

We dismounted and looked, without speaking a dozen sentences, across the wide intervening valley for an hour or more; and noted those prominent features of the city that pictures make familiar to all men from their school-days till their death. We could recognize the Tower of Hippicus, the Mosque of Omar, the Damascus Gate, the Mount of Olives, the Valley of Jehoshaphat, the Tower of David, and the Garden of Gethsemane—and dating from these landmarks could tell very nearly the localities of many others we were not able to distinguish.

I record it here as a notable but not discreditable fact that not even our pilgrims wept. I think there was no individual in the party whose brain was not teeming with thoughts and images and memories invoked by the grand history of the venerable city that lay before us, but still among them all was no "voice of them that wept."

There was no call for tears. Tears would have been out of place. The thoughts Jerusalem suggests are full of poetry, sublimity, and more than all, dignity. Such thoughts do not find their appropriate expression in the emotions of the nursery.

Just after noon we entered these narrow, crooked streets, by the ancient and the famed Damascus Gate, and now for several hours I have been trying to comprehend that I am actually in the illustrious old city where Solomon dwelt, where Abraham held converse with the Deity, and where walls still stand that witnessed the spectacle of the Crucifixion.

A fast walker could go outside the walls of Jerusalem and walk entirely around the city in an hour. I do not know how else to make one understand how small it is. The appearance of the city is peculiar. It is as knobby with countless little domes as a prison door is with bolt-heads. Every house has from one to half a dozen of these white plastered domes of stone, broad and low, sitting in the center of, or in a cluster upon, the flat roof. Wherefore, when one looks down from an eminence, upon the compact mass of houses (so closely crowded together, in fact, that there is no appearance of streets at all, and so the city looks solid) he sees the knobbiest town in the world, except Constantinople. It looks as if it might be roofed, from center to circumference, with inverted saucers. The monotony of the view is interrupted only by the great Mosque of Omar, the Tower of Hippicus, and one or two other buildings that rise into commanding prominence.

The houses are generally two stories high, built strongly of masonry, whitewashed or plastered outside, and have a cage of wooden latticework projecting in front of every window. To reproduce a Jerusalem street, it would only be necessary to up-end a chicken-coop and hang it before each window in an alley of American houses.

The streets are roughly and badly paved with stone, and are tolerably crooked—enough so to make each street appear to close together constantly and come to an end about a hundred yards ahead of a pilgrim as long as he chooses to walk in it. Projecting from the top of the lower story of many of the houses is a very narrow porch-roof or shed, without supports from below; and I have several times seen cats jump across the street from one shed to the other when they were out calling. The cats could have jumped double the distance without extraordinary exertion. I mention these things to give an idea of how narrow the streets are. Since a cat can jump across them without the least inconvenience, it is hardly necessary to state that such streets are too narrow for carriages. These vehicles cannot navigate the Holy City.

The population of Jerusalem is composed of Moslems, Jews, Greeks, Latins, Armenians, Syrians, Copts, Abyssinians, Greek Catholics, and a handful of Protestants. One hundred of the latter sect are all that dwell now in this birthplace of Christianity. The nice shades of nationality comprised in the above list, and the languages spoken by them, are altogether too numerous to mention. It seems to me that all the races and colors and tongues of the earth must be represented among the fourteen thousand souls that dwell in Jerusalem. Rags, wretchedness, poverty, and dirt, those signs and symbols that indicate the presence of Moslem rule more surely than the crescent flag itself, abound. Lepers, cripples, the blind, and the idiotic, assail you on every hand, and they know but one word of but one language apparently—the eternal "bucksheesh." To see the numbers of maimed, malformed, and diseased humanity that throng the holy places and obstruct the gates, one might suppose that the ancient days had come again, and that the angel of the Lord was expected to descend at any moment to stir the waters of Bethesda. Jerusalem is mournful, and dreary, and lifeless. I would not desire to live here.

One naturally goes first to the Holy Sepulcher. It is right in the city, near the western gate; it and the place of the Crucifixion, and, in fact, every other place intimately connected with that tremendous event, are ingeniously massed together and covered by one roof—the dome of the Church of the Holy Sepulcher.

Entering the building, through the midst of the usual assemblage of beggars, one sees on his left a few Turkish guards—for Christians of different sects will not only quarrel, but fight, also, in this sacred place, if allowed to do it. Before you is a marble slab, which covers the Stone of Unction, whereon the Saviour's body was laid to prepare it for burial. It was found necessary to conceal the real stone in this way in order to save it from destruction. Pilgrims were too much given to chipping off pieces of it to carry home. Near by is a circular railing which marks the spot where the Virgin stood when the Lord's body was anointed.

Entering the great Rotunda, we stand before the most sacred locality in Christendom—the grave of Jesus. It is in the center of the church, and immediately under the great dome. It is inclosed in a sort of little temple of yellow and white stone, of fanciful design. Within the little temple is a portion of the very stone which was rolled away from the door of the Sepulcher, and on which the angel was sitting when Mary came thither "at early dawn." Stooping low, we enter the vault—the Sepulcher itself. It is only about six feet by seven, and the stone couch on which the dead Saviour lay extends from end to end of the apartment and occupies half its width. It is covered with a marble slab which had been much worn by the lips of pilgrims. This slab serves as an altar now. Over it hang some fifty gold and silver lamps, which are kept always burning, and the place is otherwise scandalized by trumpery gewgaws and tawdry ornamentation.

All sects of Christians (except Protestants) have chapels under the roof of the Church of the Holy Sepulcher, and each must keep to itself and not venture upon another's ground. It has been proven conclusively that they cannot worship together around the grave of the Saviour of the World in peace. The chapel of the Syrians is not handsome; that of the Copts is the humblest of them all. It is nothing but a dismal cavern, roughly hewn in the living rock of the Hill of Calvary. In one side of it two ancient tombs are hewn, which are claimed to be those in which Nicodemus and Joseph of Arimathea were buried.

As we moved among the great piers and pillars of another part of the church, we came upon a party of black-robed, animal-looking Italian monks, with candles in their hands, who were chanting something in Latin, and going through some kind of religious performance around a disk of white marble let into the floor. It was there that the risen Saviour appeared to Mary Magdalen in the likeness of a gardener. Near by was a similar stone, shaped like a star—here the Magdalen herself stood, at the same time. Monks were performing in this place, also. They perform everywhere—all over the vast building, and at all hours. Their candles are always flitting about in the gloom, and making the dim old church more dismal than there is any necessity that it should be, even though it is a tomb.

We were shown the place where our Lord appeared to His mother after the Resurrection. Here, also, a marble slab marks the place where St. Helena, the mother of the Emperor Constantine, found the crosses about three hundred years after the Crucifixion.

According to the legend, this great discovery elicited extravagant demonstrations of joy. But they were of short duration. The question intruded itself: "Which bore the blessed Saviour, and which the thieves?" To be in doubt, in so mighty a matter as this—to be uncertain which one to adore—was a grievous misfortune. It turned the public joy to sorrow. But when lived there a holy priest who could not set so simple a trouble as this at rest? One of these soon hit upon a plan that would be a certain test. A noble lady lay very ill in Jerusalem. The wise priests ordered that the three crosses be taken to her bedside one at a time. It was done. When her eyes fell upon the first one, she uttered a scream that was heard beyond the Damascus Gate, and even upon the Mount of Olives, it was said, and then fell back in a deadly swoon. They recovered her and brought the second cross. Instantly she went into fearful convulsions, and it was with the greatest difficulty that six strong men could hold her. They were afraid, now, to bring in the third cross. They began to fear that possibly they had fallen upon the wrong crosses, and that the true cross was not with this number at all. However, as the woman seemed likely to die with the convulsions that were tearing her, they concluded that the third could do no more than put her out of her misery with a happy despatch. So they brought it, and behold, a miracle! The woman sprang from her bed, smiling and joyful, and perfectly restored to health. When we listen to evidence like this, we cannot but believe. We would be ashamed to doubt, and properly, too. Even the very part of Jerusalem where this all occurred is there yet. So there is really no room for doubt.

The priest tried to show us, through a small screen, a fragment of the genuine Pillar of Flagellation, to which Christ was bound when they scourged him. But we could not see it, because it was dark inside the screen. However, a baton is kept here, which the pilgrim thrusts through a hole in the screen, and then he no longer doubts that the true Pillar of Flagellation is in there. He cannot have any excuse to doubt it, for he can feel it with the stick. He can feel it as distinctly as he could feel anything.

Not far from here was a niche where they used to preserve a piece of the True Cross, but it is gone now. This piece of the cross was discovered in the sixteenth century. The Latin priests say it was stolen away, long ago, by priests of another sect. That seems like a hard statement to make, but we know very well that it *was* stolen, because we have seen it ourselves in several of the cathedrals of Italy and France.

But the relic that touched us most was the plain old sword of that stout Crusader, Godfrey of Bouillon—King Godfrey of Jerusalem. No blade in Christendom wields such enchantment as this—no blade of all that rust in the ancestral halls of Europe is able to invoke such visions of romance in the brain of him who looks upon it—none that can prate of such chivalric deeds or tell such brave tales of the warrior days of old. It stirs within a man every memory of the Holy Wars that has been sleeping in his brain for years, and peoples his thoughts with mail-clad images, with marching armies, with battles and with sieges. It speaks to him of Baldwin, and Tancred, the princely Saladin, and great Richard of the Lion Heart. It was with just such blades as these that these splendid heroes of romance used to segregate a man, so to speak, and leave the half of him to fall one way and the other half the other. This very sword has cloven hundreds of Saracen Knights from crown to chin in those old times when Godfrey wielded it. It was enchanted, then, by a genius that was under the command of King Solomon. When danger approached its master's tent it always struck the shield and clanged out a fierce alarm upon the startled ear of night. In times of doubt, or in fog or darkness, if it were drawn from its sheath it would point instantly toward the foe, and thus reveal the way—and it would also attempt to start after them of its own accord. A Christian could not be so disguised that it would not know him and refuse to hurt him —nor a Moslem so disguised that it would not leap from its scabbard and take his life. These statements are all well authenticated in many legends that are among the most trustworthy legends the good old Catholic monks preserve. I can never forget old Godfrey's sword now. I tried it on a Moslem, and clove him in twain like a doughnut. The spirit of Grimes was upon me, and if I had had a graveyard I would have destroyed all the infidels in Jerusalem. I wiped the blood off the old sword and handed it back to the priest—I did not want the fresh gore to obliterate those sacred spots that crimsoned its brightness one day six hundred years ago and thus gave Godfrey warning that before the sun went down his journey of life would end.

Still moving through the gloom of the Church of the Holy

Sepulcher we came to a small chapel, hewn out of the rock—a place which has been known as "The Prison of Our Lord" for many centuries. Tradition says that here the Saviour was confined just previously to the crucifixion. Under an altar by the door was a pair of stone stocks for human legs. These things are called the "Bonds of Christ," and the use they were once put to has given them the name they now bear.

The Greek Chapel is the most roomy, the richest and the showiest chapel in the Church of the Holy Sepulcher. Its altar, like that of all the Greek churches, is a lofty screen that extends clear across the chapel, and is gorgeous with gilding and pictures. The numerous lamps that hang before it are of gold and silver, and cost great sums.

But the feature of the place is a short column that rises from the middle of the marble pavement of the chapel, and marks the exact *center of the earth.* The most reliable traditions tell us that this was known to be the earth's center, ages ago, and that when Christ was upon earth he set all doubts upon the subject at rest forever, by stating with his own lips that the tradition was correct. Remember he said that that particular column stood upon the center of the world. If the center of the world changes, the column changes its position accordingly. This column has moved three different times, of its own accord. This is because, in great convulsions of nature, at three different times, masses of the earth—whole ranges of mountains, probably—have flown off into space, thus lessening the diameter of the earth, and changing the exact locality of its center by a point or two. This is a very curious and interesting circumstance, and is a withering rebuke to those philosophers who would make us believe that it is not possible for any portion of the earth to fly off into space.

To satisfy himself that this spot was really the center of the earth, a skeptic once paid well for the privilege of ascending to the dome of the church to see if the sun gave him a shadow at noon. He came down perfectly convinced. The day was very cloudy and the sun threw no shadows at all; but the man was satisfied that if the sun had come out and made shadows it could not have made any for him. Proofs like these are not to be set aside by the idle tongues of cavilers. To such as are not bigoted, and are willing to be convinced, they carry a conviction that nothing can ever shake.

If even greater proofs than those I have mentioned are wanted, to satisfy the headstrong and the foolish that this is the genuine center of the earth, they are here. The greatest of them lies in the fact that from under this very column was taken the *dust from which Adam was made.* This can surely be regarded in the light of a settler. It is not likely that the original first man would have been made from an inferior quality of earth when it was entirely convenient to get first quality from the world's center. This will strike any reflecting mind forcibly. That Adam was formed of dirt procured in this very spot is amply proven by the fact that in six thousand years no man has ever been able to prove that the dirt was *not* procured here whereof he was made.

It is a singular circumstance that right under the roof of this same great church, and not far away from that illustrious column, Adam himself, the father of the human race, lies buried. There is no question that he is actually buried in the grave which is pointed out as his—there can be none—because it has never yet been proven that that grave is not the grave in which he is buried.

The tomb of Adam! How touching it was, here in a land of strangers, far away from home, and friends, and all who cared for me, thus to discover the grave of a blood relation. True, a distant one, but still a relation. The unerring instinct of nature thrilled its recognition. The fountain of my filial affection was stirred to its profoundest depths, and I gave way to tumultuous emotion. I leaned upon a pillar and burst into tears. I deem it no shame to have wept over the grave of my poor dead relative. Let him who would sneer at my emotion close this volume here, for he will find little to his taste in my journeys through Holy Land. Noble old man—he did not live to see me—he did not live to see his child. And I—I—alas, I did not live to see *him.* Weighed down by sorrow and disappointment, he died before I was born—six thousand brief summers before I was born. But let us try to bear it with fortitude. Let us trust that he is better off where he is. Let us take comfort in the thought that his loss is our eternal gain.

The next place the guide took us to in the holy church was an altar dedicated to the Roman soldier who was of the military guard that attended at the Crucifixion to keep order, and who—when the veil of the Temple was rent in the awful darkness that followed; when the rock of Golgotha was split asunder by an earthquake;

when the artillery of heaven thundered, and in the baleful glare of the lightnings the shrouded dead flitted about the streets of Jerusalem—shook with fear and said, "Surely this was the Son of God!" Where this altar stands now, that Roman soldier stood then, in full view of the crucified Saviour—in full sight and hearing of all the marvels that were transpiring far and wide about the circumference of the Hill of Calvary. And in this selfsame spot the priests of the Temple beheaded him for those blasphemous words he had spoken.

In this altar they used to keep one of the most curious relics that human eyes ever looked upon—a thing that had power to fascinate the beholder in some mysterious way and keep him gazing for hours together. It was nothing less than the copper plate Pilate put upon the Saviour's cross, and upon which he wrote, "THIS IS THE KING OF THE JEWS." I think St. Helena, the mother of Constantine, found this wonderful memento when she was here in the third century. She traveled all over Palestine, and was always fortunate. Whenever the good old enthusiast found a thing mentioned in her Bible, Old or New, she would go and search for that thing, and never stop until she found it. If it was Adam, she would find Adam; if it was the Ark, she would find the Ark; if it was Goliah, or Joshua, she would find *them*. She found the inscription here that I was speaking of, I think. She found it in this very spot, close to where the martyred Roman soldier stood. That copper plate is in one of the churches in Rome now. Any one can see it there. The inscription is very distinct.

We passed along a few steps and saw the altar built over the very spot where the good Catholic priests say the soldiers divided the raiment of the Saviour.

Then we went down into a cavern which cavilers say was once a cistern. It is a chapel now, however—the Chapel of St. Helena. It is fifty-one feet long by forty-three wide. In it is a marble chair which Helena used to sit in while she superintended her workmen when they were digging and delving for the True Cross. In this place is an altar dedicated to St. Dimas, the penitent thief. A new bronze statue is here—a statue of St. Helena. It reminded us of poor Maximilian, so lately shot. He presented it to this chapel when he was about to leave for his throne in Mexico.

From the cistern we descended twelve steps into a large roughly shaped grotto, carved wholly out of the living rock. Helena blasted it out when she was searching for the true cross. She had a laborious piece of work here, but it was richly rewarded. Out of this place she got the crown of thorns, the nails of the cross, the true cross itself, and the cross of the penitent thief. When she thought she had found everything and was about to stop, she was told in a dream to continue a day longer. It was very fortunate. She did so, and found the cross of the other thief.

The walls and roof of this grotto still weep bitter tears in memory of the event that transpired on Calvary, and devout pilgrims groan and sob when these sad tears fall upon them from the dripping rock. The monks call this apartment the "Chapel of the Invention of the Cross"—a name which is unfortunate, because it leads the ignorant to imagine that a tacit acknowledgment is thus made that the tradition that Helena found the true cross here is a fiction—an invention. It is a happiness to know, however, that intelligent people do not doubt the story in any of its particulars.

Priests of any of the chapels and denominations in the Church of the Holy Sepulcher can visit this sacred grotto to weep and pray and worship the gentle Redeemer. Two different congregations are not allowed to enter at the same time, however, because they always fight.

Still marching through the venerable Church of the Holy Sepulcher, among chanting priests in coarse long robes and sandals; pilgrims of all colors and many nationalities, in all sorts of strange costumes; under dusky arches and by dingy piers and columns; through a somber cathedral gloom, freighted with smoke and incense, and faintly starred with scores of candles that appeared suddenly and as suddenly disappeared, or drifted mysteriously hither and thither about the distant aisles like ghostly jack-o'-lanterns—we came at last to a small chapel which is called the "Chapel of the Mocking." Under the altar was a fragment of a marble column; this was the seat Christ sat on when he was reviled, and mockingly made King, crowned with a crown of thorns and sceptered with a reed. It was here that they blindfolded him and struck him, and said in derision, "Prophesy who it is that smote thee." The tradition that this is the identical spot of the mocking is a very ancient one. The guide said that Saewulf was the first to mention it. I do not know Saewulf, but still, I cannot well refuse to receive his evidence—none of us can.

They showed us where the great Godfrey and his brother Baldwin, the first Christian Kings of Jerusalem, once lay buried by that sacred sepulcher they had fought so long and so valiantly to wrest from the hands of the infidel. But the niches that had contained the ashes of these renowned crusaders were empty. Even the coverings of their tombs were gone—destroyed by devout members of the Greek church, because Godfrey and Baldwin were Latin princes, and had been reared in a Christian faith whose creed differed in some unimportant respects from theirs.

We passed on, and halted before the tomb of Melchisedek! You will remember Melchisedek, no doubt; he was the King who came out and levied a tribute on Abraham the time that he pursued Lot's captors to Dan, and took all their property from them. That was about four thousand years ago, and Melchisedek died shortly afterward. However, his tomb is in a good state of preservation.

When one enters the Church of the Holy Sepulcher, the Sepulcher itself is the first thing he desires to see, and really is almost the first thing he does see. The next thing he has a strong yearning to see is the spot where the Saviour was crucified. But this they exhibit last. It is the crowning glory of the place. One is grave and thoughtful when he stands in the little Tomb of the Saviour—he could not well be otherwise in such a place—but he has not the slightest possible belief that ever the Lord lay there, and so the interest he feels in the spot is very, very greatly marred by that reflection. He looks at the place where Mary stood, in another part of the church, and where John stood, and Mary Magdalen; where the mob derided the Lord; where the angel sat; where the crown of thorns was found, and the true cross; where the risen Saviour appeared—he looks at all these places with interest, but with the same conviction he felt in the case of the Sepulcher, that there is nothing genuine about them, and that they are imaginary holy places created by the monks. But the place of the Crucifixion affects him differently. He fully believes that he is looking upon the very spot where the Saviour gave up his life. He remembers that Christ was very celebrated, long before he came to Jerusalem; he knows that his face was so great that crowds followed him all the time; he is aware that his entry into the city produced a stirring sensation, and that his reception was a kind of ovation; he cannot overlook the fact that when he was crucified there were very many in Jerusalem who believed that he was the true Son of God. To publicly execute such a personage was sufficient in itself to make the locality of the execution a memorable place for ages; added to this, the storm, the darkness, the earthquake, the rending of the veil of the Temple, and the untimely waking of the dead, were events calculated to fix the execution and the scene of it in the memory of even the most thoughtless witness. Fathers would tell their sons about the strange affair, and point out the spot; the sons would transmit the story to their children, and thus a period of three hundred years would easily be spanned [1]—at which time Helena came and built a church upon Calvary to commemorate the death and burial of the Lord and preserve the sacred place in the memories of men; since that time there has always been a church there. It is not possible that there can be any mistake about the locality of the Crucifixion. Not half a dozen persons knew where they buried the Saviour, perhaps, and a burial is not a startling event, anyhow; therefore, we can be pardoned for unbelief in the Sepulcher, but not in the place of the Crucifixion. Five hundred years hence there will be no vestige of Bunker Hill Monument left, but America will still know where the battle was fought and where Warren fell. The crucifixion of Christ was too notable an event in Jerusalem, and the Hill of Calvary made too celebrated by it, to be forgotten in the short space of three hundred years. I climbed the stairway in the church which brings one to the top of the small inclosed pinnacle of rock, and looked upon the place where the true cross once stood, with a far more absorbing interest than I had ever felt in anything earthly before. I could not believe that the three holes in the top of the rock were the actual ones the crosses stood in, but I felt satisfied that those crosses had stood so near the place now occupied by them, that the few feet of possible difference were a matter of no consequence.

When one stands where the Saviour was crucified, he finds it all he can do to keep it strictly before his mind that Christ was not crucified in a Catholic church. He must remind himself every now and then that the great event transpired in the open air, and not in a gloomy, candle-lighted cell in a little corner of a vast church, upstairs—a small cell all bejeweled and bespangled with flashy ornamentation in execrable taste.

[1] The thought is Mr. Prime's, not mine, and is full of good sense. I borrowed it from his *Tent Life*.—M. T.

Under a marble altar like a table, is a circular hole in the marble floor, corresponding with the one just under it in which the true cross stood. The first thing every one does is to kneel down and take a candle and examine this hole. He does this strange prospecting with an amount of gravity that can never be estimated or appreciated by a man who has not seen the operation. Then he holds his candle before a richly engraved picture of the Saviour, done on a massy slab of gold, and wonderfully rayed and starred with diamonds, which hangs above the hole within the altar, and his solemnity changes to lively admiration. He rises and faces the finely wrought figures of the Saviour and the malefactors uplifted upon their crosses behind the altar, and bright with a metallic luster of many colors. He turns next to the figures close to them of the Virgin and Mary Magdalen; next to the rift in the living rock made by the earthquake at the time of the Crucifixion, and an extension of which he had seen before in the wall of one of the grottoes below; he looks next at the showcase with a figure of the Virgin in it, and is amazed at the princely fortune in precious gems and jewelry that hangs so thickly about the form as to hide it like a garment almost. All about the apartment the gaudy trappings of the Greek church offend the eye and keep the mind on the rack to remember that this is the Place of the Crucifixion—Golgotha—the Mount of Calvary. And the last thing he looks at is that which was also the first—the place where the true cross stood. That will chain him to the spot and compel him to look once more, and once again, after he has satisfied all curiosity and lost all interest concerning the other matters pertaining to the locality.

And so I close my chapter on the Church of the Holy Sepulcher—the most sacred locality on earth to millions and millions of men, and women, and children, the noble and the humble, bond and free. In its history from the first, and in its tremendous associations, it is the most illustrious edifice in Christendom. With all its claptrap side-shows and unseemly impostures of every kind, it is still grand, reverend, venerable—for a god died there; for fifteen hundred years its shrines have been wet with the tears of pilgrims from the earth's remotest confines; for more than two hundred, the most gallant knights that ever wielded sword wasted their lives away in a struggle to seize it and hold it sacred from infidel pollution. Even in our own day a war, that cost millions of treasure and rivers of blood, was fought because two rival nations claimed the sole right to put a new dome upon it. History is full of this old Church of the Holy Sepulcher—full of blood that was shed because of the respect and the veneration in which men held the last resting-place of the meek and lowly, the mild and gentle Prince of Peace!

From *The Innocents Abroad,* 1869.

42 : Bethlehem

In the huge Church of the Nativity, in Bethlehem, built fifteen hundred years ago by the inveterate St. Helena, they took us below-ground, and into a grotto cut in the living rock. This was the "manger" where Christ was born. A silver star set in the floor bears a Latin inscription to that effect. It is polished with the kisses of many generations of worshiping pilgrims. The grotto was tricked out in the usual tasteless style observable in all the holy places of Palestine. As in the Church of the Holy Sepulcher, envy and uncharitableness were apparent here. The priests and the members of the Greek and Latin churches cannot come by the same corridor to kneel in the sacred birthplace of the Redeemer, but are compelled to approach and retire by different avenues, lest they quarrel and fight on this holiest ground on earth.

I have no "meditations," suggested by this spot where the very first "Merry Christmas!" was uttered in all the world, and from whence the friend of my childhood, Santa Claus, departed on his first journey to gladden and continue to gladden roaring firesides on wintry mornings in many a distant land forever and forever. I touch, with reverent finger, the actual spot where the infant Jesus lay, but I think—nothing.

You *cannot* think in this place any more than you can in any other in Palestine that would be likely to inspire reflection. Beggars, cripples, and monks compass you about, and make you think only of bucksheesh when you would rather think of something more in keeping with the character of the spot.

I was glad to get away, and glad when we had walked through the grottoes where Eusebius wrote, and Jerome fasted, and Joseph prepared for the flight into Egypt, and the dozen other distinguished grottoes, and knew we were done. The Church of the Nativity is almost as well packed with exceeding holy places as the Church of the Holy Sepulcher itself. They even have in it a grotto wherein twenty thousand children were slaughtered by Herod when he was seeking the life of the infant Saviour.

We went to the Milk Grotto, of course—a cavern where Mary hid herself for a while before the flight into Egypt. Its walls were black before she entered, but in suckling the Child, a drop of her milk fell upon the floor and instantly changed the darkness of the walls to its own snowy hue. We took many little fragments of stone from here, because it is well known in all the East that a barren woman hath need only to touch her lips to one of these and her failing will depart from her. We took many specimens, to the end that we might confer happiness upon certain households that we wot of.

We got away from Bethlehem and its troops of beggars and relic-peddlers in the afternoon, and after spending some little time at Rachel's tomb, hurried to Jerusalem as fast as possible. I never was *so* glad to get home again before. I never have enjoyed rest as I have enjoyed it during these last few hours. The journey to the Dead Sea, the Jordan, and Bethlehem was short, but it was an exhausting one. Such roasting heat, such oppressive solitude, and such dismal desolation cannot surely exist elsewhere on earth. And *such* fatigue!

The commonest sagacity warns me that I ought to tell the customary pleasant lie, and say I tore myself reluctantly away from every noted place in Palestine. Everybody tells that, but with as little ostentation as I may, I doubt the word of every he who tells it. I could take a dreadful oath that I have never heard any one of our forty pilgrims say anything of the sort, and they are as worthy and as sincerely devout as any that come here. They will say it when they get home, fast enough, but why should they not? They do not wish to array themselves against all the Lamartines and Grimeses in the world. It does not stand to reason that men are reluctant to leave places where the very life is almost badgered out of them by importunate swarms of beggars and peddlers who hang in strings to one's sleeves and coat-tails and shriek and shout in his ears and horrify his vision with the ghastly sores and malformations they exhibit. One is *glad* to get away. I have heard shameless people say they were glad to get away from Ladies' Festivals where they were importuned to buy by bevies of lovely young ladies. Transform those houris into dusky hags and ragged savages, and replace their rounded forms with shrunken and knotted distortions, their soft hands with scarred and hideous deformities, and the persuasive music of their voices with the discordant din of a hated language, and *then* see how much lingering reluctance to leave could be mustered. No, it is the neat thing to say you were reluctant, and then append the profound thoughts that "struggled for utterance" in your brain; but it is the true thing to say you were not reluctant, and found it impossible to think at all—though in good sooth it is not respectable to say it, and not poetical, either.

We do not think, in the holy places; we think in bed, afterward, when the glare, and the noise, and the confusion are gone, and in fancy we revisit alone the solemn monuments of the past, and summon the phantom pageants of an age that has passed away.

From *The Innocents Abroad,* 1869.

43 : Bombay

JANUARY 20. BOMBAY! A bewitching place, a bewildering place, an enchanting place—the Arabian Nights come again! It is a vast city; contains about a million inhabitants. Natives, they are, with a slight sprinkling of white people—not enough to have the slightest modifying effect upon the massed dark complexion of the public. It is winter here, yet the weather is the divine weather of June, and the foliage is the fresh and heavenly foliage of June. There is a rank of noble great shade trees across the way from the hotel, and under them sit groups of picturesque natives of both sexes; and the juggler in his turban is there with his snakes and his magic; and all day long the cabs and the multitudinous varieties of costumes flock by. It does not seem as if one could ever get tired of watching this moving show, this shining and shifting spectacle. . . . In the great bazar the pack and jam of natives was marvelous, the sea of rich-colored turbans and draperies an inspiring sight, and the quaint and showy Indian architecture was just the right setting for it. Toward sunset another show; this is the drive around the seashore to Malabar Point, where Lord Sandhurst, the Governor of the Bombay Presidency, lives. Parsee palaces all along the first part of the drive; and past them all the world is driving; the private carriages of wealthy Englishmen and natives of rank are manned by a driver and three footmen in stunning oriental liveries—two of these turbaned statues standing up behind, as fine as monuments. Sometimes even the public carriages have this superabundant crew, slightly modified—one to drive, one to sit by and see it done, and one to stand up behind and yell—yell when there is anybody in the way, and for practice when there isn't. It all helps to keep up the liveliness and augment the general sense of swiftness and energy and confusion and pow-wow.

In the region of Scandal Point—felicitous name—where there are handy rocks to sit on and a noble view of the sea on the one hand, and on the other the passing and repassing whirl and tumult of gay carriages, are great groups of comfortably-off Parsee women—perfect flower-beds of brilliant color, a fascinating spectacle. Tramp, tramp, tramping along the road, in singles, couples, groups, and gangs, you have the workingman and the workingwoman—but not clothed like ours. Usually the man is a nobly-built great athlete, with not a rag on but his loin-handkerchief; his color a deep dark brown, his skin satin, his rounded muscles knobbing it as if it had eggs under it. Usually the woman is a slender and shapely creature, as erect as a lightning-rod, and she has but one thing on—a bright-colored piece of stuff which is wound about her head and her body down nearly half-way to her knees, and which clings like her own skin. Her legs and feet are bare, and so are her arms, except for her fanciful bunches of loose silver rings on her ankles and on her arms. She has jewelry bunched on the side of her nose also, and showy cluster-rings on her toes. When she undresses for bed she takes off her jewelry, I suppose. If she took off anything more she would catch cold. As a rule, she has a large shiny brass water-jar of graceful shape on her head, and one of her naked arms curves up and the hand holds it there. She is so straight, so erect, and she steps with such style, and such easy grace and dignity; and her curved arm and her brazen jar are such a help to the picture—indeed, our workingwomen cannot begin with her as a road decoration.

It is all color, bewitching color, enchanting color—everywhere—all around—all the way around the curving great opaline bay clear to Government House, where the turbaned big native *chuprassies* stand grouped in state at the door in their robes of fiery red, and do most properly and stunningly finish up the splendid show and make it theatrically complete. I wish I were a chuprassy.

This is indeed India; the land of dreams and romance, of fabulous wealth and fabulous poverty, of splendor and rags, of palaces and hovels, of famine and pestilence, of genii and giants and Aladdin lamps, of tigers and elephants, the cobra and the jungle, the country of a hundred nations and a hundred tongues, of a thousand religions and two million gods, cradle of the human race, birthplace of human speech, mother of history, grandmother of legend, great-grandmother of tradition, whose yesterdays bear date with the mouldering antiquities of the rest of the nations—the one sole country under the sun that is endowed with an imperishable interest for alien prince and alien peasant, for lettered and ignorant, wise and fool, rich and poor, bond and free, the one land that *all* men desire to see, and having seen once, by even a glimpse, would not give that glimpse for the shows of all the rest of the globe combined . . .

And India did not wait for morning, it began at the hotel—straight away. The lobbies and halls were full of turbaned and fez'd and embroidered, cap'd, and barefooted, and cotton-clad dark natives, some of them rushing about, others at rest squatting, or sitting on the ground; some of them chattering with energy, others still and dreamy; in the dining-room every man's own private native servant standing behind his chair, and dressed for a part in the Arabian Nights.

Our rooms were high up, on the front. A white man—he was a burly German—went up with us, and brought three natives along to see to arranging things. About fourteen others followed in procession, with the hand-baggage; each carried an article—and only one; a bag, in some cases, in other cases less. One strong native carried my overcoat, another a parasol, another a box of cigars, another a novel, and the last man in the procession had no load but a fan. It was all done with earnestness and sincerity, there was not a smile in the procession from the head of it to the tail of it. Each man waited patiently, tranquilly, in no sort of hurry, till one of us found time to give him a copper, then he bent his head reverently, touched his forehead with his fingers, and went his way. They seemed a soft and gentle race, and there was something both winning and touching about their demeanor.

There was a vast glazed door which opened upon the balcony. It needed closing, or cleaning, or something, and a native got down on his knees and went to work at it. He seemed to be doing it well enough, but perhaps he wasn't, for the burly German put on a look that betrayed dissatisfaction, then without *explaining* what was wrong, gave the native a brisk cuff on the jaw and *then* told him where the defect was. It seemed such a shame to do that before us all. The native took it with meekness, saying nothing, and not showing in his face or manner any resentment. I had not seen the like of this for fifty years. It carried me back to my boyhood, and flashed upon me the forgotten fact that this was the *usual* way of explaining one's desires to a slave. I was able to remember that the method seemed right and natural to me in those days, I being born to it and unaware that elsewhere there were other methods; but I was also able to remember that those unresented cuffings made me sorry for the victim and ashamed for the punisher. My father was a refined and kindly gentleman, very grave, rather austere, of rigid probity, a sternly just and upright man, albeit he attended no church and never spoke of religious matters, and had no part nor lot in the pious joys of his Presbyterian family, nor ever seemed to suffer from this deprivation. He laid his hand upon me in punishment only twice in his life, and then not heavily; once for telling him a lie—which surprised me, and showed me how unsuspicious he was, for that was not my maiden effort. He punished me those two times only, and never any other member of the family at all; yet every now and then he cuffed our harmless slave boy, Lewis, for trifling little blunders and awkwardnesses. My father had passed his life among the slaves from his cradle up, and his cuffings proceeded from the custom of the time, not from his nature. When I was ten years old I saw a man fling a lump of iron-ore at a slave-man in anger, for merely doing something awkwardly—as if that were a crime. It bounded from the man's skull, and the man fell and never spoke again. He was dead in an hour. I knew the man had a right to kill his slave if he wanted to, and yet it seemed a pitiful thing and somehow wrong, though why wrong I was not deep enough to explain if I had been asked to do it. Nobody in the village approved of that murder, but of course no one said much about it.

It is curious—the space-annihilating power of thought. For just one second, all that goes to make the *me* in me was in the Missourian village, on the other side of the globe, vividly seeing again these forgotten pictures of fifty years ago, and wholly unconscious of all things but just those; and in the next second I was back in Bombay, and that kneeling native's smitten cheek was not done tingling yet! Back to boyhood—fifty years; back to age again; another fifty; and a flight equal to the circumference of the globe—all in two seconds by the watch!

Some natives—I don't remember how many—went into my bedroom, now, and put things to rights and arranged the mosquito-bar, and I went to bed to nurse my cough. It was about nine in the evening. What a state of things! For three hours the yelling and shouting of natives in the hall continued, along with the velvety patter of their swift bare feet—what a racket it was! They were yelling orders and messages down three flights. Why, in the matter of noise it amounted to a riot, an insurrection, a revolution. And then there were other noises mixed up with these and at intervals tremendously accenting them—roofs falling in, I judged, windows smashing, persons being murdered, crows squawking, and deriding, and cursing, canaries screeching, monkeys jabbering, macaws blaspheming, and every now and then fiendish bursts of laughter and explosions of dynamite. By midnight I had suffered all the different kinds of shocks there are, and knew that I could never more be disturbed by them, either isolated or in combination. Then came peace—stillness deep and solemn—and lasted till five.

Then it all broke loose again. And who restarted it? The Bird of Birds—the Indian crow. I came to know him well, by and by, and be infatuated with him. I suppose he is the hardest lot that wears feathers. Yes, and the cheerfulest, and the best satisfied with himself. He never arrived at what he is by any careless process, or any sudden one; he is a work of art, and "art is long"; he is the product of immemorial ages, and of deep calculation; one can't make a bird like that in a day. He has been re-incarnated more times than Shiva; and he has kept a sample of each incarnation, and fused it into his constitution. In the course of his evolutionary promotions, his sublime march toward ultimate perfection, he has been a gambler, a low comedian, a dissolute priest, a fussy woman, a blackguard, a scoffer, a liar, a thief, a spy, an informer, a trading politician, a swindler, a professional hypocrite, a patriot for cash, a reformer, a lecturer, a lawyer, a conspirator, a rebel, a royalist, a democrat, a practicer and propagator of irreverence, a meddler, an intruder, a busybody, an infidel, and a wallower in sin for the mere love of it. The strange result, the incredible result, of this patient accumulation of all damnable traits is, that he does not know what care is, he does not know what sorrow is, he does not know what remorse is; his life is one long thundering ecstasy of happiness, and he will go to his death untroubled, knowing that he will soon turn up again as an author or something, and be even more intolerably capable and comfortable than ever he was before.

In his straddling wide forward-step, and his springy sidewise series of hops, and his impudent air, and his cunning way of canting his head to one side upon occasion, he reminds one of the American blackbird. But the sharp resemblances stop there. He is much bigger than the blackbird; and he lacks the blackbird's trim and slender and beautiful build and shapely beak; and of course his sober garb of gray and rusty black is a poor and humble thing compared with the splendid luster of the blackbird's metallic sables and shifting and flashing bronze glories. The blackbird is a perfect gentleman, in deportment and attire, and is not noisy, I believe, except when holding religious services and political conventions in a tree; but this Indian sham Quaker is just a rowdy, and is always noisy when awake—always chaffing, scolding, scoffing, laughing, ripping, and cursing, and carrying on about something or other. I never saw such a bird for delivering opinions. Nothing escapes him; he notices everything that happens, and brings out his opinion about it, particularly if it is a matter that is none of his business. And it is never a mild opinion, but always violent—violent and profane—the presence of ladies does not affect him. His opinions are not the outcome of reflection, for he never thinks about anything, but heaves out the opinion that is on top in his mind, and which is often an opinion about some quite different thing and does not fit the case. But that is his way;

his main idea is to get out an opinion, and if he stopped to think he would lose chances.

I suppose he has no enemies among men. The whites and Mohammedans never seemed to molest him; and the Hindoos, because of their religion, never take the life of any creature, but spare even the snakes and tigers and fleas and rats. If I sat on one end of the balcony, the crows would gather on the railing at the other end and talk about me; and edge closer, little by little, till I could almost reach them; and they would sit there, in the most unabashed way, and talk about my clothes, and my hair, and my complexion, and probable character and vocation and politics, and how I came to be in India, and what I had been doing, and how many days I had got for it, and how I had happened to go unhanged so long, and when would it probably come off, and might there be more of my sort where I came from, and when would *they* be hanged,—and so on, and so on, until I could not longer endure the embarrassment of it; then I would shoo them away, and they would circle around in the air a little while, laughing and deriding and mocking, and presently settle on the rail and do it all over again.

They were very sociable when there was anything to eat—oppressively so. With a little encouragement they would come in and light on the table and help me eat my breakfast; and once when I was in the other room and they found themselves alone, they carried off everything they could lift; and they were particular to choose things which they could make no use of after they got them. In India their number is beyond estimate, and their noise is in proportion. I suppose they cost the country more than the government does; yet that is not a light matter. Still, they pay; their company pays; it would sadden the land to take their cheerful voice out of it.

From *Following the Equator,* 1897.

44 : *Bombay to Allahabad*

IT WAS A LONG JOURNEY—two nights, one day, and part of another day, from Bombay eastward to Allahabad; but it was always interesting, and it was not fatiguing. At first the night travel promised to be fatiguing, but that was on account of *pyjamas*. This foolish nightdress consists of jacket and drawers. Sometimes they are made of silk, sometimes of a raspy, scratchy, slazy woolen material with a sandpaper surface. The drawers are loose elephant-legged and elephant-waisted things, and instead of buttoning around the body there is a draw-string to produce the required shrinkage. The jacket is roomy, and one buttons it in front. Pyjamas are hot on a hot night and cold on a cold night—defects which a nightshirt is free from. I tried the pyjamas in order to be in the fashion; but I was obliged to give them up, I couldn't stand them. There was no sufficient change from day-gear to night-gear. I missed the refreshing and luxurious sense, induced by the nightgown, of being undressed, emancipated, set free from restraints and trammels. In place of that, I had the worried, confined, oppressed, suffocated sense of being abed with my clothes on. All through the warm half of the night the coarse surfaces irritated my skin and made it feel baked and feverish, and the dreams which came in the fitful flurries of slumber were such as distress the sleep of the damned, or ought to; and all through the cold other half of the night I could get no time for sleep because I had to employ it all in stealing blankets. But blankets are of no value at such a time; the higher they are piled the more effectively they cork the cold in and keep it from getting out. The result is that your legs are ice, and you know how you will feel by and by when you are buried. In a sane interval I discarded the pyjamas, and led a rational and comfortable life thenceforth.

Out in the country in India, the day begins early. One sees a plain, perfectly flat, dust-colored and brick-yardy, stretching limitlessly away on every side in the dim gray light, striped everywhere with hard-beaten narrow paths, the vast flatness broken at wide intervals by bunches of spectral trees that mark where villages are; and along all the paths are slender women and the black forms of lanky naked men moving to their work, the women with brass water-jars on their heads, the men carrying hoes. The man is not entirely naked; always there is a bit of white rag, a loin cloth; it amounts to a bandage, and is a white accent on his black person, like the silver band around the middle of a pipe-stem. Sometimes he also wears a fluffy and voluminous white turban, and this adds a second accent. He then answers properly to Miss Gordon Cumming's flashlight picture of him—as a person who is dressed in "a turban and a pocket handkerchief."

All day long one has this monotony of dust-colored dead levels and scattering bunches of trees and mud villages. You soon realize that India is not beautiful; still there is an enchantment about it that is beguiling, and which does not pall. You cannot tell just what it is that makes the spell, perhaps, but you feel it and confess it, nevertheless. Of course, at bottom, you know in a vague way that it is *history;* it is that that affects you, a haunting sense of the myriads of human lives that have blossomed, and withered, and perished here, repeating and repeating and repeating, century after century, and age after age, the barren and meaningless process; it is this sense that gives to this forlorn, uncomely land power to speak to the spirit and make friends with it; to speak to it with a voice bitter with satire, but eloquent with melancholy. The deserts of Australia and the ice-barrens of Greenland have no speech, for they have no venerable history; with nothing to tell of man and his vanities, his fleeting glories and his miseries, they have nothing wherewith to spiritualize their ugliness and veil it with a charm.

There is nothing pretty about an Indian village—a mud one—and I do not remember that we saw any but mud ones on that long flight to Allahabad. It is a little bunch of dirt-colored mud hovels jammed together within a mud wall. As a rule, the rains had beaten down parts of some of the houses, and this gave the village the aspect of a mouldering and hoary ruin. I believe the cattle and the vermin live inside the wall; for I saw cattle coming out and cattle going in; and whenever I saw a villager, he was scratching. This last is only circumstantial evidence, but I think it has value. The village has a battered little temple or two, big enough to hold an idol, and with custom enough to fat-up a priest and keep him comfortable. Where there are Mohammedans there are generally a few sorry tombs outside the village that have a decayed and neglected look. The villages interested me because of things which Major Sleeman says about them in his books—particularly what he says about the division of labor in them. He says that the whole face of India is parceled out into estates of villages; that nine-tenths of the vast population of the land consist of cultivators of the soil; that it is these cultivators who inhabit the villages; that there are certain "established" village servants—mechanics and others who are apparently paid a wage by the village at large, and whose callings remain in certain families and are handed down from father to son, like an estate. He gives a list of these established servants: Priest, blacksmith, carpenter, accountant, washerman, basket-maker, potter, watchman, barber, shoemaker, brazier, confectioner, weaver, dyer, etc. In his day witches abounded, and it was not thought good business wisdom for a man to marry his daughter into a family that hadn't a witch in it, for she would need a witch on the premises to protect her children from the evil spells which would certainly be cast upon them by the witches connected with the neighboring families.

The office of midwife was hereditary in the family of the basket-maker. It belonged to his wife. She might not be competent, but the office was hers, anyway. Her pay was not high—25 cents for a boy, and half as much for a girl. The girl was not desired, because she would be a disastrous expense by and by. As soon as she should be old enough to begin to wear clothes for propriety's sake, it would be a disgrace to the family if she were not married; and to marry her meant financial ruin; for by custom the father must spend upon feasting and wedding-display everything he had and all he could borrow—in fact, reduce himself to a condition of poverty which he might never more recover from.

It was the dread of this prospective ruin which made the killing of girl-babies so prevalent in India in the old days before England laid the iron hand of her prohibitions upon the piteous slaughter. One may judge of how prevalent the custom was, by one of Sleeman's casual electrical remarks, when he speaks of children at play in villages—*where girl-voices were never heard!*

The wedding-display folly is still in full force in India, and by consequence the destruction of girl-babies is still furtively practiced; but not largely, because of the vigilance of the government and the sternness of the penalties it levies.

In some parts of India the village keeps in its pay three other servants: an astrologer to tell the villager when he may plant his crop, or make a journey, or marry a wife, or strangle a child, or borrow a dog, or climb a tree, or catch a rat, or swindle a neighbor, without offending the alert and solicitous heavens; and what his dream means, if he has had one and was not bright enough to interpret it himself by the details of his dinner; the two other established servants were the tiger-persuader and the hailstorm discourager. The one kept away the tigers if he could, and collected the wages anyway, and the other kept off the hailstorms, or explained why he failed. He charged the same for explaining a failure that he did for scoring a success. A man is an idiot who can't earn a living in India.

Major Sleeman reveals the fact that the trade union and the boycott are antiquities in India. India seems to have originated everything. The "sweeper" belongs to the bottom caste; he is the lowest of the low—all other castes despise him and scorn his office. But that does not trouble him. His caste is a caste, and that is sufficient for him, and so he is proud of it, not ashamed. Sleeman says:

> "It is perhaps not known to many of my countrymen, even in India, that in every town and city in the country the right of sweeping the houses and streets is a monopoly, and is supported entirely by the pride of caste among the scavengers, who are all of the lowest class. The right of sweeping within a certain range is recognized by the caste to belong to a certain member; and if any other member presumes to sweep within that range, he is excommunicated—no other member will smoke out of his pipe or drink out of his jug; and he can get restored to caste only by a feast to the whole body of sweepers. If any housekeeper within a particular circle happens to offend the sweeper of that range, none of his filth will be removed until he pacifies him, because no other sweeper will dare to touch it; and the people of a town are often more tyrannized over by these people than by any other."

A footnote by Major Sleeman's editor, Mr. Vincent Arthur Smith, says that in our day this tyranny of the sweepers' guild is one of the many difficulties which bar the progress of Indian sanitary reform. Think of this:

> "The sweepers cannot be readily coerced, because no Hindoo or Mussulman would do their work to save his life, nor will he pollute himself by beating the refractory scavenger."

They certainly do seem to have the whip-hand; it would be difficult to imagine a more impregnable position. "The vested rights described in the text are so fully recognized in practice that *they are frequently the subject of sale or mortgage.*" Just like a milk-route; or like a London crossing-sweepership. It is said that the London crossing-sweeper's right to his crossing is recognized by the rest of the guild; that they protect him in its possession; that certain choice crossings are valuable property, and are salable at high figures. I have noticed that the man who sweeps in front of the Army and Navy Stores has a wealthy South African aristocratic style about him; and when he is off his guard, he has exactly that look on his face which you always see in the face of a man who is saving up his daughter to marry her to a duke.

It appears from Sleeman that in India the occupation of elephant-driver is confined to Mohammedans. I wonder why that is. The water-carrier (*bheestie*) is a Mohammedan, but it is said that the reason of that is, that the Hindoo's religion does not allow him to touch the skin of dead kine, and that is what the water-sack is made of; it would defile him. And it doesn't allow him to eat meat; the animal that furnished the meat was murdered, and to take any creature's life is a sin. It is a good and gentle religion, but inconvenient.

A great Indian river, at low water, suggests the familiar anatomical picture of a skinned human body, the intricate mesh of interwoven muscles and tendons to stand for water-channels, and the archipelagoes of fat and flesh inclosed by them to stand for the sandbars. Somewhere on this journey we passed such a river, and on a later journey we saw in the Sutlej the duplicate of that river. Curious rivers they are; low shores a dizzy distance apart, with nothing between but an enormous acreage of sand-flats with sluggish little veins of water dribbling around amongst them; Saharas of sand, smallpox-pitted with footprints punctured in belts as straight as the equator clear from the one shore to the other (barring the channel-interruptions)—a dry-shod ferry, you see. Long railway bridges are required for this sort of rivers, and India has them. You approach Allahabad by a very long one. It was now carrying us across the bed of the Jumna, a bed which did not seem to have been slept in for one while or more. It wasn't all river-bed—most of it was overflow ground.

Allahabad means "City of God." I get this from the books. From a printed curiosity—a letter written by one of those brave and confident Hindoo strugglers with the English tongue, called a "babu"—I got a more compressed translation: "Godville." It is perfectly correct, but that is the most that can be said for it.

We arrived in the forenoon, and short-handed; for Satan [1] got left behind somewhere that morning, and did not overtake us until after nightfall. It seemed very peaceful without him. The world seemed asleep and dreaming.

I did not see the native town, I think. I do not remember why; for an incident connects it with the Great Mutiny, and that is enough to make any place interesting. But I saw the English part of the city. It is a town of wide avenues and noble distances, and is comely and alluring, and full of suggestions of comfort and leisure, and of the serenity which a good conscience buttressed by a sufficient bank account gives. The bungalows (dwellings) stand well back in the seclusion and privacy of large inclosed compounds (private grounds, as we should say) and in the shade and shelter of trees. Even the photographer and the prosperous merchant ply their industries in the elegant reserve of big compounds, and the citizens drive in there upon their business occasions. And not in cabs—no; in the Indian cities cabs are for the drifting stranger; all the white citizens have private carriages; and each carriage has a flock of white-turbaned black footmen and drivers all over it. The vicinity of a lecture-hall looks like a snowstorm, and makes the lecturer feel like an opera. India has many names, and they are correctly descriptive. It is the Land of Contradictions, the Land of Subtlety and Superstition, the Land of Wealth and Poverty, the Land of Splendor and Desolation, the Land of Plague and Famine, the Land of the Thug and the Poisoner, and of the Meek and the Patient, the Land of the Suttee, the Land of the Unreinstatable Widow, the Land where All Life is Holy, the Land of Cremation, the Land where

[1] A servant.—C. N.

the Vulture is a Grave and a Monument, the Land of the Multitudinous Gods; and if signs go for anything, it is the Land of the Private Carriage.

In Bombay the forewoman of a millinery shop came to the hotel in her private carriage to take the measure for a gown—not for me, but for another. She had come out to India to make a temporary stay, but was extending it indefinitely; indeed, she was purposing to end her days there. In London, she said, her work had been hard, her hours long; for economy's sake she had had to live in shabby rooms and far away from the shop, watch the pennies, deny herself many of the common comforts of life, restrict herself in effect to its bare necessities, eschew cabs, travel third-class by underground train to and from her work, swallowing coal-smoke and cinders all the way, and sometimes troubled with the society of men and women who were less desirable than the smoke and the cinders. But in Bombay, on almost any kind of wages, she could live in comfort, and keep her carriage, and have six servants in place of the woman-of-all-work she had had in her English home. Later, in Calcutta, I found that the Standard Oil clerks had small one-horse vehicles, and did no walking; and I was told that the clerks of the other large concerns there had the like equipment. But to return to Allahabad.

I was up at dawn, the next morning. In India the tourist's servant does not sleep in a room in the hotel, but rolls himself up head and ears in his blanket and stretches himself on the veranda, across the front of his master's door, and spends the night there. I don't believe anybody's servant occupies a room. Apparently, the bungalow servants sleep on the veranda; it is roomy, and goes all around the house. I speak of men-servants; I saw none of the other sex. I think there are none, except child-nurses. I was up at dawn, and walked around the veranda, past the rows of sleepers. In front of one door a Hindoo servant was squatting, waiting for his master to call him. He had polished the yellow shoes and placed them by the door, and now he had nothing to do but wait. It was freezing cold, but there he was, as motionless as a sculptured image, and as patient. It troubled me. I wanted to say to him, "Don't crouch there like that and freeze; nobody requires it of you; stir around and get warm." But I hadn't the words. I thought of saying *jeldy jow,* but I couldn't remember what it meant, so I didn't say it. I knew another phrase, but it wouldn't come to my mind. I moved on, purposing to dismiss him from my thoughts, but his bare legs and bare feet kept him there. They kept drawing me back from the sunny side to a point whence I could see him. At the end of an hour he had not changed his attitude in the least degree. It was a curious and impressive exhibition of meekness and patience, or fortitude, or indifference, I did not know which. But it worried me, and it was spoiling my morning. In fact, it spoiled two hours of it quite thoroughly. I quitted this vicinity, then, and left him to punish himself as much as he might want to. But up to that time the man had not changed his attitude a hair. He will always remain with me, I suppose; his figure never grows vague in my memory. Whenever I read of Indian resignation, Indian patience under wrongs, hardships, and misfortunes, he comes before me. He becomes a personification, and stands for India in trouble. And for untold ages India in trouble has been pursued with the very remark which I was going to utter but didn't, because its meaning had slipped me: *Feldy jow!* ("Come, shove along!") Why, it was the very thing.

In the early brightness we made a long drive out to the Fort. Part of the way was beautiful. It led under stately trees and through groups of native houses and by the usual village well, where the picturesque gangs are always flocking to and fro and laughing and chattering; and this time brawny men were deluging their bronze bodies with the limpid water, and making a refreshing and enticing show of it; enticing, for the sun was already transacting business, firing India up for the day. There was plenty of this early bathing going on, for it was getting toward breakfast time, and with an unpurified body the Hindoo must not eat.

Then we struck into the hot plain, and found the roads crowded with pilgrims of both sexes, for one of the great religious fairs of India was being held, just beyond the Fort, at the junction of the sacred rivers, the Ganges and the Jumna. Three sacred rivers, I should have said, for there is a subterranean one. Nobody has seen it, but that doesn't signify. The fact that it is there is enough. These pilgrims had come from all over India; some of them had been months on the way, plodding patiently along in the heat and dust, worn, poor, hungry, but supported and sustained by an unwavering faith and belief; they were supremely happy and content, now; their full and sufficient reward was at hand; they were going to be cleansed from every vestige of sin and corruption by these holy waters which make utterly pure whatsoever thing they touch, even the dead and rotten. It is wonderful, the power of a faith like that, that can make multitudes upon multitudes of the old and weak and the young and frail enter without hesitation or complaint upon such incredible journeys and endure the resultant miseries without repining. It is done in love, or it is done in fear; I do not know which it is. No matter what the impulse is, the act born of it is beyond imagination marvelous to our kind of people, the cold whites. There are choice great natures among us that could exhibit the equivalent of this prodigious self-sacrifice, but the rest of us know that we should not be equal to anything approaching it. Still, we all talk self-sacrifice, and this makes me hope that we are large enough to honor it in the Hindoo.

Two millions of natives arrive at this fair every year. How many start, and die on the road, from age and fatigue and disease and scanty nourishment, and how many die on the return, from the same causes, no one knows; but the toll is great, one may say enormous. Every twelfth year is held to be a year of peculiar grace; a greatly augmented volume of pilgrims results then. The twelfth year has held this distinction since the remotest times, it is said. It is said also that there is to be but one more twelfth year—for the Ganges. After that, that holiest of all sacred rivers will cease to be holy, and will be abandoned by the pilgrims for many centuries; how many, the wise men have not stated. At the end of that interval it will become holy again. Meantime, the data will be arranged by those people who have charge of all such matters, the great chief Brahmins. It will be like shutting down a mint. At a first glance it looks most unbrahminically uncommercial, but I am not disturbed, being soothed and tranquillized by their reputation. "Brer fox he lay low," as Uncle Remus says; and at the judicious time he will spring something on the Indian public which will show that he was not financially asleep when he took the Ganges out of the market.

Great numbers of the natives along the roads were bringing away holy water from the rivers. They would carry it far and wide in India and sell it. Tavernier, the French traveler (17th century), notes that Ganges water is often given at weddings, "each guest receiving a cup or two, according to the liberality of the host; sometimes 2,000 or 3,000 rupees' worth of it is consumed at a wedding."

The Fort is a huge old structure, and has had a large experience in religions. In its great court stands a monolith which was placed there more than 2,000 years ago to preach Buddhism by its pious inscription; the Fort was built three centuries ago by a Mohammedan Emperor—a resanctification of the place in the interest of *that* religion. There is a Hindoo temple, too, with subterranean ramifications stocked with shrines and idols; and now the Fort belongs to the English, it contains a Christian Church. Insured in all the companies.

From the lofty ramparts one has a fine view of the sacred rivers. They join at that point—the pale blue Jumna, apparently clean and clear, and the muddy Ganges, dull yellow and not clean. On a long curved spit between the rivers, towns of tents were visible, with a multitude of fluttering pennons, and a mighty swarm of pilgrims. It was a troublesome place to get down to, and not a quiet place when you arrived; but it was interesting. There was a world of activity and turmoil and noise, partly religious, partly commercial; for the Mohammedans were there to curse and sell, and the Hindoos to buy and pray. It is a fair as well as a religious festival. Crowds were bathing, praying, and drinking the purifying waters, and many sick pilgrims had come long journeys in palanquins to be healed of their maladies by a bath; or if that might not be, then to die on the blessed banks and so make sure of heaven. There were fakeers in plenty, with their bodies dusted over with ashes and their long hair caked together with cow-dung; for the cow is holy and so is the rest of it; so holy that the good Hindoo peasant frescoes the walls of his hut with this refuse, and also constructs ornamental figures out of it for the gracing of his dirt floor. There were seated families, fearfully and wonderfully painted, who by attitude and grouping represented the families of certain great gods. There was a holy man who sat naked by the day and by the week on a cluster of iron spikes, and did not seem to mind it; and another holy man, who stood all day holding his withered arms motionless aloft, and was said to have been doing it for years. All of these performers have a cloth on the ground beside them for the reception of contributions, and even the poorest of the people give a trifle and hope that the sacrifice will be blessed to him. At last came a procession of naked holy people marching by and chanting, and I wrenched myself away.

From *Following the Equator,* 1897.

45 : Benares

THE JOURNEY TO BENARES was all in daylight, and occupied but a few hours. It was admirably dusty. The dust settled upon you in a thick ashy layer and turned you into a fakeer, with nothing lacking to the rôle but the cow manure and the sense of holiness. There was a change of cars about mid-afternoon at Moghul-serai—if that was the name—and a wait of two hours there for the Benares train. We could have found a carriage and driven to the sacred city, but we should have lost the wait. In other countries a long wait at a station is a dull thing and tedious, but one has no right to have that feeling in India. You have the monster crowd of bejeweled natives, the stir, the bustle, the confusion, the shifting splendors of the costumes—dear me, the delight of it, the charm of it are beyond speech. The two-hour wait was over too soon. Among other satisfying things to look at was a minor native prince from the backwoods somewhere, with his guard of honor, a ragged but wonderfully gaudy gang of fifty dark barbarians armed with rusty flintlock muskets. The general show came so near to exhausting variety that one would have said that no addition to it could be conspicuous, but when this Falstaff and his motleys marched through it one saw that that seeming impossibility had happened.

We got away by and by, and soon reached the outer edge of Benares; then there was another wait; but, as usual, with something to look at. This was a cluster of little canvas-boxes—palanquins. A canvas-box is not much of a sight—when empty; but when there is a lady in it, it is an object of interest. These boxes were grouped apart, in the full blaze of the terrible sun, during the three-quarters of an hour that we tarried there. They contained zenana ladies. They had to sit up; there was not room enough to stretch out. They probably did not mind it. They are used to the close captivity of their dwellings all their lives; when they go on a journey they are carried to the train in these boxes; in the train they have to be secluded from inspection. Many people pity them, and I always did it myself and never charged anything; but it is doubtful if this compassion is valued. While we were in India some good-hearted Europeans in one of the cities proposed to restrict a large park to the use of zenana ladies, so that they could go there and in assured privacy go about unveiled and enjoy the sunshine and air as they had never enjoyed them before. The good intentions back of the proposition were recognized, and sincere thanks returned for it, but the proposition itself met with a prompt declination at the hands of those who were authorized to speak for the zenana ladies. Apparently, the idea was shocking to the ladies—indeed, it was quite manifestly shocking. Was that proposition the equivalent of inviting European ladies to assemble scantily and scandalously clothed in the seclusion of a private park? It seemed to be about that.

Without doubt modesty is nothing less than a holy feeling; and without doubt the person whose rule of modesty has been transgressed feels the same sort of wound that he would feel if something made holy to him by his religion had suffered a desecration. I say "rule of modesty" because there are about a million rules in the world, and this makes a million standards to be looked out for. Major Sleeman mentions the case of some high-caste veiled ladies who were profoundly scandalized when some English young ladies passed by with faces bare to the world; so scandalized that they spoke out with strong indignation and wondered that people could be so shameless as to expose their persons like that. And yet "the legs of the objectors were naked to mid-thigh." Both parties were clean-minded and irreproachably modest, while abiding by their separate rules, but they couldn't have traded rules for a change without suffering considerable discomfort. All human rules are more or less idiotic, I suppose. It is best so, no doubt. The way it is now, the asylums can hold the sane people, but if we tried to shut up the insane we should run out of building materials.

You have a long drive through the outskirts of Benares before you get to the hotel. And all the aspects are melancholy. It is a vision of dusty sterility, decaying temples, crumbling tombs, broken mud walls, shabby huts. The whole region seems to ache with age and penury. It must take ten thousand years of want to produce such an aspect. We were still outside of the great native city when we reached the hotel. It was a quiet and homelike house, inviting, and manifestly comfortable. But we liked its annex better, and went thither. It was a mile away, perhaps, and stood in the midst of a large compound, and was built bungalow fashion, everything on the ground floor, and a veranda all around. They have doors in India, but I don't know why. They don't fasten, and they stand open, as a rule, with a curtain hanging in the door-space to keep out the glare of the sun. Still, there is plenty of privacy, for no white person will come in without notice, of course. The native men-servants will, but they don't seem to count. They glide in, barefoot and noiseless, and are in the midst before one knows it. At first this is a shock, and sometimes it is an embarrassment; but one has to get used to it, and does.

There was one tree in the compound, and a monkey lived in it. At first I was strongly interested in the tree, for I was told that it was the renowned *peepul*—the tree in whose shadow you cannot tell a lie. This one failed to stand the test, and I went away from it disappointed. There was a softly creaking well close by, and a couple of oxen drew water from it by the hour, superintended by two natives dressed in the usual "turban and pocket handkerchief." The tree and the well were the only scenery, and so the compound was a soothing and lonesome and satisfying place; and very restful after so many activities. There was nobody in our bungalow but ourselves; the other guests were in the next one, where the table d'hôte was furnished. A body could not be more pleasantly situated. Each room had the customary bath attached—a room ten or twelve feet square, with a roomy stone-paved pit in it and abundance of water. One could not easily improve upon this arrangement, except by furnishing it with cold water and excluding the hot, in deference to the fervency of the climate; but that is forbidden. It would damage the bather's health. The stranger is warned against taking cold baths in India, but even the most intelligent strangers are fools, and they do not obey, and so they presently get laid up. I was the most intelligent fool that passed through, that year. But I am still more intelligent now. Now that it is too late.

I wonder if the *dorian,* if that is the name of it, is another superstition, like the peepul tree. There was a great abundance and variety of tropical fruits, but the dorian was never in evidence. It was never the season for the dorian. It was always going to arrive from Burmah some time or other, but it never did. By all accounts, it was a most strange fruit, and incomparably delicious to the taste, but not to the smell. Its rind was said to exude a stench of so atrocious a nature that when a dorian was in the room even the presence of a polecat was a refreshment. We found many who had eaten the dorian, and they all spoke of it with a sort of rapture. They said that if you could hold your nose until the fruit was in your mouth a sacred joy would suffuse you from head to foot that would make you oblivious to the smell of the rind, but that if your grip slipped and you caught the smell of the rind before the fruit was in your mouth, you would faint. There is a fortune in that rind. Some day somebody will import it into Europe and sell it for cheese.

Benares was not a disappointment. It justified its reputation as a curiosity. It is on high ground, and overhangs a grand curve of the Ganges. It is a vast mass of building, compactly crusting a hill, and is cloven in all directions by an intricate confusion of cracks which stand for streets. Tall, slim minarets and beflagged temple-spires rise out of it and give it picturesqueness, viewed from the river. The city is as busy as an ant-hill, and the hurly-burly of human life swarming along the web of narrow streets reminds one of the ants. The sacred cow swarms along, too, and goes whither she pleases, and takes toll of the grain-shops, and is very much in the way, and is a good deal of a nuisance, since she must not be molested.

Benares is older than history, older than tradition, older even than legend, and looks twice as old as all of them put together. From a Hindoo statement quoted in Rev. Mr. Parker's compact and lucid Guide to Benares, I find that the site of the town was the beginning-place of the Creation. It was merely an upright "lingam," at first, no larger than a stovepipe, and stood in the midst of a shoreless ocean. This was the work of the God Vishnu. Later he spread the lingam out till its surface was ten miles across. Still it was not large enough for the business; therefore he presently built the globe around it. Benares is thus the center of the earth. This is considered an advantage.

It has had a tumultuous history, both materially and spiritually. It started Brahminically, many ages ago; then by and by Buddha came in recent times 2,500 years ago, and after that it was Buddhist during many centuries—twelve, perhaps—but the Brahmins got the upper-hand again, then, and have held it ever since. It is unspeakably sacred in Hindoo eyes, and is as unsanitary as it is sacred, and smells like the rind of the dorian. It is the headquarters of the Brahmin faith, and one-eighth of the population are priests of that church. But it is not an overstock, for they have all India as a prey. All India flocks thither on pilgrimage, and pours its savings into the pockets of the priests in a generous stream, which never fails. A priest with a good stand on the shore of the Ganges is much better off than the sweeper of the best crossing in London. A good stand is worth a world of money. The holy proprietor of it sits under his grand spectacular umbrella and blesses people all his life, and collects his commission, and grows fat and rich; and the stand passes from father to son, down and down and down through the ages, and remains a permanent and lucrative estate in the family. As Mr. Parker suggests, it can become a subject of dispute, at one time or another, and then the matter will be settled, not by prayer and fasting and consultations with Vishnu, but by the intervention of a much more puissant power—an English court. In Bombay I was told by an American missionary that in India there are 640 Protestant missionaries at work. At first it seemed an immense force, but of course that was a thoughtless idea. One missionary to 500,000 natives—no, that is not a force; it is the reverse of it; 640 marching against an intrenched camp of 300,000,000—the odds are too great. A force of 640 in Benares alone would have its hands over-full with 8,000 Brahmin priests for adversary. Missionaries need to be well equipped with hope and confidence, and this equipment they seem to have always had in all parts of the world. Mr. Parker has it. It enables him to get a favorable outlook out of statistics which might add up differently with other mathematicians. For instance:

"During the past few years competent observers declare that the number of pilgrims to Benares has increased."

And then he adds up this fact and gets this conclusion:

"But the revival, if so it may be called, has in it the marks of death. It is a spasmodic struggle before dissolution."

In this world we have seen the Roman Catholic power dying, upon these same terms, for many centuries. Many a time we have gotten all ready for the funeral and found it postponed again, on account of the weather or something. Taught by experience, we ought not to put on our things for this Brahminical one till we see the procession move. Apparently one of the most uncertain things in the world is the funeral of a religion.

I should have been glad to acquire some sort of idea of Hindoo theology, but the difficulties were too great, the matter was too intricate. Even the mere A, B, C of it is baffling. There is a trinity —Brahma, Shiva, and Vishnu—independent powers, apparently, though one cannot feel quite sure of that, because in one of the temples there is an image where an attempt has been made to concentrate the three in one person. The three have other names and plenty of them, and this makes confusion in one's mind. The three have wives and the wives have several names, and this increases the confusion. There are children, the children have many names, and thus the confusion goes on and on. It is not worth while to try to get any grip upon the cloud of minor gods, there are too many of them.

It is even a justifiable economy to leave Brahma, the chiefest god of all, out of your studies, for he seems to cut no great figure in India. The vast bulk of the national worship is lavished upon Shiva and Vishnu and their families. Shiva's symbol—the "lingam" with which Vishnu began the Creation—is worshiped by everybody, apparently. It is the commonest object in Benares. It is on view everywhere, it is garlanded with flowers, offerings are made to it, it suffers no neglect. Commonly it is an upright stone, shaped like a thimble—sometimes like an elongated thimble. This priapus-worship, then, is older than history. Mr. Parker says that the lingams in Benares *"outnumber the inhabitants."*

In Benares there are many Mohammedan mosques. There are Hindoo temples without number—these quaintly shaped and elaborately sculptured little stone jugs crowd all the lanes. The Ganges itself and every individual drop of water in it are temples. Religion, then, is the *business* of Benares, just as gold-production is the business of Johannesburg. Other industries count for nothing as compared with the vast and all-absorbing rush and drive and boom of the town's specialty. Benares is the sacredest of sacred cities. The moment you step across the sharply-defined line which separates it from the rest of the globe, you stand upon ineffably and unspeakably holy ground. Mr. Parker says: "It is impossible to convey any adequate idea of the intense feelings of veneration and affection with which the pious Hindoo regards 'Holy Kashi' (Benares)." And then he gives you this vivid and moving picture:

> "Let a Hindoo regiment be marched through the district, and as soon as they cross the line and enter the limits of the holy place they rend the air with cries of 'Kashi ji ki jai–jai!' (Holy Kashi! Hail to thee! Hail! Hail! Hail!) The weary pilgrim, scarcely able to stand with age and weakness, blinded by the dust and heat, and almost dead with fatigue, crawls out of the oven-like railway carriage, and as soon as his feet touch the ground he lifts up his withered hands and utters the same pious exclamation. Let a European in some distant city in casual talk in the bazar mention the fact that he has lived at Benares, and at once voices will be raised to call down blessings on his head, for a dweller in Benares is of all men most blessed."

It makes our own religious enthusiasm seem pale and cold. Inasmuch as the life of reliigon is in the heart, not the head, Mr. Parker's touching picture seems to promise a sort of indefinite postponement of that funeral.

Yes, the city of Benares is in effect just a big church, a religious hive, whose every cell is a temple, a shrine, or a mosque, and whose every conceivable earthly and heavenly good is procurable under one roof, so to speak—a sort of Army and Navy Stores, theologically stocked.

I will make out a little itinerary for the pilgrim; then you will see how handy the system is, how convenient, how comprehensive. If you go to Benares with a serious desire to spiritually benefit yourself, you will find it valuable. I got some of the facts from conversations with the Rev. Mr. Parker and the others from his Guide to Benares; they are therefore trustworthy.

1. *Purification.* At sunrise you must go down to the Ganges and bathe, pray, and drink some of the water. This is for your general purification.

2. *Protection against Hunger.* Next, you must fortify yourself against the sorrowful earthly ill just named. This you will do by worshiping for a moment in the Cow Temple. By the door of it you will find an image of Ganesh, son of Shiva; it has the head of an elephant on a human body; its face and hands are of silver.

You will worship it a little, and pass on, into a covered veranda, where you will find devotees reciting from the sacred books, with the help of instructors. In this place are groups of rude and dismal idols. You may contribute something for their support; then pass into the temple, a grim and stenchy place, for it is populous with sacred cows and with beggars. You will give something to the beggars, and "reverently kiss the tails" of such cows as pass along, for these cows are peculiarly holy, and this act of worship will secure you from hunger for the day.

3. *"The Poor Man's Friend."* You will next worship this god. He is at the bottom of a stone cistern in the temple of Dalbhyeswar, under the shade of a noble peepul tree on the bluff overlooking the Ganges, so you must go back to the river. The Poor Man's Friend is the god of *material prosperity* in general, and the god of the *rain* in particular. You will secure material prosperity, or both, by worshiping him. He is Shiva, under a new alias, and he abides in the bottom of that cistern in the form of a stone lingam. You pour Ganges water over him and in return for this homage you get the promised benefits. If there is any delay about the rain you must pour water in until the cistern is full; the rain will then be sure to come.

4. *Fever.* At the Kedar Ghat you will find a long flight of stone steps leading down to the river. Half way down is a tank filled with sewage. Drink as much of it as you want. It is for fever.

5. *Smallpox.* Go straight from there to the central Ghat. At its upstream end you will find a small whitewashed building, which is a temple sacred to Sitala, goddess of smallpox. Her under-study is there—a rude human figure behind a brass screen. You will worship this for reasons to be furnished presently.

6. *The Well of Fate.* For certain reasons you will next go and do homage at this well. You will find it in the Dandpan Temple, in the city. The sunlight falls into it from a square hole in the masonry above. You will approach it with awe, for your life is now at stake. You will bend over and look. If the fates are propitious, you will see your face pictured in the water far down in the well. If matters have been otherwise ordered, a sudden cloud will mask the sun and you will see nothing. This means that you have not six months to live. If you are already at the point of death, your circumstances are now serious. There is no time to lose. Let this world go, arrange

for the next one. Handily situated, at your very elbow, is opportunity for this. You turn and worship the image of Maha Kal, the Great Fate, and happiness in the life to come is secured. If there is breath in your body yet, you should now make an effort to get a further lease of the present life. You have a chance. There is a chance for everything in this admirably stocked and wonderfully systemized Spiritual and Temporal Army and Navy Store. You must get yourself carried to the

7. *Well of Long Life.* This is within the precincts of the mouldering and venerable Briddhkal Temple, which is one of the oldest in Benares. You pass in by a stone image of the monkey god, Hanuman, and there, among the ruined court-yards, you will find a shallow pool of stagnant sewage. It smells like the best limburger cheese, and is filthy with the washings of rotting lepers, but that is nothing, bathe in it; bathe in it gratefully and worshipfully, for this is the Fountain of Youth; these are the Waters of Long Life. Your gray hairs will disappear, and with them your wrinkles and your rheumatism, the burdens of care and the weariness of age, and you will come out young, fresh, elastic, and full of eagerness for the new race of life. Now will come flooding upon you the manifold desires that haunt the dear dreams of the morning of life. You will go whither you will find

8. *Fulfillment of Desire.* To wit, to the Kameshwar Temple, sacred to Shiva as the Lord of Desires. Arrange for yours there. And if you like to look at idols among the pack and jam of temples, there you will find enough to stock a museum. You will begin to commit sins now with a fresh, new vivacity; therefore, it will be well to go frequently to a place where you can get

9. *Temporary Cleansing from Sin.* To wit, to the Well of the Earring. You must approach this with the profoundest reverence, for it is unutterably sacred. It is, indeed, the most sacred place in Benares, the very Holy of Holies, in the estimation of the people. It is a railed tank, with stone stairways leading down to the water. The water is not clean. Of course it could not be, for people are always bathing in it. As long as you choose to stand and look, you will see the files of sinners descending and ascending—descending soiled with sin, ascending purged from it. "The liar, the thief, the murderer, and the adulterer may here wash and be clean," says the Rev. Mr. Parker, in his book. Very well. I know Mr. Parker,

and I believe it; but if anybody else had said it, I should consider him a person who had better go down in the tank and take another wash. The god Vishnu dug this tank. He had nothing to dig with but his "discus." I do not know what a discus is, but I know it is a poor thing to dig tanks with, because, by the time this one was finished, it was full of sweat—Vishnu's sweat. He constructed the site that Benares stands on, and afterward built the globe around it, and thought nothing of it, yet sweated like that over a little thing like this tank. One of these statements is doubful. I do not know which one it is, but I think it difficult not to believe that a god who could build a world around Benares would not be intelligent enough to build it around the tank too, and not have to dig it. Youth, long life, temporary purification from sin, salvation through propitiation of the Great Fate—these are all good. But you must do something more. You must

10. *Make Salvation Sure.* There are several ways. To get drowned in the Ganges is one, but that is not pleasant. To die within the limits of Benares is another; but that is a risky one, because you might be out of town when your time came. The best one of all is the Pilgrimage Around the City. You must walk; also, you must go barefoot. The tramp is forty-four miles, for the road winds out into the country a piece, and you will be marching five or six days. But you will have plenty of company. You will move with throngs and hosts of happy pilgrims whose radiant costumes will make the spectacle beautiful and whose glad songs and holy pæans of triumph will banish your fatigues and cheer your spirit; and at intervals there will be temples where you may sleep and be refreshed with food. The pilgrimage completed, you have purchased salvation, and paid for it. But you may not get it unless you

11. *Get Your Redemption Recorded.* You can get this done at the Sakhi Binayak Temple, and it is best to do it, for otherwise you might not be able to prove that you had made the pilgrimage in case the matter should some day come to be disputed. That temple is in a lane back of the Cow Temple. Over the door is a red image of Ganesh of the elephant head, son and heir of Shiva, and Prince of Wales to the Theological Monarchy, so to speak. Within is a god whose office it is to record your pilgrimage and be responsible for you. You will not see him, but you will see a Brahmin who will attend to the matter and take the money. If he should forget to

collect the money, you can remind him. *He* knows that your salvation is now secure, but of course you would like to know it yourself. You have nothing to do but go and pray, and pay at the

12. *Well of the Knowledge of Salvation.* It is close to the Golden Temple. There you will see, sculptured out of a single piece of black marble, a bull which is much larger than any living bull you have ever seen, and yet is not a good likeness after all. And there also you will see a very uncommon thing—an image of Shiva. You have seen his lingam fifty thousand times already, but this is Shiva himself, and said to be a good likeness. It has three eyes. He is the only god in the firm that has three. "The well is covered by a fine canopy of stone supported by forty pillars," and around it you will find what you have already seen at almost every shrine you have visited in Benares, a mob of devout and eager pilgrims. The sacred water is being ladled out to them; with it comes to them the knowledge, clear, thrilling, absolute, that they are saved; and you can see by their faces that there is one happiness in this world which is supreme, and to which no other joy is comparable. You receive your water, you make your deposit, and now what more would you have? Gold, diamonds, power, fame? All in a single moment these things have withered to dirt, dust, ashes. The world has nothing to give you now. For you it is bankrupt. . . .

However, let me not deceive any one. My Itinerary lacks a detail. I must put it in. The truth is, that after the pilgrim has faithfully followed the requirements of the Itinerary through to the end and secured his salvation and also the personal knowledge of that fact, there is still an accident possible to him which can annul the whole thing. If he should ever cross to the other side of the Ganges and get caught out and die there he would at once come to life again in the form of an ass. Think of that, after all this trouble and expense. You see how capricious and uncertain salvation is there. The Hindoo has a childish and unreasoning aversion to being turned into an ass. It is hard to tell why. One could properly expect an ass to have an aversion to being turned into a Hindoo. One could understand that he could lose dignity by it; also self-respect, and nine-tenths of his intelligence. But the Hindoo changed into an ass wouldn't lose anything, unless you count his religion. And he would gain much—release from his slavery to two million gods and twenty million priests, fakeers, holy mendicants, and other sacred bacilli; he would escape the Hindoo hell; he would also escape the Hindoo heaven. These are advantages which the Hindoo ought to consider; then he would go over and die on the other side.

Benares is a religious Vesuvius. In its bowels the theological forces have been heaving and tossing, rumbling, thundering and quaking, boiling, and weltering and flaming and smoking for ages. But a little group of missionaries have taken post at its base, and they have hopes. There are the Baptist Missionary Society, the Church Missionary Society, the London Missionary Society, the Wesleyan Missionary Society, and the Zenana Bible and Medical Mission. They have schools, and the principal work seems to be among the children. And no doubt that part of the work prospers best, for grown people everywhere are always likely to cling to the religion they were brought up in.

From *Following the Equator,* 1897.

4 / *Africa*

46 : *Tangier*

THIS IS ROYAL! Let those who went up through Spain make the best of it—these dominions of the Emperor of Morocco suit our little party well enough. We have had enough of Spain at Gibraltar for the present. Tangier is the spot we have been longing for all the time. Elsewhere we have found foreign-looking things and foreign-looking people, but always with things and people intermixed that we were familiar with before, and so the novelty of the situation lost a deal of its force. We wanted something thoroughly and uncompromisingly foreign—foreign from top to bottom—foreign from center to circumference—foreign inside and outside and all around—nothing anywhere about it to dilute its foreignness—nothing to remind us of any other people or any other land under the sun. And lo! in Tangier we have found it. Here is not the slightest thing that ever we have seen save in pictures—and we always mistrusted the pictures before. We cannot any more. The pictures used to seem exaggerations—they seemed too weird and fanciful for reality. But behold, they were not wild enough—they were not fanciful enough—they have not told half the story. Tangier is a foreign land if ever there was one; and the true spirit of it can never be found in any book save the Arabian Nights. Here are no white men visible, yet swarms of humanity are all about us. Here is a packed and jammed city inclosed in a massive stone wall which is more than a thousand years old. All the houses nearly are one and two story; made of thick walls of stone; plastered outside; square as a dry-goods box; flat as a floor on top; no cornices; whitewashed all over—a crowded city of snowy tombs! And the doors are arched with a peculiar arch we see in Moorish pictures; the floors are laid in vari-colored diamond flags; in tessellated many-colored porcelain squares wrought in the furnaces of Fez; in red tiles and broad bricks that time cannot wear; there is no furniture in the rooms (of Jewish dwellings) save divans—what there is in Moorish ones no man may know; within their sacred walls no Christian dog can enter. And the streets are oriental—some of them three feet wide, some six, but only two that are over a dozen; a man can blockade the most of them by extending his body across them. Isn't it an oriental picture?

There are stalwart Bedouins of the desert here, and stately Moors, proud of a history that goes back to the night of time; and Jews, whose fathers fled hither centuries upon centuries ago; and swarthy Riffians from the mountains—born cutthroats—and original, genuine negroes, as black as Moses; and howling dervishes, and a hundred breeds of Arabs—all sorts and descriptions of people that are foreign and curious to look upon.

And their dresses are strange beyond all description. Here is a bronzed Moor in a prodigious white turban, curiously embroidered jacket, gold and crimson sash of many folds, wrapped round and round his waist, trousers that only come a little below his knee, and yet have twenty yards of stuff in them, ornamented simitar, bare shins, stockingless feet, yellow slippers, and gun of preposterous length—a mere soldier!—I thought he was the Emperor at least. And here are aged Moors with flowing white beards, and long white robes with vast cowls; and Bedouins with long, cowled, striped cloaks, and negroes and Riffians with heads clean-shaven, except a kinky scalp-lock back of the ear, or rather up on the after corner of the skull, and all sorts of barbarians in all sorts of weird costumes, and all more or less ragged. And here are Moorish women who are enveloped from head to foot in coarse white robes and whose sex can only be determined by the fact that they only leave one eye visible, and never look at men of their own race, or are looked at by them in public. Here are five thousand Jews in blue gaberdines, sashes upon their waists, slippers upon their feet, little skull-caps upon the backs of their heads, hair combed down on the forehead, and cut straight across the middle of it from side to side—the self-same fashion their Tangier ancestors have worn for I don't know how many bewildering centuries. Their feet and ankles are bare. Their noses are all hooked, and hooked alike. They all resemble each other so much that one could almost believe they were of one family. Their women are plump and pretty, and do smile upon a Christian in a way which is in the last degree comforting.

What a funny old town it is! It seems like profanation to laugh and jest and bandy the frivolous chat of our day amid its hoary relics. Only the stately phraseology and the measured speech of the sons of the Prophet are suited to a venerable antiquity like this. Here is a crumbling wall that was old when Columbus discovered America; was old when Peter the Hermit roused the knightly men of the Middle Ages to arm for the first Crusade; was old when Charlemagne and his paladins beleaguered enchanted castles and battled with giants and genii in the fabled days of the olden time; was old when Christ and his disciples walked the earth; stood where it stands to-day when the lips of Memnon were vocal, and men bought and sold in the streets of ancient Thebes!

The Phœnicians, the Carthaginians, the English, Moors, Romans, all have battled for Tangier—all have won it and lost it. Here is a ragged, oriental-looking negro from some desert place in interior Africa, filling his goatskin with water from a stained and battered fountain built by the Romans twelve hundred years ago. Yonder is a ruined arch of a bridge built by Julius Cæsar nineteen hundred years ago. Men who had seen the infant Saviour in the Virgin's arms have stood upon it, maybe.

Near it are the ruins of a dockyard where Cæsar repaired his ships and loaded them with grain when he invaded Britain, fifty years before the Christian era.

Here, under the quiet stars, these old streets seemed thronged with the phantoms of forgotten ages. My eyes are resting upon a spot where stood a monument which was seen and described by Roman historians less than two thousand years ago, whereon was inscribed:

"WE ARE THE CANAANITES. WE ARE THEY THAT HAVE BEEN DRIVEN OUT OF THE LAND OF CANAAN BY THE JEWISH ROBBER, JOSHUA."

Joshua drove them out, and they came here. Not many leagues from here is a tribe of Jews whose ancestors fled thither after an unsuccessful revolt against King David, and these their descendants are still under a ban and keep to themselves.

Tangier has been mentioned in history for three thousand years. And it was a town, though a queer one, when Hercules, clad in his lion-skin, landed here, four thousand years ago. In these streets he met Anytus, the king of the country, and brained him with his club, which was the fashion among gentlemen in those days. The people of Tangier (called Tingis, then) lived in the rudest possible huts, and dressed in skins and carried clubs, and were as savage as the wild beasts they were constantly obliged to war with. But they were a gentlemanly race, and did no work. They lived on the natural products of the land. Their king's country residence was at the famous Garden of Hesperides, seventy miles down the coast from here. The garden, with its golden apples (oranges), is gone now—no vestige of it remains. Antiquarians concede that such a personage as Hercules did exist in ancient times, and agree that he was an enterprising and energetic man, but decline to believe him a good, bona fide god, because that would be unconstitutional.

Down here at Cape Spartel is the celebrated cave of Hercules, where that hero took refuge when he was vanquished and driven out of the Tangier country. It is full of inscriptions in the dead languages, which fact makes me think Hercules could not have traveled much, else he would not have kept a journal.

Five days' journey from here—say two hundred miles—are the ruins of an ancient city, of whose history there is neither record nor tradition. And yet its arches, its columns, and its statues proclaim it to have been built by an enlightened race.

The general size of a store in Tangier is about that of an ordinary shower-bath in a civilized land. The Mohammedan merchant, tinman, shoemaker, or vender of trifles sits cross-legged on the floor, and reaches after any article you may want to buy. You can rent a whole block of these pigeonholes for fifty dollars a month. The market-people crowd the market-place with their baskets of figs, dates, melons, apricots, etc., and among them file trains of laden asses, not much larger, if any, than a Newfoundland dog. The scene is lively, is picturesque, and smells like a police court. The Jewish money-changers have their dens close at hand; and all day long are counting bronze coins and transferring them from one bushel basket to another. They don't coin much money nowadays, I think. I saw none but what was dated four or five hundred years back, and was badly worn and battered. These coins are not very valuable. Jack went out to get a napoleon changed, so as to have money suited to the general cheapness of things, and came back and said he had "swamped the bank; had bought eleven quarts of coin, and the head of the firm had gone on the street to negotiate for the balance of the change." I bought nearly half a pint of their money for a shilling myself. I am not proud on account of having so much money, though. I care nothing for wealth. The Moors have some small silver coins, and also some silver slugs worth a dollar each. The latter are exceedingly scarce—so much so that when poor ragged Arabs see one they beg to be allowed to kiss it.

They have also a small gold coin worth two dollars. And that reminds me of something. When Morocco is in a state of war, Arab couriers carry letters through the country, and charge a liberal postage. Every now and then they fall into the hands of marauding bands and get robbed. Therefore, warned by experience, as soon as they have collected two dollars' worth of money they exchange it for one of those little gold pieces, and when robbers come upon them, swallow it. The stratagem was good while it was unsuspected, but after that the marauders simply gave the sagacious United States mail an emetic and sat down to wait.

The Emperor of Morocco is a soulless despot, and the great officers under him are despots on a smaller scale. There is no regular system of taxation, but when the Emperor or the Bashaw wants money, they levy on some rich man, and he has to furnish the cash or go to prison. Therefore, few men in Morocco dare to be rich. It is too dangerous a luxury. Vanity occasionally leads a man to display wealth, but sooner or later the Emperor trumps up a charge against him—any sort of one will do—and confiscates his property. Of course, there are many rich men in the empire, but their money is buried, and they dress in rags and counterfeit poverty. Every now and then the Emperor imprisons a man who is suspected of the crime of being rich, and makes things so uncomfortable for him that he is forced to discover where he has hidden his money.

Moors and Jews sometimes place themselves under the protection of the foreign consuls, and then they can flout their riches in the Emperor's face with impunity.

About the first adventure we had yesterday afternoon, after landing here, came near finishing that heedless Blucher. We had just mounted some mules and asses, and started out under the guardianship of the stately, the princely, the magnificent Hadji Mohammed Lamarty (may his tribe increase!), when we came upon a fine Moorish mosque, with tall tower, rich with checker-work of many-colored porcelain, and every part and portion of the edifice adorned with the quaint architecture of the Alhambra, and Blucher started to ride into the open doorway. A startling "Hi-hi!" from our camp followers, and a loud "Halt!" from an English gentleman in the party, checked the adventurer, and then we were informed that so dire a profanation is it for a Christian dog to set foot upon the sacred threshold of a Moorish mosque, that no amount of purification can ever make it fit for the faithful to pray in again. Had Blucher succeeded in entering the place, he would no doubt have been chased through the town and stoned; and the time has been, and not many years ago either, when a Christian would have been most ruthlessly slaughtered, if captured in a mosque. We caught a glimpse of the handsome tessellated pavements within, and of the devotees performing their ablutions at the fountains; but even that we took that glimpse was a thing not relished by the Moorish bystanders.

Some years ago the clock in the tower of the mosque got out of order. The Moors of Tangier have so degenerated that it has been long since there was an artificer among them capable of curing so delicate a patient as a debilitated clock. The great men of the city met in solemn conclave to consider how the difficulty was to be met. They discussed the matter thoroughly but arrived at no solution. Finally, a patriarch arose and said:

"Oh, children of the Prophet, it is known unto you that a Portuguee dog of a Christian clockmender pollutes the city of Tangier with his presence. Ye know, also, that when mosques are builded, asses bear the stones and the cement, and cross the sacred threshold. Now, therefore, send the Christian dog on all fours, and barefoot, into the holy place to mend the clock, and let him go as an ass!"

And in that way it was done. Therefore, if Blucher ever sees the inside of a mosque, he will have to cast aside his humanity and go in his natural character. We visited the jail, and found Moorish prisoners making mats and baskets. (This thing of utilizing crime savors of civilization.) Murder is punished with death. A short time ago three murderers were taken beyond the city walls and shot. Moorish guns are not good, and neither are Moorish marksmen. In this instance, they set up the poor criminals at long range, like so many targets, and practised on them—kept them hopping about and dodging bullets for half an hour before they managed to drive the center.

When a man steals cattle, they cut off his right hand and left leg, and nail them up in the market-place as a warning to everybody. Their surgery is not artistic. They slice around the bone a little; then break off the limb. Sometimes the patient gets well; but, as a general thing, he don't. However, the Moorish heart is stout. The Moors were always brave. These criminals undergo the fearful operation without a wince, without a tremor of any kind, without a groan! No amount of suffering can bring down the pride of a Moor, or make him shame his dignity with a cry.

Here, marriage is contracted by the parents of the parties to it. There are no valentines, no stolen interviews, no riding out, no courting in dim parlors, no lovers' quarrels and reconciliations—no nothing that is proper to approaching matrimony. The young man takes the girl his father selects for him, marries her, and after that she is unveiled, and he sees her for the first time. If, after due acquaintance, she suits him, he retains her; but if he suspects her purity, he bundles her back to her father; if he finds her diseased, the same; or if, after just and reasonable time is allowed her, she neglects to bear children, back she goes to the home of her childhood.

Mohammedans here, who can afford it, keep a good many wives on hand. They are called wives, though I believe the Koran only allows four genuine wives—the rest are concubines. The Emperor of Morocco don't know how many wives he has, but thinks he has five hundred. However, that is near enough—a dozen or so, one way or the other, don't matter.

Even the Jews in the interior have a plurality of wives.

I have caught a glimpse of the faces of several Moorish women (for they are only human, and will expose their faces for the admiration of a Christian dog when no male Moor is by), and I am full of veneration for the wisdom that leads them to cover up such atrocious ugliness.

They carry their children at their backs, in a sack, like other savages the world over.

Many of the negroes are held in slavery by the Moors. But the moment a female slave becomes her master's concubine her bonds are broken, and as soon as a male slave can read the first chapter of the Koran (which contains the creed) he can no longer be held in bondage.

They have three Sundays a week in Tangier. The Mohammedan's

comes on Friday, the Jew's on Saturday, and that of the Christian Consuls on Sunday. The Jews are the most radical. The Moor goes to his mosque about noon on his Sabbath, as on any other day, removes his shoes at the door, performs his ablutions, makes his salaams, pressing his forehead to the pavement time and again, says his prayers, and goes back to his work.

But the Jew shuts up shop; will not touch copper or bronze at all; soils his fingers with nothing meaner than silver and gold; attends the synagogue devoutly; will not cook or have anything to do with fire; and religiously refrains from embarking in any enterprise.

The Moor who has made a pilgrimage to Mecca is entitled to high distinction. Men call him Hadji, and he is thenceforward a great personage. Hundreds of Moors come to Tangier every year, and embark for Mecca. They go part of the way in English steamers; and the ten or twelve dollars they pay for passage is about all the trip costs. They take with them a quantity of food, and when the commissary department fails they "skirmish," as Jack terms it in his sinful, slangy way. From the time they leave till they get home again, they never wash, either on land or sea. They are usually gone from five to seven months, and as they do not change their clothes during all that time, they are totally unfit for the drawing-room when they get back.

Many of them have to rake and scrape a long time to gather together the ten dollars their steamer passage costs; and when one of them gets back he is a bankrupt forever after. Few Moors can ever build up their fortunes again in one short lifetime, after so reckless an outlay. In order to confine the dignity of Hadji to gentlemen of patrician blood and possessions, the Emperor decreed that no man should make the pilgrimage save bloated aristocrats who were worth a hundred dollars in specie. But behold how iniquity can circumvent the law! For a consideration, the Jewish money-changer lends the pilgrim one hundred dollars long enough for him to swear himself through, and then receives it back before the ship sails out of the harbor!

Spain is the only nation the Moors fear. The reason is, that Spain sends her heaviest ships of war and her loudest guns to astonish these Moslems; while America, and other nations, send only a little contemptible tub of a gunboat occasionally. The Moors, like other savages, learn by what they see; not what they hear or read. We have great fleets in the Mediterranean, but they seldom touch at African ports. The Moors have a small opinion of England, France and America, and put their representatives to a deal of red-tape circumlocution before they grant them their common rights, let alone a favor. But the moment the Spanish minister makes a demand, it is acceded to at once, whether it be just or not.

Spain chastised the Moors five or six years ago, about a disputed piece of property opposite Gibraltar, and captured the city of Tetouan. She compromised on an augmentation of her territory; twenty million dollars indemnity in money; and peace. And then she gave up the city. But she never gave it up until the Spanish soldiers had eaten up all the cats. They would not compromise as long as the cats held out. Spaniards are very fond of cats. On the contrary, the Moors reverence cats as something sacred. So the Spaniards touched them on a tender point that time. Their unfeline conduct in eating up all the Tetouan cats aroused a hatred toward them in the breasts of the Moors, to which even the driving them out of Spain was tame and passionless. Moors and Spaniards are foes forever now. France had a minister here once who embittered the nation against him in the most innocent way. He killed a couple of battalions of cats (Tangier is full of them) and made a parlor carpet out of their hides. He made his carpet in circles—first a circle of old gray tomcats, with their tails all pointing toward the center; then a circle of yellow cats; next a circle of black cats and a circle of white ones; then a circle of all sorts of cats; and, finally, a centerpiece of assorted kittens. It was very beautiful; but the Moors curse his memory to this day.

When we went to call on our American Consul-General, to-day, I noticed that all possible games for parlor amusement seemed to be represented on his center-tables. I thought that hinted at lonesomeness. The idea was correct. His is the only American family in Tangier. There are many foreign consuls in this place; but much visiting is not indulged in. Tangier is clear out of the world, and what is the use of visiting when people have nothing on earth to talk about? There is none. So each consul's family stays at home chiefly, and amuses itself as best it can. Tangier is full of interest for one day, but after that it is a weary prison. The Consul-General has been here five years, and has got enough of it to do him for a century, and is going home shortly. His family seize upon their letters and papers when the mail arrives, read them over and over again for two days or three, talk them over and over again for two or three more, till they wear them out, and after that, for days together, they eat and drink and sleep, and ride out over the same old road, and see the same old tiresome things that even decades of centuries have scarcely changed, and say never a single word! They have literally nothing whatever to talk about. The arrival of an American man-of-war is a godsend to them. "Oh, solitude, where are the charms which sages have seen in thy face?" It is the completest exile that I can conceive of. I would seriously recommend to the government of the United States that when a man commits a crime so heinous that the law provides no adequate punishment for it, they make him Consul-General to Tangier.

I am glad to have seen Tangier—the second oldest town in the world. But I am ready to bid it good-by, I believe.

From *The Innocents Abroad,* 1869.

47 : *Alexandria*

AFTER A PLEASANT VOYAGE and a good rest, we drew near to Egypt, and out of the mellowest of sunsets we saw the domes and minarets of Alexandria rise into view. As soon as the anchor was down, Jack and I got a boat and went ashore. It was night by this time, and the other passengers were content to remain at home and visit ancient Egypt after breakfast. It was the way they did at Constantinople. They took a lively interest in new countries, but their school-boy impatience had worn off, and they had learned that it was wisdom to take things easy and go along comfortably—these old countries do not go away in the night; they stay till after breakfast.

When we reached the pier we found an army of Egyptian boys with donkeys no larger than themselves, waiting for passengers—for donkeys are the omnibuses of Egypt. We preferred to walk, but we could not have our own way. The boys crowded about us, clamored around us, and slewed their donkeys exactly across our path, no matter which way we turned. They were good-natured rascals, and so were the donkeys. We mounted, and the boys ran behind us and kept the donkeys in a furious gallop, as is the fashion at Damascus. I believe I would rather ride a donkey than any beast in the world. He goes briskly, he puts on no airs, he is docile, though opinionated. Satan himself could not scare him, and he is convenient—very convenient. When you are tired riding you can rest your feet on the ground and let him gallop from under you.

We found the hotel and secured rooms, and were happy to know that the Prince of Wales had stopped there once. They had it everywhere on signs. No other princes had stopped there since, till Jack and I came. We went abroad through the town, then, and found it a city of huge commercial buildings, of broad, handsome streets brilliant with gaslight. By night it was a sort of reminiscence of Paris. But finally Jack found an ice-cream saloon, and that closed investigations for that evening. The weather was very hot, it had been many a day since Jack had seen ice-cream, and so it was useless to talk of leaving the saloon till it shut up.

In the morning the lost tribes of America came ashore and infested the hotels and took possession of all the donkeys and other open barouches that offered. They went in picturesque procession to the American Consul's; to the great gardens; to Cleopatra's Needles; to Pompey's Pillar; to the palace of the Viceroy of Egypt; to the Nile; to the superb groves of date-palms. One of our most inveterate relic-hunters had his hammer with him, and tried to break a fragment off the upright Needle and could not do it; he tried the prostrate one and failed; he borrowed a heavy sledge-hammer from a mason and failed again. He tried Pompey's Pillar, and this baffled him. Scattered all about the mighty monolith were sphinxes of noble countenance, carved out of Egyptian granite as hard as blue steel, and whose shapely features the wear of five thousand years had failed to mark or mar. The relic-hunter battered at these persistently, and sweated profusely over his work. He might as well have attempted to deface the moon. They regarded him serenely with the stately smile they had worn so long, and which seemed to say, "Peck away, poor insect; we were not made to fear such as you; in tenscore dragging ages we have seen more of your kind than there are sands at your feet; have they left a blemish upon us?"

From *The Innocents Abroad,* 1869.

48 : The Pyramids

THE DONKEYS WERE ALL GOOD, all handsome, all strong and in good condition, all fast and all willing to prove it. They were the best we had found anywhere, and the most *recherché*. I do not know what *recherché* is, but that is what these donkeys were, anyhow. Some were of a soft mouse-color, and the others were white, black, and vari-colored. Some were close-shaven, all over, except that a tuft like a paint-brush was left on the end of the tail. Others were so shaven in fanciful landscape-garden patterns, as to mark their bodies with curving lines, which were bounded on one side by hair and on the other by the close plush left by the shears. They had all been newly barbered, and were exceedingly stylish. Several of the white ones were barred like zebras with rainbow stripes of blue and red and yellow paint. These were indescribably gorgeous. Dan and Jack selected from this lot because they brought back Italian reminiscences of the "old masters." The saddles were the high, stuffy, frog-shaped things we had known in Ephesus and Smyrna. The donkey-boys were lively young Egyptian rascals who could follow a donkey and keep him in a canter half a day without tiring. We had plenty of spectators when we mounted, for the hotel was full of English people bound overland to India and officers getting ready for the African campaign against the Abyssinian King Theodorus. We were not a very large party, but as we charged through the streets of the great metropolis, we made noise for five hundred, and displayed activity and created excitement in proportion. Nobody can steer a donkey, and some collided with camels, dervishes, effendis, asses, beggars, and everything else that offered to the donkeys a reasonable chance for a collision. When we turned into the broad avenue that leads out of the city toward Old Cairo, there was plenty of room. The walls of stately date-palms that fenced the gardens and bordered the way, threw their shadows down and made the air cool and bracing. We rose to the spirit of the time and the race became a wild rout, a stampede, a terrific panic. I wish to live to enjoy it again.

Somewhere along this route we had a few startling exhibitions of Oriental simplicity. A girl apparently thirteen years of age came along the great thoroughfare dressed like Eve before the fall. We would have called her thirteen at home; but here girls who look thirteen are often not more than nine, in reality.

Occasionally we saw stark-naked men of superb build, bathing, and making no attempt at concealment. However, an hour's acquaintance with this cheerful custom reconciled the pilgrims to it, and then it ceased to occasion remark. Thus easily do even the most startling novelties grow tame and spiritless to these sight-surfeited wanderers.

Arrived at Old Cairo, the camp-followers took up the donkeys and tumbled them bodily aboard a small boat with a lateen sail, and we followed and got under way. The deck was closely packed with donkeys and men; the two sailors had to climb over and under and through the wedged mass to work the sails, and the steersman had to crowd four or five donkeys out of the way when he wished to swing his tiller and put his helm hard down. But what were their troubles to us? We had nothing to do; nothing to do but enjoy the trip; nothing to do but shove the donkeys off our corns and look at the charming scenery of the Nile.

On the island at our right was the machine they call the Nilometer, a stone column whose business it is to mark the rise of the river and prophesy whether it will reach only thirty-two feet and produce a famine, or whether it will properly flood the land at forty and produce plenty, or whether it will rise to forty-three and bring death and destruction to flocks and crops—but how it does all this they could not explain to us so that we could understand. On the same island is still shown the spot where Pharaoh's daughter found Moses in the bulrushes. Near the spot we sailed from, the Holy Family dwelt when they sojourned in Egypt till Herod should complete his slaughter of the innocents. The same tree they rested under when they first arrived was there a short time ago, but the Viceroy of Egypt sent it to the Empress Eugénie lately. He was just in time, otherwise our pilgrims would have had it.

The Nile at this point is muddy, swift, and turbid, and does not lack a great deal of being as wide as the Mississippi.

We scrambled up the steep bank at the shabby town of Ghizeh, mounted the donkeys again, and scampered away. For four or five miles the route lay along a high embankment which they say is to be the bed of a railway the Sultan means to build for no other reason than that when the Empress of the French comes to visit him she can go to the Pyramids in comfort. This is true Oriental hospitality. I am very glad it is our privilege to have donkeys instead of cars.

At the distance of a few miles the Pyramids, rising above the palms, looked very clean-cut, very grand and imposing, and very soft and filmy, as well. They swam in a rich haze that took from them all suggestions of unfeeling stone, and made them seem only the airy nothings of a dream—structures which might blossom into tiers of vague arches, or ornate colonnades, maybe, and change and change again into all graceful forms of architecture while we looked, and then melt deliciously away and blend with the tremulous atmosphere.

At the end of the levee we left the mules and went in a sailboat across an arm of the Nile or an overflow, and landed where the sands of the Great Sahara left their embankment, as straight as a wall, along the verge of the alluvial plain of the river. A laborious walk in the flaming sun brought us to the foot of the great Pyramid of Cheops. It was a fairy vision no longer. It was a corrugated, unsightly mountain of stone. Each of its monstrous sides was a wide stairway which rose upward, step above step, narrowing as it went, till it tapered to a point far aloft in the air. Insect men and women —pilgrims from the *Quaker City*—were creeping about its dizzy perches, and one little black swarm were waving postage-stamps from the airy summit—handkerchiefs will be understood.

Of course we were besieged by a rabble of muscular Egyptians and Arabs who wanted the contract of dragging us to the top—all tourists are. Of course you could not hear your own voice for the din that was around you. Of course the Sheiks said *they* were the only responsible parties; that all contracts must be made with them, all moneys paid over to them, and none exacted from us by any but themselves alone. Of course they contracted that the varlets who dragged us up should not mention bucksheesh once. For such is the usual routine. Of course we contracted with them, paid them, were delivered into the hands of the draggers, dragged up the Pyramids, and harried and bedeviled for bucksheesh from the foundation clear to the summit. We paid it, too, for we were purposely spread very far apart over the vast side of the Pyramid. There was no help near if we called, and the Herculeses who dragged us had a way of asking sweetly and flatteringly for bucksheesh, which was seductive, and of looking fierce and threatening to throw us down the precipice, which was persuasive and convincing.

Each step being full as high as a dinner-table; there being very, very many of the steps; an Arab having hold of each of our arms and springing upward from step to step and snatching us with them, forcing us to lift our feet as high as our breasts every time, and do it rapidly and keep it up till we were ready to faint,—who shall say it is not a lively, exhilarating, lacerating, muscle-straining, bone-wrenching, and perfectly excruciating and exhausting pastime, climbing the Pyramids? I beseeched the varlets not to twist *all* my joints asunder; I iterated, reiterated, even *swore* to them that I did not wish to beat anybody to the top; did all I could to convince them that if I got there the last of all I would feel blessed above men and grateful to them forever; I begged them, prayed them, pleaded with them to let me stop and rest a moment—only one little moment: and they only answered with some more frightful springs, and an unenlisted volunteer behind opened a bombardment of determined boosts with his head which threatened to batter my whole political economy to wreck and ruin.

Twice, for one minute, they let me rest while they extorted bucksheesh, and then continued their maniac flight up the Pyramid. They wished to beat the other parties. It was nothing to them that I, a stranger, must be sacrificed upon the altar of their unholy ambition. But in the midst of sorrow joy blooms. Even in this dark hour I had a sweet consolation. For I knew that except these Mohammedans repented they would go straight to perdition some day. And *they* never repent—they never forsake their paganism. This thought calmed me, cheered me, and I sank down, limp and exhausted, upon the summit, but happy, *so* happy and serene within.

On the one hand, a mighty sea of yellow sand stretched away toward the ends of the earth, solemn, silent, shorn of vegetation, its solitude uncheered by any forms of creature life; on the other, the Eden of Egypt was spread below us—a broad green floor, cloven by the sinuous river, dotted with villages, its vast distances measured and marked by the diminishing stature of receding clusters of palms. It lay asleep in an enchanted atmosphere. There was no sound, no motion. Above the date-plumes in the middle distance, swelled a domed and pinnacled mass, glimmering through a tinted, exquisite mist; away toward the horizon a dozen shapely pyramids watched over ruined Memphis; and at our feet the bland impassible Sphinx looked out upon the picture from her throne in the sands as placidly and pensively as she had looked upon its like full fifty lagging centuries ago.

We suffered torture no pen can describe from the hungry appeals for bucksheesh that gleamed from Arab eyes and poured incessantly from Arab lips. Why try to call up the traditions of vanished Egyptian grandeur; why try to fancy Egypt following dead Rameses to his tomb in the Pyramid, or the long multitude of Israel departing over the desert yonder? Why try to think at all? The thing was impossible. One must bring his meditations cut and dried, or else cut and dry them afterward.

The traditional Arab proposed, in the traditional way, to run down Cheops, cross the eighth of a mile of sand intervening between it and the tall pyramid of Cephren, ascend to Cephren's summit and return to us on the top of Cheops—all in nine minutes by the watch, and the whole service to be rendered for a single dollar. In the first flush of irritation, I said let the Arab and his exploits go to the mischief. But stay. The upper third of Cephren was coated with dressed marble, smooth as glass. A blessed thought entered my brain. He must infallibly break his neck. Close the contract with despatch, I said, and let him go. He started. We watched. He went bounding down the vast broadside, spring after spring, like an ibex. He grew small and smaller till he became a bobbing pygmy, away down toward the bottom—then disappeared. We turned and peered over the other side—forty seconds—eighty seconds—a hundred—happiness, he is dead already?—two minutes—and a quarter—"There he goes!" Too true—it was too true. He was very small, now. Gradually, but surely, he overcame the level ground. He began to spring and climb again. Up, up, up—at last he reached the smooth coating—now for it. But he clung to it with toes and fingers, like a fly. He crawled this way and that—away to the right, slanting upward—away to the left, still slanting upward—and stood at last, a black peg on the summit, and waved his pygmy scarf! Then he crept downward to the raw steps again, then picked up his agile heels and flew. We lost him presently. But presently again we saw him under us, mounting with undiminished energy. Shortly he bounded into our midst with a gallant war-whoop. Time, eight minutes, forty-one seconds. He had won. His bones were intact. It was a failure. I reflected. I said to myself, he is tired, and must grow dizzy. I will risk another dollar on him.

He started again. Made the trip again. Slipped on the smooth coating—I almost had him. But an infamous crevice saved him. He was with us once more—perfectly sound. Time, eight minutes, forty-six seconds.

I said to Dan, "Lend me a dollar—I can beat this game, yet."

Worse and worse. He won again. Time, eight minutes, forty-eight seconds. I was out of all patience, now. I was desperate. Money was no longer of any consequence. I said, "Sirrah, I will give you a hundred dollars to jump off this pyramid head first. If you do not like the terms, name your bet. I scorn to stand on expenses now. I will stay right here and risk money on you as long as Dan has got a cent."

I was in a fair way to win, now, for it was a dazzling opportunity for an Arab. He pondered a moment, and would have done it, I think, but his mother arrived, then, and interfered. Her tears moved me—I never can look upon the tears of woman with indifference—and I said I would give her a hundred to jump off, too.

But it was a failure. The Arabs are too high-priced in Egypt. They put on airs unbecoming to such savages.

We descended, hot and out of humor. The dragoman lit candles, and we all entered a hole near the base of the pyramid, attended by a crazy rabble of Arabs who thrust their services upon us uninvited. They dragged us up a long inclined chute, and dripped candle-grease all over us. This chute was not more than twice as wide and high as a Saratoga trunk, and was walled, roofed, and floored with solid blocks of Egyptian granite as wide as a wardrobe, twice as thick, and three times as long. We kept on climbing, through the oppressive gloom, till I thought we ought to be nearing the top of the pyramid again, and then came to the "Queen's

Chamber," and shortly to the Chamber of the King. These large apartments were tombs. The walls were built of monstrous masses of smoothed granite, neatly joined together. Some of them were nearly as large square as an ordinary parlor. A great stone sarcophagus like a bathtub stood in the center of the King's Chamber. Around it were gathered a picturesque group of Arab savages and soiled and tattered pilgrims, who held their candles aloft in the gloom while they chattered, and the winking blurs of light shed a dim glory down upon one of the irrepressible memento-seekers who was pecking at the venerable sarcophagus with his sacrilegious hammer. We struggled out to the open air and the bright sunshine, and for the space of thirty minutes received ragged Arabs by couples, dozens, and platoons, and paid them bucksheesh for services they swore and proved by each other that they had rendered, but which we had not been aware of before—and as each party was paid, they dropped into the rear of the procession and in due time arrived again with a newly invented delinquent list for liquidation.

We lunched in the shade of the pyramid, and in the midst of this encroaching and unwelcome company, and then Dan and Jack and I started away for a walk. A howling swarm of beggars followed us—surrounded us—almost headed us off. A sheik, in flowing white burnoose and gaudy headgear, was with them. He wanted more bucksheesh. But we had adopted a new code—it was millions for defense, but not a cent for bucksheesh. I asked him if he could persuade the others to depart if we paid him. He said yes—for ten francs. We accepted the contract, and said—

"Now persuade your vassals to fall back."

He swung his long staff round his head and three Arabs bit the dust. He capered among the mob like a very maniac. His blows fell like hail, and wherever one fell a subject went down. We had to hurry to the rescue and tell him it was only necessary to damage them a little, he need not kill them. In two minutes we were alone with the sheik, and remained so. The persuasive powers of this illiterate savage were remarkable.

Each side of the Pyramid of Cheops is about as long as the Capitol at Washington, or the Sultan's new palace on the Bosporus, and is longer than the greatest depth of St. Peter's at Rome —which is to say that each side of Cheops extends seven hundred and some odd feet. It is about seventy-five feet higher than the cross on St. Peter's. The first time I ever went down the Mississippi, I thought the highest bluff on the river between St. Louis and New Orleans—it was near Selma, Missouri—was probably the highest mountain in the world. It is four hundred and thirteen feet high. It still looms in my memory with undiminished grandeur. I can still see the trees and bushes growing smaller and smaller as I followed them up its huge slant with my eye, till they became a feathery fringe on the distant summit. This symmetrical Pyramid of Cheops—this solid mountain of stone reared by the patient hands of men—this mighty tomb of a forgotten monarch—dwarfs my cherished mountain. For it is four hundred and eighty feet high. In still earlier years than those I have been recalling, Holliday's Hill, in our town, was to me the noblest work of God. It appeared to pierce the skies. It was nearly three hundred feet high. In those days I pondered the subject much, but I never could understand why it did not swathe its summit with never-failing clouds, and crown its majestic brow with everlasting snows. I had heard that such was the custom of great mountains in other parts of the world. I remembered how I worked with another boy, at odd afternoons stolen from study and paid for with stripes, to undermine and start from its bed an immense boulder that rested upon the edge of that hilltop; I remembered how, one Saturday afternoon, we gave three hours of honest effort to the task, and saw at last that our reward was at hand; I remembered how we sat down, then, and wiped the perspiration away, and waited to let a picnic party get out of the way in the road below—and then we started the boulder. It was splendid. It went crashing down the hillside, tearing up saplings, mowing bushes down like grass, ripping and crushing and smashing everything in its path—eternally splintered and scattered a woodpile at the foot of the hill, and then sprang from the high bank clear over a dray in the road—the negro glanced up once and dodged—and the next second it made infinitesimal mincemeat of a frame cooper shop, and the coopers swarmed out like bees. Then we said it was perfectly magnificent, and left. Because the coopers were starting up the hill to inquire.

Still, that mountain, prodigious as it was, was nothing to the Pyramid of Cheops. I could conjure up no comparison that would convey to my mind a satisfactory comprehension of the magnitude of a pile of monstrous stones that covered thirteen acres of ground and stretched upward four hundred and eighty tiresome feet, and so I gave it up and walked down to the Sphinx.

From *The Innocents Abroad,* 1869.

49 : The Sphinx

AFTER YEARS OF WAITING it was before me at last. The great face was so sad, so earnest, so longing, so patient. There was a dignity not of earth in its mien, and in its countenance a benignity such as never anything human wore. It was stone, but it seemed sentient. If ever image of stone thought, it was thinking. It was looking toward the verge of the landscape, yet looking *at* nothing—nothing but distance and vacancy. It was looking over and beyond everything of the present, and far into the past. It was gazing out over the ocean of Time—over lines of century-waves which, further and further receding, closed nearer and nearer together, and blended at last into one unbroken tide, away toward the horizon of remote antiquity. It was thinking of the wars of departed ages; of the empires it had seen created and destroyed; of the nations whose birth it had witnessed, whose progress it had watched, whose annihilation it had noted; of the joy and sorrow, the life and death, the grandeur and decay, of five thousand slow revolving years. It was the type of an attribute of man—of a faculty of his heart and brain. It was MEMORY—RETROSPECTION—wrought into visible, tangible form. All who know what pathos there is in memories of days that are accomplished and faces that have vanished—albeit only a trifling score of years gone by—will have some appreciation of the pathos that dwells in these grave eyes that look so steadfastly back upon the things they knew before History was born—before Tradition had being—things that were, and forms that moved, in a vague era which even Poetry and Romance scarce know of—and passed one by one away and left the stony dreamer solitary in the midst of a strange new age, and uncomprehended scenes.

The Sphinx is grand in its loneliness; it is impossible in its magnitude; it is impressive in the mystery that hangs over its story. And there is that in the overshadowing majesty of this eternal figure of stone, with its accusing memory of the deeds of all ages, which reveals to one something of what he shall feel when he shall stand at last in the awful presence of God.

There are some things which, for the credit of America, should be left unsaid, perhaps; but these very things happen sometimes to be the very things which, for the real benefit of Americans, ought to have prominent notice. While we stood looking, a wart, or an excrescence of some kind, appeared on the jaw of the Sphinx. We heard the familiar clink of a hammer, and understood the case at once. One of our well-meaning reptiles—I mean relic-hunters—had crawled up there and was trying to break a "specimen" from the face of this the most majestic creation the hand of man has wrought. But the great image contemplated the dead ages as calmly as ever, unconscious of the small insect that was fretting at its jaw. Egyptian granite that has defied the storms and earthquakes of all time has nothing to fear from the tack-hammers of ignorant excursionists—highwaymen like this specimen. He failed in his enterprise. We sent a sheik to arrest him if he had the authority, or to warn him, if he had not, that by the laws of Egypt the crime he was attempting to commit was punishable with imprisonment or the bastinado. Then he desisted and went away.

The Sphinx: a hundred and twenty-five feet long, sixty feet high, and a hundred and two feet around the head, if I remember rightly—carved out of one solid block of stone harder than any iron. The block must have been as large as the Fifth Avenue Hotel before the usual waste (by the necessities of sculpture) of a fourth or a half of the original mass was begun. I only set down these figures and these remarks to suggest the prodigious labor the carving of it so elegantly, so symmetrically, so faultlessly, must have cost. This species of stone is so hard that figures cut in it remain sharp and unmarred after exposure to the weather for two or three thousand years. Now did it take a hundred years of patient toil to carve the Sphinx? It seems probable.

From *The Innocents Abroad,* 1869.

50 : *Boers and Natives*

I HAVE BEEN UNDER THE IMPRESSION all along that I had an unpleasant paragraph about the Boers somewhere in my note-book, and also a pleasant one. I have found them now. The unpleasant one is dated at an interior village, and says:

"Mr. Z. called. He is an English Afrikander; is an old resident, and has a Boer wife. He speaks the language, and his professional business is with the Boers exclusively. He told me that the ancient Boer families in the great region of which this village is the commercial center are falling victims to their inherited indolence and dullness in the materialistic latter-day race and struggle, and are dropping one by one into the grip of the usurer—getting hopelessly in debt—and are losing their high place and retiring to second and lower. The Boer's farm does not go to another Boer when he loses it, but to a foreigner. Some have fallen so low that they sell their daughters to the blacks."

Under date of another South African town I find the note which is creditable to the Boers:

"Dr. X. told me that in the Kafir war 1,500 Kafirs took refuge in a great cave in the mountains about 90 miles north of Johannesburg, and the Boers blocked up the entrance and smoked them to death. Dr. X. has been in there and seen the great array of bleached skeletons—one a woman with the skeleton of a child hugged to her breast."

The great bulk of the savages must go. The white man wants their lands, and all must go excepting such percentage of them as he will need to do his work for him upon terms to be determined by himself. Since history has removed the element of guesswork from this matter and made it certainty, the humanest way of diminishing the black population should be adopted, not the old cruel ways of the past. Mr. Rhodes and his gang have been following the old ways. They are chartered to rob and slay, and they lawfully do it, but not in a compassionate and Christian spirit. They rob the Mashonas and the Matabeles of a portion of their territories in the hallowed old style of "purchase" for a song, and then they force a quarrel and take the rest by the strong hand. They rob the natives of their cattle under the pretext that all the cattle in the country belonged to the king whom they have tricked and assassinated. They issue "regulations" requiring the incensed and harassed natives to work for the white settlers, and neglect their own affairs to do it. This is slavery, and is several times worse than was the American slavery which used to pain England so much; for when this Rhodesian slave is sick, superannuated, or otherwise disabled, he must support himself or starve—his master is under no obligation to support him.

The reduction of the population by Rhodesian methods to the desired limit is a return to the old-time slow-misery and lingering-death system of a discredited time and a crude "civilization." We humanely reduce an overplus of dogs by swift chloroform; the Boer humanely reduced an overplus of blacks by swift suffocation; the nameless but right-hearted Australian pioneer humanely reduced his overplus of aboriginal neighbors by a sweetened swift death concealed in a poisoned pudding. All these are admirable, and worthy of praise; you and I would rather suffer either of these deaths thirty times over in thirty successive days than linger out one of the Rhodesian twenty-year deaths, with its daily burden of insult, humiliation, and forced labor for a man whose entire race the victim hates. Rhodesia is a happy name for that land of piracy and pillage, and puts the right stain upon it.

Several long journeys gave us experience of the Cape Colony railways; easy-riding, fine cars; all the conveniences; thorough cleanliness; comfortable beds furnished for the night trains. It was in the first days of June, and winter; the daytime was pleasant, the night-time nice and cold. Spinning along all day in the cars it was ecstasy to breathe the bracing air and gaze out over the vast brown solitudes of the velvet plains, soft and lovely near by, still softer and lovelier further away, softest and loveliest of all in the remote distances, where dim island-hills seemed afloat, as in a sea—a sea made of dreamstuff and flushed with colors faint and rich; and dear me, the depth of the sky, and the beauty of the strange new cloud-forms, and the glory of the sunshine, the lavishness, the wastefulness of it! The vigor and freshness and inspiration of the air and the sun—well, it was all just as Olive Schreiner had made it in her books.

To me the veldt, in its sober winter garb, was surpassingly beautiful. There were unlevel stretches where it was rolling and swelling, and rising and subsiding, and sweeping superbly on and on, and still on and on like an ocean, toward the far-away horizon, its pale brown deepening by delicately-graduated shades of rich orange, and finally to purple and crimson where it washed against the wooded hills and naked red crags at the base of the sky.

Everywhere, from Cape Town to Kimberley, and from Kimberley to Port Elizabeth and East London, the towns were well populated with tamed blacks; tamed and Christianized too, I suppose, for they wore the dowdy clothes of our Christian civilization. But for that, many of them would have been remarkably handsome. These fiendish clothes, together with the proper lounging gait, good-natured face, happy air, and easy laugh, made them precise counterparts of our American blacks; often where all the other aspects were strikingly and harmoniously and thrillingly African, a flock of these natives would intrude, looking wholly out of place, and spoil it all, making the thing a grating discord, half African and half American.

One Sunday in King William's Town a score of colored women came mincing across the great barren square dressed—oh, in the last perfection of fashion, and newness, and expensiveness, and showy mixture of unrelated colors,—all just as I had seen it so often at home; and in their faces and their gait was that languishing, aristocratic, divine delight in their finery which was so familiar to me, and had always been such a satisfaction to my eye and my heart. I seemed among old, old friends; friends of fifty years, and I stopped and cordially greeted them. They broke into a good-fellowship laugh, flashing their white teeth upon me, and all answered at once. I did not understand a word they said. I was astonished; I was not dreaming that they would answer in anything but American.

The voices, too, of the African women, were familiar to me—sweet and musical, just like those of the slave women of my early days. I followed a couple of them all over the Orange Free State—no, over its capital—Bloemfontein, to hear their liquid voices and the happy ripple of their laughter. Their language was a large improvement upon American. Also upon the Zulu. It had no Zulu click in it; and it seemed to have no angles or corners, no roughness, no vile *s's* or other hissing sounds, but was very, very mellow and rounded and flowing.

In moving about the country in the trains, I had opportunity to see a good many Boers of the veldt. One day at a village station a hundred of them got out of the third-class cars to feed. Their clothes were very interesting. For ugliness of shapes, and for miracles of ugly colors inharmoniously associated, they were a record.

The effect was nearly as exciting and interesting as that produced by the brilliant and beautiful clothes and perfect taste always on view at the Indian railway stations. One man had corduroy trousers of a faded chewing-gum tint. And they were new—showing that this tint did not come by calamity, but was intentional; the very ugliest color I have ever seen. A gaunt, shackly country lout six feet high, in battered gray slouched hat with wide brim, and old resin-colored breeches, had on a hideous brand-new woolen coat which was imitation tiger skin—wavy broad stripes of dazzling yellow and deep brown. I thought he ought to be hanged, and asked the stationmaster if it could be arranged. He said no; and not only that, but said it rudely; said it with a quite unnecessary show of feeling. Then he muttered something about my being a jackass, and walked away and pointed me out to people, and did everything he could to turn public sentiment against me. It is what one gets for trying to do good.

In the train that day a passenger told me some more about Boer life out in the lonely veldt. He said the Boer gets up early and sets his "niggers" at their tasks (pasturing the cattle, and watching them); eats, smokes, drowses, sleeps; toward evening superintends the milking, etc.; eats, smokes, drowses; goes to bed at early candle-light in the fragrant clothes he (and she) have worn all day and every week-day for years. I remember that last detail, in Olive Schreiner's "Story of an African Farm." And the passenger told me that the Boers were justly noted for their hospitality. He told me a story about it. He said that his grace the Bishop of a certain See was once making a business-progress through the tavernless veldt, and one night he stopped with a Boer; after supper was shown to bed; he undressed, weary and worn out, and was soon sound asleep;

in the night he woke up feeling crowded and suffocated, and found the old Boer and his fat wife in bed with him, one on each side, with all their clothes on, and snoring. He had to stay there and stand it—awake and suffering—until toward dawn, when sleep again fell upon him for an hour. Then he woke again. The Boer was gone, but the wife was still at his side.

Those Reformers detested that Boer prison; they were not used to cramped quarters and tedious hours, and weary idleness, and early to bed, and limited movement, and arbitrary and irritating rules, and the absence of the luxuries which wealth comforts the day and the night with. The confinement told upon their bodies and their spirits; still, they were superior men, and they made the best that was to be made of the circumstances. Their wives smuggled delicacies to them, which helped to smooth the way down for the prison fare.

In the train Mr. B. told me that the Boer jail-guards treated the black prisoners—even political ones—mercilessly. An African chief and his following had been kept there nine months without trial, and during all the time they had been without shelter from rain and sun. He said that one day the guards put a big black in the stocks for dashing his soup on the ground; they stretched his legs painfully wide apart, and set him with his back down hill; he could not endure it, and put back his hands upon the slope for a support. The guard ordered him to withdraw the support—and kicked him in the back. "Then," said Mr. B., "the powerful black wrenched the stocks asunder and went for the guard; a Reform prisoner pulled him off, and thrashed the guard himself."

From *Following the Equator,* 1897.

5 / *Australia*

51 : *Sydney*

WE ENTERED AND CAST ANCHOR, and in the morning went oh-ing and ah-ing in admiration up through the crooks and turns of the spacious and beautiful harbor—a harbor which is the darling of Sydney and the wonder of the world. It is not surprising that the people are proud of it, nor that they put their enthusiasm into eloquent words. A returning citizen asked me what I thought of it, and I testified with a cordiality which I judged would be up to the market rate. I said it was beautiful—superbly beautiful. Then by a natural impulse I gave God the praise. The citizen did not seem altogether satisfied. He said:

"It *is* beautiful, of course it's beautiful—the Harbor; but that isn't all of it, it's only half of it; Sydney's the other half, and it takes both of them together to ring the supremacy-bell. God made the Harbor, and that's all right; but Satan made Sydney."

Of course I made an apology; and asked him to convey it to his friend. He was right about Sydney being half of it. It would be beautiful without Sydney, but not above half as beautiful as it is now, with Sydney added. It is shaped somewhat like an oak-leaf—a roomy sheet of lovely blue water, with narrow off-shoots of water running up into the country on both sides between long fingers of land, high wooden ridges with sides sloped like graves. Handsome villas are perched here and there on these ridges, snuggling amongst the foliage, and one catches alluring glimpses of them as the ship swims by toward the city. The city clothes a cluster of hills and a ruffle of neighboring ridges with its undulating masses of masonry, and out of these masses spring towers and spires and other architectural dignities and grandeurs that break the flowing lines and give picturesqueness to the general effect.

The narrow inlets which I have mentioned go wandering out

into the land everywhere and hiding themselves in it, and pleasure-launches are always exploring them with picnic parties on board. It is said by trustworthy people that if you explore them all you will find that you have covered 700 miles of water passage. But there are liars everywhere this year, and they will double that when their works are in good going order.

October was close at hand, spring was come. It was really spring—everybody said so; but you could have sold it for summer in Canada, and nobody would have suspected. It was the very weather that makes our home summers the perfection of climatic luxury; I mean, when you are out in the wood or by the sea. But these people said it was cool, now—a person ought to see Sydney in the summer time if he wanted to know what warm weather is; and he ought to go north ten or fifteen hundred miles if he wanted to know what hot weather is. They said that away up there toward the equator the hens laid fried eggs. Sydney is the place to go to get information about other people's climates. It seems to me that the occupation of Unbiased Traveler Seeking Information is the pleasantest and most irresponsible trade there is. The traveler can always find out anything he wants to, merely by asking. He can get at all the facts, and more. Everybody helps him, nobody hinders him. Anybody who has an old fact in stock that is no longer negotiable in the domestic market will let him have it at his own price. An accumulation of such goods is easily and quickly made. They cost almost nothing and they bring par in the foreign market. Travelers who come to America always freight up with the same old nursery tales that their predecessors selected, and they carry them back and always work them off without any trouble in the home market.

One is sure to be struck by the liberal way in which Australasia spends money upon public works—such as legislative buildings, town halls, hospitals, asylums, parks, and botanical gardens. I should say that where minor towns in America spend a hundred dollars on the town hall and on public parks and gardens, the like towns in Australasia spend a thousand. And I think that this ratio will hold good in the matter of hospitals, also. I have seen a costly and well-equipped, and architecturally handsome hospital in an Australian village of fifteen hundred inhabitants. It was built by private funds furnished by the villagers and the neighboring planters, and its running expenses were drawn from the same sources. I suppose it would be hard to match this in any country. This village was about to close a contract for lighting the streets with the electric light, when I was there. That is ahead of London. London is still obscured by gas—gas pretty widely scattered, too, in some of the districts; so widely indeed, that except on moonlight nights it is difficult to find the gas lamps.

The botanical garden of Sydney covers thirty-eight acres, beautifully laid out and rich with the spoil of all the lands and all the climes of the world. The garden is on high ground in the middle of the town, overlooking the great harbor, and it adjoins the spacious grounds of Government House—fifty-six acres; and at hand, also, is a recreation ground containing eighty-two acres. In addition, there are the zoölogical gardens, the race-course, and the great cricket-grounds where the international matches are played. Therefore there is plenty of room for reposeful lazying and lounging, and for exercise too, for such as like that kind of work.

There are four specialties attainable in the way of social pleasure. If you enter your name on the Visitor's Book at Government House you will receive an invitation to the next ball that takes place there, if nothing can be proven against you. And it will be very pleasant; for you will see everybody except the Governor, and add a number of acquaintances and several friends to your list. The Governor will be in England. He always is. The continent has four or five governors, and I do not know how many it takes to govern the outlying archipelago; but anyway you will not see them. When they are appointed they come out from England and get inaugurated, and give a ball, and help pray for rain, and get aboard ship and go back home. And so the Lieutenant-Governor has to do all the work. I was in Australasia three months and a half, and saw only one Governor. The others were at home.

The Australasian Governor would not be so restless, perhaps, if he had a war, or a veto, or something like that to call for his reserve-energies, but he hasn't. There isn't any war, and there isn't any veto in his hands. And so there is really little or nothing doing in his line. The country governs itself, and prefers to do it; and is so strenuous about it and so jealous of its independence that it grows restive if even the Imperial Government at home proposes to help; and so the Imperial veto, while a fact, is yet mainly a name.

Thus the Governor's functions are much more limited than are a Governor's functions with us. And therefore more fatiguing. He is the apparent head of the State, he is the real head of Society. He represents culture, refinement, elevated sentiment, polite life, religion; and by his example he propagates these, and they spread and flourish and bear fruit. He creates the fashion, and leads it. His ball is the ball of balls, and his countenance makes the horse-race thrive.

He is usually a lord, and this is well; for his position compels him to lead an expensive life, and an English lord is generally well equipped for that.

Another of Sydney's social pleasures is the visit to the Admiralty House; which is nobly situated on high ground overlooking the water. The trim boats of the service convey the guests thither; and there, or on board the flagship, they have the duplicate of the hospitalities of Government House. The Admiral commanding a station in British waters is a magnate of the first degree, and he is sumptuously housed, as becomes the dignity of his office.

Third in the list of special pleasures is the tour of the harbor in a fine steam pleasure launch. Your richer friends own boats of this kind, and they will invite you, and the joys of the trip will make a long day seem short.

And finally comes the shark-fishing. Sydney Harbor is populous with the finest breeds of man-eating sharks in the world. Some people make their living catching them; for the Government pays a cash bounty on them. The larger the shark the larger the bounty, and some of the sharks are twenty feet long. You not only get the bounty, but everything that is in the shark belongs to you. Sometimes the contents are quite valuable. . . .

The people of Sydney ought to be afraid of the sharks, but for some reason they do not seem to be. On Saturdays the young men go out in their boats, and sometimes the water is fairly covered with the little sails. A boat upsets now and then, by accident, a result of tumultuous skylarking; sometimes the boys upset their boat for fun —such as it is—with sharks visibly waiting around for just such an occurrence. The young fellows scramble aboard whole—sometimes—not always. Tragedies have happened more than once. While I was in Sydney it was reported that a boy fell out of a boat in the mouth of the Paramatta river and screamed for help and a boy jumped overboard from another boat to save him from the assembling sharks; but the sharks made swift work with the lives of both.

The government pays a bounty for the shark; to get the bounty the fishermen bait the hook or the seine with agreeable mutton; the news spreads and the sharks come from all over the Pacific Ocean to get the free board. In time the shark culture will be one of the most successful things in the colony.

From *Following the Equator,* 1897.

52 : *Melbourne*

MELBOURNE SPREADS AROUND over an immense area of ground. It is a stately city architecturally as well as in magnitude. It has an elaborate system of cable-car service; it has museums, and colleges, and schools, and public gardens, and electricity, and gas, and libraries, and theaters, and mining centers, and wool centers, and centers of the arts and sciences, and boards of trade, and ships, and railroads, and a harbor, and social clubs, and journalistic clubs, and racing clubs, and a squatter club sumptuously housed and appointed, and as many churches and banks as can make a living. In a word, it is equipped with everything that goes to make the modern great city. It is the largest city of Australasia, and fills the post with honor and credit. It has one specialty; this must not be jumbled in with those other things. It is the mitred Metropolitan of the Horse-Racing Cult. Its race-ground is the Mecca of Australasia. On the great annual day of sacrifice—the 5th of November, Guy Fawkes' Day—business is suspended over a stretch of land and sea as wide as from New York to San Francisco, and deeper than from the northern lakes to the Gulf of Mexico; and every man and woman, of high degree or low, who can afford the expense, put away their other duties and come. They begin to swarm in by ship and rail a fortnight before the day, and they swarm thicker and thicker day after day, until all the vehicles of transportation are taxed to their uttermost to meet the demands of the occasion, and all hotels and lodgings are bulging outward because of the pressure from within. They come a hundred thousand strong, as all the best authorities say, and they pack the spacious grounds and grand-stands and make a spectacle such as is never to be seen in Australasia elsewhere.

It is the "Melbourne Cup" that brings this multitude together. Their clothes have been ordered long ago, at unlimited cost, and without bounds as to beauty and magnificence, and have been kept in concealment until now, for unto this day are they consecrate. I am speaking of the *ladies'* clothes; but one might know that.

And so the grand-stands make a brilliant and wonderful spectacle, a delirium of color, a vision of beauty. The champagne flows, everybody is vivacious, excited, happy; everybody bets, and gloves and fortunes change hands right along, all the time. Day after day the races go on, and the fun and the excitement are kept at white heat; and when each day is done, the people dance all night so as to be fresh for the race in the morning. And at the end of the great week the swarms secure lodgings and transportations for next year, then flock away to their remote homes and count their gains and losses, and order next year's Cup-clothes, and then lie down and sleep two weeks, and get up sorry to reflect that a whole year must be put in somehow or other before they can be wholly happy again.

The Melbourne Cup is the Australasian National Day. It would be difficult to overstate its importance. It overshadows all other holidays and specialized days of whatever sort in that congeries of colonies. Overshadows them? I might almost say it blots them out. Each of them gets attention, but not everybody's; each of them evokes interest, but not everybody's; each of them rouses enthusiasm, but not everybody's; in each case a part of the attention, interest, and enthusiasm is a matter of habit and custom, and another part of it is official and perfunctory. Cup Day, and Cup Day only, commands an attention, an interest, and an enthusiasm which are universal—and spontaneous, not perfunctory. Cup Day is supreme—it has no rival. I can call to mind no specialized annual day, in any country, which can be named by that large name—Supreme. I can call to mind no specialized annual day, in any country, whose approach fires the whole land with a conflagration of conversation and preparation and anticipation and jubilation. No day save this one; but this one does it.

In America we have no annual supreme day; no day whose approach makes the whole nation glad. We have the Fourth of July, and Christmas, and Thanksgiving. Neither of them can claim the primacy; neither of them can arouse an enthusiasm which comes near to being universal. Eight grown Americans out of ten dread the coming of the Fourth, with its pandemonium and its perils, and they rejoice when it is gone—if still alive. The approach of Christmas brings harassment and dread to many excellent people. They have to buy a cart-load of presents, and they never know what to buy to hit the various tastes; they put in three weeks of hard and anxious work, and when Christmas morning comes they are so dissatisfied with the result, and so disappointed that they want to sit down and cry. Then they give thanks that Christmas comes but once a year. The observance of Thanksgiving Day—as a function—has become general of late years. The Thankfulness is not so general. This is natural. Two-thirds of the nation have always had hard luck and a hard time during the year, and this has a calming effect upon their enthusiasm.

We *have* a supreme day—a sweeping and tremendous and tumultuous day, a day which commands an absolute universality of interest and excitement; but it is not annual. It comes but once in four years; therefore it cannot count as a rival of the Melbourne Cup.

In Great Britain and Ireland they have two great days—Christmas and the Queen's birthday. But they are equally popular; there is no supremacy.

I think it must be conceded that the position of the Australasian Day is unique, solitary, unfellowed; and likely to hold that high place a long time. . . .

In the museums you will find acres of the most strange and fascinating things; but all museums are fascinating, and they do so tire your eyes, and break your back, and burn out your vitalities with their consuming interest. You always say you will never go again, but you do go. The palaces of the rich, in Melbourne, are much like the palaces of the rich in America, and the life in them is the same; but there the resemblance ends. The grounds surrounding the American palace are not often large, and not often beautiful, but in the Melbourne case the grounds are often ducally spacious, and the climate and the gardeners together make them as beautiful as a dream. It is said that some of the country seats have grounds—domains—about them which rival in charm and magnitude those which surround the country mansion of an English lord; but I was not out in the country; I had my hands full in town.

And what was the origin of this majestic city and its efflorescence of palatial town houses and country seats? Its first brick was laid and its first house built by a passing convict. Australian history is almost always picturesque; indeed, it is so curious and strange, that it is itself the chiefest novelty the country has to offer, and so it pushes the other novelties into second and third place. It does not read like history, but like the most beautiful lies. And all of a fresh new sort, no moldy old stale ones. It is full of surprises, and adventures, and incongruities, and contradictions, and incredibilities; but they are all true, they all happened.

From *Following the Equator,* 1897.

53 : Ballarat

FREQUENTLY, IN AUSTRALIA, one has cloud-effects of an unfamiliar sort. We had this kind of scenery, finely staged, all the way to Ballarat. Consequently we saw more sky than country on that journey. At one time a great stretch of the vault was densely flecked with wee ragged-edged flakes of painfully white cloud-stuff, all of one shape and size, and equidistant apart, with narrow cracks of adorable blue showing between. The whole was suggestive of a hurricane of snow-flakes drifting across the skies. By and by these flakes fused themselves together in interminable lines, with shady faint hollows between the lines, the long satin-surfaced rollers following each other in simulated movement, and enchantingly counterfeiting the majestic march of a flowing sea. Later, the sea solidified itself; then gradually broke up its mass into innumerable lofty white pillars of about one size, and ranged these across the firmament, in receding and fading perspective, in the similitude of a stupendous colonnade—a mirage without a doubt flung from the far Gates of the Hereafter.

The approaches to Ballarat were beautiful. The features, great green expanses of rolling pastureland, bisected by eye-contenting hedges of commingled new-gold and old-gold gorse—and a lovely lake. One must put in the pause, there, to fetch the reader up with a slight jolt, and keep him from gliding by without noticing the lake. One *must* notice it; for a lovely lake is not as common a thing along the railways of Australia as are the dry places. Ninety-two in the shade again, but balmy and comfortable, fresh and bracing. A perfect climate.

Forty-five years ago the site now occupied by the City of Ballarat was a sylvan solitude as quiet as Eden and as lovely. Nobody had ever heard of it. On the 25th of August, 1851, the first *great* gold-strike made in Australia was made here. The wandering prospectors who made it scraped up two pounds and a half of gold the first day —worth $600. A few days later the place was a hive—a town. The news of the strike spread everywhere in a sort of instantaneous way —spread like a flash to the very ends of the earth. A celebrity so prompt and so universal has hardly been paralleled in history, perhaps. It was as if the name BALLARAT had suddenly been written on the sky, where all the world could read it at once.

The smaller discoveries made in the colony of New South Wales three months before had already started emigrants toward Australia; they had been coming as a stream, but they came as a flood, now. A hundred thousand people poured into Melbourne from England and other countries in a single month, and flocked away to the mines. The crews of the ships that brought them flocked with them; the clerks in the government offices followed; so did the cooks, the maids, the coachmen, the butlers, and the other domestic servants; so did the carpenters, the smiths, the plumbers, the painters, the reporters, the editors, the lawyers, the clients, the barkeepers, the bummers, the blacklegs, the thieves, the loose women, the grocers, the butchers, the bakers, the doctors, the druggists, the nurses; so did the police; even officials of high and hitherto envied place threw up their positions and joined the procession. This roaring avalanche swept out of Melbourne and left it desolate, Sunday-like, paralyzed, everything at a stand-still, the ships lying idle at anchor, all signs of life departed, all sounds stilled save the rasping of the cloud-shadows as they scraped across the vacant streets.

That grassy and leafy paradise at Ballarat was soon ripped open, and lacerated and sacrificed and gutted, in the feverish search for its hidden riches. There is nothing like surface-mining to snatch the graces and beauties and benignities out of a paradise, and make an odious and repulsive spectacle of it.

What fortunes were made! Immigrants got rich while the ship unloaded and reloaded—and went back home for good in the same cabin they had come out in! Not all of them. Only some. I saw the others in Ballarat myself, forty-five years later—what were left of them by time and death and the disposition to rove. They were young and gay, then; they are patriarchal and grave, now; and they do not get excited any more. They talk of the Past. They live in it. Their life is a dream, a retrospection.

Ballarat was a great region for "nuggets." No such nuggets were found in California as Ballarat produced. In fact, the Ballarat region has yielded the largest ones known to history. Two of them weighed about 180 pounds each, and together were worth $90,000. They were offered to any poor person who would shoulder them and carry them away. Gold was so plentiful that it made people liberal like that.

Ballarat was a swarming city of tents in the early days. Everybody was happy, for a time, and apparently prosperous. Then came trouble. The government swooped down with a mining tax. And in its worst form, too; for it was not a tax upon what the miner had taken out, but upon what he was *going* to take out—if he could find it. It was a license tax—license to work his claim—and it had to be paid before he could begin digging.

Consider the situation. No business is so uncertain as surface-mining. Your claim may be good, and it may be worthless. It may make you well off in a month; and then again you may have to dig and slave for half a year, at heavy expense, only to find out at last that the gold is not there in cost-paying quantity, and that your time and your hard work have been thrown away. It might be wise policy to advance the miner a monthly sum to encourage him to develop the country's riches; but to tax him monthly in advance instead—why, such a thing was never dreamed of in America. There, neither the claim itself nor its products, howsoever rich or poor, were taxed.

The Ballarat miners protested, petitioned, complained—it was of no use; the government held its ground, and went on collecting the tax. And not by pleasant methods, but by ways which must have been very galling to free people. The rumblings of a coming storm began to be audible.

By and by there was a result; and I think it may be called the finest thing in Australasian history. It was a revolution—small in size, but great politically; it was a strike for liberty, a struggle for a principle, a stand against injustice and oppression. It was the Barons and John, over again; it was Hampden and Ship-Money; it was Concord and Lexington; small beginnings, all of them, but all of them great in political results, all of them epoch-making. It is another instance of a victory won by a lost battle. It adds an honorable page to history; the people know it and are proud of it. They keep green the memory of the men who fell at the Eureka Stockade, and Peter Lalor has his monument.

The surface-soil of Ballarat was full of gold. This soil the miners ripped and tore and trenched and harried and disemboweled, and made it yield up its immense treasure. Then they went down into the earth with deep shafts, seeking the gravelly beds of ancient rivers and brooks—and found them. They followed the courses of these streams, and gutted them, sending the gravel up in buckets to the upper world, and washing out of it its enormous deposits of gold. The next biggest of the two monster nuggets mentioned above came from an old river-channel 180 feet under ground.

Finally the quartz lodes were attacked. That is not poor man's mining. Quartz-mining and milling require capital, and staying-power, and patience. Big companies were formed, and for several decades, now, the lodes have been successfully worked, and have yielded great wealth. Since the gold discovery in 1853 the Ballarat mines—taking the three kinds of mining together—have contributed to the world's pocket something over *three hundred millions of dollars,* which is to say that this nearly invisible little spot on the earth's surface has yielded about one-fourth as much gold in forty-four years as all California has yielded in forty-seven. The Californian aggregate, from 1848 to 1895, inclusive, as reported by the Statistician of the United States Mint, is $1,265,217,217.

A citizen told me a curious thing about those mines. With all my experience of mining I had never heard of anything of the sort before. The main gold reef runs about north and south—of course

—for that is the custom of a rich gold reef. At Ballarat its course is between walls of slate. Now the citizen told me that throughout a stretch of twelve miles along the reef, the reef is crossed at intervals by a straight black streak of a carbonaceous nature—a streak in the slate; a streak no thicker than a pencil—and that wherever it crosses the reef you will certainly find gold at the junction. It is called the Indicator. Thirty feet on each side of the Indicator (and down in the slate, of course) is a still finer streak—a streak as fine as a pencil mark; and indeed, that is its name—Pencil Mark. Whenever you find the Pencil Mark you know that thirty feet from it is the Indicator; you measure the distance, excavate, find the Indicator, trace it straight to the reef, and sink your shaft; your fortune is made, for certain. If that is true, it is curious. And it is curious any way.

Ballarat is a town of only 40,000 population; and yet, since it is in Australia, it has every essential of an advanced and enlightened big city. This is pure matter of course. I must stop dwelling upon these things. It is hard to keep from dwelling upon them, though; for it is difficult to get away from the surprise of it. I will let the other details go, this time, but I must allow myself to mention that this little town has a park of 326 acres; a flower garden of 83 acres, with an elaborate and expensive fernery in it and some costly and unusually fine statuary; and an artificial lake covering 600 acres, equipped with a fleet of 200 shells, small sail boats, and little steam yachts.

At this point I strike out some other praiseful things which I was tempted to add. I do not strike them out because they were not true or not well said, but because I find them better said by another man —and a man more competent to testify, too, because he belongs on the ground, and knows. I clip them from a chatty speech delivered some years ago by Mr. William Little, who was at that time mayor of Ballarat:

"The language of our citizens, in this as in other parts of Australasia, is mostly healthy Anglo-Saxon, free from Americanisms, vulgarisms, and the conflicting dialects of our Fatherland, and is pure enough to suit a Trench or a Latham. Our youth, aided by climatic influence, are in point of physique and comeliness unsurpassed in the Sunny South. Our young men are well ordered; and our maidens, 'not stepping over the bounds of modesty,' are as fair as Psyches, dispensing smiles as charming as November flowers."

The closing clause has the seeming of a rather frosty compliment, but that is apparent only, not real. November is summer-time there. His compliment to the local purity of the language is warranted. It is quite free from impurities; this is acknowledged far and wide. As in the German Empire all cultivated people claim to speak Hanoverian German, so in Australasia all cultivated people claim to speak Ballarat English. Even in England this cult has made considerable progress, and now that it is favored by the two great Universities, the time is not far away when Ballarat English will come into general use among the educated classes of Great Britain at large. Its great merit is, that it is shorter than ordinary English—that is, it is more compressed. At first you have some difficulty in understanding it when it is spoken as rapidly as the orator whom I have quoted speaks it. An illustration will show what I mean. When he called and I handed him a chair, he bowed and said:

"Q."

Presently, when we were lighting our cigars, he held a match to mine and I said:

"Thank you," and he said:

"Km."

Then I saw. Q is the end of the phrase "I thank you." Km is the end of the phrase "You are welcome." Mr. Little puts no emphasis upon either of them, but delivers them so reduced that they hardly have a sound. All Ballarat English is like that, and the effect is very soft and pleasant; it takes all the hardness and harshness out of our tongue and gives to it a delicate whispery and vanishing cadence which charms the ear like the faint rustling of the forest leaves.

From *Following the Equator,* 1897.

6 / Islands

54 : *The Sandwich Islands**

On a certain bright morning the Islands hove in sight, lying low on the lonely sea, and everybody climbed to the upper deck to look. After two thousand miles of watery solitude the vision was a welcome one. As we approached, the imposing promontory of Diamond Head rose up out of the ocean, its rugged front softened by the hazy distance, and presently the details of the land began to make themselves manifest; first the line of beach; then the plumed cocoanut trees of the tropics; then cabins of the natives; then the white town of Honolulu, said to contain between twelve and fifteen thousand inhabitants, spread over a dead level; with streets from twenty to thirty feet wide, solid and level as a floor, most of them straight as a line and few as crooked as a corkscrew.

The further I traveled through the town the better I liked it. Every step revealed a new contrast—disclosed something I was unaccustomed to. In place of the grand mud-colored brown fronts of San Francisco, I saw dwellings built of straw, adobes, and cream-colored pebble-and-shell-conglomerated coral, cut into oblong blocks and laid in cement; also a great number of neat white cottages, with green window-shutters; in place of front yards like billiard-tables with iron fences around them, I saw these homes surrounded by ample yards, thickly clad with green grass, and shaded by tall trees, through whose dense foliage the sun could scarcely penetrate; in place of the customary geranium, calla, lily, etc., languishing in dust and general debility, I saw luxurious banks and thickets of flowers, fresh as a meadow after a rain, and glowing with the richest dyes; in place of the dingy horrors of San Francisco's pleasure grove, the "Willows," I saw huge-bodied, wide-spreading forest trees, with strange names and stranger appearance—trees that cast a shadow like a thunder-cloud, and were able to stand alone without being tied

* Former name of the Hawaiian Islands.—C. N.

to green poles; in place of gold-fish, wiggling around in glass globes, assuming countless shades and degrees of distortion through the magnifying and diminishing qualities of their transparent prison-house, I saw cats—Tom cats, Mary Ann cats, long-tailed cats, bob-tailed cats, blind cats, one-eyed cats, wall-eyed cats, cross-eyed cats, gray cats, black cats, white cats, yellow cats, striped cats, spotted cats, tame cats, wild cats, singed cats, individual cats, groups of cats, platoons of cats, companies of cats, regiments of cats, armies of cats, multitudes of cats, millions of cats, and all of them sleek, fat, lazy, and sound asleep.

I looked on a multitude of people, some white, in white coats, vests, pantaloons, even white cloth shoes, made snowy with chalk duly laid on every morning; but the majority of the people were almost as dark as negroes—women with comely features, fine black eyes, rounded forms, inclining to the voluptuous, clad in a single bright red or white garment that fell free and unconfined from shoulder to heel, long black hair falling loose, gypsy hats, encircled with wreaths of natural flowers of a brilliant carmine tint; plenty of dark men in various costumes, and some with nothing on but a battered stove-pipe hat tilted on the nose, and a very scant breech-clout; certain smoke-dried children were clothed in nothing but sunshine—a very neat fitting and picturesque apparel indeed.

In place of roughs and rowdies staring and black-guarding on the corners, I saw long-haired, saddle-colored Sandwich Island maidens sitting on the ground in the shade of corner houses, gazing indolently at whatever or whoever happened along; instead of wretched cobblestone pavements I walked on a firm foundation of coral, built up from the bottom of the sea by the absurd but persevering insect of that name, with a light layer of lava and cinders overlying the coral, belched up out of fathomless perdition long ago through the seared and blackened crater that stands dead and harmless in the distance now; instead of cramped and crowded street-cars, I met dusky native women sweeping by, free as the wind, on fleet horses and astride, with gaudy riding-sashes, streaming like banners behind them; instead of the combined stenches of Chinadom and Brannan Street slaughter-houses, I breathed the balmy fragrance of jasmine, oleander, and the Pride of India; in place of the hurry and bustle and noisy confusion of San Francisco, I moved in the midst of a summer calm as tranquil as dawn in the Garden of Eden; in place of the Golden City's skirting sand-hills and the placid bay, I saw on the one side a framework of tall, precipitous mountains close at hand, clad in refreshing green, and cleft by deep, cool, chasm-like valleys—and in front the grand sweep of the ocean: a brilliant, transparent green near the shore, bound and bordered by a long white line of foamy spray dashing against the reef, and further out the dead blue water of the deep sea, flecked with "white caps," and in the far horizon a single, lonely sail—a mere accent-mark to emphasize a slumberous calm and a solitude that were without sound or limit. When the sun sunk down—the one intruder from other realms and persistent in suggestions of them—it was tranced luxury to sit in the perfumed air and forget that there was any world but these enchanted islands.

It was such ecstasy to dream and dream—till you got a bite. A scorpion bite. Then the first duty was to get up out of the grass and kill the scorpion; and the next to bathe the bitten place with alcohol or brandy; and the next to resolve to keep out of the grass in the future. Then came an adjournment to the bedchamber and the pastime of writing up the day's journal with one hand and the destruction of mosquitoes with the other—a whole community of them at a slap. Then, observing an enemy approaching—a hairy tarantula on stilts—why not set the spittoon on him? It is done, and the projecting ends of his paws give a luminous idea of the magnitude of his reach. Then to bed and become a promenade for a centipede with forty-two legs on a side and every foot hot enough to burn a hole through a rawhide. More soaking with alcohol, and a resolution to examine the bed before entering it, in future. Then wait, and suffer, till all the mosquitoes in the neighborhood have crawled in under the bar, then slip out quickly, and shut them in and sleep peacefully on the floor till morning. Meantime it is comforting to curse the tropics in occasional wakeful intervals.

We had an abundance of fruit in Honolulu, of course. Oranges, pineapples, bananas, strawberries, lemons, limes, mangoes, guavas, melons, and a rare and curious luxury called the chirimoya, which is deliciousness itself. Then there is the tamarind. I thought tamarinds were made to eat, but that was probably not the idea. I ate several, and it seemed to me that they were rather sour that year. They pursed up my lips, till they resembled the stem-end of a tomato, and I had to take my sustenance through a quill for twenty-four hours. They sharpened my teeth till I could have shaved with them, and gave them a "wire edge" that I was afraid would stay; but a citizen said "no, it will come off when the enamel does"—which was comforting, at any rate. I found, afterward, that only strangers eat tamarinds—but they only eat them once.

Passing through the market-place we saw that feature of Honolulu under its most favorable auspices—that is, in the full glory of Saturday afternoon, which is a festive day with the natives. The native girls, by twos and threes and parties of a dozen, and sometimes in whole platoons and companies, went cantering up and down the neighboring streets astride of fleet but homely horses, and with their gaudy riding-habits streaming like banners behind them. Such a troop of free and easy riders, in their natural home, the saddle, makes a gay and graceful spectacle. The riding-habit I speak of is simply a long broad scarf, like a tavern table-cloth, brilliantly colored, wrapped around the loins once, then apparently passed between the limbs and each end thrown backward over the same, and floating and flapping behind on both sides beyond the horse's tail like a couple of fancy flags; then, slipping the stirrup-irons between her toes, the girl throws her chest forward, sits up like a major-general, and goes sweeping by like the wind.

The girls put on all the finery they can on Saturday afternoon—fine black-silk robes; flowing red ones that nearly put your eyes out; others as white as snow; still others that discount the rainbow; and they wear their hair in nets, and trim their jaunty hats with fresh flowers, and encircle their dusky throats with home-made necklaces of the brilliant vermilion-tinted blossom of the *ohia;* and they fill the markets and the adjacent streets with their bright presences, and smell like a rag factory on fire with their offensive cocoanut oil.

Occasionally, you see a heathen from the sunny isles away down in the South Seas, with his face and neck tattooed till he looks like the customary mendicant from Washoe who has been blown up in a mine. Some are tattooed a dead blue color down to the upper lip—masked, as it were—leaving the natural light-yellow skin of Micronesia unstained from thence down; some with broad marks drawn down from hair to neck, on both sides of the face, and a strip of the original yellow skin, two inches wide, down the center—a gridiron with a spoke broken out; and some with the entire face discolored with the popular mortification tint, relieved only by one or two thin, wavy threads of natural yellow running across the face from ear to ear, and eyes twinkling out of this darkness, from under shadowing hat-brims, like stars in the dark of the moon.

Moving among the stirring crowds, you come to the poi-merchants, squatting in the shade on their hams, in true native fashion, and surrounded by purchasers. (The Sandwich-Islanders always squat on their hams, and who knows but they may be the original "ham sandwiches"? The thought is pregnant with interest.) The poi looks like common flour paste, and is kept in large bowls formed of a species of gourd, and capable of holding from one to three or four gallons. Poi is the chief article of food among the natives, and is prepared from the *taro* plant. The taro root looks like a thick, or, if you please, a corpulent sweet-potato, in shape, but is of a light-purple color when boiled. When boiled it answers as a passable substitute for bread. The buck Kanakas bake it underground, then mash it up well with a heavy lava pestle, mix water with it until it becomes a paste, set it aside and let it ferment, and then it is poi—and an unseductive mixture it is, almost tasteless before it ferments and too sour for a luxury afterward. But nothing is more nutritious. When solely used, however, it produces acrid humors, a fact which sufficiently accounts for the humorous character of the Kanakas. I think there must be as much of a knack in handling poi as there is in eating with chopsticks. The forefinger is thrust into the mess and stirred quickly round several times and drawn as quickly out, thickly coated, just as if it were poulticed; the head is thrown back, the finger inserted in the mouth and the delicacy stripped off and swallowed—the eye closing gently, meanwhile, in a languid sort of ecstasy. Many a different finger goes into the same bowl and many a different kind of dirt and shade and quality of flavor is added to the virtues of its contents.

Around a small shanty was collected a crowd of natives buying the *awa* root. It is said that but for the use of this root the destruction of the people in former times by certain imported diseases would have been far greater than it was, and by others it is said that this is merely a fancy. All agree that poi will rejuvenate a man who is used up and his vitality almost annihilated by hard drinking, and that in some kinds of diseases it will restore health after all medicines have failed; but all are not willing to allow to the *awa* the virtues claimed for it. The natives manufacture an intoxicating drink from it which is fearful in its effects when persistently indulged in. It covers the body with dry, white scales, inflames the eyes, and causes premature decrepitude. Although the man before whose establishment we stopped has to pay a government license of eight hundred dollars a year for the exclusive right to sell *awa* root, it is said that he makes a small fortune every twelvemonth; while saloon-keepers, who pay a thousand dollars a year for the privilege of retailing whisky, etc., only make a bare living.

We found the fish market crowded; for the native is very fond of fish, and *eats the article raw and alive!* Let us change the subject.

In old times here Saturday was a grand gala day indeed. All the native population of the town forsook their labors, and those of the surrounding country journeyed to the city. Then the white folks had to stay indoors, for every street was so packed with charging cavaliers and cavalieresses that it was next to impossible to thread one's way through the cavalcades without getting crippled.

At night they feasted and the girls danced the lascivious *hula hula* —a dance that is said to exhibit the very perfection of educated motion of limb and arm, hand, head, and body, and the exactest uniformity of movement and accuracy of "time." It was performed by a circle of girls with no raiment on them to speak of, who went through an infinite variety of motions and figures without prompting, and yet so true was their "time," and in such perfect concert did they move that when they were placed in a straight line, hands, arms, bodies, limbs, and heads waved, swayed, gesticulated, bowed, stooped, whirled, squirmed, twisted, and undulated as if they were part and parcel of a single individual; and it was difficult to believe they were not moved in a body by some exquisite piece of mechanism.

Of late years, however, Saturday has lost most of its quondam gala features. This weekly stampede of the natives interfered too much with labor and the interests of the white folks, and by sticking in a law here, and preaching a sermon there, and by various other means, they gradually broke it up.

The demoralizing *hula hula* was forbidden to be performed, save at night, with closed doors, in presence of few spectators, and only by permission duly procured from the authorities and the payment of ten dollars for the same. There are few girls nowadays able to dance this ancient national dance in the highest perfection of the art.

The missionaries have christianized and educated all the natives. They all belong to the church, and there is not one of them, above the age of eight years, but can read and write with facility in the native tongue. It is the most universally educated race of people outside of China. They have any quantity of books, printed in the Kanaka language, and all the natives are fond of reading. They are inveterate church-goers—nothing can keep them away. All this ameliorating cultivation has at last built up in the native women a profound respect for chastity—in other people. Perhaps that is enough to say on that head. The national sin will die out when the race does, but perhaps not earlier. But doubtless this purifying is not far off, when we reflect that contact with civilization and the whites has reduced the native population from *four hundred thousand* (Captain Cook's estimate) to *fifty-five thousand* in something over eighty years!

Society is a queer medley in this notable missionary, whaling, and governmental center. If you get into conversation with a stranger and experience that natural desire to know what sort of ground you are treading on by finding out what manner of man your stranger is, strike out boldly and address him as "Captain." Watch him narrowly, and if you see by his countenance that you are on the wrong track, ask him where he preaches. It is a safe bet that he is either a missionary or captain of a whaler. I am now personally acquainted with seventy-two captains and ninety-six missionaries. The captains and ministers form one-half of the population; the third fourth is composed of common Kanakas and mercantile foreigners and their families, and the final fourth is made up of high officers of the Hawaiian government. And there are just about cats enough for three apiece all around. . . .

From *Roughing It,* 1872.

55 : *The Fiji Islands*

FROM DIARY:—For a day or two we have been plowing among an invisible vast wilderness of islands, catching now and then a shadowy glimpse of a member of it. There does seem to be a prodigious lot of islands this year; the map of this region is freckled and fly-specked all over with them. Their number would seem to be uncountable. We are moving among the Fijis now—224 islands and islets in the group. In front of us, to the west, the wilderness stretches toward Australia, then curves upward to New Guinea, and still up and up to Japan; behind us, to the east, the wilderness stretches sixty degrees across the wastes of the Pacific; south of us is New Zealand. Somewhere or other among these myriads Samoa is concealed, and not discoverable on the map. Still, if you wish to go there, you will have no trouble about finding it if you follow the directions given by Robert Louis Stevenson to Dr. Conan Doyle and to Mr. J. M. Barrie. "You go to America, cross the continent to San Francisco, and then it's the second turning to the left." To get the full flavor of the joke one must take a glance at the map.

Wednesday, September 11.—Yesterday we passed close to an island or so, and recognized the published Fiji characteristics: a broad belt of clean white coral sand around the island; back of it a graceful fringe of leaning palms, with native huts nestling cosily among the shrubbery at their bases; back of these a stretch of level land clothed in tropic vegetation; back of that, rugged and picturesque mountains. A detail of the immediate foreground: a mouldering ship perched high up on a reef-bench.

This completes the composition, and makes the picture artistically perfect.

In the afternoon we sighted Suva, the capital of the group, and threaded our way into the secluded little harbor—a placid basin of brilliant blue and green water tucked snugly in among the sheltering hills. A few ships rode at anchor in it—one of them a sailing vessel flying the American flag; and they said she came from Duluth! There's a journey! Duluth is several thousand miles from the sea, and yet she is entitled to the proud name of Mistress of the Commercial Marine of the United States of America. There is only one free, independent, unsubsidized American ship sailing the foreign seas, and Duluth owns it. All by itself that ship is the American fleet. All by itself it causes the American name and power to be respected in the far regions of the globe. All by itself it certifies to the world that the most populous civilized nation in the earth has a just pride in her stupendous stretch of sea-front, and is determined to assert and maintain her rightful place as one of the Great Maritime Powers of the Planet. All by itself it is making foreign eyes familiar with a Flag which they have not seen before for forty years, outside of the museum. For what Duluth has done, in building, equipping, and maintaining at her sole expense the American Foreign Commercial Fleet, and in thus rescuing the American name from shame and lifting it high for the homage of the nations, we owe her a debt of gratitude which our hearts shall confess with quickened beats whenever her name is named henceforth. Many national toasts will die in the lapse of time, but while the flag flies and the Republic survives, they who live under their shelter will still drink this one, standing and uncovered: Health and prosperity to Thee, O Duluth, American Queen of the Alien Seas!

Rowboats began to flock from the shore; their crews were the first natives we had seen. These men carried no overplus of clothing, and this was wise, for the weather was hot. Handsome, great dusky men they were, muscular, clean-limbed, and with faces full of character and intelligence. It would be hard to find their superiors anywhere among the dark races, I should think.

Everybody went ashore to look around, and spy out the land, and have that luxury of luxuries to sea-voyagers—a land-dinner. And there we saw more natives: Wrinkled old women, with their flat mammals flung over their shoulders, or hanging down in front like the cold-weather drip from the molasses faucet; plump and smily young girls, blithe and content, easy and graceful, a pleasure to look at; young matrons, tall, straight, comely, nobly built, sweeping by with chin up, and a gait incomparable for unconscious stateliness and dignity; majestic young men—athletes for build and muscle —clothed in a loose arrangement of dazzling white, with bronze breast and bronze legs naked, and the head a cannon-swab of solid hair combed straight out from the skull and dyed a rich brick-red. Only sixty years ago they were sunk in darkness; now they have the bicycle.

We strolled about the streets of the white folks' little town, and around over the hills by paths and roads among European dwellings and gardens and plantations, and past clumps of hibiscus that made a body blink, the great blossoms were so intensely red; and by and by we stopped to ask an elderly English colonist a question or two, and to sympathize with him concerning the torrid weather; but he was surprised, and said:

"This? This is not hot. You ought to be here in the summer time once."

"We supposed that this was summer; it has the earmarks of it. You could take it to almost any country and deceive people with it. But if it isn't summer, what does it lack?"

"It lacks half a year. This is mid-winter."

I had been suffering from colds for several months, and a sudden change of season, like this, could hardly fail to do me hurt. It brought on another cold. It is odd, these sudden jumps from season to season. A fortnight ago we left America in mid-summer, now it is mid-winter; about a week hence we shall arrive in Australia in the spring.

After dinner I found in the billiard-room a resident whom I had known somewhere else in the world, and presently made some new friends and drove with them out into the country to visit His Excellency the head of the State, who was occupying his country residence, to escape the rigors of the winter weather, I suppose, for it was on breezy high ground and much more comfortable than the lower regions, where the town is, and where the winter has full swing, and often sets a person's hair afire when he takes off his hat to bow. There is a noble and beautiful view of ocean and islands and castellated peaks from the governor's high-placed house, and its immediate surroundings lie drowsing in that dreamy repose and serenity which are the charm of life in the Pacific Islands.

One of the new friends who went out there with me was a large man, and I had been admiring his size all the way. I was still admiring it as he stood by the governor on the veranda, talking; then the Fijian butler stepped out there to announce tea, and dwarfed him. Maybe he did not quite dwarf him, but at any rate the contrast was quite striking. Perhaps that dark giant was a king in a condition of political suspension. I think that in the talk there on the veranda it was said that in Fiji, as in the Sandwich Islands, native kings and chiefs are of much grander size and build than the commoners. This man was clothed in flowing white vestments, and they were just the thing for him; they comported well with his great stature and his kingly port and dignity. European clothes would have degraded him and made him commonplace. I know that, because they do that with everybody that wears them.

It was said that the old-time devotion to chiefs and reverence for their persons still survive in the native commoner, and in great force. The educated young gentleman who is chief of the tribe that live in the region about the capital dresses in the fashion of high-class European gentlemen, but even his clothes cannot damn him in the reverence of his people. Their pride in his lofty rank and ancient lineage lives on, in spite of his lost authority and the evil magic of his tailor. He has no need to defile himself with work, or trouble his heart with the sordid cares of life; the tribe will see to it that he shall not want, and that he shall hold up his head and live like a gentleman. I had a glimpse of him down in the town. Perhaps he is a descendant of the last king, the king with the difficult name whose memory is preserved by a notable monument of cut stone which one sees in the enclosure in the middle of the town. Thakombau—I remember, now; that is the name. It is easier to preserve it on a granite block than in your head.

Fiji was ceded to England by this king in 1858. One of the gentlemen present at the governor's quoted a remark made by the king at the time of the session—a neat retort, and with a touch of pathos in it, too. The English Commissioner had offered a crumb of comfort to Thakombau by saying that the transfer of the kingdom to Great Britain was merely "a sort of hermit-crab formality, you know." "Yes," said poor Thakombau, "but with this difference—the crab moves into an unoccupied shell, but mine isn't."

However, as far as I can make out from the books, the King was between the devil and the deep sea at the time, and hadn't much choice. He owed the United States a large debt—a debt which he could pay if allowed time, but time was denied him. He must pay up right away or the war-ships would be upon him. To protect his people from this disaster he ceded his country to Britain, with a clause in the contract providing for the ultimate payment of the American debt.

In old times the Fijians were fierce fighters; they were very religious, and worshiped idols; the big chiefs were proud and haughty, and they were men of great style in many ways; all chiefs had several wives, the biggest chiefs sometimes had as many as fifty; when a chief was dead and ready for burial, four or five of his wives were strangled and put into the grave with him. In 1804 twenty-seven British convicts escaped from Australia to Fiji, and brought guns and ammunition with them. Consider what a power they were, armed like that, and what an opportunity they had. If they had been energetic men and sober, and had had brains and known how to use them, they could have achieved the sovereignty of the archipelago—twenty-seven kings and each with eight or nine islands under his scepter. But nothing came of this chance. They lived worthless lives of sin and luxury, and died without honor—in most cases by violence. Only one of them had any ambition; he was an Irishman named Connor. He tried to raise a family of fifty children, and scored forty-eight. He died lamenting his failure. It was a foolish sort of avarice. Many a father would have been rich enough with forty.

It is a fine race, the Fijians, with brains in their heads and an inquiring turn of mind. It appears that their savage ancestors had a doctrine of immortality in their scheme of religion—with limitations. That is to say, their dead friend would go to a happy hereafter if he could be accumulated, but not otherwise. They drew the line; they thought that the missionary's doctrine was too sweeping, too comprehensive. They called his attention to certain facts. For instance, many of their friends had been devoured by sharks; the sharks, in their turn, were caught and eaten by other men; later, these men were captured in war, and eaten by the enemy. The original persons had entered into the composition of the sharks; next, they and the sharks had become part of the flesh and blood and bone of the cannibals. How, then, could the particles of the original men be searched out from the final conglomerate and put together again? The inquirers were full of doubts, and considered that the missionary had not examined the matter with the gravity and attention which so serious a thing deserved.

The missionary taught these exacting savages many valuable things, and got from them one—a very dainty and poetical idea: Those wild and ignorant poor children of Nature believed that the flowers, after they perish, rise on the winds and float away to the fair fields of heaven, and flourish there forever in immortal beauty!

From *Following the Equator,* 1897.

56 : Ceylon

JANUARY 14. Hotel Bristol. Servant Brompy. Alert, gentle, smiling, winning young brown creature as ever was. Beautiful shining black hair combed back like a woman's, and knotted at the back of his head—tortoise-shell comb in it, sign that he is a Singhalese; slender, shapely form; jacket; under it is a beltless and flowing white cotton gown—from neck straight to heel; he and his outfit quite unmasculine. It was an embarrassment to undress before him.

We drove to the market, using the Japanese jinriksha—our first acquaintanceship with it. It is a light cart, with a native to draw it. He makes good speed for half-an-hour, but it is hard work for him; he is too slight for it. After the half-hour there is no more pleasure for you; your attention is all on the man, just as it would be on a tired horse, and necessarily your sympathy is there, too. There's a plenty of these 'rickshas, and the tariff is incredibly cheap.

I was in Cairo years ago. That was Oriental, but there was a lack. When you are in Florida or New Orleans you are in the South—that is granted; but you are not in *the* South; you are in a modified South, a tempered South. Cairo was a tempered Orient—an Orient with an indefinite something wanting. That feeling was not present in Ceylon. Ceylon was Oriental in the last measure of completeness—utterly Oriental; also utterly tropical; and indeed to one's unreasoning spiritual sense the two things belong together. All the requisites were present. The costumes were right; the black and brown exposures, unconscious of immodesty, were right; the juggler was there, with his basket, his snakes, his mongoose, and his arrangements for growing a tree from seed to foliage and ripe fruitage before one's eyes; in sight were plants and flowers familiar to one in books but in no other way—celebrated, desirable, strange, but in production restricted to the hot belt of the equator; and out a little way in the country were the proper deadly snakes, and fierce beasts of prey, and the wild elephant and the monkey. And there was that swoon in the air which one associates with the tropics, and that smother of heat, heavy with odors of unknown flowers, and that sudden invasion of purple gloom fissured with lightnings,—then the tumult of crashing thunder and the downpour—and presently all sunny and smiling again; all these things were there; the conditions were complete, nothing was lacking. And away off in the deeps of the jungle and in the remotenesses of the mountains were the ruined cities and mouldering temples, mysterious relics of the pomps of a forgotten time and a vanished race—and this was as it should be, also, for nothing is quite satisfyingly Oriental that lacks the somber and impressive qualities of mystery and antiquity.

The drive through the town and out to the Gallè Face by the seashore, what a dream it was of tropical splendors of bloom and blossom, and Oriental conflagrations of costume! The walking groups of men, women, boys, girls, babies—each individual was a flame, each group a house afire for color. And such stunning colors, such intensely vivid colors, such rich and exquisite minglings and fusings of rainbows and lightnings! And all harmonious, all in perfect taste; never a discordant note; never a color on any person swearing at another color on him or failing to harmonize faultlessly with the colors of any group the wearer might join. The stuffs were silk—thin, soft, delicate, clinging; and, as a rule, each piece a solid color: a splendid green, a splendid blue, a splendid yellow, a splendid purple, a splendid ruby, deep and rich with smouldering fires—they swept continuously by in crowds and legions and multitudes, glowing, flashing, burning, radiant; and every five seconds came a burst of blinding red that made a body catch his breath, and filled his heart with joy. And then, the unimaginable grace of those costumes! Sometimes a woman's whole dress was but a scarf wound about her person and her head, sometimes a man's was but a turban and a careless rag or two—in both cases generous areas of polished dark skin showing—but always the arrangement compelled the homage of the eye and made the heart sing for gladness.

I can see it to this day, that radiant panorama, that wilderness of rich color, that incomparable dissolving-view of harmonious tints, and lithe half-covered forms, and beautiful brown faces, and gracious and graceful gestures and attitudes and movements, free, unstudied, barren of stiffness and restraint, and—

Just then, into this dream of fairyland and paradise a grating dissonance was injected. Out of a missionary school came marching, two and two, sixteen prim and pious little Christian black girls, Europeanly clothed—dressed, to the last detail, as they would have been dressed on a summer Sunday in an English or American village. Those clothes—oh, they were unspeakably ugly! Ugly, barbarous, destitute of taste, destitute of grace, repulsive as a shroud. I looked at my women folk's clothes—just full-grown duplicates of the outrages disguising those poor little abused creatures—and was ashamed to be seen in the street with them. Then I looked at my own clothes, and was ashamed to be seen in the street with myself.

However, we must put up with our clothes as they are—they have their reason for existing. They are on us to expose us—to advertise what we wear them to conceal. They are a sign; a sign of insincerity; a sign of suppressed vanity; a pretense that we despise gorgeous colors and the graces of harmony and form; and we put them on to propagate that lie and back it up. But we do not deceive our neighbor; and when we step into Ceylon we realize that we have not even deceived ourselves. We do love brilliant colors and graceful costumes; and at home we will turn out in a storm to see them when the procession goes by—and envy the wearers. We go to the theater to look at them and grieve that we can't be clothed like that. We go to the King's ball, when we get a chance, and are glad of a sight of the splendid uniforms and the glittering orders. When we are granted permission to attend an imperial drawing-room we shut ourselves up in private and parade around in the theatrical court-dress by the hour, and admire ourselves in the glass, and are utterly happy; and every member of every governor's staff in democratic America does the same with his grand new uniform—and if he is not watched he will get himself photographed in it, too. When I see the Lord Mayor's footman I am dissatisfied with my lot. Yes, our clothes are a lie, and have been nothing short of that these hundred years. They are insincere, they are the ugly and appropriate outward exposure of an inward sham and a moral decay.

The last little brown boy I chanced to notice in the crowds and swarms of Colombo had nothing on but a twine string around his waist, but in my memory the frank honesty of his costume still stands out in pleasant contrast with the odious flummery in which the little Sunday-school dowdies were masquerading.

From *Following the Equator,* 1897.